# COMPUTATIONAL SOCIAL PSYCHOLOGY

*Computational Social Psychology* showcases a new approach to social psychology that enables theorists and researchers to specify social psychological processes in terms of formal rules that can be implemented and tested using the power of high-speed computing technology and sophisticated software. This approach allows for previously infeasible investigations of the multidimensional nature of human experience as it unfolds in accordance with different temporal patterns on different timescales. In effect, the computational approach represents a redis-covery of the themes and ambitions that launched the field over a century ago.

This book brings together social psychologists with varying topical interests who are taking the lead in this redirection of the field. Many present formal models that are implemented in computer simulations to test basic assumptions and investigate the emergence of higher-order properties; others develop models to fit the real-time evolution of people's inner states, overt behavior, and social interactions. Collectively, the contributions illustrate how the methods and tools of the computational approach can investigate, and transform, the diverse land-scape of social psychology.

**Robin R. Vallacher** is Professor of Psychology at Florida Atlantic University, a Research Associate in the Center for Complex Systems, University of Warsaw, Poland, and a Research Affiliate in the Advanced Consortium on Cooperation, Conflict, and Complexity at Columbia University. He has been a visiting scholar at University of Texas at Austin, University of Bern (Switzerland), Max Planck Institute for Psychological Research (Germany), and University of Montpellier (France). Dr. Vallacher has authored or edited seven professional texts, and has published over 100 book chapters and journal articles on a wide range of topics in social psychology, including self-concept, self-regulation, social judgment, close relationships, prejudice and discrimination, sport psychology, social justice, and intergroup conflict. In recent years, he and his colleagues have adapted concepts and methods from the study of nonlinear dynamical systems in the natural sciences to the investigation of personal, interpersonal, and societal processes.

**Stephen J. Read** is Professor of Psychology at the University of Southern California, head of the social psychology area, and a Fellow of the Association for Psychological Science and the Society for Experimental Social Psychology. Dr. Read has edited three books and published over 100 journal articles and book chapters on person perception, causal reasoning, attachment theory, decision-making, use of interactive media (DVD and game) for changing risky sexual behavior, personality, and the neurobiology of risky decision-making. He has developed and published neural network models of person perception, causal reasoning, cognitive dissonance, personality and motivation, and risky decision-making. He has also worked on computational models of personality in intelligent agents and models of the role of narrative representations in military decision-making. Recently, he has focused on integrating work on the neurobiological bases of risky decision-making with neural network models of the neural systems involved in risky decision-making.

**Andrzej Nowak** is Professor of Psychology at Florida Atlantic University, University of Warsaw, Poland, where he directs the Center for Complex Systems, and Warsaw University of Humanities and Social Sciences. He is also a Fellow at the European Center for Living Technologies, and a Research Affiliate in the Advanced Consortium on Cooperation, Conflict, and Complexity at Columbia University. Dr. Nowak has authored or edited 16 professional texts, and has published over 100 book chapters and journal articles on a wide range of topics in social psychology, including social influence, social change, self-concept, self-regulation, social judgment, sport psychology, intergroup conflict, and psychological aspects of new media. Working with his colleagues, he has adapted concepts and methods from the study of complex systems and nonlinear dynamics in the natural sciences to the investigation of personal, interpersonal, and societal processes. He publishes in psychology, physics, and interdisciplinary journals.

# Frontiers of Social Psychology

Series Editors:

**Arie W. Kruglanski**, *University of Maryland at College Park*
**Joseph P. Forgas**, *University of New South Wales*

*Frontiers of Social Psychology* is a series of domain-specific handbooks. Each volume provides readers with an overview of the most recent theoretical, methodological, and practical developments in a substantive area of social psychology, in greater depth than is possible in general social psychology handbooks. The editors and contributors are all internationally renowned scholars whose work is at the cutting edge of research.

Scholarly, yet accessible, the volumes in the *Frontiers* series are an essential resource for senior undergraduates, postgraduates, researchers, and practitioners, and are suitable as texts in advanced courses in specific subareas of social psychology.

**Published Titles**

*Social Metacognition*, Briñol & DeMarree

*Goal-Directed Behavior*, Aarts & Elliot

*Social Judgment and Decision Making*, Krueger

*Intergroup Conflicts and Their Resolution*, Bar-Tal

*Social Motivation*, Dunning

*Social Cognition*, Strack & Förster

*Social Psychology of Consumer Behavior*, Wänke

**Forthcoming Titles**

For continually updated information about published and forthcoming titles in the *Frontiers of Social Psychology* series, please visit: **https://www.routledge.com/ psychology/series/FSP**

# COMPUTATIONAL SOCIAL PSYCHOLOGY

*Edited by Robin R. Vallacher, Stephen J. Read, and Andrzej Nowak*

Routledge
Taylor & Francis Group

NEW YORK AND LONDON

First published 2017
by Routledge
711 Third Avenue, New York, NY 10017

and by Routledge
2 Park Square, Milton Park, Abingdon, Oxon, OX14 4RN

*Routledge is an imprint of the Taylor & Francis Group, an informa business*

© 2017 Taylor & Francis

*Library of Congress Cataloging in Publication Data*
Names: Vallacher, Robin R., 1946- editor. | Read, Stephen J., editor. |
    Nowak, Andrzej (Andrzej Krzysztof), editor.
Title: Computational social psychology / edited by Robin R. Vallacher,
    Stephen J. Read, and Andrzej Nowak.
Description: New York : Routledge, 2017. | Series: Frontiers of social
    psychology | Includes bibliographical references and index.
Identifiers: LCCN 2017000667| ISBN 9781138951648 (hb : alk. paper) |
    ISBN 9781138951655 (pb : alk. paper) | ISBN 9781315173726 (ebook)
Subjects: LCSH: Social psychology.
Classification: LCC HM1033 .C636 2017 | DDC 302—dc23
LC record available at https://lccn.loc.gov/2017000667

ISBN: 978-1-138-95164-8 (hbk)
ISBN: 978-1-138-95165-5 (pbk)
ISBN: 978-1-315-17372-6 (ebk)

Typeset in Bembo
by Swales & Willis Ltd, Exeter, Devon, UK

# CONTENTS

# CONTRIBUTORS

**Kobus Barnard**, *University of Arizona*

**Brian R. Baucom**, *University of Utah*

**Arwen A. Behrends**, *University of Utah*

**Ernesto Brau**, *Boston College*

**Emily A. Butler**, *University of Arizona*

**Jonathan E. Butner**, *University of Utah*

**Daniel Chen**, *Biocomplexity Institute of Virginia Tech*

**Vita Droutman**, *University of Southern California*

**Brian A. Eiler**, *Center for Cognition, Action and Perception, University of Cincinnati*

**Ilya Farber**, *Institute of High Performance Computing (IHPC): Agency for Science, Technology, and Research (A*STAR), Singapore*

**Jinyan Guan**, *University of Arizona*

**Swati Gupta**, *Callaghan Innovation, New Zealand*

**Rachel W. Kallen**, *Center for Cognition, Action and Perception, University of Cincinnati*

**Yoshihisa Kashima**, *University of Melbourne*

**Michael Kirley**, *University of Melbourne*

**Tei Laine**, *Université Grenoble Alpes*

**Kerry L. Marsh**, *University of Connecticut*

**Robert J. MacCoun**, *Stanford University Law School*

**Lynn C. Miller**, *University of Southern California*

**Brian M. Monroe**, *University of Alabama*

**Andrzej Nowak**, *Warsaw University* and *Warsaw School of Social Sciences and Humanities*

**Mark G. Orr**, *Biocomplexity Institute of Virginia Tech*

**Andrew Predoehl**, *University of Arizona*

**Michael J. Richardson**, *Center for Cognition, Action and Perception, University of Cincinnati*

**Stephen J. Read**, *University of Southern California*

**Garry Robins**, *University of Melbourne*

**David Serfass**, *Florida Atlantic University*

**Ryne Sherman**, *Florida Atlantic University*

**DaHee Shon**, *Columbia University*

**Kyle Simek**, *University of Arizona*

**Paul E. Smaldino**, *University of California, Merced*

**Alexander Stivala**, *University of Melbourne*

**Jennifer Rose Talevich**, *University of Southern California*

**Robin R. Vallacher**, *Florida Atlantic University*

**James D. Westaby**, *Columbia University*

# PREFACE

Human behavior is complex and often difficult to understand or predict, making its meaning a preoccupation throughout history for lay people and scholars alike. Some of the ambiguities and mysteries are localized, referring to specific actions that can presumably be traced to momentary motives or immediate external influences. At other times, the focus is on the bigger picture—the driving forces in human nature responsible for action generally. Insight into both the local causes and general features of thought and behavior underwent a dramatic transformation with the advent of the scientific method and its adaptation to the unique subject matter of human experience. The history of scientific social psychology is brief compared to that of other disciplines such as physics and chemistry, however, and it is not entirely clear that the field has hit upon the adaptation of science that is best suited to the challenge the field faces.

This book examines this issue, noting the limitations of the approach that has dominated theory construction and research for most of social psychology's existence as a field of scientific inquiry. Rather than lamenting this state of affairs, we showcase an alternative approach that has emerged in recent years because of significant advances in computer technology and its increased availability. These developments enable theorists and researchers to specify social psychological processes in terms of formal rules that can be implemented and tested using the power of high-speed computing technology and sophisticated software. Because of its reliance on computer technology and its expression in formal rules, we refer to this approach as *computational social psychology*.

Computational social psychology casts a very broad net within which specific theories and research platforms find expression. This state of affairs is to be expected at this stage in its development. Whereas the methods and tools for traditional research (e.g. analyses of variance, significance testing) have been available for over a century, the powerful computers, sophisticated software, and electronic communications technology defining the computational approach have been around for a mere generation and have only recently found their way into the conduct of research in social psychology. Tremendous progress has been made in reframing social psychological phenomena in computational terms, but this work is still in its nascent stage, so it is unclear at this point how the selective pressures of theoretical and applied gain will sort out the winners and losers.

To showcase the computational approach and demonstrate its added value, we have brought together social psychologists with varying topical interests who are taking the lead in this redirection of the field. Operating within the computational framework, each contributor brings to bear a unique method focusing on a distinct facet of human experience. Collectively, the contributions illustrate how the diverse topical landscape of social psychology can be investigated with the benefits of the methods and tools associated with the computational approach.

In so doing, the book goes beyond providing new strategies for *how* to investigate social processes to provide direction for *what* should be investigated. Human experience is inherently complex and dynamic, defining features that were emphasized in the formative years of social psychology. Because complexity and dynamism have proven difficult to investigate with traditional methods, however, social psychological theory and research have tended instead to focus on simple causal relations and one-step processes. Computational social psychology, by contrast, is explicitly concerned with the multidimensional nature of human experience that unfolds in accordance with different temporal patterns on different timescales. In effect, the computational approach represents a rediscovery of the themes that launched the field over a century ago.

## Overview of Chapters

The contributions we have assembled each provide a unique way of showcasing the computational approach to social psychology. Most present formal models that are implemented in computer simulations to test basic assumptions and investigate the emergence of higher-order properties, but some develop models to fit the real-time evolution of people's inner states, overt behavior, and social interactions. The diversity of methods is essential at this stage in the development of computational social psychology, but it is also testament to the flexibility of this approach in tackling how psychological systems behave.

In an introductory chapter, we provide an overview of the computational approach and its contrast to the traditional approach that has defined social psychological research for decades. We emphasize that this emerging paradigm not only provides precise tools for assessing social processes, it also shines the light on important features of human experience that have gone largely unexamined in traditional approaches—features that were recognized as crucial in the early years of social psychology but were not investigated for want of appropriate tools and methods.

The next three sets of chapters are organized to reflect expanding levels of experience, from processes that reflect intra-individual dynamics to those that operate at the group and societal level. In Part I, the emphasis is on *intrapersonal dynamics*. Read, Droutman, and Miller (Chapter 2) present a neural network model that captures in parsimonious fashion the interplay of personality structure and dynamics. Monroe, Tei Laine, Gupta, and Farber (Chapter 3) illustrate how connectionist modeling can represent the basic factors at work in impression formation. Talevich (Chapter 4) discusses the integrative potential of complex systems generally, and demonstrates this potential for modeling different attachment styles. Orr and Chen (Chapter 5) show how computational modeling can be used to represent how people manage (and mismanage) their health behavior.

The chapters comprising Part II offer different, though complementary, means of modeling *interpersonal dynamics*. Eiler, Kallen, and Richardson (Chapter 6) illustrate a central feature of interaction-dominant dynamical systems: how local interactions between social agents give rise to global patterns that subsequently feed back to constrain future micro- and macroscopic social processes. Butler, Guan, Predoehl, Brau, Simek, and Barnard (Chapter 7) investigate the emergence of shared emotions among interacting individuals and present a model that captures the essence and detail of this temporal trajectory. Butner, Behrends and Baucom (Chapter 8) employ topological analysis to capture how individuals come to regulate one another in their social relations. Marsh (Chapter 9) presents evidence showing how the multidimensional context in which thought and behavior are embedded promotes the emergence of synchronization and joint action among interacting individuals. Vallacher and Nowak (Chapter 10) use coupled dynamical systems to model the synchronization of overt behavior and internal states that underlies the evolution of social relations in the course of social interaction.

Part III consists of three chapters that illustrate the added value of computational models for providing insight into *collective dynamics*. Westaby and Shon (Chapter 11) present a simulation model that shows how individual goal-striving is expressed in the context of dynamic social networks. MacCoun (Chapter 12) shows how many classic principles and phenomena in collective behavior can be represented as various special cases of a single computational model. Kashima, Kirley, Stivala, and Robins (Chapter 13) show how basic dimensions of culture variation can be modeled by the iteration of a few simple formal rules.

Part IV addresses the potential of the computational approach for *transforming social psychology*. Smaldino (Chapter 14) discusses how the very simplicity of computational models is what enables them to capture the essential features that give rise to the complexity of human experience at all levels of psychological reality. Serfass, Nowak, and Sherman (Chapter 15) discuss the recent emergence of Big Data as a tool for understanding social processes, and consider the expanding role that this approach is destined to have in the years to come. In a concluding chapter, Nowak and Vallacher (Chapter 16) forecast future developments in the computational approach and suggest how these emerging trends are likely, in combination with traditional approaches, to provide a new paradigm for social psychology.

# ACKNOWLEDGMENTS

To an important extent, this book has its genesis in the pre-conference, *Dynamical Systems and Computational Modeling in Social Psychology*, that was initiated at the annual meeting of the Society of Personality and Social Psychology (SPSP) in 2012. This pre-conference has attracted increased attention since that time and is now a regular feature of the annual meeting of the SPSP. Many of the contributors to the pre-conference are represented in this book.

We wish to thank Joseph Forgas and Arie Kruglanski, the co-editors of the *Frontiers of Social Psychology* series, for the invitation to prepare this volume. They appreciated the potential of the computational approach to become a dominant paradigm for the field, and they felt that the time was right to showcase the variety of strategies that have emerged in recent years. They entrusted us to assemble the set of contributions to provide this showcase. Their foresight, support, and trust in this endeavor are greatly appreciated.

Andrzej Nowak acknowledges the support of a grant from the Polish Committee for Scientific Research [DEC-2011/02/A/HS6/00231].

# Overview

# 1

# RETHINKING HUMAN EXPERIENCE

## The Promise of Computational Social Psychology

*Robin R. Vallacher, Andrzej Nowak, and Stephen J. Read*[1]

Social psychology adopted the scientific method over a hundred years ago, and in that time has generated an enormous literature concerning every conceivable aspect of human experience, from internal mechanisms of mind and emotion to basic principles that underlie societal functioning. Although the field consists of numerous theories, some of which are mutually contradictory, researchers for the most part have not called into question the means by which such theories are generated. After all, for psychological research to be published in the field's top journals, it must meet stringent standards of scientific practice. The results emanating from psychology labs over the past decades are thus beyond reproach and can be assumed to capture important features of how people think, feel, and behave. If there is conflict among theoretical interpretations, all one need do is perform further research to settle the conflict. Like every other scientific field, psychology is built upon the resolution of such conflicts, and through this dialectic provides progressive understanding, with increases in both the nuance and generality of the phenomena it is designed to investigate.

Or so we thought. In recent years, the meaningfulness of effects generated in psychology labs, and hence the value of theories based on such efforts, has come under intense scrutiny. Most notably, the findings of the Open Science Collaboration (OSC, 2015) have raised concerns that what are presented as solid generalizations about psychological processes may instead be unreliable effects observed under idiosyncratic laboratory conditions, often analyzed with inadequate statistical methods. These concerns have generated considerable discussion and created a crisis of confidence among many in the field. Not surprisingly, there has been pushback against the conclusions of the OSC (e.g., Gilbert, King, Pettigrew, & Wilson, 2016). But even if the OSC findings are eventually qualified, one can ask whether the standard paradigm of psychological research is sufficient for generating important insights into the complexity and dynamism at the heart of human experience in real-world contexts. People's internal states and overt actions are embedded in a multidimensional context, unfold over time in accordance with temporal patterns on various timescales, and often display reciprocal rather than unidirectional causality. Standard experimental designs that isolate specific relationships and concentrate on the immediate effect of independent variables are not designed to capture these defining features of human experience.

In recent years, a viable alternative to the traditional approach has begun to gain acceptance in social psychology. This approach is made possible by the explosive growth in computer technology and sophisticated software that enables researchers to identify fundamental principles that incorporate the complexity and dynamism of human thought, emotion, and behavior. Because this approach uses computers and rule-based algorithms to model and quantify psychological processes, we refer to it as *computational social psychology*.[2] The contributions to this volume, though different in their respective topics of interest and specific research strategies, are all built on the assumption that formal models can be generated to provide quantitative rather than merely qualitative understanding of social psychological phenomena.

## Overview of the Chapter

Our aim in this chapter is to describe the computational approach and high-light its added value for theory construction and verification. The first section describes the qualitative changes in research that have emerged in recent years as a result of new technologies and statistical methods. The new approaches currently co-exist alongside traditional research methods in social psychology, but there is reason to suspect that the shift toward computational methods will accelerate as they become increasingly familiar to psychologists, particularly to those who have grown up in an era of high-speed computers, electronic communication, and social networks.

The second section describes significant changes in theoretical focus engendered by the computational approach. As in other areas of science, the tools that are available constrain the phenomena that can be investigated. Traditional social psychological methods have served a useful purpose in addressing many important topics but they are not designed to capture some defining features of human experience, many of which, ironically, were the focus of social psychology in its formative years last century—well before the advent of electronic calculators, let alone high-speed computers. The technology and statistical methods available today allow psychologists to gain insight into the complexity and dynamism of human experience that figured so prominently in the insights of such luminaries as Kurt Lewin and William James.

In a concluding section, we describe the integrative potential of computational social psychology. This approach is clearly heuristic, generating new lines of research and opening the door on a host of important phenomena. But the approach also holds potential for identifying basic properties that underlie topics that have traditionally been conceptualized in very different terms. Indeed, a guiding vision for computational researchers is the development of a foundational science consisting of a small set of basic principles that provide conceptual integration for the fragmented topical landscape that characterizes social psychology. The fragmentation issue has been a persistent sore point in the field, fueling a crisis in the 1970s that was never resolved and which continues to provoke consternation among theorists and researchers today.

## Methods of Computational Social Psychology

At one level, computational social psychology simply means gaining knowledge about the subject matter of social psychology using computers. This potential is manifest in several ways. Modern computer technology, first of all, has made available new and extensive sources of data. The internet, Big Data, social media, and smart phones provide an unimaginable amount of information concerning people's attitudes and values, the structure of social contacts and social relations, and the spread of ideas, rumors, fads, and awareness of events. This frees researchers to go beyond simple laboratory studies to extract large volumes of data from the real world. This source of information, moreover, is becoming increasingly representative of people's spontaneous thoughts, attitudes, desires, and openness to social influence as computers, smart phones, and social media have become the personal tools of the majority of people worldwide.

Beyond providing a wealth of data concerning people, the growing availability of computer software enables social psychologists to formulate their theories in terms of rules expressed in computer code, to check the consistency of their theoretical assumptions, to observe how the model behaves over time, and to examine results for unexpected and emergent properties. Computers also offer unprecedented analytical power for advanced statistics and automatic model building. Finally, because of their visualization capability, computers enable psychologists to see patterns in complex data sets that might not be apparent with recourse to statistics or verbal descriptions (Nowak, Rychwalska, & Borkowski, 2013).

In more general terms, computational social psychology refers to a revolutionary new way of doing research. Traditionally, theories in social psychology have been formulated in natural language, stating the qualitative relations among variables of interest—which variables influence other variables, and the direction of such influence. Natural language, however, does not offer the precision necessary to describe the quantitative nature of the relationship among variables, especially when the relations involve complex interactions and nonlinear dependencies. In contrast, describing social theories in terms of computational models enables researchers to combine many factors and to capture the complex relations among them.

Computer simulations are especially useful in this regard because there is virtually no limit to the number of factors that can be investigated, nor is there a limit to the number and complexity of relationships among such factors that can be assessed (see, e.g., Gilbert & Troitzsch, 2011; Liebrand, Nowak, & Hegselman, 1998; Nowak & Vallacher, 1998; Read & Miller, 1998; Smith & Conrey, 2007). Computer simulations provide an ideal compromise between the freedom but imprecision of natural language and the daunting requirements of mathematical formulas. For this reason, computer simulations have been described as the third pillar of the scientific method, alongside experimentation and theory building (cf. Ostrom, 1988).

Within the computational framework, of course, empirical data are essential to provide assumptions for a model and to test a model's predictions. In contrast to traditional empirical methods, which are designed to show that a relationship is probably not due to chance, the computational approach describes the relationship among variables in quantitative terms, and can do so with a vast number of cases rather than with small convenience samples. In this endeavor, the computational approach uses statistics in a fundamentally different way. Instead of $t$-tests and ANOVAs designed for significance testing, there is an emphasis on advanced methods for model-fitting, including structural equation modeling, log linear models, and multilevel modeling. The computational approach is also reflected in new statistics, such as boot-strapping methods and machine learning.

These advanced tools are proving useful in time series methodology, which can be employed to characterize the temporal patterns in thought, emotion, and behavior (e.g., Boker & Wenger, 2007; Butner, Gagnon, Geuss, Lessard, & Story, 2014; Freeman & Ambady, 2010; Hollenstein, 2013; Kuppens, Oravecz, & Tuerlinckx, 2010; Spivey & Dale, 2006; Vallacher, Van Geert, & Nowak, 2015). This strategy differs from the computer simulation approach in a fundamental way: whereas the strategy of computer simulations is to *formulate* rules and observe their operation as they are iterated over time, the strategy in time series analyses is to *discover* the rules that produce the structure and temporal patterns in empirical data. Clearly, the two strategies work together synergistically. The rules discovered in time series can provide the basis for the rules implemented in computer simulations, and the results of simulations can provide insight into the properties to look for in time series of empirical data.

## Theories in Computational Social Psychology

Computational social psychology is more than a recipe for *how* research should be conducted. In a fundamental sense, it enables researchers to address features of social life that were largely off limits within traditional experimental designs—in effect, it is a blueprint for *what* can be investigated. For one thing, more complex theories can be formulated and tested. Theorists no longer need to be bound by independent, moderating, mediating, and dependent variables. Instead, they can formulate theories in terms of multiple feedback loops, reciprocal causality, complex interactions, and temporal changes in these properties.

It is particularly noteworthy that the topics and issues rendered open to investigation within the computational approach represent central concerns that were at the forefront during the field's formative years (e.g., Cooley, 1902; James, 1890; Lewin, 1936; Mead, 1934). Psychologists have known all along that human experience is embedded in a multidimensional field of forces and displays internally generated change on various timescales, but they did not have the tools necessary to capture the complexity and dynamism of mind and action. Largely due to the sophistication and availability of computer technology and software, we can now observe behavior unfold in ecologically meaningful settings and we can implement the rules for such behavior in computer simulations that reveal the consequences of these rules on relevant time scales. In a concrete sense, the availability of modern technological advances enables psychologists to finally address questions that have gone unanswered since they were raised in the early 20th century.

This potential has been realized in recent years in the adaptation of complexity science and nonlinear dynamical systems to social processes (e.g., Guastello, Koopmans, & Pincus, 2009; Vallacher, Read, & Nowak, 2002). This perspective introduces such concepts as self-organization, emergence, attractors, fractals, and nonlinearity, which are central to the study of complex systems in the natural sciences (e.g., Schuster, 1984; Strogatz, 1994; Waldrop, 1992; Wolfram, 2002; Weisbuch, 1992), to theory construction and research in social psychology (Nowak & Vallacher, 1998; Read & Miller, 1998; Vallacher & Nowak, 1994, 1997, 2007). The methods and tools made available by the computational approach have been indispensable in this endeavor.

Computer simulations employing agent-based modeling, for example, have shown how higher-order structures emerge in both mental systems and social systems through the self-organization of the system's basic elements. With respect to mental systems, computer simulations have shown how the mutual influence among specific thoughts and feelings give rise to higher-order mental states such as attitudes (e.g., Read, Vanman, & Miller, 1997; Monroe & Read, 2008), self-concepts (e.g., Nowak, Vallacher, Tesser, & Borkowski, 2000), stereotypes (e.g., Queller, 2002), and enduring moods (Thagard & Nerb, 2002). With respect to social systems, simulation work has revealed how the local interactions among individuals in a society promote the emergence of public opinion (e.g., Nowak, Szamrej, & Latané, 1990), cooperation versus competition in social dilemmas (e.g., Messick & Liebrand, 1995), social norms surrounding mating (e.g., Kenrick, Li, & Butner, 2003), societal change (e.g., Nowak & Vallacher, 2001), and the survival versus collapse of minority opinions (e.g., Jarman et al., 2015).

In another simulation approach, social relationships are modeled as the progressive synchronization of individuals' internal states (e.g., temperament, personality). Individuals are represented as separate dynamical systems (logistic equations) with unique control parameters signifying their internal states (Nowak, Vallacher, & Zochowski, 2005). The degree of coupling (mutual influence) between individuals and the similarity in the initial settings of their respective control parameters are varied, and the individual systems are given the chance to synchronize the dynamics of their overt behavior over many trials (iterations of the program). After synchronization is achieved, the coupling is reduced to zero and the program assesses how well the two systems remain synchronized.

The results show that synchronization in dynamics is achieved very quickly under strong coupling, but that the systems diverge when mutual influence is broken. Under moderate coupling, synchronization is achieved more slowly, but it persists after the coupling is broken because the systems converge on a common control parameter (internal state) to compensate for the lack of strong mutual influence. In recent years, synchronization has emerged as a prominent way to conceptualize social relations (e.g., emotional coordination); the computer simulations of this process identify the optimal degree of influence that facilitates the development of lasting synchrony between individuals.

Time series methodology, meanwhile, has been employed to identify dynamical properties in the stream of thought (e.g., Delignières, Fortes, & Ninot, 2004; Vallacher et al., 2015). James (1890) clearly saw value in focusing on the flow of thought, feeling that it provided a better characterization of mental process than did the central tendency of thought collapsed over time (e.g., an average judgment), but he pretty much left it at that. The tools for measuring the dynamical properties of thought simply did not exist in his time. Because of the concepts and tools adapted from nonlinear dynamical systems in recent years, researchers can now extract meaningful information from the temporal trajectories of thought.

Research employing the mouse paradigm (cf. Vallacher, Nowak, & Kaufman, 1994) illustrates this strategy. Participants first verbalize, in private, their thoughts and feelings regarding a topic (e.g., a relationship partner, a social issue, themselves) for several minutes and then listen to a recording of their narrative. As they hear themselves talk, they use the computer mouse to adjust the position of the cursor on the monitor to indicate the evaluation of the topic conveyed at each point in the narrative. Because the cursor's position is tracked on a moment-to-moment basis, participants' stream of thought can be displayed as a temporal trajectory of evaluation. Analytical tools are then applied to the trajectory to reveal the dynamics of participants' thinking.

This strategy has proven useful in capturing basic dynamical properties, including attractors, repellers, multistability, and fractals in the temporal patterns of thought, as well as individual differences in these properties. For example, individual differences in self-concept clarity (Campbell, 1990) are reflected in the landscape of attractors and repellers in people's self-evaluative narratives (Wong, Vallacher, & Nowak, 2016). People with higher clarity (signaling a well-integrated self-concept) have positive self-evaluation attractors and weaker self-esteem repellers in their trajectories of self-evaluation, whereas those with lower clarity have less positive attractors and stronger repellers when they reflect on themselves. Fractal structure also has been observed in people's self-evaluation narratives (Wong, Vallacher, & Nowak, 2014) and in their stream of thought regarding close friends (Vallacher et al., 1994).

## The Integrative Potential of Computational Social Psychology

The current consternation regarding the state of social psychology is somewhat reminiscent of the so-called "crisis" in social psychology in the 1970s (e.g., Gauld & Shotter, 1977; Gergen, 1978; Harré & Secord, 1972). The concerns at that time were partly philosophical in nature, questioning whether human behavior was deterministic and whether logical positivism in general, and reductionism in particular, were appropriate for understanding psychological phenomena. But concern was also voiced regarding the proliferation of localized "mini-theories" devoted to different topics and that were devoid of contact with one another. The field was fragmented, lacking an agreed-upon conceptual or empirical foundation. Lacking a way out of the dilemmas that were identified, researchers maintained the status quo in their approach to psychological phenomena. The crisis thus eventually abated without any change in the conduct of "normal" psychological research.

This is not surprising in view of how normal science operates. As Kuhn (1970) observed, established paradigms are highly resistant to challenges, maintaining their status when problems are exposed. In social psychology, as in other disciplines, the implicit attitude seems to be that "a bad theory is better than no theory at all." For a paradigm shift to occur, an alternative to normal science must be forwarded that resolves the problems of the existing paradigm and provides a better depiction of the phenomena of interest.

Computational social psychology holds promise as the needed alternative. The properties that provide the underpinnings and focus of computational social psychology—intrinsic dynamics, self-organization, coordination, attractors and repellers—characterize all levels of psychological reality. At the intrapersonal level, thoughts and emotions display patterns of change on fairly short timescales and tend to become progressively more coherent due to their mutual influence. At the interpersonal level, the dynamics of interacting individuals tend to become progressively coordinated, enabling them to co-regulate one another's feelings, thoughts, and actions. At the collective level, group dynamics are characterized by the synchronization of moods, attitudes, norms, and behavior—both in local circumstances (e.g., deindividuation, groupthink) and with respect to societal norms, preferences, and values. And at each level, a shared tool kit is available for identifying and modeling the phenomenon of interest.

By viewing social processes through the lens of computational models, then, it may be possible to establish commonalities among topics as seemingly distinct as attitudes, close relations, and social change. Beyond providing redirection for the field, computational social psychology holds potential for integrating a field that is acknowledged as fragmented and in need of such integration. We are not there yet, but there is reason to be optimistic that the scalability of the computational approach will someday create the foundational science that the field has lacked all these years.

## Notes

1 Andrzej Nowak acknowledges the support of a grant from the Polish Committee for Scientific Research [DEC-2011/02/A/HS6/00231].
2 Nowak, Vallacher, and Burnstein (1998) coined this term to describe the approach of computer simulations in investigating social processes. "Computational social psychology" as employed in this book encompasses a wider range of approaches.

## References

Boker, S. M., & Wenger, M. J. (2007). *Data analytic techniques for dynamical systems in the social and behavioral sciences.* Mahwah, NJ: Lawrence Erlbaum.

Butner, J., Gagnon, K. T., Geuss, M. N., Lessard, D. A., & Story, T. N. (2014). Using topology to generate and test theories of change. *Psychological Methods, 20,* 1–25.

Campbell, J. D. (1990). Self-esteem and clarity of the self-concept. *Journal of Personality and Social Psychology, 59,* 538–549.

Cooley, C. H. (1902). *Human nature and the social order.* New York: Scribner.

Delignières, D., Fortes, M., & Ninot, G. (2004). The fractal dynamics of self-esteem and physical self. *Nonlinear Dynamics in Psychology and Life Sciences, 8,* 479–510.

Freeman, J. B., & Ambady, N. (2010). MouseTracker: Software for studying real-time mental processing using a computer mouse-tracking method. *Behavior Research Methods, 42,* 226–241.

Gauld, A., & Shotter, J. (1977). *Human action and its psychological investigation.* London: Routledge & Kegan Paul.

Gergen, K. J. (1978). Toward generative theory. *Journal of Personality and Social Psychology, 36,* 1344–1360.

Gilbert, D., King, G., Pettigrew, S., & Wilson, T. (2016). Comment on "Estimating the reproducibility of psychological science." *Science, 351,* 1037a–1037b.

Gilbert, N., & Troitzsch, K. G. (2011). *Simulation for the social scientist* (2nd ed.). New York: Open University Press.

Guastello, S., Koopmans, M., & Pincus, D. (Eds.) (2009). *Chaos and complexity in psychology: The theory of nonlinear dynamical systems.* New York: Cambridge University Press.

Harré, R., & Secord, P. F. (1972). *The explanation of social behavior.* Oxford: Blackwell.

Hollenstein, T. (2013). *State space grids: Depicting dynamics across development.* New York: Springer.

James, W. (1890). *Principles of psychology.* New York: Holt.

Jarman, M., Nowak, A., Borkowski, W., Serfass, D., Wong, A., & Vallacher, R. R. (2015). The critical few: Anticonformists at the crossroads of minority survival and collapse. *Journal of Artificial Societies and Social Simulation, 18*(1), 6. Retrieved from http://jasss.soc.surrey.ac.uk/18/1/6.html

Kenrick, D. T., Li, N. P., & Butner, J. (2003). Dynamical evolutionary psychology: Individual decision-rules and emergent social norms. *Psychological Review, 110*, 3–28.

Kuhn, T. S. (1970). *The structure of scientific revolutions* (2nd ed.). Chicago, IL: University of Chicago Press.

Kuppens, P., Oravecz, Z., & Tuerlinckx, F. (2010). Feelings change: Accounting for individual differences in the temporal dynamics of affect. *Journal of Personality and Social Psychology, 99*, 1042–1060.

Lewin, K. (1936). *Principles of topological psychology*. New York: McGraw-Hill.

Liebrand, W., Nowak, A., & Hegselman, R. (Eds.) (1998). *Computer modeling of social processes*. New York: SAGE.

Mead, G. H. (1934). *Mind, self, and society*. Chicago, IL: University of Chicago Press.

Messick, D. M., & Liebrand, V. B. G. (1995). Individual heuristics and the dynamics of cooperation in large groups. *Psychological Review, 102*, 131–145.

Monroe, B. M., & Read, S. J. (2008). A general connectionist model of attitudes and attitude change: The ACS (Attitudes as Constraint Satisfaction) Model. *Psychological Review, 115*, 733–759.

Nowak, A., Rychwalska, A., & Borkowski, W. (2013). Why simulate? To develop a mental model. *Journal of Artificial Societies and Social Simulation, 16*(3), 12. Retrieved from http://jasss.soc.surrey.ac.uk/16/3/12.html

Nowak, A., Szamrej, J., & Latané, B. (1990). From private attitude to public opinion: A dynamic theory of social impact. *Psychological Review, 97*, 362–376.

Nowak, A., & Vallacher, R. R. (1998). *Dynamical social psychology*. New York: Guilford Press.

Nowak, A., & Vallacher, R. R. (2001). Societal transition: Toward a dynamical model of social change. In W. Wosinska, R. B. Cialdini, D. W. Barrett, & J. Reykowski (Eds.), *The practice of social influence in multiple cultures* (pp. 151–171). Mahwah, NJ: Lawrence Erlbaum.

Nowak, A., Vallacher, R. R., & Burnstein, E. (1998). Computational social psychology: A neural network approach to interpersonal dynamics. In W. Liebrand, A. Nowak, & R. Hegselman (Eds.), *Computer modeling and the study of dynamic social processes* (pp. 97–125). New York: SAGE.

Nowak, A., Vallacher, R. R., Tesser, A., & Borkowski, W. (2000). Society of self: The emergence of collective properties in self-structure. *Psychological Review, 107*, 39–61.

Nowak, A., Vallacher, R. R., & Zochowski, M. (2005). The emergence of personality: Dynamic foundations of individual variation. *Developmental Review, 25*, 351–385.

Open Science Collaboration (2015). Estimating the reproducibility of psychological science. *Science, 349*(6251), aac4716–aac4716. http://doi.org/10.1126/science.aac4716

Ostrom, T. M. (1988). Computer simulation: The third symbol system. *Journal of Experimental Social Psychology, 24*, 381–392.

Queller, S. (2002). Stereotype change in a recurrent network. *Personality and Social Psychology Review, 6*, 295–303.

Read, S. J., & Miller, L. C. (Eds.) (1998). *Connectionist models of social reasoning and social behavior*. Mahwah, NJ: Lawrence Erlbaum.

Read, S. J., Vanman, E. J., & Miller, L. C. (1997). Connectionism, parallel constraint satisfaction processes, and Gestalt principles: (Re)introducing cognitive dynamics to social psychology. *Personality and Social Psychology Review, 1*, 26–53.

Schuster, H. G. (1984). *Deterministic chaos*. Vienna: Physik Verlag.

Smith, E. R., & Conrey, F. R. (2007). Agent-based modeling: A new approach for theory building in social psychology. *Personality and Social Psychology Review, 11*, 87–104.

Spivey, M. J., & Dale, R. (2006). Continuous dynamics in real-time cognition. *Current Directions in Psychological Science, 15*, 207–211.

Strogatz, S. (1994). *Nonlinear dynamics and chaos*. Cambridge, MA: Perseus Books.

Thagard, P., & Nerb, J. (2002). Emotional Gestalts: Appraisal, change, and the dynamics of affect. *Personality and Social Psychology Review, 6*, 274–282.

Vallacher, R. R., & Nowak, A. (Eds.) (1994). *Dynamical systems in social psychology*. San Diego, CA: Academic Press.

Vallacher, R. R., & Nowak, A. (1997). The emergence of dynamical social psychology. *Psychological Inquiry, 4*, 73–99.

Vallacher, R. R., & Nowak, A. (2007). Dynamical social psychology: Finding order in the flow of human experience. In A. W. Kruglanski & E. T. Higgins (Eds.), *Social psychology: Handbook of basic principles* (pp. 734–758). New York: Guilford Press.

Vallacher, R. R., Nowak, A., & Kaufman, J. (1994). Intrinsic dynamics of social judgment. *Journal of Personality and Social Psychology, 67*, 20–34.

Vallacher, R. R., Read, S. J., & Nowak, A. (Eds.) (2002). The dynamical perspective in social psychology. *Personality and Social Psychology Review, 6*, 264–388.

Vallacher, R. R., Van Geert, P., & Nowak, A. (2015). The intrinsic dynamics of psychological process. *Current Directions in Psychological Science, 24*, 58–64.

Waldrop, M. M. (1992). *Complexity: The emerging science at the edge of order and chaos*. New York: Schuster.

Weisbuch, G. (1992). *Complex system dynamics*. Redwood City, CA: Addison-Wesley.

Wolfram, S. (2002). *A new kind of science*. Champaign, IL: Wolfram Media.

Wong, A., Vallacher, R. R., & Nowak, A. (2014). Fractal dynamics in self-evaluation reveal self-concept clarity. *Nonlinear Dynamics, Psychology, and Life Sciences, 18*, 349–370.

Wong, A. E., Vallacher, R. R., & Nowak, A. (2016). Intrinsic dynamics of self-evaluation: The role of self-concept clarity. *Personality and Individual Differences, 100*, 167–172.

# PART I
# Intrapersonal Dynamics

# 2

# VIRTUAL PERSONALITIES

## A Neural Network Model of the Structure and Dynamics of Personality

*Stephen J. Read, Vita Droutman, and Lynn C. Miller*

There is a long-standing split in personality between structural and dynamic approaches to understanding personality (for recent discussions, see Funder, 2001; Mischel & Shoda, 1998). These two approaches typically rely on different theories and constructs. The structural approach typically focuses on determining the psychometric structure of personality tests (e.g., Lee & Ashton, 2004; McCrae & Costa, 1999) or the everyday language used to describe personality (Digman, 1997; Goldberg, 1981; John & Srivastava, 1999), and a major (although not the only) focus is on understanding stable personality dispositions. In contrast, dynamic approaches, such as Mischel's Cognitive-Affective Systems theory (Mischel & Shoda, 1995, 2008), Atkinson's Dynamics of Action model (Atkinson & Birch, 1970) or McAdams' narrative approach to personality (McAdams, 2008; McAdams, Josselson, & Lieblich, 2006) typically focus on uncovering and understanding the psychological mechanisms that underlie individual differences and changes in behavior across situations and time, and are less interested in understanding stable, broad dispositions. Although some personality researchers have suggested that there is no need to try to bring these two approaches together, many researchers have become increasingly concerned with doing so.

In the current chapter we argue that modeling personality in terms of the behavior of organized motivational systems can help unify the two approaches. We present a neural network model of personality in terms of structured motivational systems (Read et al., 2010; Read & Miller, 2002) that both demonstrates how the structure of personality, such as the Big Five, can arise from these motivational systems and how the dynamics of everyday behavior can arise from the interaction between these structured motivational systems and the changing affordances of situations over time and the bodily states of individuals. Our goal is to show

how personality structure and personality dynamics can arise from the same psychological architecture in interactions with the social and physical environment.

People differ considerably in their behavior and how they respond to the same situations. Personality psychologists who take the psychometric approach to personality often try to understand these individual differences by asking people to respond to items on a personality test, which typically ask people to characterize themselves in terms of typical behaviors, beliefs, emotions, and sometimes motivation. The response to these items across a large sample of individuals is factor analyzed, and the result is typically something like the Big Five (John, Naumann, & Soto, 2008; John & Srivastava, 1999) or similar structures such as the six-factor HEXACO model (Ashton & Lee, 2007; Lee & Ashton, 2004), which essentially adds an Honesty/Humility factor to the Big Five. The Big Five (often referred to by the acronym OCEAN) consists of five major dimensions of human personality: Openness to experience, Conscientiousness, Extraversion, Agreeableness, and Neuroticism.

Differences between individuals can then be considered in terms of different individuals' relative standing on each of the Big Five dimensions. Each individual can be thought of as having a relative profile across each dimension that describes their standing relative to others on the various dimensions.

But something is typically missing in the various structural approaches to personality: an explanation of *why* this particular structure is found and what are the underlying mechanisms or processes. We have argued that this particular structure is the result of underlying structured motivational systems.

Our neural network model of personality (Read et al., 2010; see also Read & Miller, 1989) argues that personality traits, and specifically the Big Five, arise from the interaction between structured motivational systems and the goal affordances of situations. We have argued that a number of relatively specific brain systems manage a variety of different motivational domains and their related behavior, and that these specific systems are then organized into two higher-level Approach and Avoidance systems that integrate over the lower-level systems. The *structure* of these motivational systems is responsible for the *structure* of human personality. But additionally, the *dynamics* of personality can be understood in terms of the ways in which these structured motivational systems interact with the affordances of different situations that the individual encounters and with the individual's current bodily state.

As noted above, personality researchers have largely addressed the structure and dynamics of personality independently. However, researchers have become increasingly interested in how those two important approaches can be related. Here we use our neural network model of personality to show how the structure and dynamics of personality can arise from the dynamics of structured motivational systems.

In the first section of the chapter, we demonstrate how such structured motivational systems can transform variability in chronic motivations across individuals into patterns of behavior from which we can recover the Big Five. We will do this by constructing a neural network model of a set of structured motivational systems, and then training the network to associate different clusters of behavior with different underlying motives. This network will then be used to simulate the behavior of a large number of different individuals as they respond to a variety of different situations. We will then factor analyze the resulting behavior. The result of this factor analysis will map onto the underlying motivational structures in the model.

In the second section of the chapter, we will show how both within- and between-person variability in personality-related behavior can be understood in terms of the dynamics of the interaction between individual's motives, the affordances of situations, and current bodily states. In a series of recent experience-sampling studies of everyday behavior, Fleeson has shown that while there are clear individual differences, consistent with the Big Five, in trends in personality related behavior over time, at the same time the within person variability over situations is at least as large as the between person differences (Fleeson, 2012; Fleeson & Jayawickreme, 2015).

In the final section of the chapter, we will discuss the implications of our computational model for thinking about person–situation interactions.

## General Theoretical Background

The Virtual Personalities model draws upon a wide range of research from personality, neuroscience, developmental psychology, and evolutionary approaches to human behavior that have helped us identify the basic motivational structures that underlie human behavior. Here we briefly review some of the relevant research.

### The Big Five Structure

A large body of research examining the structure of trait scales (e.g., Lee & Ashton, 2004; McCrae & Costa, 1999; Wiggins & Trapnell, 1996) and another body of research that has examined the structure of trait language used in everyday language (e.g., Digman, 1997; Goldberg, 1981; Peabody & De Raad, 2002; Saucier & Ostendorf, 1999) has demonstrated that the overall structure of human personality can be described in terms of five broad factors, typically referred to as the Big Five, or OCEAN, as explained above. Other research, such as HEXACO (Ashton & Lee, 2007; Lee & Ashton, 2004), has argued for six factors, most of which largely overlap with the Big Five.

### Traits as Goal-Based Structures

We and others have argued for a Motive/Goal-based model of traits: the central idea is that personality traits can be viewed as configurations of chronic goals, plans, resources, beliefs, and styles (e.g., Fleeson, 2012; Fleeson & Jayawickreme, 2015; Miller & Read, 1987; Read & Miller, 1989; Yang et al., 2014). Probably most central is the role of motives and goals: at the center of most traits is something people want or something they want to avoid.

### Evolutionary Tasks

A number of researchers (e.g., Bugental, 2000; Kenrick & Trost, 1997) have noted that there are a wide range of problems and tasks that all humans must solve if they are to survive and successfully reproduce, and they have identified a number of motivational systems that have evolved to handle these tasks (e.g., Maslow, 1943; Murray, 1938). Among the various tasks that must be solved and the relevant system are mating, nurturance of young, affiliation and bonding with peers, establishing dominance hierarchies, insuring attachment to caregivers, avoidance of social rejection, and avoidance of physical harm. Over the last 15 years we have developed two extensive motive taxonomies from which we draw in our work (Chulef, Read, & Walsh, 2001; Talevich, Read, Walsh, Chopra, & Iyer, 2015).

### Biological Temperament

In addition, work from neuroscience and work on biological temperament has demonstrated that there are at least three major biologically based dimensions of personality or temperament that map onto three dimensions of the Big Five: Extraversion, Neuroticism, and Conscientiousness. Each of these three dimensions corresponds to a major aspect of motivation. A number of researchers have argued that there is a general Approach (Clark & Watson, 1999; Rothbart & Bates, 1998) or Behavioral Approach System (BAS) (Gray, 1987; Gray & McNaughton, 2000) that governs sensitivity to cues signaling rewards and, when activated, results in an active approach. This maps onto Extraversion. There is considerable evidence that the neurotransmitter dopamine plays a major role in this Approach or Reward system.

In addition, there is a general Avoidance or Behavioral Inhibition System (BIS) (Carver & White, 1994; Clark & Watson, 1999; Gray, 1987; Gray & McNaughton, 2000) that governs sensitivity to cues of punishment and loss and manages avoidance of threatening situations. This maps onto Neuroticism. A third broad dimension concerns a General Disinhibition/Constraint System (Derryberry & Rothbart, 1997; Rothbart & Bates, 1998) which is related to executive function and inhibitory control. This probably maps onto Conscientiousness.

### Overview of the Simulations and Their Implications

The section below on "The Dynamics of Motivation" details how we go from a structured motivational model to how resulting motivational dynamics across hundreds of virtual personalities produce emergent outcomes resembling the Big Five.

The section on "Within-Person versus Between-Person Variability" describes a simulation of how our neural network model captures motivational dynamics and changes in behavior over time.

The section on "Person–Situation Interactions" discusses the implications of this computational model for thinking about person–situation interactions.

## Overview of Neural Networks

A neural network model consists of nodes and weighted links between them. Processing in the network proceeds by the passing of activation among nodes along these weighted links. The activation of a node is a function of the inputs it receives from the other nodes with which it is linked. Typically, the input is a weighted average (or sum) of the activations from other nodes, where the activations are weighted by the strength of the link:

- *Nodes*—These represent various features or concepts, analogous to neurons or systems of neurons. Their level of activation represents their importance and their readiness to fire and send activation to other nodes with which they are linked.
- *Layers*—Nodes are organized in layers, corresponding to systems (Situational Input, Approach and Avoidance Motives, Behavior) of nodes that interact in terms of excitatory and inhibitory relations among them. In the neural architecture that we use in the current simulations (Leabra; Aisa, Mingus, & O'Reilly, 2008), nodes within a layer compete with each other for activation. The degree of competition is a parameter that can be manipulated in Leabra.
- *Links*—These represent the relations among nodes. The strength and direction of weight represents degree and direction of influence. Nodes can be connected either unidirectionally or bidirectionally, depending on the type of model. When there is a unidirectional connection between two nodes, then activation can only flow in one direction and only the first node can influence the subsequent one. However, when nodes are bidirectionally connected, then activation can flow in both directions and the nodes can mutually influence one another.

## *Current Neural Network Model*

The current networks are modeled in the *emergent* (Aisa et al., 2008; O'Reilly & Munakata, 2000) neural network modeling system, using the Leabra architecture. Leabra (Local, error-driven and associative, biologically realistic algorithm) is a specific architecture developed by O'Reilly that attempts to use biologically realistic algorithms, based on actual neural systems, to capture both the activation of nodes and the process of learning the weights between nodes. A learning rule allows us to model changes in association between nodes as a function of their frequency of co-occurrence.

Figure 2.1 shows the version of the Virtual Personality model used for the Big Five simulations. There are five meaningful layers. The *Input* or *Situational Features* layer is the initial input layer to the network that represents information about the different situations or situational features to which the network is exposed. There are 30 input nodes, representing 30 different situations. Processing in the network starts by applying activation from the available features to these nodes and then having activation spread across the weighted links to subsequent nodes.

The *Approach* and the *Avoid(ance)* layers organize specific approach-related and avoidance-related motives. Each node represents a different motive. The Approach layer has two nodes, corresponding to two different potential factors, each with a corresponding motive, whereas the Avoid layer has three nodes, corresponding to three different motives and factors. The specific motives are described in the following. Nodes within a layer compete for activation, and the amount of competition can be manipulated, which influences how many nodes can be active. This allows us to control how many motives can be active at any one time and trying to influence behavior. In the current network, competition is set so that only one motive within a layer will tend to be active at any one time.

The *Motivation Level* layer is used to represent chronic individual differences in specific motive activation. Each node in this layer has a one-to-one connection with a node in the Approach and Avoid layers. By setting activations in the Motivation Level nodes, we can control the baseline activation for the motive nodes in the Approach and Avoid layers, which influences the likelihood that motive nodes will be active.

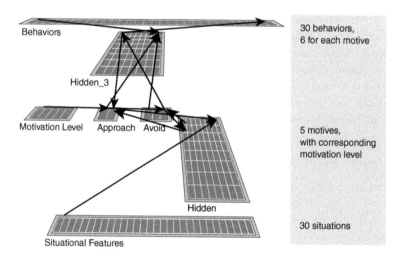

**FIGURE 2.1** Version of the Virtual Personality model used for the Big Five simulations.

The *Behaviors* layer represents the personality-related behaviors, and in this model there are 30 different behaviors. (For this simulation, the behaviors are abstract—e.g., Behavior 1, Behavior 2, etc.—since the concrete nature of a behavior is not important here.) Competition is set in this layer so that only one node (behavior) at a time can be active, to capture the obvious idea that only one action can be enacted at any given time.

The two *Hidden* layers allow the network to learn complex or conjunctive combinations of features that represent a more abstract concept. For example, in the visual system, hidden layers enable the visual system to learn a hierarchy of visual representations, such as from dots on the retina to lines, from lines to shapes, and then from shapes to entire objects.

## Activation of Node and Output Activation

The activation level of a node is calculated as a function of its current activation plus its input activation. In Leabra, input activation is calculated as the sum of three terms: (1) excitatory input from other neurons, (2) inhibitory input from other neurons, and (3) leak current, which is a constant inhibitory term. The sum of these three terms provides the membrane potential $V_m$ of the node. Whether and the extent to which a node will fire or send activation is a function of the extent to which the current activation of the node exceeds a threshold value that is a function of the degree of inhibitory input and leak current.[1]

The excitatory input to a node is a function of two terms: (1) the number of ion channels which can be potentially open ($\bar{g}_e$), and (2) the proportion of ion channels that are actually open ($g_e$). As we discuss later, the number of ion channels that are potentially open can serve as a gain or sensitivity parameter for the node. Higher sensitivity results in a steeper activation function. The proportion of ion channels that are currently open $g_e$ can be calculated as:

$$g_e(t) = \frac{1}{n}\sum_i x_i w_i \tag{2.1}$$

where $x_i$ is the activity of a particular sending neuron indexed by the subscript $i$, $w_i$ s the synaptic weight strength that connects sending neuron $i$ to the receiving neuron, and $n$ is the total number of channels of that type (in this case, excitatory) across all synaptic inputs to the cell. This equation is essentially the same equation that is used in all neural network models to calculate the input activation as a function of the activation being sent by input nodes, multiplied by the weights between the input and output nodes. A similar equation applies to inhibitory inputs. From this information, the overall levels of excitation, inhibition, and leak current can be calculated:

- **excitatory conductance:**

$$\bar{g}_e g_e(t)$$

- **inhibitory conductance:**

$$\bar{g}_i g_i(t)$$

- **leak conductance:**

$$\bar{g}_l$$

(The leak current does not have a time varying component, it is a constant.)

From these terms one can calculate the membrane potential, with the conductance terms explicitly broken out into the "g-bar" constants and the time-varying "g(t)" parts. The $E$ terms correspond to what is called the "driving potential" for the particular kind of channel:

$$v_m = \frac{\bar{g}_e g_e(t)}{\bar{g}_e g_e(t) + \bar{g}_i g_i(t) + \bar{g}_l} E_e + \frac{\bar{g}_i g_i(t)}{\bar{g}_e g_e(t) + \bar{g}_i g_i(t) + \bar{g}_l} E_i$$

$$+ \frac{\bar{g}_l}{\bar{g}_e g_e(t) + \bar{g}_i g_i(t) + \bar{g}_l} E_l \tag{2.2}$$

The membrane potential can then be used to calculate the threshold $g_e^\theta$, which is the threshold that the total excitatory conductance must exceed in order to fire:

$$g_e^\theta = \frac{g_i(E_i - \Theta) + g_l(E_l - \Theta)}{\Theta - E_e} \tag{2.3}$$

The output activation of the node is a sigmoidal or S-shaped function of the extent to which the excitatory input to the node exceeds the threshold for firing.

$$y = \frac{1}{\left(1 + \dfrac{1}{\gamma\left[g_e - g_e^\theta\right]+}\right)} \tag{2.4}$$

$y$ is the output value, $g_e$ is excitatory input, $g_e^\theta$ is the threshold for firing, $\gamma$ is the gain parameter, which governs the steepness of the slope, and the + indicates that only a positive value will be returned.

## Learning

Weights between nodes are modified to capture two different kinds of information. One kind of learning is Hebbian learning, which captures the covariance or correlation among the activation of nodes. In Hebbian learning, the weight between two nodes will increase if they are active at the same time, whereas they will decrease if one is active and the other is not. A second kind of learning is error-correcting learning, where weights will change to capture the extent to which activation of the input node successfully predicts activation of the output node. Error-correcting learning changes the weights to reduce the degree of error in predicting an outcome.[2]

## Processing

Processing starts by applying situational or input features to the Input layer. Activation then flows from there through the hidden layer and then to the Approach and Avoidance layers. Activation also flows from the Motivation level to the Approach and Avoidance layers to set the baseline or chronic activation of each motive. Activations of the motives are a function of: (1) the current situation, (2) individual differences in chronic motive activations, set by the Chronic Motive level, and (3) individual differences in the sensitivities or gains of the Approach and Avoidance systems (a parameter that can be set in Leabra), which captures individual differences in sensitivity to reward and punishment.

Activated motives in the Approach and Avoidance layers then compete with one another for activation. Competition takes place independently in each of the two layers. The amount of competition, and thus the number of nodes that can be active, can be manipulated in Leabra. The relevant parameter is set so that only one or so motives can be active in each layer. Motive nodes that are active then send activation to behaviors that can help to satisfy those motives. Behaviors in the Behavior layer then compete for which behavior will be enacted. Competition is set within the Behavior layer so that only one behavior node can be active at a time, capturing the idea that multiple behaviors cannot typically be enacted at the same time.

In the simulation of the Big Five, two important parameters will be manipulated: (1) the conductances (or gains) for the Approach and Avoidance layers, which influence the sensitivity or gain of all nodes within the relevant layer, and (2) the baseline or chronic activation of individual motives within the relevant layer, which is set by activation from the Chronic Motive Level layer.

## Simulation of the Structure of Personality: The Big Five

If personality traits, and specifically the Big Five, arise from the interaction between organized motivational systems and the goal affordances of situations, then we should be able to use this neural network model to simulate a pattern of behavior across situations and different individuals that will result in the Big Five. Specifically, if we: (1) model several hundred individuals (or Virtual Personalities—VPs) by varying the parameters of appropriately structured underlying motivational systems, (2) measure the resulting behavior from these hundreds of VPs, and (3) factor analyze that behavior, then the factor analysis will result in something like the Big Five.

For the current simulation, we have structured the motivational systems as follows. We have divided the underlying motivational systems into two broad systems, corresponding to the Approach and Avoidance layers, in the network. Within each of these two layers or systems, we represent multiple motives, corresponding to multiple Big Five factors. Following DeYoung's (2015) work on the structure of the two broad factors underlying the Big Five, in the Approach system we have Extraversion and Openness to Experience, whereas in the Avoidance system we have Neuroticism, as well as Agreeableness and Conscientiousness. In this simple simulation, we have five nodes, two in the Approach layer and three in the Avoidance layer. Each node represents a plausible motive for the corresponding factor.

The Big Five factors and plausible underlying motives are:

- Extraversion—relating and belonging; being with others;
- Openness to Experience—appreciating beauty; enjoying intellectual experiences;
- Neuroticism—avoiding rejection by others;
- Agreeableness—helping others; wanting others to like you;
- Conscientiousness—doing my duty; being disciplined.

## Training of the Model/Learning

This instantiation of the model has 30 input nodes, corresponding to 30 different situations, five motive nodes, two in the Approach layer and three in the Avoidance layer, and 30 different behavior nodes, corresponding to 30 different behaviors. The network is trained to learn the following patterns of associations among the different nodes by repeatedly presenting it with 150 different instances that are structured as follows.

Each of the 30 situations co-occurs equally often with each of the five motives, creating 150 instances. This results in roughly equal weight strengths between each situation and each motive. Thus, each motive is equally likely to be activated by a given situation.

Within these 150 instances, each of the five motives co-occurs equally often (five times) with each behavior in a cluster of six behaviors. That is, each motive is highly related to six behaviors, but unrelated to the other 24. So when a particular motive is activated, each of the six associated behaviors will tend to be equally activated, on average. Thus, activation of a specific motive will tend to activate a set of six behaviors. This will lead to correlations among the activations of the behaviors. However, because random noise leads to slightly different levels of activation for each behavior, the competitive dynamics among the behaviors ensure that on any given trial only one behavior will end up being enacted.[3]

## Testing

To test whether we could get something like the structure of the Big Five from this network, we first generated 576 instances of the neural network (576 "individuals") with different patterns of individual differences, by doing the following: (1) We generated all 32 possible combinations of the five binary (0,1) motive levels in the Chronic Motive layer ($2 \times 2 \times 2 \times 2 \times 2 = 32$), (2) generated all possible combinations of three levels of sensitivity for both the Approach and Avoidance layers ($3 \times 3 = 9$), and (3) trained two different networks, with different random starting weights. This gave us a total of 576 unique "individuals" ($9 \times 32 \times 2 = 576$). We could get many more instances by more continuously varying the parameters. However, we felt that 576 individuals would be enough to test our predictions.

Once we had the 576 individuals, we then tested each one on five passes through the 30 situations (150 total test situations). Each of the 30 nodes in the Situation layer was treated as a different situation. Because of random noise in the Input or Situation layer, each time a situation was presented, it should have had a slightly different activation.

For each of the 150 "situations" presented, we recorded the net activation across each of the 30 behavior nodes and then averaged the net activation for each node across the 150 test cases. We can think of the net activation as the tendency to enact that behavior. Thus, for each individual we have a profile of the net activation or behavioral tendency across the 30 behaviors. The 30 behavior nodes can be thought of as 30 items on a scale. And because of the way the behavior nodes are linked to the five motives, there are six items for each motive. Essentially we have the scores for 576 "individuals" on 30 different items in a scale, with six items measuring each of the Big Five. From this, we can calculate a correlation matrix among the 30 behaviors and then factor analyze the correlation matrix to look for evidence of the Big Five structure.

We then did a Principal Factor Analysis on the correlation matrix. Figure 2.2 shows the Scree plot, which has a very clear bend between five and six factors, indicating that there are five factors.

Figure 2.3 shows the factor loadings for a five-factor solution, with Varimax (orthogonal) rotation. The figure is set to only display loadings that are 0.4 or greater. There are five clear factors, corresponding to the five clusters of items associated with the five motives. With one minor exception, each item is very highly loaded on only one factor and the pattern of loadings corresponds to the relationship of the behaviors to the five motives.

One way to think about these results that might be helpful is to think of this as analogous to a Latent Variable Factor model, with specific motivations as latent variables and behaviors as manifest variables that are indicators of the latent, motivational variable. Different behaviors that are influenced by the same motivation will tend to occur frequently within the same individual.

# Scree plot of eigenvalues after factor

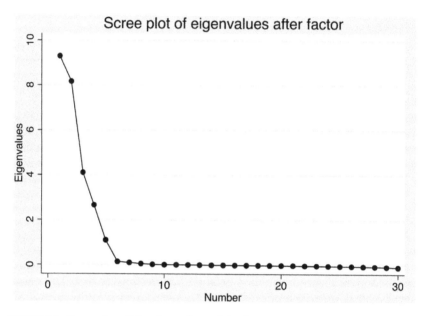

**FIGURE 2.2**  Scree plot of the eigenvalues of the factors in a Principal Factors solution. There is a very clear bend between 5 and 6, indicating that five factors is probably the best number for this data set.

## Principal Factor Analysis
### 5 factors, orthogonal rotation. Mean activation

Rotated factor loadings (pattern matrix) and unique variances

| Variable | Factor1 | Factor2 | Factor3 | Factor4 | Factor5 |
|---|---|---|---|---|---|
| behav_net_-1 | | | | | 0.8588 |
| behav_n-n210 | | | | | 0.8401 |
| behav_n-n220 | | | | | 0.8292 |
| behav_n-n230 | | | | | 0.8240 |
| behav_n-n240 | | | | | 0.6761 |
| behav_n-n250 | | | | | 0.8239 |
| behav_n-n260 | | | | 0.8231 | |
| behav_n-n270 | | | | 0.8144 | |
| behav_n-n280 | | | | 0.8209 | |
| behav_n-n290 | | | | 0.7902 | |
| behav_n-2100 | | | | 0.8181 | |
| behav_n-2110 | -0.4168 | | | 0.6610 | |
| behav_n-2120 | 0.8890 | | | | |
| behav_n-2130 | 0.9000 | | | | |
| behav_n-2140 | 0.9135 | | | | |
| behav_n-2150 | 0.8468 | | | | |
| behav_n-2160 | 0.8957 | | | | |
| behav_n-2170 | 0.8956 | | | | |
| behav_n-2180 | | | 0.8355 | | |
| behav_n-2190 | | | 0.8717 | | |
| behav_n-2200 | | | 0.8117 | | |
| behav_n-2210 | | | 0.8336 | | |
| behav_n-2220 | | | 0.8592 | | |
| behav_n-2230 | | | 0.8568 | | |
| behav_n-2240 | | 0.9079 | | | |
| behav_n-2250 | | 0.9205 | | | |
| behav_n-2260 | | 0.9227 | | | |
| behav_n-2270 | | 0.9218 | | | |
| behav_n-2280 | | 0.9328 | | | |
| behav_n-2290 | | 0.8225 | | | |

Extraversion
Openness to experience
Neuroticism
Agreeableness
Conscientiousness

**FIGURE 2.3**  Factor loadings for a five-factor solution, after Varimax (orthogonal) rotation.

## Interim Conclusions

Read and Miller (e.g., Miller & Read, 1991; Read & Miller, 1989) and others, such as Fleeson (e.g., Fleeson & Jayawickreme, 2015) in his Whole Trait Theory, argue that goals and motives play a fundamental role in the nature of personality traits, and that personality structure can be understood in terms of underlying motivational structures. Here we have used a computer simulation to show how the Big Five could arise from suitably organized motivational systems. This further suggests how stable underlying motivational systems (structure) can nevertheless produce considerable variability in behavior across individuals.

## The Dynamics of Motivation: Changes in Behavior over Time and Situation

Recently, various researchers have raised the question of how the structure and dynamics of personality can be related. Among the questions that have been raised are: Can stable personality structures result in dynamic, changing behavior over time and situations? If so, how? What are the mechanisms by which underlying stable structures can result in dynamic behavior?

Although there are strong differences between individuals in their dispositions or general levels of different kinds of behavior, behavior is highly dynamic and varies considerably over time and situations. The same individual may be highly talkative at a party or a meeting, but quiet when in church or studying at the library. A major source of those behavioral dynamics is motivational dynamics—changes in what we "want" over time and situations. Motivation changes—in the short term—due to changes in opportunities in the environment for motive or goal-related behavior (Gibson, 1979 called this "affordances") and our current bodily or interoceptive state.

As a result of changes in our motivation and the motivational affordances of situations, our behavior will vary over time and situations. In this section, we show how our personality model, based on structured motivational systems can also capture the variability of individuals' behavior over time and situations. Our approach to motivational dynamics is influenced by Atkinson and Birch's (1970) Dynamics of Action (DOA), which presented a model of how the ebb and flow of competing motives over time and situations would lead to major changes in behavior. It is also influenced by Revelle and Condon's (2015) recent reparameterization of Atkinson and Birch's model. In particular, Revelle and Condon suggest that the DOA model can actually be modeled as a neural network model. Although our model does not precisely follow their parameterization, it does have some similarities with their description.

In both the DOA and Revelle and Condon's reparameterization, they treat the strength of current motivation as a function of previous motivation, instigating forces and consummatory forces resulting from actions such as eating or drinking that reduce the strength of motivation. In their approach, instigating forces are solely a function of the strength or attractiveness of a cue. However, Berridge and colleagues (e.g., Berridge, 2007; Zhang, Berridge, Tindell, Smith, & Aldridge, 2009) argue that motivation for a behavior or the strength of "wanting" is also strongly influenced by current bodily or interoceptive state. Specifically, they argue that the strength of "wanting" is a multiplicative function of both cue strength (attractiveness of approach cue and aversiveness of avoidance cue) and current bodily state (e.g., Hunger, Thirst, etc.). For example, Food is more wanted when it is highly attractive *and* when one is very hungry. In terms of the DOA model, this view of the nature of wanting argues that instigating forces are a joint function of cue strength and bodily state, rather than just a function of cue strength. We follow this idea in the current model, and we add a layer that represents current interoceptive or bodily state to our simulation of the dynamics of motivation.

## Not a Cybernetic Model

One important point to note is that our model is not a cybernetic or homeostatic model of control. There is no set point or comparator, such as a thermostat on a heating system. Instead, it is an open control model (see Bolles, 1980), in which the level of motivation is the result of the balance between instigating forces and consummatory forces.

## Structure of the Computational Model and Flow of Processing

In the current simulation, we start out with a simple model system to simulate behavioral dynamics over time and situations. The simple model system is a rat, with basic motives, bodily states, and situational affordances. Model systems are typically used in biology to provide a simple and clearly understood system for a phenomenon that still captures the central characteristics of the system. In previous modeling work, we have started with much more complex models and have ended up spending much of our time trying to understand the complexities of the model, rather than the central principles. However, we believe that once we understand this model system well, it should be fairly easy to scale up to more complicated systems.

A picture of the model, as represented in the Emergent software system can be seen in Figure 2.4. The Environment layer represents cues in the environment that have strong motivational affordances, here Food, Water, and a Cat. The Bodily State layer represents the strength of current interoceptive or bodily states: Hunger, Thirst, and Fear.

The Environment layer and the Bodily State layer jointly send activation to the Approach and Avoidance layers. Both the Approach and Avoidance layers are implemented as Multiplicative layers, which take the inputs from two layers and multiplies them together. Thus, the activation of each motive node is a multiplicative function of the corresponding Environment cues and Bodily State.

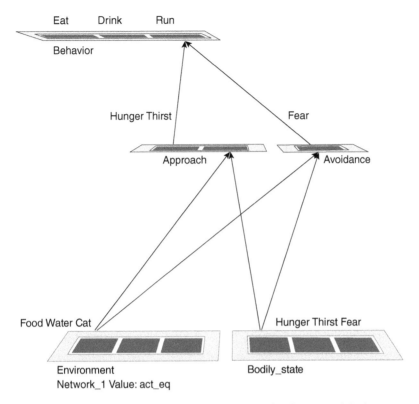

Eat      Drink      Run

Behavior

Hunger Thirst                    Fear

Approach                         Avoidance

Food Water Cat                   Hunger Thirst Fear

Environment                      Bodily_state
Network_1 Value: act_eq

**FIGURE 2.4**  A screenshot of the Emergent network for the rat model of Motivation.

Note that one important implication of this is that typically neither a strong cue nor a strong bodily state is sufficient by itself to strongly activate wanting. However, in subsequent work (Read, Smith, Droutman, & Miller, in press) we have begun to investigate how to model the possibility that a highly activated bodily state will lead the animal to start looking for objects that can satisfy that state. So high levels of hunger, with no food present in the current environment, would instigate animals to start looking for food.

In general, consistent with a large body of work suggesting organisms are more sensitive to potential negative events than to potential positive events (e.g., Cacioppo & Berntson, 1994; Cacioppo, Gardner, & Berntson, 1997), the network is more sensitive to Threat cues than to Approach cues, so Threat will typically override Approach-related motives. Thus, even with strong affordances and strong Bodily State, Threat (Cat) will override the other systems. The strong impact of the Threat cue is implemented by giving a higher weight scaling to the weight from the Avoidance layer (Fear) to the Run node in the Behavior layer.

The Motive nodes then send activation to the Behavior layer, where the three behaviors of Eat, Drink, and Run compete with each other for activation. When a behavior is activated, it then can reduce the level of its corresponding bodily state. Thus, engaging in a consummatory behavior, such as eating or drinking, or running away will reduce the relevant bodily state and thus reduce the likelihood of the relevant behavior. (In the current version of the model, this direct effect on bodily state is not currently implemented, but instead is simulated by changing the input to the bodily state from the Inputs. In ongoing work, we have implemented this direct effect: Read et al., in press).

An important implication of the fact that motives and behaviors compete with each other for activation is that the likelihood of a behavior being activated is not a function solely of the strength of the relevant motive, but rather is a function of the strength of wanting something compared to the strength of wanting other things. For example, if there are both food and water around and we are moderately hungry but are also very thirsty, we will drink. However, in the absence of thirst, the same level of hunger and food will lead to eating.

## Factors Influencing Dynamics

Behavior from this network is highly dynamic and will shift over time as a function of a variety of different factors: (1) changes in situational *affordances*—as affordances appear and disappear as situations change, behavior will change even with consistent bodily state; (2) Changes in current *bodily state*—as bodily state waxes and wanes, behavior will change even with consistent affordances, and behaviors will influence motivation, and thus future behavior, by influencing both bodily state and situational affordances. For example, eating will reduce the bodily state cue associated with hunger, and by reducing bodily state allows motivation or "wanting" to be higher for another behavior, and thus allow another behavior to be enacted. Behaviors can also influence situational affordances, by moving the organism into different situations that have different affordances or by removing affordances, such as eating all the food or drinking all the water. All of these components acting together over time and situations will result in a highly dynamic situation in which the organism's behavior will change across time and place.

## Simulation

In the following simulations, we provide an example of how the model behaves as both affordances and bodily state change over time. The columns in the figures below show the activation values of the different layers and their nodes over time. The Environment and Bodily State columns represent the Inputs to the network, the Motivation layer represents the intervening Motivational state, and the Behavior layers represent the outputs.

### Simulation 1

In Figure 2.5a, the three columns labeled "Environment" indicate the strength of the activation of three cues in the Environment—Food, Water, and Cat—at each time point. The strength of the cues stays constant, and the strength of the Food cue is stronger than the strength of the Water cue. The second column, "Bodily State," indicates the strength of the activation of each Bodily State at each time point. Over time, the Hunger state decreases and the Thirst state increases. The third column, "Motivation", represents the multiplicative value of the Environment activations and the Bodily State activations. The final column, "Behavior," represents the activation of each behavior after the competitive dynamics have played out in this layer. The most strongly activated behavior is the one that will be enacted.

As can be seen in Figure 2.5a, with a constant set of environmental cues to Food and Water, changes in bodily state over time lead to a shift in motivation

**(a)**

**Bodily State change**

| Time | Environment | | | Bodily State | | | Motivation | | | Behavior | | |
|---|---|---|---|---|---|---|---|---|---|---|---|---|
| | Food | Water | Cat | Hunger | Thirst | Fear | Hunger | Thirst | Fear | Eat | Drink | Run |
| 1 | 0.80 | 0.50 | 0.00 | 0.80 | 0.50 | 0.00 | 0.64 | 0.25 | 0.00 | 0.89 | 0.00 | 0.00 |
| 2 | 0.80 | 0.50 | 0.00 | 0.70 | 0.50 | 0.00 | 0.56 | 0.25 | 0.00 | 0.86 | 0.00 | 0.00 |
| 3 | 0.80 | 0.50 | 0.00 | 0.60 | 0.60 | 0.00 | 0.48 | 0.30 | 0.00 | 0.79 | 0.00 | 0.00 |
| 4 | 0.80 | 0.50 | 0.00 | 0.50 | 0.60 | 0.00 | 0.40 | 0.30 | 0.00 | 0.71 | 0.00 | 0.00 |
| 5 | 0.80 | 0.50 | 0.00 | 0.40 | 0.70 | 0.00 | 0.32 | 0.35 | 0.00 | 0.08 | 0.58 | 0.00 |
| 6 | 0.80 | 0.50 | 0.00 | 0.30 | 0.70 | 0.00 | 0.24 | 0.35 | 0.00 | 0.00 | 0.68 | 0.00 |
| 7 | 0.80 | 0.50 | 0.00 | 0.30 | 0.80 | 0.00 | 0.24 | 0.40 | 0.00 | 0.00 | 0.74 | 0.00 |

**(b)**

**Environment change**

| Time | Environment | | | Bodily State | | | Motivation | | | Behavior | | |
|---|---|---|---|---|---|---|---|---|---|---|---|---|
| | Food | Water | Cat | Hunger | Thirst | Fear | Hunger | Thirst | Fear | Eat | Drink | Run |
| 1 | 0.80 | 0.50 | 0.00 | 0.80 | 0.50 | 0.00 | 0.64 | 0.25 | 0.00 | 0.89 | 0.00 | 0.00 |
| 2 | 0.70 | 0.50 | 0.00 | 0.80 | 0.50 | 0.00 | 0.56 | 0.25 | 0.00 | 0.86 | 0.00 | 0.00 |
| 3 | 0.60 | 0.60 | 0.00 | 0.80 | 0.50 | 0.00 | 0.48 | 0.30 | 0.00 | 0.79 | 0.00 | 0.00 |
| 4 | 0.50 | 0.60 | 0.00 | 0.80 | 0.50 | 0.00 | 0.40 | 0.30 | 0.00 | 0.71 | 0.00 | 0.00 |
| 5 | 0.40 | 0.70 | 0.00 | 0.80 | 0.50 | 0.00 | 0.32 | 0.35 | 0.00 | 0.08 | 0.58 | 0.00 |
| 6 | 0.30 | 0.70 | 0.00 | 0.80 | 0.50 | 0.00 | 0.24 | 0.35 | 0.00 | 0.00 | 0.68 | 0.00 |
| 7 | 0.30 | 0.80 | 0.00 | 0.80 | 0.50 | 0.00 | 0.24 | 0.40 | 0.00 | 0.00 | 0.74 | 0.00 |

**(c)**

**Cat**

| Time | Environment | | | Bodily State | | | Motivation | | | Behavior | | |
|---|---|---|---|---|---|---|---|---|---|---|---|---|
| | Food | Water | Cat | Hunger | Thirst | Fear | Hunger | Thirst | Fear | Eat | Drink | Run |
| 1 | 0.80 | 0.60 | 0.00 | 0.80 | 0.50 | 0.00 | 0.64 | 0.30 | 0.00 | 0.88 | 0.00 | 0.00 |
| 2 | 0.80 | 0.70 | 0.00 | 0.80 | 0.50 | 0.00 | 0.64 | 0.35 | 0.00 | 0.87 | 0.00 | 0.00 |
| 3 | 0.80 | 0.70 | 0.50 | 0.80 | 0.50 | 0.50 | 0.64 | 0.35 | 0.25 | 0.00 | 0.00 | 0.72 |
| 4 | 0.80 | 0.70 | 0.50 | 0.80 | 0.50 | 0.50 | 0.64 | 0.35 | 0.25 | 0.00 | 0.00 | 0.72 |
| 5 | 0.80 | 0.70 | 0.50 | 0.80 | 0.50 | 0.50 | 0.64 | 0.35 | 0.25 | 0.00 | 0.00 | 0.72 |
| 6 | 0.80 | 0.70 | 0.50 | 0.80 | 0.50 | 0.50 | 0.64 | 0.35 | 0.25 | 0.00 | 0.00 | 0.72 |
| 7 | 0.80 | 0.80 | 0.50 | 0.80 | 0.50 | 0.50 | 0.64 | 0.40 | 0.25 | 0.00 | 0.00 | 0.69 |

**FIGURE 2.5** Tables representing the Environment and Bodily State inputs, and the resulting Motivation and Behavior activations for the rat model. (a) With a constant set of environmental cues to Food and Water, changes in bodily state over time lead to a shift in motivation and a sudden shift in behavior. (b) Bodily State remains constant over time, but changes in the strength of Environmental cues lead to nonlinear shifts in Motivation and the corresponding behavior. (c) Because of the stronger weights from Fear to Behavior (representing greater fear sensitivity), relatively weak Fear cues can override much stronger Environment and Bodily State cues.

and a sudden shift in behavior. Moreover, this shift from Eating to Drinking can occur even though the strength of the Food cue is consistently stronger than the strength of the Water cue.

## Simulation 2

The results of the simulation in Figure 2.5b show that when Bodily State remains constant over time, changes in strength of Environmental cues leads to a shift in Motivation and a corresponding shift in Behavior. Moreover, the shift is highly nonlinear.

## Simulation 3

The results of the simulation in Figure 2.5c simply show that because of the stronger weights from the Fear motivation to Behavior and because of the competitive dynamics in the Behavior layer, even relatively weak Fear cues can override much stronger Environment and Bodily State cues. This captures the idea that the Avoid- or Threat-related motivational system is more sensitive to Environmental cues than is the Approach system. Again, the change in behavior is highly nonlinear.

Taken together, these three simulations demonstrate how behavior can change quite strongly over time and situations, in a highly nonlinear fashion, as a function of changes in bodily state and changes in the strength of environmental cues. This shows how a stable structure can nevertheless lead to considerable variability over time and space as the inputs to the structure change over time and with exposure to different situations.

## Within-Person versus Between-Person Variability

Both within- and between-person variability can be understood in terms of motive dynamics. Fleeson has observed, over a number of studies (Fleeson, 2001, 2012; Fleeson & Jayawickreme, 2015), that within-person variability in personality-related behaviors over time and situations can be as large as between-person variability in personality-related behavior. But how can this be if there are stable individual differences, and more specifically, how can this be if there are stable individual differences in the structure of motivation?

We argue that this pattern makes sense because both within- and between-person variability in personality-related behavior can be understood in terms of motivational dynamics: specifically, the dynamics of the interaction among individuals' chronic motive activations, motive affordances of situations, and individuals' current "bodily" or interoceptive state.

*Within-person variability* in personality-related behavior can be understood in terms of changes in motive affordances as people move through different situations and changes in current "bodily" state over time (e.g., due to satiation, deprivation, etc.).

*Between-person variability* in personality-related behavior can be understood in terms of between-person differences in chronic motive activations, between-person differences in sensitivity to situations, and between-person differences in choice of situations with different affordances.

The preceding suggests that the ratio of between-person variability to within-person variability in personality-related behavior depends on:

> ratio of between-person variability in chronic activation of different motives
>
> to
>
> within-person variability in momentary motive activation as individuals move through time and situations

Thus, within-person variability can easily be equivalent to typical between-person variability as long as the motive affordances of situations vary strongly over time and there is strong variability in bodily state.

## Person–Situation Interactions

Related to the above discussion on within- versus between-person variability, a key question in personality over the years has been how stable personality dispositions can nevertheless result in different kinds of behaviors in different situations. In the preceding simulations, we have shown how this question can be addressed through the role of structured motivational systems interacting with the motive affordances of situations. Specifically, we have argued that behavior is a joint function of individual differences in chronic motives, motive affordances of the specific situations an individual is in, and current bodily state. Thus, an individual's behavior in a situation will be the result of the interaction of the motive affordances of the situation with both chronic and temporary differences in motivational state within the individual. As a result, stable dispositions based on chronic motives can lead to very different behaviors as the nature of the situation and the current bodily states change.

In the current chapter, we have focused on the role of motive affordances in explaining why people may behave quite differently in different situations. However, we acknowledge and have discussed extensively in other work (e.g., Miller & Read, 1991; Read & Miller, 1989) how behavior is strongly influenced by other aspects of situations, such as roles, and rules and scripts for appropriate and typical behavior. In this current work, we are attempting to see how much of the variability across situations can be explained by the concept of affordances. But other aspects of situations could be implemented in an expanded version of this model. For example, we could simulate individual differences in situational knowledge or reinforcement history in different situations.

## Conclusion and Discussion

This chapter has outlined how the structural and dynamic approaches to personality can be integrated and understood in terms of the interaction between structured motivational systems within the individual, and affordances for goal pursuit within the situation. In the first simulation, we showed how structured motivational systems can result in personality *structures*, such as the Big Five, when we look at the behavior of a large number of individuals. In the second simulation, we showed how such structured motivational systems can result in personality *dynamics* over time and situations, such that the variability in behavior *within* individuals can be large, and potentially as large as the variability in behavior between individuals. Following on this simulation, we have discussed how person–situation interactions can be understood in terms of the interaction between underlying motivational structures and the varying affordances for goal pursuit that characterize different situations.

In sum, our models and the simulations using them demonstrate that the same kind of underlying motivational systems can be responsible for both the structure and dynamics of personality. Although the field has tended to approach personality structure and personality dynamics independently and to view them as very different types of things, we have shown how they can arise out of the same psychological architecture in interactions with the environment.

## Notes

1 For a detailed description of how activation is calculated in Leabra, see the chapter "CCNBook/Neuron" in the online wiki textbook *Computational Cognitive Neuroscience* (2nd ed.), Boulder, CO: CCNLab, University of Colorado. Retrieved from https://grey.colorado.edu/CompCogNeuro/index.php/CCNBook/Neuron.
2 For a detailed description of the learning rule in Leabra, see the chapter "CCNBook/Learning" in *Computational Cognitive Neuroscience* (2nd ed.). Retrieved from https://grey.colorado.edu/CompCogNeuro/index.php/CCNBook/Learning.
3 This only looks at the impact of behaviors depending on common motives. It does not examine the impact of situation–goal links.

## References

Aisa, B., Mingus, B., & O'Reilly, R. (2008). The Emergent neural modeling system. *Neural Networks, 21*(8), 1146–1152. http://doi.org/10.1016/j.neunet.2008.06.016
Ashton, M. C., & Lee, K. (2007). Empirical, theoretical, and practical advantages of the HEXACO model of personality structure. *Personality and Social Psychology Review, 11*(2), 150–166. http://doi.org/10.1177/1088868306294907

Atkinson, J. W., & Birch, D. (1970). *The dynamics of action.* New York: John Wiley.

Berridge, K. C. (2007). The debate over dopamine's role in reward: The case for incentive salience. *Psychopharmacology, 191*(3), 391–431.

Bolles, R. (1980). Some functionalistic thoughts about regulation. In F. M. Toates & T. Halliday (Eds.), *Analysis of motivational processes* (pp. 77–102). London: Academic Press.

Bugental, D. B. (2000). Acquisition of the algorithms of social life: A domain-based approach. *Psychological Bulletin, 126*(2), 187–219. http://doi.org/10.1037/0033-2909.126.2.187

Cacioppo, J. T., & Berntson, G. G. (1994). Relationship between attitudes and evaluative space: A critical review, with emphasis on the separability of positive and negative substrates. *Psychological Bulletin, 115*(3), 401.

Cacioppo, J. T., Gardner, W. L., & Berntson, G. G. (1997). Beyond bipolar conceptualizations and measures: The case of attitudes and evaluative space. *Personality and Social Psychology Review, 1*(1), 3–25.

Carver, C. S., & White, T. L. (1994). Behavioral inhibition, behavioral activation, and affective responses to impending reward and punishment: The BIS/BAS scales. *Journal of Personality and Social Psychology, 67*, 319–333.

Chulef, A. S., Read, S. J., & Walsh, D. A. (2001). A hierarchical taxonomy of human goals. *Motivation and Emotion, 25*(3), 191–232.

Clark, L. A., & Watson, D. (1999). Temperament: A new paradigm for trait psychology. In L. A. Pervin & O. P. John (Eds.), *Handbook of personality: Theory and research* (2nd ed.) (pp. 399–423). New York: Guilford Press.

Derryberry, D., & Rothbart, M. K. (1997). Reactive and effortful processes in the organization of temperament. *Development and Psychopathology, 9*(04), 633–652. http://doi.org/10.1017/S0954579497001375

DeYoung, C. G. (2015). Cybernetic Big Five Theory. *Journal of Research in Personality, 56*, 33–58. http://doi.org/10.1016/j.jrp.2014.07.004

Digman, J. M. (1997). Higher-order factors of the Big Five. *Journal of Personality and Social Psychology, 73*(6), 1246–1256. http://doi.org/10.1037/0022-3514.73.6.1246

Fleeson, W. (2001). Toward a structure- and process-integrated view of personality: Traits as density distributions of states. *Journal of Personality and Social Psychology, 80*(6), 1011.

Fleeson, W. (2012). Perspectives on the person: Rapid growth and opportunities for integration. In K. Deaux & M. Snyder (Eds.), *The Oxford handbook of personality and social psychology* (pp. 33–63). New York: Oxford University Press.

Fleeson, W., & Jayawickreme, E. (2015). Whole trait theory. *Journal of Research in Personality, 56*, 82–92.

Funder, D. C. (2001). Personality. *Annual Review of Psychology, 52*(1), 197–221. http://doi.org/10.1146/annurev.psych.52.1.197

Gibson, J. J. (1979). *The ecological approach to visual perception.* Boston, MA: Houghton Mifflin.

Goldberg, L. R. (1981). Language and individual differences: The search for universals in personality lexicons. In L. Wheeler (Ed.), *Review of personality and social psychology* (Vol. 2, pp. 141–165). Beverly Hills, CA: SAGE.

Gray, J. A. (1987). *The psychology of fear and stress* (2nd ed.). New York: Cambridge University Press.

Gray, J. A., & McNaughton, N. (2000). *The neuropsychology of anxiety: An enquiry into the functions of the septo-hippocampal system* (2nd ed.). New York: Oxford University Press.

John, O. P., Naumann, L. P., & Soto, C. J. (2008). Paradigm shift to the integrative Big Five trait taxonomy. In P. John, R. W. Robins, & L. A. Pervin (Eds.), *Handbook of personality: Theory and research* (3rd ed.) (pp. 114–158). New York: Guilford Press.

John, O. P., & Srivastava, S. (1999). The Big Five trait taxonomy: History, measurement, and theoretical perspectives. In L. A. Pervin & O. P. John (Eds.), *Handbook of personality: Theory and research* (2nd ed.) (pp. 102–138). New York: Guilford Press.

Kenrick, D. T., & Trost, M. R. (1997). Evolutionary approaches to relationships. In S. Duck (Ed.), *Handbook of personal relationships: Theory, research, and interventions* (pp. 151–177). Chichester: Wiley.

Lee, K., & Ashton, M. C. (2004). Psychometric properties of the HEXACO Personality Inventory. *Multivariate Behavioral Research, 39*(2), 329–358. http://doi.org/10.1207/s15327906mbr3902_8

Maslow, A. H. (1943). A theory of human motivation. *Psychological Review, 50*, 370–396.

McAdams, D. P. (2008). Personal narratives and the life story. In O. P. John, R. W. Robins, & L. A. Pervin (Eds.), *Handbook of personality: Theory and research* (3rd ed.) (pp. 242–262). New York: Guilford Press.

McAdams, D. P., Josselson, R. E., & Lieblich, A. E. (2006). *Identity and story: Creating self in narrative.* Washington, DC: American Psychological Association.

McCrae, R. R., & Costa, P. T., Jr., (1999). A five-factor theory of personality. In L. A. Pervin & O. P. John (Eds.), *Handbook of personality: Theory and research* (2nd ed.) (pp. 139–153). New York: Guilford Press.

Miller, L. C., & Read, S. J. (1987). Why am I telling you this? Self-disclosure in a goal-based model of personality. In V. J. Derlega & J. Berg (Eds.), *Self-disclosure: Theory, research, and therapy.* Plenum.

Miller, L. C., & Read, S. J. (1991). On the coherence of mental models of persons and relationships: A knowledge structure approach. In G. J. O. Fletcher & F. Fincham (Eds.), *Cognition in close relationships* (pp. 69–99). Hillsdale, NJ: Erlbaum.

Mischel, W., & Shoda, Y. (1995). A cognitive-affective system theory of personality: Reconceptualizing situations, dispositions, dynamics, and invariance in personality structure. *Psychological Review, 102*(2), 246–268. http://doi.org/10.1037/0033-295X.102.2.246

Mischel, W., & Shoda, Y. (1998). Reconciling processing dynamics and personality dispositions. *Annual Review of Psychology, 49*(1), 229–258. http://doi.org/10.1146/annurev.psych.49.1.229

Mischel, W., & Shoda, Y. (2008). Toward a unified theory of personality: Integrating dispositions and processing dynamics within the cognitive-affective processing system. In O. P. John, R. W. Robins, & L. A. Pervin (Eds.), *Handbook of personality: Theory and research* (3rd ed.) (pp. 208–241). New York: Guilford Press.

Murray, H. A. (1938). *Explorations in personality: A clinical and experimental study of fifty men of college age.* Oxford: Oxford University Press. http://psycnet.apa.org/psycinfo/1938-15040-000

O'Reilly, R. C., & Munakata, Y. (2000). *Computational explorations in cognitive neuroscience: Understanding the mind by simulating the brain.* Cambridge, MA: MIT Press.

Peabody, D., & De Raad, B. (2002). The substantive nature of psycholexical personality factors: A comparison across languages. *Journal of Personality and Social Psychology, 83*(4), 983–997. http://doi.org/10.1037/0022-3514.83.4.983

Read, S. J., & Miller, L. C. (1989). Inter-personalism: Toward a goal-based theory of persons in relationships. In Lawrence A. Pervin (Ed), *Goal Concepts in Personality and Social Psychology* (pp. 413–472). Hillsdale, NJ: Lawrence Erlbaum,

Read, S. J., & Miller, L. C. (2002). Virtual personalities: A neural network model of personality. *Personality and Social Psychology Review, 6*(4), 357–369.

Read, S. J., Monroe, B. M., Brownstein, A. L., Yang, Y., Chopra, G., & Miller, L. C. (2010). A neural network model of the structure and dynamics of human personality. *Psychological Review, 117*(1), 61–92.

Read, S. J., Smith, B., Droutman, V., & Miller, L. C. (in press). Virtual personalities: Using computational modeling to understand within-person variability. *Journal of Research in Personality.*

Revelle, W., & Condon, D. M. (2015). A model for personality at three levels. *Journal of Research in Personality, 56,* 70–81. http://doi.org/10.1016/j.jrp.2014.12.006

Rothbart, M. K., & Bates, J. E. (1998). Temperament. In N. Eisenberg (Ed.), *Handbook of child psychology, Vol. 3: Social, emotional, and personality development* (5th ed.) (pp. 105–176). New York: Wiley.

Saucier, G., & Ostendorf, F. (1999). Hierarchical subcomponents of the Big Five personality factors: A cross-language replication. *Journal of Personality and Social Psychology, 76*(4), 613–627. http://doi.org/10.1037/0022-3514.76.4.613

Talevich, J. R., Read, S. J., Walsh, D. A., Chopra, G., & Iyer, R. (2015). A comprehensive taxonomy of human motives. Unpublished manuscript, University of Southern California.

Wiggins, J. S., & Trapnell, P. D. (1996). A dyadic-interactional perspective on the five-factor model. In J. S. Wiggins (Ed.), *The five-factor model of personality: Theoretical perspectives* (pp. 88–162). New York: Guilford Press.

Yang, Y., Read, S. J., Denson, T. F., Xu, Y., Zhang, J., & Pedersen, W. C. (2014). The key ingredients of personality traits: Situations, behaviors, and explanations. *Personality and Social Psychology Bulletin, 40*(1), 79–91.

Zhang, J., Berridge, K. C., Tindell, A. J., Smith, K. S., & Aldridge, J. W. (2009). A neural computational model of incentive salience. *PLoS Computational Biology, 5*(7), e1000437.

# 3

# USING CONNECTIONIST MODELS TO CAPTURE THE DISTINCTIVE PSYCHOLOGICAL STRUCTURE OF IMPRESSION FORMATION

*Brian M. Monroe, Tei Laine, Swati Gupta, and Ilya Farber*

## Introduction

In this chapter we present a novel connectionist architecture for modeling first impression formation, the process whereby a person makes judgments about another person based on limited observational data with no prior knowledge. Our purposes are twofold. First, as scientists interested in the process of impression formation, we are interested in seeing whether it is possible to develop a computational model which captures more of the subtleties and distinctive features of this process than the existing, relatively straightforward models have done, thus potentially underpinning an enhanced understanding of the process more broadly. Second, as computational modelers, we here describe and attempt to show the value of a particular strategy for creating connectionist models of psychological processes: rather than employing a general-purpose network structure and relying on connection weights to provide all the structure, we start by identifying key features of the target phenomenon and find ways to represent those directly in the architecture of the network, before training occurs. As we will demonstrate, this makes it possible to efficiently create a network model which captures more of the distinctive properties and dynamics of impression formation than has been possible with more conventional network architectures.

### Neural Network Models

Connectionist-type models have been the most commonly adopted by person perception researchers (e.g., Read & Miller, 1993; Kunda & Thagard 1996; see Chapter 2 in this volume for a more extended introduction in the context of personality processes; see also Read, Vanman, & Miller, 1997 and Smith, 1996 for more general discussions of their uses; for explorations of learning effects, see

Van Overwalle, 2007). The interplay among different abstract concepts in these explanatory networks using a parallel constraint satisfaction framework has shown how stimuli can be flexibly interpreted, which allows coherent inferences to become active simultaneously while inhibiting inconsistent cognitions—a hallmark of social psychology theory (cf. Abelson et al., 1968) and an approach more powerful than simple algebraic approaches to integration (cf. Anderson, 1968, 1981). While these networks typically do not represent memories of specific episodes or people, other connectionist networks have shown that experience with individuals could lead to abstractions being produced and subsequently represented (Smith & DeCoster, 1998), which allows the networks to exhibit properties like generalization to new stimuli. Another advantage of neural networks is their ability to handle parallel processing; findings suggest that different person inferences can spontaneously become simultaneously activated (Uleman & Moskowitz, 1994; Ham & Vonk, 2003; Freeman & Ambady, 2009), and it is not clear how a serial model or a model that makes forced categorizations at an early stage (e.g., Srull & Wyer, 1989; Fiske & Neuberg, 1990) would handle this. Findings showing that forcing people to use deliberative (versus automatic) judgment strategies decreases accuracy in a person perception task (Ambady & Rosenthal, 1993; Patterson & Stockbridge, 1998) also suggest, albeit indirectly, that serial processes make it hard to integrate information that is routinely used, and that parallel integration is more natural and efficient.

## Extensions to a Cognitive Neural Network Model

We have mentioned that connectionist models addressing impression formation already exist and seem like a good candidate to explain relevant processes. So what's left to explain? The current chapter suggests how, by focusing on improving the fidelity of connectionist networks in reproducing human judgments, we can refine and make more accurate a psychological theory of how impression judgments are made. Without accounting for the abilities and biases that people demonstrate in making their judgments, computational models simply will fall short of embodying a valid explanation for these processes. The specific psychological features, and corresponding additions to the computational model that we focus on are:

1.  *Prior probabilities*—how one makes judgments when there is a lack of specific diagnostic information; base rates or prior probabilities in belief for the attributes in the network (e.g., the likelihood of being a serial killer is small in the absence of other information) can be useful in making these judgments.
2.  *Asymmetric connections*—there is often an asymmetry in the nature of learned associations between pairs of attributes (such that $P(A|B) \neq P(B|A)$). Consequently, we have incorporated asymmetry into the bi-directional connections between attributes in the network.

3. *Evaluation feedback*—the process of evaluating the target runs automatically and concurrently to the attribute inference process; this suggests a feedback loop between the inferences and the evaluation that influences the representation.
4. *Limited attention*—the impact of differing levels of available processing capacity (attention) to devote to the judgment task is an important determinant of the output judgment; we implement this as a variable limit on the activation available for the impression formation task.

Of course, the lack of inclusion of anything on the above list does not preclude its potential importance for understanding the impression formation process. The aim is to build a framework essentially from the ground up, and to test the idea of incorporating these features into the structure of the model itself. If successful, it could form a solid foundation that could in turn hopefully incorporate more complicated processing as needed.

We will use a combination of thought experiments and demonstration simulations with a limited version of our model in order to argue for its validity. In the end, though, the question is if a model of this type can reproduce human judgments. It is worth noting that none of the published models presented have actually tried to reproduce actual human data by using a training process derived from human data. Instead, they have used hand-wired connections and attempted only to replicate general patterns like we do in our preliminary demonstrations. So we then present an abbreviated set of results from the human studies we conducted with a larger version of the model.

## The Present Model

Our concern is with how the representation of person-relevant information when combined with some basic processing mechanisms might lead to the types of actual human judgments we see. A conceptual outline is presented here.

Because of the potential complexity of perceiving and interpreting each type of information that could potentially be input into the person judgment process (e.g., interpreting the meaning of language or figuring out the intention of the actor in a behavior for which one doesn't have an existing schema), we stick to a level of analysis where schematic knowledge already exists and can be integrated—a level that we believe can help us understand critical aspects of this process without being overwhelming. Like many previous connectionist models of social cognition, our instantiation of a network (Figure 3.1) is intended to represent contents of schematic knowledge at a level that is somewhat abstracted from individual experiences or memories. We also do not attempt to model explicit mechanisms for acquisition of knowledge through experience (but see Smith & Decoster, 1998; Van Overwalle & Labiouse, 2004). While not exhaustive, hopefully it is rich enough to represent a mental model of another person.

Each node in the network represents one of two things: either (1) an attribute that a person might have, including but not limited to physical features, personality traits, values, and other enduring mental states like beliefs, goals, or interests;[1] or (2) an observation, of a behavioral cue or other feature, that could be predictive of these attributes.

Our connectionist network architecture, a modified autoassociator (cf. McClelland & Rumelhart, 1981), is separated into two layers: the input layer that consists of nodes representing observations and have only feed-forward connections to the attribute nodes, and an inference layer that consists of attribute nodes, which can be fully and recurrently connected with excitatory and inhibitory links. The nodes corresponding to observations about a person are externally activated, and the activation feeds to the attribute nodes, and among them, until the network settles in some stable configuration of activations. The final activation of each attribute node represents the degree of belief that the target person has the given attribute. The activation levels also can be positive or negative, representing a range of belief from likely to unlikely. (See the appendix for extended details.)

## Base Rates/Prior Probabilities

Imagine the situation where you are waiting in line at your regular coffee place and you find yourself in casual banter with one of the other waiting customers.

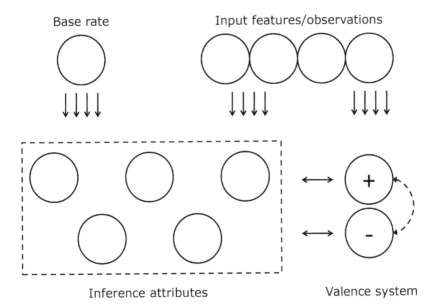

**FIGURE 3.1**   Schematic depiction of the network model. An inferred attribute (within the box) can potentially be connected to any other inferred attribute, but these connections are not shown, to retain simplicity.

You must to some degree make assumptions about what they know or might be interested in, in order to carry on a simple conversation. You might be able to predict some of these things merely from their appearance, and the fact that they are in a coffee joint to begin with. But some of the assumptions you make about them might be based on the fact that they are a female whose age can be approximated visually, rather than on the aforementioned. This represents knowledge averaged over a larger pool of experience. And still other assumptions might be based merely on overall experience with people, the largest possible pool. Another term that can describe this most general inference is a normative expectation about people in general.

We reason that if none of the possible predictive cues for a judgment of interest is present and available, or one merely doesn't notice any of the cues that could be predictive, one must rely on what the other customer knows, in the absence of knowledge of these predictors. Importantly, there is no single cue that is always present, but as people, that doesn't stop us from making assumptions about the target. We take advantage of the fact that a person must at some level recognize that the entity they are perceiving is a person. Therefore it makes sense to include a node that represents this "person" feature of the judgment object. It also makes sense that this node will always be active, since that defines the domain of the model. This node has the power to account for inferences that are not accounted for by other nodes in the network, and which it will have acquired through experience with every person who has been encountered. Through associative learning, this connection would naturally have built up to form stronger links for common attributes, and weaker links for rarer attributes, making common attributes more likely to be recruited in forming an impression. It is important to note that this base rate implementation also influences the impression even when the other predictive cues are present, in combination with them.

### Base Rate Simulations

In our simulation of this first thought experiment (Figure 3.2), one can imagine that if an arbitrary feature such as having earned a college degree is not diagnostic of lawfulness, but rather is the normative expectation of people in general that leads to this conclusion, it is important for a connectionist model to be able to represent this, resulting in the same conclusion whether the arbitrary feature is there or not. A model that lacked this would either not be able to make a prediction at all, or misattribute the predictive value to the arbitrary feature, in essence leading the knowledge structure to inaccurately represent what the perceiver has learned through experience.

In the second thought experiment (Figure 3.3), we can see what happens when we combine a base rate with another attribute that is diagnostic.

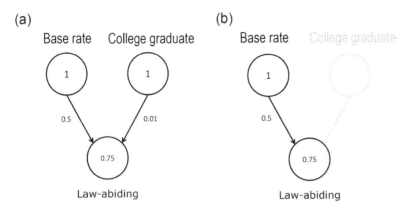

**FIGURE 3.2**   Base rates between conditions. Numbers displayed inside nodes are
settled activations for inferred attributes, or external activations for
input observations. Numbers accompanying arrows are the connection
weights. (a) Observed attribute is only "College graduate" (plus
"Non-diagnostic appearance," not shown). (b) Observed attribute
is only "Appearance" (not shown). Grayed-out nodes are inactive,
representing observations that are not currently present, but are kept
for comparison purposes.

Inferences can be equally sensitive to diagnostic inputs, even though they
have different levels of likelihood in absolute terms. This is easily illustrated
by contrasting an inference to an attribute that is relatively common with an
inference to an attribute that is rare. Here we assume that being intelligent is
likely to increase judgments of friendliness and also judgments of being a scam
artist, both slightly. If one did not take into account their overall prevalence
level, the model would make predictions that each was equally likely to be
true. But since that does not match the intuition that people are not likely
to assume someone is a scam artist based on the observation of being a smart
person, we show that adding the base rate node allows the model to make the
correct prediction.

## Asymmetric Relations between Nodes

The model we are presenting is ultimately a model of inference about person
qualities that have not been directly observed, based on those things that are
observed. A common way for inferences under uncertainty to be expressed is
in terms of conditional probabilities. There is no requirement that $P(A|B) =
P(B|A)$; that would be a special case. These probabilities usually represent
degrees of belief in a certain proposition. Even when using subjective beliefs
as opposed to objective frequentist probabilities, observation of A can be more

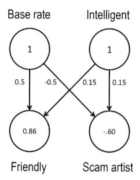

**FIGURE 3.3** Base rates within-condition.

revealing about B than vice versa. Especially when A and B are related by a deductive rule, it is likely that the inference is stronger in one direction than the other. When making predictions of continuous variables, regression coefficients (as well as semipartial correlations) are asymmetric when used among the same set of variables in the alternate roles of predictor and outcome. These asymmetric conditional probabilities and regression coefficients are the quantities that are learned by standard network learning algorithms (O'Reilly & Munakata, 2000).

Considering this situation, it is somewhat surprising that other models of person inference have exclusively used symmetric relationships between nodes (e.g., Read & Miller, 1993; Kunda & Thagard, 1996). It is possible these models did not explore cases where precise discrimination was necessary, and so could get away with only symmetric relationships. Thagard (2004) argued that using (unidirectional) conditional probabilities as instantiated in a Bayesian network, instead of symmetric weights, did not improve the quality of prediction in certain inference networks. We believe the focus of Thagard's explanation networks is typically of facts of physical occurrences that either can both happen or are mutually exclusive, for which "consistent" or "inconsistent" symmetrical coherence relationships might be more appropriate. The judgments those models produce are also interpreted as either accepting or rejecting a proposition or explanation. Impression judgments, in contrast, do not require complete acceptance or rejection, but instead seem to involve combining predictions of the diagnostic value of available pieces of information. Even if a symmetric model is able to produce data that match human coherence judgments well when they are interpreted dichotomously, it is less certain that it will work for more graded strength-of-prediction judgments. The base rate exploration suggests a case where it is important to judge attributes on the full continuum from likely to unlikely, rather than only allowing extremely likely or extremely unlikely judgments.

Regardless of the above, one could imagine that a well-trained network will eventually learn to predict correctly based on symmetric inference weights, plus the weights coming from the input nodes (in the latter case only the weight going from observation to inference matters because input activations are fixed.) In the previous impression formation models with symmetric weights, the number of judgments that were correctly made was fewer than the number of free parameters (the connection strengths) in the network, so it was always possible to use a set of parameters in combination to get those judgments to come out correctly (a situation that could be described as an overfit model). The issues this raises are that symmetric weight patterns might not work when a much larger set of predictions is attempted, and subsequently this casts doubt that it meaningfully reproduces the psychological representation. For all the above reasons, we believe using asymmetric connections instead is an appropriate solution to accomplishing the types of inference one must make for impression judgments. This is a case where the result is an increase in the number of parameters in models that are often already overfit, but we feel it is justified.

## *Asymmetry Simulation*

The advantage is demonstrated in the simulation of the following thought experiment (Figure 3.4). The two inferences of interest are whether someone is an ignorant person, and whether someone is an intolerant person. In the first case, the perceiver observes the target person pepper spraying the participants at a pride parade for a minority group (a hateful act). In the second case, it arises in conversation that someone doesn't know a relatively common fact. These are fairly straightforward unambiguous inferences, to intolerance in the first case, and ignorance in the second case. What is of importance is how, given one attribute, the perceiver judges the likelihood of the other (ignorance in the first case, and intolerance in the second). If a network with symmetric-only connections is used, and the observations are equally strong predictors of their respective traits, the judgments in the two cases would be identical. In contrast, in a model with asymmetric connections,[2] the person who pepper sprays is judged to be ignorant more than the person who doesn't know the common fact is judged to be intolerant. This is because intolerance has a higher cue value for ignorance than vice versa. This can be thought of as a knowledge structure where ignorance is a requirement for intolerance, but intolerance is not a requirement for ignorance.

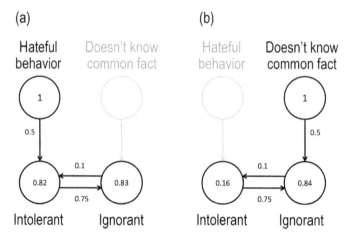

**FIGURE 3.4** Asymmetry. Grayed-out nodes show inactive inputs. Base rates for this simulation were assumed to be similar, and were not included in the network. (a) Observation of intolerant behavior. (b) Observation of ignorant behavior.

## Summary Evaluation and Valence Feedback

When people judge entities in their world, evaluation on a positive–negative dimension is one of the most fundamental aspects of that. Studies of abstract concepts, items, or adjectives show that evaluation accounts for much of the variance in their cognitive representation (e.g., Osgood, Suci, & Tannenbaum, 1957; Heise, 1969). In person perception research, positive qualities are typically correlated with each other, as are negative qualities (e.g., Asch 1946; Nisbett & Wilson, 1977; Cooper, 1981; Anderson & Sedikides, 1991; Eagly, Ashmore, Makhijani, & Longo, 1991). Further, trait qualities that are evaluatively tinged seem to be judged less reliably than neutral items (John & Robins, 1993). This suggests that valence is an indispensible part of the representation of a person, and further, that somehow the evaluation of someone actively influences the process of forming a judgment of them or their qualities.

These findings make sense when looking at the role of evaluation in an agent who must then act on their judgments. Echoing the premise that "thinking is for doing" (cf. Ferguson & Bargh, 2004), it has been theorized that systems exist with the specific function of resolving conflicts and removing ambivalence from judgments so we can act decisively (Harmon-Jones, Harmon-Jones, Fearn, Sigelman, & Johnson, 2008; Harmon-Jones, Amodio, & Harmon-Jones, 2009). The evaluation system serves to inform the agent whether they should approach or avoid the object of interest—a critical decision-based mechanism for an individual. Consistent with this mechanism, it has more specifically been suggested that once an evaluation has formed, it shapes subsequent information processing (Srull & Wyer, 1989), and also that there is a bi-directional pathway of influence between evaluation and beliefs as examined from perspectives in decision modeling (Wagar & Thagard, 2004), emotional appraisal coherence (Nerb, 2007), social neuroscience (Cunningham & Zelazo, 2007), and attitude modeling (Monroe & Read, 2008; Ehret, Monroe, & Read, 2014). Previous modeling efforts have also recognized that influences from valenced emotional responses can account for judgments made from available evidence (Thagard, 2003). This general valence mechanism in some form could plausibly account for a broad range of biased reasoning phenomena (e.g., Kunda, 1990).

In order to account for this, we have implemented connections to two valence nodes (positive and negative)[3] that not only read out the evaluative components of the other inferences, but their own activations influence the activation of the other nodes by means of a bi-directional connection. We have little basis to assume the exact strength of this feedback connection, so in the current exercise the connections between attribute nodes and valence nodes are symmetric; a looser condition that we would agree with only requires that the feedback connections be positively correlated with the respective connections from attribute to valence. In this model, the strength of the connections from the attribute nodes to the valence nodes is fixed.

The valence nodes in our model provide a functional-level implementation of this dynamic inhibition without representing a commitment to any particular hypothesis about the underlying brain mechanisms. Theories of how valenced representations directly affect propositional representations have not been tested directly (but see Thagard & Aubie, 2008 for one proposed mechanism that specifically includes emotion appraisals) and there are several possibilities; we have chosen to implement the minimum essential element that is able to highlight the advantages of putting in a valence loop. The advantage of incorporating this element into the model is best illustrated through simulations.

An empirical finding that evidences the operation of a valence-driven process is one that suggests impression consistency ratings are far more sensitive to valence than they are to semantic relations. In experiments by Roese & Morris (1999), subjects were given several hypotheses to judge simultaneously about both momentary and dispositional attributes that could be suggested by the behavior of a target person in a scenario. When rating the likelihood that certain attributes or behavioral explanations were compatible with each other, the judgments of valence were far more important than merely how the explanations covaried, or what other causal mechanisms they might share. So, for example, if someone is known to be humorous, the ratings of their conscientiousness tend to be higher than ratings of their dishonesty, and the most critical factor in these ratings across different combinations of attributes (as determined by multiple regression analyses) is the consistency of valence of those attributes rather than a perceived covariation of the attributes or even the other personality-behavioral mechanisms they entail. These experiments and corresponding simulation also allow us to illustrate how valence effects are important within the same judgment episode.

## Valence Simulation

In our thought experiment and simulation, inspired by the Roese & Morris (1999) experiments (Figure 3.5), we externally activate the default explanation (humorous, which was the attribute given to the participants in the example above). Activation spreads to both the inferred attributes equally, but also to the valence nodes. The pattern of weights only among the attributes is effectively symmetric, and so on its own would result in both attributes being equally active. However, the activation of the valence nodes sends excitatory input to the valence-compatible attribute, conscientious, and inhibits the valence-incompatible attribute, dishonest. A test for the ratings of likelihood of the secondary explanations, which is represented by the resulting activation value of the relevant attribute or behavior inference, confirms the pattern. The simulations show that the valence-compatible attributes are favored, while the valence-incompatible attributes are suppressed, which is consistent with the ratings of the likelihood that the conjunction of attributes is present as indicated in the results from the experiment.

One could imagine similar results possible, without the process being mediated by a valence pathway, as long as the relevant attributes were already significantly positively correlated or negatively correlated in their schematic knowledge or shared common personality-behavioral mechanisms. But this only pushes the question back a step, where one has to ask where the consistent positive and negative correlations between same and oppositely valenced items come from

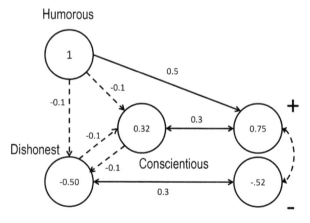

**FIGURE 3.5**   Valence feedback within-condition. Base rates were assumed to be similar and not included in the network.

in the first place. The sheer difference in size of the effects of Roese & Morris (1999) between covariation and valence also calls into question the potential for genuine covariation to account for the valence effect. Therefore we would argue the mechanism we have demonstrated is a much more parsimonious explanation for this pattern of results.

## Cognitive Capacity

Cognitive capacity, or the amount of available attentional capacity one devotes to the target task, is a central variable of interest in many social cognitive models of information processing. In addition to being prominent in cognitive theories of attitude change (Petty & Cacioppo, 1986; Kruglanski & Thompson, 1999), person perception researchers have also noted that the amount of attention or processing one devotes to person stimuli can have significant effects on the conclusions one draws about the target (Brewer & Feinstein, 1999; Fiske, Lin, & Neuberg, 1999). Low attention promotes reliance on well-learned associations like stereotypes (Macrae, Hewstone, & Griffiths, 1993; Wigboldus, Sherman, Franzese, & Van Knippenberg, 2004) and insufficient consideration of situational constraints on behavior (Gilbert, Pelham, & Krull, 1988; Trope & Alfieri, 1997). High attention promotes consideration of individuating information and more detailed representations of the target person (Fiske, Neuberg, Beattie, & Milberg, 1987; Pendry & Macrae, 1994). Knowing that even when presented with the same information people can come to completely different characterizations merely based on the amount of attention paid to the target, we believe it is important to incorporate a mechanism to allow this type of processing into the model.

### Implementation of Cognitive Capacity

While it is very important to understand how perceptual features are identified and fit together to build up a conceptual interpretation of an observation and how processing capacity might affect this, it is beyond the scope of the current model. So for this exploration we bypass the issue of low-level perception and focus only on how high versus low capacity differentially affects concept activation. Therefore we only put a hard ceiling on the amount of activation available for processing in the combined pool of downstream inferred concepts.[4] Perhaps most consequential of the potential factors that can interact with capacity in these limited circumstances is the order in which information is received through time, which we explore at length here.

### Order Effects

It is well documented that when people are given pieces of information in series about a target person, the overall impression is sensitive to the order, even though the overall pool of information is the same (e.g., Asch, 1946;

Anderson, 1965; Dreben, Fiske, & Hastie, 1979). Aside from artificial lab manipulations of order, the manner in which observations about a person are made in a natural environment suggests that it is important to address this aspect of impression judgments. The cliché of saying that one should not judge a book by its cover reflects the inescapability of perceiving some pieces of information before others, and the potential for the initially encountered stimuli to drive the judgment so strongly that in some cases it prevents the perceiver from even attending to further information.

A network seems appropriate to model this because its mechanisms match those proposed on the basis of empirical findings in impression formation. Specifically, the activation of categorical and/or trait schema representations has been shown to have a marked effect on resulting judgments (Srull & Wyer, 1979; Bodenhausen, 1988), and it is the interpretation of subsequent incoming stimuli via this temporarily established influence that leads to primacy effects (e.g., Jaccard & Fishbein, 1975; cf. Kunda & Thagard, 1996). However, it is important to note that this tendency doesn't always hold: when placed under sufficient competing processing demands, recency effects can be seen such that given a series of person attributes, the ones given later tend to dominate the overall judgment (Lichtenstein & Srull, 1987).

### Simulation: Primacy and Recency Effects

In these simulations (Figures 3.6 and 3.7), the network received a series of four behaviors, in counterbalanced order. The network consists of several different related attributes, intended to represent related parts of a schema. Related parts of the schema are activated, which likely activate associated attributes to some degree. In this schema, we have represented the two focal attributes (intelligent and honest) as well as two additional ones that are associated with each of them to some degree, for a total of six attributes. We have also included as the inputs to the network one behavior related to each of the two focal attributes, and corresponding negative behaviors related to the same traits. We activated the first behavior and allowed the network to settle in its own time due to the dynamic evolution of activation; then the observation nodes were turned off (but preserving the state of the rest of the network) and the new observation was activated, and this was repeated until the series was complete. When the cognitive capacity was sufficient for the schema associated with the behaviors to become sufficiently active (which was then preserved between introductions of new observations in a continuous stream), this schema constrained and inhibited new information that was inconsistent with it—so the traits that became active earlier remained active (a primacy effect). When the cognitive capacity was reduced, the activation of any given schema was not strong enough to produce this effect, so the recency advantage of the later information allowed it to influence the final pattern of activation more (a recency effect). This matches the pattern seen in Lichtenstein & Srull (1987).[5]

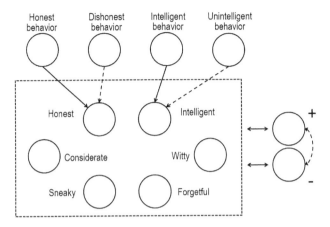

**FIGURE 3.6** Network for cognitive capacity simulation. Connections between inferred attributes are present but not shown.

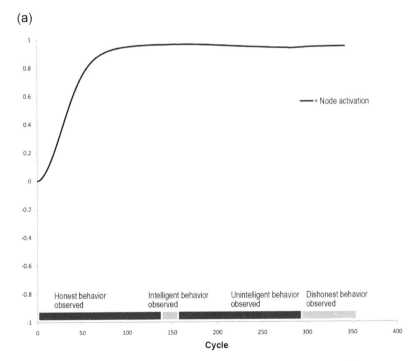

(a)

**FIGURE 3.7** Simulation results for cognitive capacity. (a) Full capacity. (b) Low capacity. Activation in trait nodes (not shown) shows a similar pattern to the valence nodes. Each subsequent observation was introduced after the network settled into a stable configuration due to its own dynamics; the number of time steps varied in each case (roughly, more disruption requires more time to resolve).

(b)

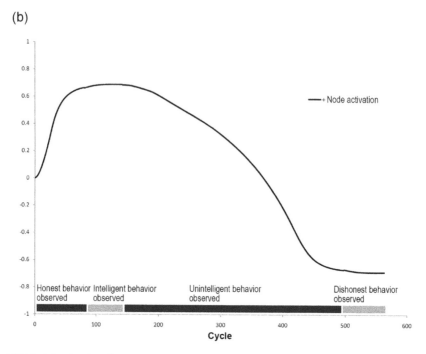

**FIGURE 3.7**  *(continued)*

## Empirical Test of the Model

The ability of the constructed models to produce the intended outcomes provides an initial form of validation. Ultimately, however, the real test of the value
of the structural features described above is whether a model that has them can
more accurately replicate human performance than a model that lacks them. In
a large-scale project, we collected human data on inferences of traits. People
provided their judgments, given either (1) single observed characteristics, or
(2) combinations of a few characteristics together in mini-profiles. Practical concerns dictated choices for the large-scale model, including data collection volume
(and thus the size of the network), and we did not manipulate attention or cognitive load during exposure to the stimuli. In the end, the large-scale model for
which we report results had 47 different characteristics as possible observed inputs
(plus base rate if applicable), and 52 traits as possible inferences. The observed
characteristics included things like gender, age, ethnicity, profession, and hob-
bies. Instead of setting weights by hand, it was trained using the human data for
single observed characteristics, with single input–inference pairs at a time and
then performance-tested on the profiles containing multiple characteristics. The
performance during training (and testing) was based on how close the model's
settled activation for a given node was to the human data, re-scaled to fit the activation range of the model. Any discrepancy was considered an error with respect

to the training data. Critically, all models were trained to the same mean-square-error (MSE) standard on the training corpus.

The main comparison of interest for us is against a model like the one used by Kunda & Thagard (1996) (hereafter KT), which is a connectionist network, but one that does not contain any of the critical features we have discussed up to this point. Rather than testing a new model with all of these features, it is important to selectively add or subtract one at a time the feature critical to demonstrating a particular effect so one could determine if it in fact caused any possible improvements in performance.

A full analysis and description of these results will be the subject of future work and is beyond the scope of this chapter. Here we present only a few key observations based on an analysis of simulations using our present model and comparison models via human judgments,[6] to illustrate some of the ways in which empirical data can be used to assess the significance of the particular architectural choices presented in this chapter.[7]

1.  Adding a base rate only to a model like KT allows the model to match human judgments on a one-to-one basis much better than a KT model. This is especially so when more observed characteristics were present in a profile, where the KT model's estimates were systematically more extreme. This suggests the model without the base rate was misattributing the diagnostic value to the observed characteristics, rather than normative expectations of people in general.
2.  Adding asymmetric weights allows a model to perform better than a KT model. This suggests the asymmetry is in fact important for replicating human inferences.
3.  Adding valence nodes allows a model to perform better than a KT model, and the strength of this advantage is positively correlated with the extremity of the evaluation of the target profile. This suggests that the valence nodes are in fact important, and influence human inferences in a causal fashion above and beyond the trait schemas that are active.
4.  Adding multiple components to the model improved performance incrementally over models with just single additional components.

## Current Limits and Future Paths

In this chapter we have demonstrated processing features that have not previously been included in models of impression formation, and which we believe are critical to account for because they capture psychological features relevant to forming these judgments. We have focused more for the time being on explaining how and why these features are necessary. But these concerns are ultimately equally important because accounting for them will result in a framework that would be more successful in accurately reproducing human judgments of target persons. We believe that existing models of impression formation, both verbal and computational, do not meet these criteria. The model is fairly limited in its scope, though. We recognize there are many aspects of impression formation that are important, which this model is not explicitly designed to account for.

For example, this model does none of the upstream processing that would be necessary to understand people in real time, such as facial expression recognition, language understanding, or parsing and interpreting actions. We have limited the processing in the network to the social meaning level, to simplify the task and examine it at a level that is manageable, but recognize that in order to understand a fuller complement of phenomena, one cannot overlook these phases of processing. For example, the inferences that are drawn from physical appearance that can be perceived immediately might typically precede inferences drawn from behaviors that are observed. Thus the inferences that have been activated first from appearance will then interact (and possibly compete) with the inferences from behavior. In this case we believe it will be important to account for the temporal order, especially when the observations are not strongly diagnostic themselves and depend on combining evidence from several sources to make a significant inference. This is an additional concern that suggests the importance of incorporating temporal differences, as we have. It is worth mentioning that a model could be extended in a manner entirely consistent with the current architecture by implementing multiple-layer representations, each layer hierarchically building up more complex or abstracted inputs from simple ones in appearance or language or behavior comprehension (cf. Read & Miller, 1998, 2005; Freeman & Ambady, 2011), each of these layers also connecting to the common pool of inferred attributes.

## Conclusion

Much of what we know about impression formation is based on experiments where one factor is manipulated to understand how it affects another variable. What is still lacking is an integrative framework of how an impression is formed. There are descriptions of the *what* of impression formation that are impressively comprehensive (Carlston, 1994), but this needs to be combined with the *how*. In order to address this, we have attempted to abide by a few guiding principles: (1) in making a computational model in particular, we are forced to be more precise than existing verbal models (e.g., Brewer, 1988; Srull & Wyer, 1989; Fiske & Neuberg, 1990) in specifying how information gets combined; (2) avoiding assumptions or distinctions in representation or processing unless the existing framework is arguably unable to account for the phenomena; and (3) advancing existing network architectures by noting where the deficiencies arise in their ability to replicate human judgments. It is our hope that by doing these things, the resulting model will have explanatory value as both a parsimonious, coherent, and broadly applicable model of certain aspects of social cognition, and also one that will be able to actually predict human judgments in real circumstances.

Towards the third aim especially, we have gone beyond the KT model, and suggested that a network without the features we have described throughout this chapter fails to capture important aspects of person judgments. Prime examples of this are: (1) the ability of the current model to make inferences that discriminate between common and rare attributes, which suggests that it is very important for the researcher to pay attention not just to what is observed about the target, but also what is not observed (in the sense that base rate expectations derived from observations containing information that is not present in the current observation will continue to influence judgments) when modeling person inferences; (2) the ability for multiple levels of abstraction or construal to simultaneously influence perceptions, such as the most general person representation (i.e., base rate) combining with the gender or ethnicity of a person; one does not need to choose only one level of abstraction from a hierarchy to construe a person, as each might have independent predictive value; and (3) allowing for rule-based inferences that are likely asymmetric.

The shift in perspective that comes out of this modeling exercise should not be overlooked. While we do not view our results as embodying a full theory of person judgments, we have tried to use an approach that has the potential to accommodate a comprehensive account of the process and outcome. Instead of positing a domain-specific (and ultimately unexplained) fixed sequence of processing, as do many entrenched verbal theories, the sequence of processing is assumed to conform to a more general perceptual-cognitive set of rules. It has been shown that sequences of judgments can often seemingly be reversed from that of prevailing theories (e.g., Krull, 1993), which suggests that those theories take too narrow a view. Specifically, impression judgments are highly dependent on the schematic knowledge structures that people have (represented in the current model by the pattern of connections and weights between nodes)—one cannot form an impression without such knowledge, and so the schema should be a major determinant of the flow of processing, along with the attention paid to the task at hand, personal motivations, and the spatiotemporal configuration in which the information about the target is observed. By taking a more general schematic view, one can, for example, start to generate hypotheses about why certain social categories seem to have the operational properties they do, rather than just assume that they rigidly result in reduced attention to other attributes as is the case in dual-process models (e.g., Brewer, 1988; Fiske & Neuberg, 1990). One can also hopefully be on firmer ground to explore more automatic versus more deliberate processing and how different judgments are produced if that processing must either be assimilated or contrasted with a mechanism that has been shown to match human judgments in a wide set of cases. More generally, in being forced to specify processing mechanisms and relationships, it can suggest gaps in our knowledge of the impression formation process, and force us to re-examine existing theories (cf. McClelland, 2009; Sun, 2009). A model like this one could be the basis for a more complete account of impression processing and judgments, and progress in understanding can indeed be made through a cycle of adequate testing and extension of the model.

## Appendix

The net input η to a node j is the sum of the activation-weight products across all nodes it is connected to. Since weights are potentially asymmetric, the model uses the incoming weight.

$$\eta_j = \sum_i x_i w_{ij} \tag{3.1}$$

And this evolves over time steps t with a leaky integration process, becoming

$$\eta_j(t) = (1 - \delta t)\eta_j(t-1) + \delta t \left(\sum_i x_i w_{ij}\right) \tag{3.2}$$

with a fractional integration parameter δ, activations x, and weights w.

The outgoing activation x of a node j is the net input transformed by a sigmoidally shaped function to bound it between -1 and 1.

$$x_j = \tanh\left(\frac{\eta_j}{2}\right) \tag{3.3}$$

Processing in the models starts with observation nodes having their activation values set externally. Processing in the model stops when the change in activation over successive time steps over all nodes in the network falls below a specified limit.

For the large model with learning implemented, the learning algorithm combines error-correcting learning with a form of purely associative learning. The error-correcting learning was implemented using contrastive Hebbian learning

$$\Delta w_{ij} = \epsilon [x_i^+ y_j^+ - x_i^- y_j^-] \tag{3.4}$$

where the superscripts denote the plus and minus phases of activation (O'Reilly & Munakata, 2000) and the associative learning used Oja's rule:

$$\Delta w_{ij} = \epsilon (x_i y_j - y_j^2 w_{ij}) \tag{3.5}$$

using the minus phase activations to calculate the weight change. The proportion of associative learning was set at 0.1% of the total weight change, with the remainder due to error-correcting learning.

## Notes

1  It is important to emphasize that not all attribute nodes need be abstract personality traits. For example, a central tenet of correspondent inference theory (Jones & Davis, 1965) is that when a behavior is observed, the perceiver naturally makes the inference that the actor desired the specific outcome(s) their behavior achieved. This inference

of present desires can then be connected to more stable personality attributes through schematic knowledge (this connection is highlighted, e.g., in Read, Jones, & Miller, 1990), but the present desire inference is an important and potentially necessary intermediate step.

2 We limit ourselves presently to cases in which the subjective base rates are roughly the same to illustrate this point in a simple demonstration, although it should apply as well even in cases when the base rates are different.

3 For present purposes these function similarly to a single bipolar node. For demonstrations of positive and negative nodes functioning independently, see Ehret, Monroe, & Read (2015).

4 For more discussion of the nature of the capacity mechanism, see Monroe & Read (2008).

5 We note that our model suggests that sufficient activation is required among the inferred attributes to achieve a primacy effect, even under full capacity, because if the pattern of activation is not strong, the more recent inputs will have more influence. Thus there are multiple factors in the model that determine whether primacy forces are strong enough to control the judgment.

6 B. M. Monroe, T. Laine, S. Gupta, & I. Farber, unpublished raw data, 2016.

7 Except where specifically noted, performance measures used a combination of within-profile correlations across the entire set of profiles, as well as MSE comparisons, all comparing the human ratings of the 52 traits per profile to the model outputs on the traits.

# References

Abelson, R. P., et al. (Eds.) (1968). *Theories of cognitive consistency: A sourcebook*. Chicago, IL: Rand-McNally.

Ambady, N., & Rosenthal, R. (1993). Half a minute: Predicting teacher evaluations from thin slices of nonverbal behavior and physical attractiveness. *Journal of Personality and Social Psychology, 64*(3), 431–441.

Anderson, C. A., & Sedikides, C. (1991). Thinking about people: Contributions of a typological alternative to associationistic and dimensional models of person perception. *Journal of Personality and Social Psychology, 60*(2), 203–217.

Anderson, N. H. (1965). Averaging versus adding as a stimulus-combination rule in impression formation. *Journal of Experimental Psychology, 70*(4), 394–400.

Anderson, N. H. (1968). Application of a linear-serial model to a personality-impression task using serial presentation. *Journal of Personality and Social Psychology, 10*(4), 354–362.

Anderson, N. H. (1981). *Foundations of information integration theory*. London: Academic Press.

Asch, S. (1946). Forming impressions of personality. *Journal of Abnormal and Social Psychology, 41*(3), 258–290.

Bodenhausen, G. V. (1988). Stereotypic biases in social decision making and memory: Testing process models of stereotype use. *Journal of Personality and Social Psychology, 55*(5), 726–737.

Brewer, M. B. (1988). A dual process model of impression formation. In T. K. Srull & R. S. Wyer (Eds.), *Advances in Social Cognition* (Vol. 1, pp. 1–36). Hillsdale, NJ: Lawrence Erlbaum.

Brewer, M. B., & Feinstein, A. S. H. (1999). Dual processes in the cognitive representation of persons and social categories. In S. Chaiken & Y. Trope (Eds.), *Dual-process theories in social psychology* (pp. 255–270). New York: Guilford Press.

Carlston, D. E. (1994). Associated Systems Theory: A systematic approach to cognitive representations of persons. In T. K. Srull & R. S. Wyer (Eds.), *Advances in Social Cognition* (Vol. X, pp. 1–78). Hillsdale, NJ: Lawrence Erlbaum.

Cooper, W. H. (1981). Ubiquitous halo. *Psychological Bulletin, 90*(2), 218–244.

Cunningham, W. A., & Zelazo, P. D. (2007). Attitudes and evaluations: A social cognitive neuroscience perspective. *Trends in Cognitive Sciences, 11*(3), 97–104.

Dreben, E. K., Fiske, S. T., & Hastie, R. (1979). The independence of evaluative and item information: Impression and recall order effects in behavior-based impression formation. *Journal of Personality and Social Psychology, 37*(10), 1758–1768.

Eagly, A. H., Ashmore, R. D., Makhijani, M. G., & Longo, L. C. (1991). What is beautiful is good, but . . .: A meta-analytic review of research on the physical attractiveness stereotype. *Psychological Bulletin, 110*(1), 109–128.

Ehret, P. J., Monroe, B. M., & Read, S. J. (2015). Modeling the dynamics of evaluation: A multilevel neural network implementation of the Iterative Reprocessing Model. *Personality and Social Psychology Review, 19*, 148–176.

Ferguson, M. J., & Bargh, J. A. (2004). Liking is for doing: The effects of goal pursuit on automatic evaluation. *Journal of Personality and Social Psychology, 87*(5), 557–572.

Fiske, S. T., Lin, M., & Neuberg, S. L. (1999). The continuum model: Ten years later. In S. Chaiken & Y. Trope (Eds.), *Dual-process theories in social psychology* (pp. 231–254). New York: Guilford Press.

Fiske, S. T., & Neuberg, S. L. (1990). A continuum of impression formation, from category-based to individuating processes: Influences of information and motivation on attention and interpretation. *Advances in Experimental Social Psychology, 23*, 1–74.

Fiske, S. T., Neuberg, S. L., Beattie, A. E., & Milberg, S. J. (1987). Category-based and attribute-based reactions to others: Some informational conditions of stereotyping and individuating processes. *Journal of Experimental Social Psychology, 23*(5), 399–427.

Freeman, J. B., & Ambady, N. (2009). Motions of the hand expose the partial and parallel activation of stereotypes. *Psychological Science, 20*(10), 1183–1188.

Freeman, J. B., & Ambady, N. (2011). A dynamic interactive theory of person construal. *Psychological Review, 118*(2), 247–279.

Gilbert, D. T., Pelham, B. W., & Krull, D. S. (1988). On cognitive busyness: When person perceivers meet persons perceived. *Journal of Personality and Social Psychology, 54*(5), 733–740.

Ham, J., & Vonk, R. (2003). Smart and easy: Co-occurring activation of spontaneous trait inferences and spontaneous situational inferences. *Journal of Experimental Social Psychology, 39*(5), 434–447.

Harmon-Jones, E., Amodio, D. M., & Harmon-Jones, C. (2009). Action-based model of dissonance: A review, integration, and expansion of conceptions of cognitive conflict. *Advances in experimental social psychology, 41*, 119–166.

Harmon-Jones, E., Harmon-Jones, C., Fearn, M., Sigelman, J. D., & Johnson, P. (2008). Left frontal cortical activation and spreading of alternatives: Tests of the action-based model of dissonance. *Journal of Personality and Social Psychology, 94*(1), 1–15.

Heise, D. R. (1969). Some methodological issues in semantic differential research. *Psychological Bulletin, 72*(6), 406–422.

Jaccard, J. J., & Fishbein, M. (1975). Inferential beliefs and order effects in personality impression formation. *Journal of Personality and Social Psychology, 31*(6), 1031–1040.

John, O. P., & Robins, R. W. (1993). Determinants of interjudge agreement on personality traits: The Big Five domains, observability, evaluativeness, and the unique perspective of the self. *Journal of Personality, 61*(4), 521–551.

Jones, E. E., & Davis, K. E. (1965). From acts to dispositions: The attribution process in person perception. *Advances in experimental social psychology*, *2*, 219–266.

Kruglanski, A. W., & Thompson, E. P. (1999). Persuasion by a single route: A view from the unimodel. *Psychological Inquiry*, *10*(2), 83–109.

Krull, D. S. (1993). Does the grist change the mill? The effect of the perceiver's inferential goal on the process of social inference. *Personality and Social Psychology Bulletin*, *19*(3), 340–348.

Kunda, Z. (1990). The case for motivated reasoning. *Psychological Bulletin*, *108*(3), 480–498.

Kunda, Z., & Thagard, P. (1996). Forming impressions from stereotypes, traits, and behaviors: A parallel-constraint-satisfaction theory. *Psychological Review*, *103*(2), 284–308.

Lichtenstein, M., & Srull, T. K. (1987). Processing objectives as a determinant of the relationship between recall and judgment. *Journal of Experimental Social Psychology*, *23*(2), 93–118.

Macrae, C., Hewstone, M., & Griffiths, R. J. (1993). Processing load and memory for stereotype-based information. *European Journal of Social Psychology*, *23*(1), 77–87.

McClelland, J. L. (2009). The place of modeling in cognitive science. *Topics in Cognitive Science*, *1*(1), 11–38.

McClelland, J. L., & Rumelhart, D. E. (1981). An interactive activation model of context effects in letter perception I: An account of basic findings. *Psychological Review*, *88*, 375–407.

Monroe, B. M., & Read, S. J. (2008). A general connectionist model of attitude structure and change: The ACS (Attitudes as Constraint Satisfaction) model. *Psychological Review*, *115*(3), 733–759.

Nerb, J. (2007). Exploring the dynamics of the appraisal–emotion relationship: A constraint satisfaction model of the appraisal process. *Cognition and Emotion*, *21*(7), 1382–1413.

Nisbett, R. E., & Wilson, T. D. (1977). The halo effect: Evidence for unconscious alteration of judgments. *Journal of Personality and Social Psychology*, *35*(4), 250–256.

O'Reilly, R. C., & Munakata, Y. (2000). *Computational explorations in cognitive neuroscience: Understanding the mind by simulating the brain*. Cambridge, MA: MIT Press.

Osgood, C. E., Suci, G. J., & Tannenbaum, P. H. (1957). *The measurement of meaning*. Oxford: University of Illinois Press.

Patterson, M. L., & Stockbridge, E. (1998). Effects of cognitive demand and judgment strategy on person perception accuracy. *Journal of Nonverbal Behavior*, *22*(4), 253–263.

Pendry, L. F., & Macrae, C. (1994). Stereotypes and mental life: The case of the motivated but thwarted tactician. *Journal of Experimental Social Psychology*, *30*(4), 303–325.

Petty, R. E., & Cacioppo, J. T. (1986). The elaboration likelihood model of persuasion. *Advances in experimental social psychology*, *19*(1), 123–205.

Read, S. J., Jones, D. K., & Miller, L. C. (1990). Traits as goal-based categories: The importance of goals in the coherence of dispositional categories. *Journal of Personality and Social Psychology*, *58*(6), 1048–1061.

Read, S. J., & Miller, L. C. (1993). Rapist or "regular guy": Explanatory coherence in the construction of mental models of others. *Personality and Social Psychology Bulletin*, *19*(5), 526–540.

Read, S. J., & Miller, L. C. (1998). On the dynamic construction of meaning: An interactive activation and competition model of social perception. In S. J. Read & L. C. Miller (Eds.), *Connectionist models of social reasoning and social behavior* (pp. 27–68). Mahwah, NJ: Lawrence Erlbaum.

Read, S. J., & Miller, L. C. (2005). Explanatory coherence and goal-based knowledge structures in making dispositional inferences. In B. F. Malle & S. D. Hodges (Eds.), *Other minds: How humans bridge the divide between self and others* (pp. 124–139). New York: Guilford Press.

Read, S. J., Vanman, E. J., & Miller, L. C. (1997). Connectionism, parallel constraint satisfaction processes, and Gestalt principles: (Re)introducing cognitive dynamics to social psychology. *Personality and Social Psychology Review, 1*(1), 26–53.

Roese, N. J., & Morris, M. W. (1999). Impression valence constrains social explanations: The case of discounting versus conjunction effects. *Journal of Personality and Social Psychology, 77*(3), 437–448.

Smith, E. R. (1996). What do connectionism and social psychology offer each other? *Journal of personality and social psychology, 70*(5), 893.

Smith, E. R., & DeCoster, J. (1998). Knowledge acquisition, accessibility, and use in person perception and stereotyping: Simulation with a recurrent connectionist network. *Journal of Personality and Social Psychology, 74*(1), 21–35.

Srull, T. K., & Wyer, R. S. (1979). The role of category accessibility in the interpretation of information about persons: Some determinants and implications. *Journal of Personality and Social Psychology, 37*(10), 1660–1672.

Srull, T. K., & Wyer, R. S. (1989). Person memory and judgment. *Psychological Review, 96*(1), 58–82.

Sun, R. (2009). Theoretical status of computational cognitive modeling. *Cognitive Systems Research, 10*(2), 124–140.

Thagard, P. (2003). Why wasn't O.J. convicted? Emotional coherence in legal inference. *Cognition and Emotion, 17*(3), 361–383.

Thagard, P. (2004). Causal inference in legal decision making: Explanatory coherence vs. Bayesian networks. *Applied Artificial Intelligence, 18*(3–4), 231–249.

Thagard, P., & Aubie, B. (2008). Emotional consciousness: A neural model of how cognitive appraisal and somatic perception interact to produce qualitative experience. *Consciousness and Cognition, 17*(3), 811–834.

Trope, Y., & Alfieri, T. (1997). Effortfulness and flexibility of dispositional judgment processes. *Journal of Personality and Social Psychology, 73*(4), 662–674.

Uleman, J. S., & Moskowitz, G. B. (1994). Unintended effects of goals on unintended inferences. *Journal of Personality and Social Psychology, 66*(3), 490–501.

Van Overwalle, F. (2007). *Social connectionism: A reader and handbook for simulations.* Hove: Psychology Press.

Van Overwalle, F., & Labiouse, C. (2004). A recurrent connectionist model of person impression formation. *Personality and Social Psychology Review, 8*(1), 28–61.

Wagar, B. M., & Thagard, P. (2004). Spiking Phineas Gage: A neurocomputational theory of cognitive-affective integration in decision making. *Psychological Review, 111*(1), 67–79.

Wigboldus, D. H., Sherman, J. W., Franzese, H. L., & Van Knippenberg, A. (2004). Capacity and comprehension: Spontaneous stereotyping under cognitive load. *Social Cognition, 22*(3), 292–309.

# 4

# THE WHOLE ELEPHANT

## Toward Psychological Integration of the Individual as a Complex System

*Jennifer Rose Talevich*[1]

As people, we intuitively understand that we are not our environment, our emotions, perceptions, motivation, or even our behavior. We have the sense that who we are is something greater than just the sum of these parts. That is, although we may not have the technical vocabulary, we intuitively understand ourselves as complex systems.

Complex systems are ubiquitously embedded throughout the human experience. In every moment, we are served by systems within ourselves (our brains, our immune system). We depend upon and contend with both natural systems (climate systems and ecological systems, etc.) and social systems (our network of friends and family, governance systems, and the economy, to name a few). Throughout the physical and social sciences, from anthropology to physics, the research on these systems is abundant.

The basic component of models in the social sciences and humanities is individual humans. It is their behavior, and the complex interactions between them, that give rise to societies, cultures, and economic systems. In these models, typically, simple agents, outfitted with a simple pre-determined map of behaviors determined by basic decision-making rules, represent the individual human. However, decision-making and behavior, in realistic human beings (in contrast to these simple agents), are the nonlinear product of the motivations, feelings and experiences of an individual's mind or psyche. Yet within complexity science, research on the complexity of this foundational component of social systems, the individual mind, is scarce.

This gaping oversight receives little attention because the field that best understands the psyche and human behavior—psychology—is not, itself, working on the entire problem. Although cognitive science and cognitive psychology have worked to develop cognitive architectures, they have largely neglected the emotional, motivational, and most importantly, the social aspects of the mind and behavior. The social mind is the bridge between the individual and the collective. How cognitive, emotional, and motivational processes interact with the social world is the particular focus of social psychology.

The purpose of this chapter is to argue for the mutually beneficial importance of psychology's full participation in complexity science. Psychology's key contribution should be integrated psychological models of the individual mind situated in the social world. The chapter will introduce an integrated social and developmental psychological model as one example of how to apply complex systems principles to integrate psychological theory.

## The Missing Field in Complexity Science

One of the foremost institutes devoted to complexity research is the Santa Fe Institute. Their most popular massive online course, "Introduction to Complexity," enrolled 4,275 students in one semester (Complexity Explorer, 2015). Of particular interest are Week 7, which discusses models of biological self-organization, and Week 8, which models cooperation in social systems. Another week, "Scaling in Biology and Society," moved from a discussion of metabolism to cities, with nothing to connect the two. To this psychologist, the lack of connection between biological and social complexity was striking. A review of the research and curriculums of several other programs in complex systems science show the same gap. It would seem that complexity science does not consider people to be complex—or, if it does, does not think understanding the individual person is critical to understanding society.

Why this oversight? Consider the following quote recently published by a physicist in the *LA Times*: "That's right. Psychology isn't science. Why can we definitively say that? Because . . . [p]sychologists can't use a ruler or a microscope, so they invent an arbitrary scale" (Berezow, 2012)—an amusing commentary from the field in which "everything is relative" and invisible particles are theoretically inferred for decades, if not centuries, before they can be measured. According to this definition, it would seem that among the physical sciences, psychology has the most in common with physics. So why this disconnect between the physical sciences and psychology—and why is the disconnect not true, at least to the same extent, for the other social sciences?

One thing that sociology, anthropology, and economics share with the physical sciences, and which much of psychology does not, is a strong emphasis on computational models. Much work in the modern natural sciences is computational in nature. Computational models require an exacting level of specification, are entirely quantifiable; conditions in experimental simulations are completely controlled, reproducible, predictable, and testable. A favored type of computational model in both these social and the physical sciences are multi-agent systems in which the interactions of numerous simple agents result in highly complex phenomena. In physics, we find the simplest of all agents: atoms! To those who study atoms, simple agents are familiar and, as such, appear intrinsically reasonable and accurate. The misunderstandings and inaccuracies of modeling people as simple would not be apparent to them.

This is a problem because the people who study atoms are numerous among the people who decide what research projects receive funding. This is because the social sciences are comparatively young. Our older siblings, the "hard sciences," were already being supported by private and public funds (and sitting on review committees) before we came on the scene. This translates into a lot of influence and, thereby, money. Consider, for instance, the Superconducting Super Collider project, for which the United States government, in 1992, approved $8.25 billion ($13.5 billion today) for a *single* project (Appell, 2013).

The National Science Foundation (NSF) supports fundamental research and education in all the non-medical fields of science and engineering. It is the major source of federal backing in mathematics, computer science, and the social sciences. The NSF grants five times as much money to anthropology, sociology, and economics ($160 million) as it does to the behavioral sciences ($31 million) (Yamaner, 2014). That is, it provides five times the support to the social sciences that utilize and contribute to complex systems science.

Complexity science is a space in which physics, and the computational social and biological sciences, all interact to discover commonalities and share methods of both experimentation and analysis. Complexity scientists are particularly concerned with the common properties of systems considered complex in nature, society and science. With that, complexity has become not just a research approach, but a movement—a movement of unprecedented interdisciplinary collaboration among the natural and social sciences.

Although psychology is not yet participating sufficiently to garner a real presence in complexity science, there is evidence its contribution would be most welcome. For instance, two of the editors of this book, Vallacher and Nowak, have been invited to give a talk on dynamical systems psychology at the Santa Fe Institute. The professor featured in the Santa Fe Institute's massive online introductory course mentioned above, Dr. Melanie Mitchell, began her scientific career with a search for an understanding of the mind (Mitchell, 2011). She has published on psychological topics. The evidence suggests the exclusion of psychology from complex systems science is not only a matter of discrimination, but also a failure of our own field to fully participate. This chapter will argue that this absence is rooted in a basic incompatibility between traditional psychological research and the study of the mind as a complex system: it comes down to the study of the whole versus study of the parts.

## Holism in Complexity Science

The special focus of complexity science is on holism. A fundamental understanding is that the whole is not necessarily greater, but rather often different from the sum of the parts, and different from the parts themselves. There is no sentience in a neuron, no tornado in a raindrop, no financial collapse in a single dollar bill. The whole is not found among the parts, but arises as something different, *and often impossible to predict*, from its individual components.

Integration of theory and sub-systems is a particular challenge for psychology, as discussed directly above. As with other fields, what separates the complex systems approach from the disciplines that contribute to it is a special focus on holism: the whole that arises from many interacting parts.

### *"System Nestedness", "System Embeddedness"*

Wholes are but parts in even larger systems. Thus, in complexity science, there is also an emphasis on the multiplicity of systems and the effect that one sub-system has upon the behavior of another. This is the concept of system embeddedness or system nestedness. Individual components self-organize into hierarchical levels.

Biological complexity is hierarchically nested. Cells are complex systems in which the simple agents are molecules. Cells form tissues, which form organs, and organs form the body-wide organ systems of which the organism is composed. The organism, then, is a complex system composed of many biological agents that are each simple relative to the whole organism.

Social complexity is also hierarchically nested. The world economy is composed of national economies, and national economies are composed of state economies. "Human" culture is composed of a great variety of cultures found throughout the world and can be studied by identifying the universals found among them. In turn, these unique cultures often include many nations, each of which are composed of a plethora of groups and organizations. Some models include groups as the basic unit, but most often individual people self-organize into hierarchically nested social groups and structures.

The individual, then, is the basic unit of social complexity. This is why psychological integration at the level of the individual is how we can most significantly contribute to complexity science. As the individual at the biological level is a complex system composed of multiple body-wide complex systems, the individual mind is a complex system composed of multiple psychological complex systems. Complex systems scientists want to know what the overall system looks like: the whole cell, the whole society. A complex systems psychologist, then, would want to know what the person, as a whole, looks like: how psychological parts (which may themselves be hierarchically nested psychological systems) interact to give rise to an emergent psyche and the behavior it produces.

### Holism in Psychology

At its founding, the purpose of the field of psychology was not to understand psychological phenomena, but to understand people. The fundamental understanding of Gestalt psychology held that the mind could only be understood as an irreducible whole, something "other than" its parts. Unfortunately, the Second World War interrupted this German school of psychology and it, thereafter, became largely circumscribed to the study of perceptual illusions. Yet Gestalt psychology was poured into the very foundation of modern social psychology by theorists such as Asch, Heider, Lewin, and by Festinger (1950) (Read, Vanman, & Miller, 1997). For instance, Heider and Simmel's animation of "interacting" geometric shapes (1944) and Asch's impression formation (1946) showed that social stimuli, like perceptual illusion, are not processed in parts, but as a whole.

Early theories were "Big Theories" such as Lewin's force-field theory (1935), Bowlby's behavioral systems theory (1969), and others such as Murray's comprehensive system of needs (1959), Maslow's psychology of being (1968), as well as work by Jung (1939) and Freud (1927 [1923]). These theorists all developed comprehensive frameworks that attempted to integrate the entire psyche. But how does one test big theory? There really has been no way to do this except to break it down, carve it up, and manipulate the pieces in lab experiments. And so, the field moved towards reduction. Now we know a lot about emotions, motivation, perception, and the like—but have we made equal strides in understanding the person, the mind, the psyche? No. The individual person isn't just the level of scale missing in complexity science, it is also the missing level of scale in modern psychological science.

Psychology is a highly fractured field. We are split into several basic subdisciplines (e.g., social psychology) and, within each sub-discipline, scholars work as artisans crafting their own theories and carving out their highly individualized niches. Psychology, as a field, does not often combine sub-systems or levels of analysis. The result is highly detailed information about specific psychological phenomena without much integration. Nowhere in modern psychology is there a movement to integrate existing psychological knowledge and theories so as to represent the individual person holistically.

This is unfortunate because, as will be discussed further below, the individual person is the basic unit of social complexity in anthropological, economic, and sociological models. Holism at the level of the individual human is the bridge between psychology and the ability of our field to contribute significantly to complexity science. Nonlinear dynamical psychologists, like those whose contributions you will read in other chapters of this book, are doing the important work of understanding different psychological processes as complex systems. The authors in this book are psychologists working to change the field. We study nonlinear psychological dynamics, chaos, catastrophe, and complexity.[2] The next step is to begin to integrate multiple dynamical systems into broader psychological systems and, eventually, to integrate these systems so as to represent the individual person in a holistic manner. Reduction was the best science possible at one time. It is no longer. The infeasible pipe-dreams of early psychologists have, with the invention of computational methods, become a manageable feat.

## Contributing the Individual

A key problem in studying the psyche as a whole is that, well, it's complicated! What is meant by "whole" is not "entire," but "integrated". Any one model need only include that which has been known to influence the particular social behavior of interest. Even so, it is difficult to build a model that integrates multiple psychological theories and phenomena (each complex systems in their own right), and nearly impossible to track, or even imagine in any detail, how these non-additively interact.

Yet this is the key problem, across fields that gave rise to complexity as a science and to common solutions. Psychologists can now draw on this new body of knowledge in the attempt to integrate their field. But to join complexity science, psychology needs to not just draw from it, but to contribute solutions. What problems, as newcomers to complexity, can psychologists solve?

## The Limitations of Multi-Agent Systems

Many complex systems models are multi-agent models in which individual agents, be they ants or people, are programmed with simple decision rules. From the interactions of these simple agents arise sophisticated collective behavior. This has led to the general consensus that only simple representations of people are necessary to model social complexity (Boero, Castellani, & Squazzoni, 2008). If the goal is to predict what collective behavior may arise given certain conditions and assumptions, then this approach is quite useful.

But if the goal is to understand social *change*, then simple-agent models are inadequate—particularly if the goal is to simulate the possible effects of social interventions such as campaigns designed to sway public opinion, strategies to prevent crime, or predicting the effects of government policy changes on the economy (Boero, 2015). The source of change in social models is individual people, and behavioral change in an actual human is fundamentally nonlinear. Simple-agent decision rules are pre-programmed. But changes in the environment such as new information, new opportunities, or new obstacles can fundamentally change individuals and their decision rules.

The human response to an event is to think, perceive, and feel. Behavior emerges from the pattern of perceptions, motivation, and emotions that become activated in response to an event. These patterns are highly individualized because they reflect the personal history of the individual. That is, personal histories become ingrained as patterns of association among psychological components. A lost opportunity is easily dismissed by one person, cause for fear in another, and cause for anger in yet another, based on their past histories. Of those who feel fear, different histories will associate different behavioral responses to fear urging fight, flight, or freeze. Each change in the environment, given time, will be encoded as new thoughts and feelings and decision-making rules.

Essentially, the modeling of social change requires the transversal of multiple hierarchically nested levels of complexity. From the complex interactions of human behavior emerge sociological phenomena. These emergent phenomena of macro models, society, culture, and the economy, are, in turn, environmental inputs to the complex psychological models from which individual behaviors emerge.

One unfortunate byproduct of the general failure to acknowledge psychological complexity is a dearth of available technologies with which to build multi-agent models with sophisticated agents (cf. Boero, 2015; Marsella, Pynadath, & Read, 2004). So even nonlinear dynamical systems psychologists, today can only build simple-agent multi-agent models. The fact that they do so, nonetheless, is meaningful. The collective dynamics chapters in this book demonstrate the fact that, ultimately, understanding human behavior requires the transversal of many scales of complexity.

As complexity science extends its reach to solve more and more complex social issues, it will become more apparent that they are missing a critical level of scale. Then one of two things will happen: psychologists will provide the missing level of scale—the complex individual—or computer scientists will reverse engineer psychology. The choice is ours.

## The Complex Behavioral System

This section describes a complex psychological system. It takes a classic psychological theory, integrates modern theories and findings within the classic framework, and then implements the final model as a neural network.

Behavioral systems theory was developed by John Bowlby in the 1950s and 1960s (Bowlby, 1969). In his early career as a physician at an orphanage, Bowlby observed that child abandonment initially caused anxiety and crying, followed by anger and acting out, then finally despair and detachment. Children responded to their situation through a predictable process—an environmental cause and behavioral effect that could not be accounted for by the psychological theories of his day, such as Freud's psychic energy model. So Bowlby looked outside of psychology to engineering and ethology. Then-new control systems theory dealt with the behavior of dynamical systems with inputs and studied how their behavior is modified by feedback. Animal reflex and fixed-action patterns (e.g., mating dances of birds) in ethology linked environmental cues to the appropriate behavior with advantageous speed. Pulling these together, Bowlby envisioned a kind of psychological control system, one in which psychological phenomena such as perception, motivation, and emotion were organized so as to link typical human circumstances to adaptive responses with a kind of immediacy approximating that found elsewhere in the animal kingdom.

The neural network presented herein fills in Bowlby's sketch of how psychological experiences link events and behavior with modern findings and theories.

Most prominent among those integrated are Smith and Lazarus's (1990) primary appraisal process, in which the adaptive function of emotion is to signal motivational assessments of well-being that trigger behavior. This is then integrated with the neuroscientific finding that approach and avoidance motivation occurs via different neural pathways (Gray, 1991) and they are learned through different experiential processes (Gable, 2006). The model presents Bowlby's framework as a complex system in which environmental inputs activate multiple, networked, psychological sub-systems. These sub-systems interact dynamically to form associations, through self-organized learning, to produce the behavioral patterns observed by Bowlby. These behaviors and the underlying psychological experiences are then fed back into the system such that the patterns become so consistent as to be trait-like: that is, the network forms a personality.

## Attachment Theory

Attachment theory, and behavioral systems theory more broadly, is both an evolutionary and developmental psychological theory (Bowlby, 1969). Humans are proposed to have evolved several behavioral systems, each with a specialized function for responding to species-typical situations such as needing protection from predators or to protect those resources necessary for survival and thriving. Bowlby proposed five systems, including the attachment, caregiving, affiliation, sexual, and exploration systems (Mikulincer & Shaver, 2012). Each of these systems overlaps fairly well with domains of adaptive problems proposed by modern evolutionary psychology (Bugental, 2000; Kenrick, Li, & Butner, 2003). In line with that literature, power has also been delineated as a behavioral system (Shaver, Segev, & Mikulincer, 2011).

Attachment is by far the best-known and most well-researched of these systems. The specialized function of the attachment system, in particular, is to obtain help in times of need. Human babies are incapable of meeting their own most basic survival needs: feeding, protecting, and cleaning themselves. To obtain this care, babies have evolved to perform certain behaviors, such as crying out, when in need of assistance. The attachment bond is a motivational and behavioral system that directs children to seek proximity to a familiar caregiver, and pair-bonded adults to seek out their significant others, with the expectation that they will receive protection and emotional support. The strength and quality of an attachment bond, at any age, depends on how much one can trust that another will be there for them in times of need.

## Modeling Psychological Complexity with Neural Networks

The model presented herein is abstracted from the neuro-architecture in order to represent the attachment system as a complex system. By communicating through chemical interaction, neurons self-organize into a biological neural network which gives rise to "the brain." By analogy, psychological components self-organize in an artificial neural network by adjusting their connection weights. Patterns of connections across a psychological network give rise to "the mind."

Connections between psychological systems in the network are adjusted according to biologically realistic learning algorithms. Not all neural net technologies are capable of modeling complex properties like self-organized learning. In feed-forward neural networks, activation flows in one direction and error signals are unnaturally back-propagated (sent backwards) against the flow of activation. This is criticized as a form of executive rather than decentralized control. However, the model herein is a recurrent neural network that is bi-directionally connected. Activations flow in a directed cycle which allows the network to have an internal state that can change over time. This, in turn, allows the network to exhibit dynamic temporal behavior in which activation states are mutually influenced by one another and settling over time leads to states that satisfy the constraints of the weights in the network. Constraint satisfaction is an *emergent* computational property of recurrent neural nets.

The current network was built in the Emergent software program and the Leabra (Local, error-driven and associative, biologically realistic algorithm) architecture (Aisa, Mingus, & O'Reilly, 2008). Learning in this architecture utilizes the extended contrastive attractor learning (XCAL) equation, which is a balance of Hebbian, associative learning, and contrastive Hebbian learning (CHL) for targeted learning. In CHL, the network learns the difference between a sequence of activation states: an expectation and then a subsequent outcome. To use a basketball analogy, back-propagation is similar to a coach saying, "You missed the basket, aim more to the left." In contrast, CHL is similar to seeing the difference between where *you expected* the ball to land and where it actually landed, and self-adjusting your aim accordingly.

In this network, the CHL algorithm adjusts weights to reduce the difference in activation between the expectation and outcome. That is, the weighted value of a connection (conceptually analogous to beta weights in a structural equation model) is adjusted so that the connection between the experience and the correct output is strengthened, and the connection to the wrong one is lessened on each trial. The "compute" or hidden layers are necessary to this error-correcting component.[3]

Finally, Leabra utilizes k-Winners-Take-All (kWTA) sparse distributed representations. This is a form of competitive learning in which k number of nodes in a given layer become active. Nodes in the network mutually activate and inhibit each other, and after some time, only the most highly activated (k-number) of nodes will be active in the output layer. Learned patterns (or representations) are composed of the winners of this competition.

## The Attachment Neural Network

The attachment neural network models the psychological circuit that has evolved to meet the demands of the species-typical requirement for social assistance to survive and thrive as a human being. Life experience tunes this evolved system to develop the set of attachment strategies most effective in the environment. This is referred to as one's attachment style. The purpose of the model is to show how the evolved circuit is represented in the mind, how these relationship processes are learned and eventually ingrained as a personality or chronic relationship style that maintains social behavior. It is a holistic psychological architecture (including social perception, emotion, motivation, and behavior) that demonstrates how, with learning over time, individual differences develop.

The network structure (Figure 4.1) begins with inputs representing features of the situation. These features are those identified as being most important to attachment in the literature: who is present, how they are behaving (e.g., are they being attentive to you?), their past behavior, and whether or not the current situation is threatening. These features of the situation activate a schema, or "working model," as it is referred to in the attachment literature. This hidden layer nonlinearly transforms the environmental inputs into a dynamic pattern to represent the situation as a whole.

The schema activates the motivation sub-system including a behavioral approach (BAS) and behavioral avoidance (BIS) motivation system. There are

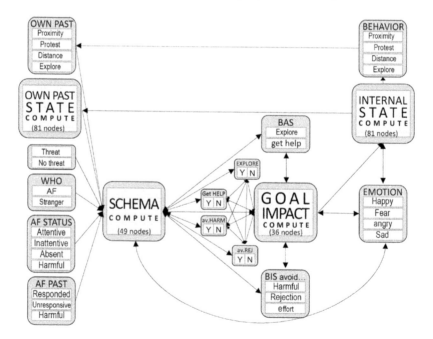

**FIGURE 4.1** The attachment neural network.

also several congruence layers, one for each motive, connected to the Situation Compute. These assess the impact that the situation will have upon one's most important goals. Activations from the BIS and BAS motive layers and each congruence layer connect to an additional hidden layer called the Goal Impact Compute. This layer nonlinearly transforms the inputs from all the motive layers into a single, dynamic pattern, to represent the state of the network's motivation system. This architecture is consistent with the primary process in appraisal models of emotion (Scherer, Schorr, & Johnstone, 2001; Smith & Lazarus, 1990) and has been formalized with human data studies in previous work by the author and colleagues (Talevich, Read, & Walsh, 2014).

The output of the motivation system, the Goal Impact Compute, then activates specific emotions in the emotions layer. Both emotions and motivation layers then converge on yet another hidden layer intended to capture the state of the network (the Internal State Compute) which will then activate behavior. This layer is analogous to Bowlby's model of the self (Bowlby, 1969), and is necessary to capture goal-corrected behavior. In the last step, the Internal State Compute and the behaviors layer are both copied and fed back into the network as inputs for the next time step.

With computational tools, it is possible to model within-person processes over time. Temporal contingencies among relevant cues and the behaviors they evoke can be simulated moment-by-moment. This allows for hypothesis testing of the dynamic social cognitive processes related to relationship formation, growth, and change at a level of detail that is otherwise impossible. Competing activations in the network feed forward and back to find balance throughout the entire system by satisfying the constraints of all the psychological forces. The final state of the system, once it has settled, is copied along with the behavior it evoked and fed back into the system on the next iteration. In this way, each experience happens in the context of "what happened last time." With learning over time, this information builds up to create a context of "what usually happens." This process will be discussed in more detail below under "Dynamics in the Psychological Network."

## Hierarchy and Scales of Complexity

Complexity is hierarchically nested. Each level of scale is a complex system whose emergent behavior is the input or comparatively "simple" agent of the next level of scale. While the lower level remains a complex system, its emergent behavior is simple *as compared to the whole* of the higher-level system. In neural networks, the "agents" are nodes analogous to neuron groups. For computational feasibility, these are the smallest units in an artificial neural network. Nodes are organized into layers analogous to functional brain regions. As a psychological network (Figure 4.1), the nodes represent concrete psychological variables (e.g., fear) while the layers represent nonlinear dynamical psychological sub-systems (e.g., emotions).

## Decentralized Learning

Another key feature of complex systems is decentralization. There is no executive control. The psychological network presented herein is a decentralized system in which the individual nodes competitively learn to associate with other nodes and whether or not to activate based on what other nodes are doing. Decision rules arise through experience as connection weights strengthen as the model learns to make associations between variables. For instance, over time, the "happiness" node of the attachment model will associate with certain motivation activations, the weights between them will increase, and happiness will learn to activate if the output from the motivation system is positive (i.e., the outlook for active goals looks good). Next, the "explore" node will learn to activate if the happiness node is active and the fear node is not.

Thus, psychological phenomena are connected, or networked, and representations in an artificial (or biological) neural network are distributed. Note that, although this is a model of attachment formation, there is no node or layer for anxious, avoidant, or secure attachment styles in Figure 4.1. That is because personality and chronic behavioral patterns like attachment are emergent—they arise from the collective actions of, and interactions between, emotions, motivation, and other psychological components.

## Dynamics in the Psychological Network

Inspired by biological brains, neural networks can model dynamics such as non-linear activation functions, thresholding, changing connections (weights), and inhibition between psychological variables.

The Leabra neural network architecture allows for the modeling of important psychological dynamics such as the development of chronic associations, differences in sensitivities to attractive or aversive stimuli, and the approach or avoidance motives they activate, etc. (For a more detailed explanation of these functions with the Leabra architecture, see Read et al., 2010.)

Like biological neurons, computational nodes can have different sensitivities to inputs (conductance and gain parameters). Greater sensitivity in one neuron/node can result in higher output in response to the same input. This is one way in which individual differences in psychological variables can be manipulated. Furthermore, each node has a firing threshold, and input to the network must exceed that threshold before the node will "fire." This plays out at the psychological level in the attachment network. For instance, the motivational appraisal that the situation looks bad for one's most important goals (a pattern represented in the Goal Impact layer) will activate different emotions based on the severity of the computed situation. While the "fear" node may learn to respond to even a mildly poor goal appraisal, the severity of the situation must reach a particularly high level before the "sadness" node will activate. This is consistent with the finding that a fear response is generally faster and has a lower threshold than positive responses for the adaptive purpose of focusing attention on goals.

Another fundamental aspect of Leabra is a general mechanism for inhibition. This is particularly important for modeling motivation. The active pursuit of one goal should inhibit competing goals because conflicting signals about what is important lead to a kind of behavioral freeze.

## Adaptation

Dynamics constitute adaptation if the changes occurring within the system are in response to an external environment. In order to evolve, a complex system must find a way to extract information from its environment and then adapt to it. If the response improves the system's fitness in that environment, then complex systems scientists call the adaptation Darwinian evolution. This is a much more basic or general sense of the word "evolution" than is used in common parlance, which refers more specifically to evolution of a species. The complex system that is a human mind develops in accordance with the constraints and affordances of biology and culture. Consistent with common parlance, evolutionary psychology theorizes about adaptations at the species level. However, several disciplines in psychology study adaptive processes: cultural psychology studies adaptation at both the societal level (e.g., cultural differences) and the species level (e.g., "human universals" such as gender differences in power). Social psychology studies adaptation more broadly and from the perspective of the immediate environment: how diverse individual human beings commonly respond (adapt) to similar situations (similar environments). Developmental psychology studies adaptation at the individual level across the lifespan. As complex systems science defines it, if these social and developmental psychological adaptations improve the individual's fitness in their social environment or culture, the adaptation is a form of Darwinian evolution.

The introduction to attachment theory at the beginning of this section was an evolutionary argument. Bowlby's behavioral systems theory theorizes about the adaptive problem that each functional system evolved to solve at the species level. The predictive power of attachment theory lies in how individuals adapt the system to maximize fitness in their social environments. These adaptations result in highly predictable patterns of behavior.

The dynamics by which individual variables within a psychological system adjust in response to one another were discussed above. But how does the system, as a whole, adapt to its environment? That is, how does an emergent psyche, or at least aspects of it, evolve?

The attachment system is designed to respond to both threats and the amount of social support currently available in the environment. The system responds to threats by seeking aid from close others—those known to the system to be more reliable sources of aid than other potential sources (a secure situation).

If, however, aid is not forthcoming, the system adjusts to "gear up" help-seeking behaviors by protesting inadequate aid (an anxious situation). But if this too fails, the system suppresses help-seeking in order to turn efforts toward self-help (an avoidant situation).

The key factor in determining the type of attachment style that develops is a function of attachment figure responsiveness in these times of need. The network formalizes this function as schedules of reinforcement where responsiveness of the attachment figure is the reward. Over time, the network forms expectancies regarding the quality of care one is likely to receive. Attachment behaviors are strategies for dealing with this expected outcome.

When responsiveness is positively reinforced, the network develops a secure attachment style. Weights throughout the network adjust to associate threat with fear. However, when responsiveness is reinforced, threat also becomes associated with the "get help" motive and its positive congruence with the situation. This is the internal state of the network: a pattern of expecting a positive response. Expecting its needs will be met, the secure network adaptively implements help-seeking or independence depending on whether there is or is not a threat, respectively.

When care is delivered on a partial reinforcement schedule, an anxious attachment style develops. Weights throughout the network adjust in expectation of having to "work for it," and the anxious system pre-emptively over-implements help-seeking and protests rejection. An attachment-avoidant network develops when care is delivered on an extinction schedule. Weights throughout the network adjust in expectation of going unaided, and independence is automatic rather than in direct response to the situation at hand.

The adjustment of these connection weights is a unique feature of neural network programming, designed to replicate the strength of connections between neurons and neuronal pathways. This is one way in which neural networks are ideally suited for the modeling of complex psychological systems.

This process of internal, nonlinear dynamics, aimed toward adapting the system to its environment, is how experiences become ingrained as a personality or chronic relationship style that maintains social behavior.

### The Emergence of Behavioral Patterns: Attachment Styles

In Figure 4.1 we have what seems to be a great omission: an attachment model without attachment styles. One might reasonably expect an "attachment layer" with three nodes for secure, anxious, and avoidant attachment. Certainly, these appear in any statistical model dealing with attachment variables. However, as with infants and adults alike, the behavior of the network is diagnostic of its attachment style. The attachment style representation is distributed in patterns of activation throughout social perceptions, motivations, emotions, and behavior.

In the above we discussed how these patterns are learned. This section shows how attachment bonds emerge from these patterns.

After training, each network was put in a simulation of the Ainsworth Strange Situation: an experiment in which mothers bring their infants into the lab and, in a series of episodes, leave the child to play alone or with a stranger for short periods of time. Human infants respond to these situations with reliable patterns of behavior that can be used to identify their attachment style (Ainsworth, Blehar, Waters, & Wall, 1978). A child is classified as secure if he or she plays contentedly with toys (exploration) when his or her mother is present (Episodes 1 and 2), but then seeks proximity to her after she returns from an absence (Episodes 5 and 8). However, if the child does not explore, and either ignores his or her mother or resists her greeting upon her return, the child is classified as avoidant or anxious, respectively.

The output of each network was coded using the Strange Situation code book (Ainsworth et al., 1978). Each neural network's behavior was consistent with the behavior of differently attached human infants in the Ainsworth Strange Situation. As hypothesized, networks trained with reinforced responsiveness behaved in accordance with the secure classification (seeking proximity only in need). The partially reinforced network behaved in accordance with the resistant (i.e., anxious) classification (marked by protest/resistance). Finally, the network receiving extinction schedules behaved in accordance with the avoidant classification (marked by dismissive behavior). The behavior of the network is consistent with the behavior of human infants.

The network output is, like infant behavior, diagnostic of its attachment style. Unlike actual human beings, we can look directly into the "minds" of these networks: we see that the attachment style representation is distributed throughout that "mind" as different patterns of learned associations between social perceptions, motivations, and emotions.

## Conclusion

Presented herein was a complex system in which psychological phenomena are networked to connect human circumstances with human behaviors. Through self-organized learning, psychological sub-systems (e.g., emotions, motivation) come to be associated and behavioral patterns emerge. Distributed among these sub-systems, and represented by the patterns of interaction that form among psychological components, an individual, a "self" as relates to close others, arises as long histories are encoded and the "self" system adapts to its external environment.

Emergent patterns of chronic behavior in known contexts allow us to identify the underlying personality representation. Identifying this representation then allows us to predict the individual's future behavior in additional contexts. Therefore, in order to change behavior, we must modify the underlying representation, the interactions among psychological components. That is, to predict people's responses to changing circumstances accurately requires a complex model that can simulate the numerous interactions of the many psychological components from which the ever-changing individual "self" arises.

As a complex system, the psyche as a whole will constrain the behavior of the individual psychological components we study in ways that we cannot yet comprehend. The difficulties with replication that currently plague psychology are not due to a lack of scientific rigor—they are due to using reductionist science to model complex phenomena. Each field currently engaged in complexity science hit a wall in its work. That we have come to the limits of reductionist psychology is a sign that our science has matured. This is reason for congratulation and excited anticipation for the next frontier.

There is much to learn from the new field of complexity science. It has arisen from the participation of multiple disciplines, and is being applied to aid discovery at every (non-psychological level) of human (and non-human) existence from cell biology to brain networks to social life. The greatest troubles of our time are not technological, but social. Yet funding for the social sciences lags behind that of the physical sciences. Further, funding for psychology as a basic science lags behind the social sciences that are currently engaged in complex systems research such as multi-agent modeling.

We have seen here that the individual is a complex system from which predictable behavior patterns (in complex systems terminology, "decision rules") are emergent phenomena. Given this, any model designed to simulate and accurately predict human social change needs to include psychologically complex, not simple, individuals. Yet most anthropological, sociological, and economic computational models are multi-agent models using simple agents pre-programmed with simple decision rules. It is fairly ironic that the individual person is the most important yet least understood level of social complexity. One might argue that behavioral science is not just *a* missing level of scale, but also the most important. While the study of emergent macro social behavior is fascinating, the ultimate utility of these models is to predict social changes such as the effects of public policies, interventions, or calamities. Collective behavior emerges from the behavior of individual decision-makers. Yet the social environment shapes the individuals that make those decisions. The social variable, "inputs," to which an individual human responds changes the decision-making rules of the individual such that the behavior they output is nonlinearly related to environmental inputs. The human mind is not simple, and simple models of the human mind are not going to be accurate—particularly when predicting social change over time.

The absence of psychology, particularly social psychology, at complex systems research centers indicates there is much work yet to do in convincing this community of the importance of the complex individual. However, it is a worthy goal, and one that has received substantial financial backing in recent years. A National Institute of Health funding opportunity entitled "Modeling Social

Behavior (R01)" (PAR-13-374, 2013–2017), involving several behavioral and mental health programs, calls for computational approaches. It puts particular emphasis on understanding the system as a whole, and further specifies that research must traverse multiple scales of social complexity—examinations at single levels of scale are not fundable.

In 2011, the John Templeton Foundation funded the massive online courses in complexity discussed in the introduction. This educational outreach was a major component of a three-year $5 million grant to the Santa Fe Institute to illuminate many hidden regularities in the biological and social systems (universal patterns in the emergence of complex societies) by capitalizing on the opportunities presented by recent advances in computational power.

In 2012, the John Templeton Foundation offered another $3 million in grants, each proposal to win approximately $250,000, in a funding competition aimed at psychologists and social scientists "designed to promote integration of existing lines of research and to generate and test new hypotheses emerging from such integration." An expansion to the attachment neural network described in this chapter was proposed. It was the only proposal for a computational model entered into the competition. This gave it a decided advantage—not because it was computational, but because only computational methods can harness the integrative potential of complex systems: holism and nestedness. The project was one of the winners of the competition and is currently being funded. An express hope, by the grantor and grantee, is that the work will encourage more integrative computational research, to the benefit of both psychology and complexity science alike.

## Summary

This chapter has argued for the importance to psychology of more fully participating in complexity science—not only its methods, but also its intellectual focus on holism and the transversal of multiple levels of scale. It has further argued that the greatest value that psychology can contribute is to integrate psychological science. Integrated models would include all the major psychological phenomena such as cognition, emotion, and motivation, and consider them in developmental and socially situated systems. When modeling the psyche rather than its parts, social-behavioral phenomena can be more easily scaled up in collaboration with the collective-oriented social sciences.

For instance, attachment behaviors influence a surprising number of social interactions: not only the parent–child bond, but also mating bonds (Miller, Christensen, Pedersen, Putcha-Bhagavatula, & Appleby, 2013), attachments to the supernatural (Kirkpatrick, 1997), and even different product brands (Park, MacInnis, & Priester, 2007). Thus, the model of attachment presented herein would be an appropriate complex agent in multi-agent models of changing family and marriage patterns, religious organizations, species-level evolution of gender differences, and even some consumer economic models.

Thus, an integrated psychological science would result in realistically complex human agents. As technology and processing power increase, these complex human agents can be integrated into multi-agent models. That technological future is not too far off, but psychology has quite a bit of integration to do before it will be ready to take part in such an endeavor.

Yet it is only by uniting the behavioral and collective social sciences, modeling both the individual decision-maker who drives social change and the social environment that shapes the decision-maker, that we will accurately predict the impact of social policy and intervention. This is the only way to understand change: how we came to be the people and peoples that we are, and who we may become.

Some might consider striving towards an integrated model of the complex human psyche as too ambitious—even mythic. But as the field of physics has demonstrated, sometimes it pays to think really big. What is psychology's—or, better yet, the social sciences'—Large Hadron Collider project? Self and societal well-being and improvement are the domain of the social sciences. Let physics have the God particle, ours is the domain of human salvation.

## Notes

1 My thanks to Stephen J. Read for reading and editing many versions of this chapter, for financial support by the John Templeton Foundation, and for the shepherding of our program manager, Nicholas Gibson.
2 For an introduction to nonlinear dynamics and complexity from a psychological perspective, see the following: Guastello, Koopmans, & Pincus (2009); Nowak & Vallacher (1998); Read et al. (1997); Vallacher & Nowak (1994, 1997, 2007); Wiese, Vallacher, & Strawinska (2010).
3 To learn more about these learning mechanisms, see O'Reilly and Munakata (2000).

## References

Ainsworth, M. D. S., Blehar, M. C., Waters, E., & Wall, S. (1978). *Patterns of attachment: A psychological study of the strange situation.* Hillsdale, NJ: Lawrence Erlbaum.
Aisa, B., Mingus, B., & O'Reilly, R. (2008). The Emergent neural modeling system. *Neural Networks, 21*(8), 1146–1152.
Appell, D. (2013). The supercollider that never was. *Scientific American,* October 15. Retrieved from www.scientificamerican.com/article/the-supercollider-that-never-was/
Asch, S. E. (1946). Forming impressions of personality. *Journal of Abnormal and Social Psychology, 41*(3), 258.
Berezow, A. B. (2012). Why psychology isn't science. *Los Angeles Times,* July 13. Retrieved from http://articles.latimes.com/2012/jul/13/news/la-ol-blowback-pscyhology-science-20120713
Boero, R. (2015). *Behavioral computational social science.* Hoboken, NJ: John Wiley & Sons.
Boero, R., Castellani, M., & Squazzoni, F. (2008). Individual behavior and macro social properties: An agent-based model. *Computational and Mathematical Organization Theory, 14*(2), 156–174.
Bowlby, J. (1969). *Attachment* (Kindle ed., Vol. 1). New York: Basic Books Classics.

Bugental, D. B. (2000). Acquisition of the algorithms of social life: A domain-based approach. *Psychological Bulletin, 126*(2), 187.

Complexity Explorer (2015). Course statistics from fall, 2014. Retrieved from www.complexityexplorer.org/news/15-course-statistics-from-fall-2014

Festinger, L. (1950). Informal social communication. *Psychological Review, 57*(5), 271.

Freud, S. (1927 [1923]). *The ego and the id.* London: Hogarth.

Gable, S. L. (2006). Approach and avoidance social motives and goals. *Journal of Personality, 74*(1), 175–222.

Gray, J. A. (1991). The neuropsychology of temperament. In J. Strelau & A. Angleitner (Eds.), *Explorations in temperament: International perspectives on theory and measurement* (pp. 105–128). New York: Plenum.

Guastello, S. J., Koopmans, M., & Pincus, D. (2009). *Chaos and complexity in psychology: The theory of nonlinear dynamical systems.* Cambridge: Cambridge University Press.

Heider, F., & Simmel, M. (1944). An experimental study of apparent behavior. *American Journal of Psychology, 57,* 243–259.

Jung, C. G. (1939). *The integration of the personality.* New York: Farrar & Rinehart.

Kenrick, D. T., Li, N. P., & Butner, J. (2003). Dynamical evolutionary psychology: Individual decision rules and emergent social norms. *Psychological Review, 110*(1), 3–28.

Kirkpatrick, L. A. (1997). A longitudinal study of changes in religious belief and behavior as a function of individual differences in adult attachment style. *Journal for the Scientific Study of Religion, 36*(2), 207–217.

Lewin, K. (1935). *A dynamic theory of personality.* New York: McGraw-Hill.

Marsella, S. C., Pynadath, D.V., & Read, S. J. (2004). PsychSim: Agent-based modeling of social interactions and influence. In *Proceedings of the International Conference on Cognitive Modeling* (pp. 243–248). Mahwah, NJ: Lawrence Erlbaum.

Maslow, A. H. (1968). *Toward a psychology of being.* Floyd, VA: Sublime Books.

Mikulincer, M., & Shaver, P. R. (2012). Attachment theory expanded. In K. Deaux & M. Snyder (Eds.), *The Oxford handbook of personality and social psychology* (pp. 467–492). New York: Oxford University Press.

Miller, L. C., Christensen, J. L., Pedersen, W. C., Putcha-Bhagavatula, A., & Appleby, P. R. (2013). Attachment fertility theory: Complex systems of mechanisms simplify sex, mating, and sexual risks. *Psychological Inquiry, 24*(3), 211–220.

Mitchell, M. (2011). *Complexity: A guided tour* (1st ed.). Oxford: Oxford University Press.

Murray, H. A. (1959). Preparations for the scaffold of a comprehensive system. *Psychology: A Study of a Science, 3,* 7–54.

Nowak, A., & Vallacher, R. R. (1998). *Dynamical social psychology.* New York: Guilford Press.

O'Reilly, R. C., & Munakata, Y. (2000). *Computational explorations in cognitive neuroscience: Understanding the mind by simulating the brain.* Cambridge, MA: MIT Press.

Park, C. W., MacInnis, D. J., & Priester, J. R. (2007). *Beyond attitudes: Attachment and consumer behavior* (SSRN Scholarly Paper No. ID 961469). Rochester, NY: Social Science Research Network.

Read, S. J., Monroe, B. M., Brownstein, A. L., Yang, Y., Chopra, G., & Miller, L. C. (2010). A neural network model of the structure and dynamics of human personality. *Psychological Review, 117*(1), 61–92.

Read, S. J., Vanman, E. J., & Miller, L. C. (1997). Connectionism, parallel constraint satisfaction processes, and Gestalt principles: (Re)introducing cognitive dynamics to social psychology. *Personality and Social Psychology Review, 1*(1), 26–53.

Scherer, K. R., Schorr, A., & Johnstone, T. (Eds.) (2001). *Appraisal processes in emotion: Theory, methods, research*. New York: Oxford University Press.

Shaver, P. R., Segev, M., & Mikulincer, M. (2011). A behavioral systems perspective on power and aggression. In P. R. Shaver & M. Mikulincer (Eds.), *Human Aggression and Violence: Causes, Manifestations, and Consequences* (pp. 71–87). Washington, DC: American Psychological Association.

Smith, C. A., & Lazarus, R. S. (1990). Emotion and adaptation. In L. A. Pervin (Ed.), *Handbook of personality theory and research* (609–637). New York: Guilford Press.

Talevich, J. R., Read, S. J., & Walsh, D. A. (2014). Goal impact: A goal systems domain-general prediction tool, applied to voluntary job turnover. *Basic and Applied Social Psychology, 36*(1), 35–50.

Vallacher, R. R., & Nowak, A. (Eds.) (1994). *Dynamical systems in social psychology*. San Diego, CA: Academic Press.

Vallacher, R. R., & Nowak, A. (1997). The emergence of dynamical social psychology. *Psychological Inquiry, 8*(2), 73–99.

Vallacher, R. R., & Nowak, A. E. (2007). Dynamical social psychology: Finding order in the flow of human experience. In A. W. Kruglanski & E. T. Higgins (Eds.), *Social psychology: Handbook of basic principles* (2nd ed.) (734–758). New York: Guilford Press.

Wiese, S. L., Vallacher, R. R., & Strawinska, U. (2010). Dynamical social psychology: Complexity and coherence in human experience. *Social and Personality Psychology Compass, 4*(11), 1018–1030.

Yamaner, M. (2014). Federal funding for basic research at universities and colleges essentially unchanged in FY 2012. National Science Foundation, NSF 14-318, September. Retrieved from www.nsf.gov/statistics/infbrief/nsf14318/#fn1

# 5

# COMPUTATIONAL MODELING OF HEALTH BEHAVIOR

*Mark G. Orr and Daniel Chen*[1]

The field of health psychology is broad, covering a variety of psychological mechanisms (e.g., stress/coping), contexts (extended hospital visits), and applications (e.g., in-clinic interventions). The distinct field of health behavior (the study of behaviors related to health), largely influenced by psychology, is equally broad, but in a different way—it addresses behavior embedded in a variety of levels of scale, from the individual to the community to the population. In this chapter, we will focus exclusively on the issues of health behavior, a perspective that puts a premium on articulating how psychological processes are implicated across levels of scale. Thus, our interest lies in modeling both an individual's behavior and a collection of individuals simultaneously. This goal clearly invokes a systems approach that leverages computational models of individual-level health behavior that can be embedded in computational social systems (e.g., social networks).

Central to the study of health behavior is the dynamics of change—in attitudes, beliefs, self-efficacy, and behavior—where the principal challenge is to explain how social and environmental contexts drive change in a person's mental representations and processes. This challenge is captured well by the notion that behavior at any point is always driven by the individual and his/her situation and context (Mischel & Shoda, 1995; Monroe & Read, 2008; Shoda, LeeTiernan, & Mischel, 2002; Shoda & Mischel, 1998). A primary context in the health behavior field is, naturally, other persons—something that is well captured in the social network literature.

The social network literature extends and formalizes what we call the person–context system. Here, a person's context is composed of other people, providing an account of the behavior of both individuals and populations of individuals simultaneously. Furthermore, some social network effects provide convergent evidence that behaviors are socially determined, evidence that comes largely from outside of the bounds of traditional experimental paradigms used in psychology and, in effect, offers a greater degree of ecological validity (for an excellent example, see Muchnik, Aral, & Taylor, 2013). However, a key limitation of the social network approach is the difficulty in interfacing with psychological processes that are informed by psychological theory (for a rare exception, see Bhattacharyya & Ohlsson, 2010)—that is, the approach is too heavy on context and too light on person.

This limitation has not been reconciled in the health behavior field. Here, when social networks are considered, it is as an auxiliary piece of information for understanding individuals' behavior, and not as an integrated part of the psychological processes related to behavior—for example, to understand the degree to which individuals should be targeted based on their position in a network (for a thorough review, see Valente, 2010). Thus, the health behavior field, although deeply wedded to the idea of people embedded in social systems, has not yet provided the theoretical infrastructure to support models of health behavior that are truly dynamic and integrated with respect to social context.

The central problem, then, is that each approach focuses too much on one level of scale—social networks on networks, health behavior on individuals. What is needed to remedy this situation is the development of computational models of health behavior. This would offer the possibility of building computational models of social systems that capture both levels of scale simultaneously. This idea is embodied well by the agent-based modeling approach ( for an introduction to this approach, see Wilensky & Rand, 2015).

The remainder of this chapter will be guided by the goal of building person–context systems of health behavior, but with equal attention to both the person and context. We will review the nascent field of what we have coined the computational health behavior modeling approach (Orr & Plaut, 2014), a subfield of health behavior that emphasizes the use of computational and mathematical modeling for representing health behavior theory. We offer the criteria in Table 5.1 as a way to organize our thoughts around computational models of health behavior. On the whole, these criteria define the desired qualities of a useful health behavior theory that can promote the unification of social networks and health behavior to scale.

## Past and Related Work

The field of computational health behavior modeling (Orr & Plaut, 2014), to date, has only used two formalisms: dynamical systems and artificial neural networks. Aligning with this dichotomy is the fact that only two labs have produced computational models of health behavior. The dynamical systems approach, led by Daniel Rivera at Arizona State University, provides a control systems engineering perspective on health behavior. The neural networks approach to

**TABLE 5.1** Criteria for useful computational models of health behavior.

| Criterion name | Description |
| --- | --- |
| Dynamic | Is it sensitive to changing contexts? Does it capture past behavior as part of its current state? |
| Learning | Is there ability for permanent change of model aspects, parameters, etc.? Is it important for well-established theory? |
| Network-ready | Is there a reasonable interface with the environment and/or with the social context? |
| Novel mechanisms | Does it pose novel theoretical entities that are testable? |
| Empirical grounding | Has the model been compared to empirical data? Have novel predictions been tested? Have novel mechanisms been tested? Have the social aspects (network-ready) been empirically tested? |
| Social psychological theory | Is it grounded in principles of social psychology? Does the model incorporate constructs from existing theory? |
| Cognitive science theory | Is the model grounded in principles of cognitive science? |

modeling health behavior, developed by our lab (Orr is lab leader), was highly influenced by work in social cognition (for a compendium, see Read & Miller, 1998), an area of research that encapsulated the first sketch of the potential promise of computational modeling of health behavior (see Shoda & Mischel, 1998).

We will review each formalism in turn.

## Modeling Health Behavior as a Dynamical System

The work by the Rivera Lab used a dynamical systems approach to represent the dynamics of health behavior (Martin et al., 2014; Navarro-Barrientos, Rivera, & Collins, 2011). Dynamical systems, a field with roots in both physics and control systems engineering, affords modeling how a set of variables change over time in relation to one another, with an emphasis on the system as a whole. Some of the common systems that can be modeled using the dynamical systems approach are the heating of a home and the spread of a virus in a population. Much of the time, the solutions of real-world applications or complex theoretical relationships are numerically estimated using computational algorithms, but for some simplified cases, analytic solutions are available (e.g., identification of equilibrium). In psychology, the dynamical systems approach is most dominant in understanding issues related to embodied and situated cognition and perception (Schoner, 2008), to development (Smith & Thelen, 1994), and to interpersonal dynamics (Marsh, Richardson, & Schmidt, 2009; Vallacher, Read, & Nowak, 2002).

The approach in the Rivera Lab has been to reconceptualize both the Theory of Planned Behavior (TPB) (Ajzen, 1991) and Social Cognitive Theory (SCT)

(Bandura, 1986), two core psychological theories that have been widely co-opted by the health behavior field, into a dynamical systems model in which each variable is considered as either an inventory (think number of units in a warehouse) or as a flow (think deliveries into and out of a warehouse). To gain some insight into this modeling method, imagine the following. A warehouse, with a capacity of 100 widgets, receives ten widgets at the open of business and sends out 10% of its inventory by the close of business that same day, that is: $X_{end} = (X_{begin} + 10)*0.90$. To run a simulation over a course of a month on this very simple system, you would first specify the number of units in the warehouse at the opening of the first day of the simulation. Then you would calculate the inventory of the warehouse at the close of business each day in the simulation. To gain insight into this simple system, it would be useful to construct a simple table of corresponding $X_{begin}$ and $X_{end}$ values under two starting conditions: $X_{begin} = 0$ and $X_{begin} = 100$.

The systems developed by the Rivera Lab use the same principle, whereby flows and inventories represent psychological constructs. Figure 5.1 shows their effort to reconceptualize the TPB (Navarro-Barrientos et al., 2011). Some of the TPB constructs are represented as inventories (attitude, subjective norms, perceived behavioral control, intention, and behavior) and some as flows ($\xi_1$, $\xi_2$, and $\xi_3$ correspond to outcome belief, normative beliefs, and perceived control beliefs, respectively). To see how this system works, consider the attitude stock. Its inflow, as per TPB, is outcome beliefs ($\xi_1$), which is scaled by $\gamma_{11}$ and time (the $\theta_1$ represents delays, so that as $\theta_1$ increases, the inflow decreases) and is perturbed by $\zeta_1$ (functioning as noise). Its outflow is split in two—some flows to the intention inventory scaled by $\beta_{41}$, and the remaining flows out of the system (inversely proportional to the flow to intention). Each of the inventories acts in this way. As per the TPB, the only external input to the system is from $\xi_1$ to $\xi_3$. That is, external modification of the system operates strictly through changes in beliefs. Another slightly later effort by the Rivera Lab was to build a dynamical systems model of Social Cognitive Theory (Martin et al., 2014).

The Rivera Lab used the TPB and SCT models in two ways. First, they conducted a series of what are called counterfactuals to explore and compare the effects of different health behavior intervention approaches. The simulations using the TPB system focused on: (a) changes in both temporal (e.g., time lag of flow between intention and behavior) and structural relations between inventories (e.g., more or less flow between inventories), and (b) the efficacy of an intervention as a function of the temporal ordering of the components of said intervention (e.g., intervene on attitude prior to subjective norms). The simulations using SCT centered around comparing how initial values of the inventories affect the dynamics of behavior, looking for potential nonlinear dynamics (e.g., if the initial levels of self-efficacy were large enough, would the system be self-sustaining and maintain itself without further external cuing from a simulated intervention).

Second, the Rivera Lab attempted to estimate the parameters of the SCT system given data from the *Mobile Interventions for Lifestyle Exercise and Eating* at

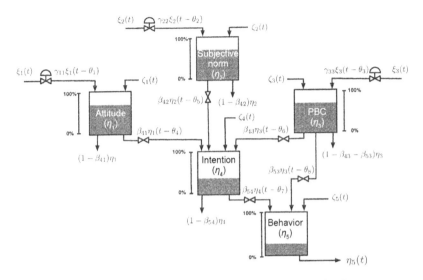

**FIGURE 5.1** A dynamical systems model of the Theory of Planned Behavior (Fishbein & Ajzen, 2010) (reproduced with permission from Navarro-Barrientos et al., 2011). See text for details.

Stanford. This data set contained dynamic data (daily, over an eight-week period) regarding some of the core inputs to and outputs of SCT (for details of the data set, see King et al., 2013). The estimation approach used gray-box system identification (Ljung, 1999), an approach developed specifically to estimate parameters of mathematical models of physical systems; it leverages statistical estimation and prior knowledge of the structure of a dynamical system. Gray-box system identification may prove to be useful for integrating dynamic empirical data on health behavior into a computational modeling framework. See Bohlin (2006) for an accessible introduction to gray-box system identification.

How does this approach stand up to the criteria offered in Table 5.1? The approach is dynamic in the sense that it can directly capture changing contexts and contains feedback loops among inventories; it is not directly network-ready, but could easily accommodate this need; these models assume several novel processes (most of the parameters in Figure 5.1). However, the Rivera Lab approach is weaker in terms of the empirical grounding of its theoretical assumptions. In our estimation, the data-driven gray-box fitting algorithm used to model the SCT had many free parameters and should be considered one of several approaches for empirical grounding—experimentation will be needed. Finally, although the use of dynamical systems has precedence in both social psychology and cognitive science as a theoretical framework, the specifics of the Rivera approach are not well grounded theoretically. Of principal concern are: (1) the conceptualization of attitudes as stocks and of causal relations as flows with rates, and (2) the assumption that information flows forward only (e.g., from beliefs to attitudes to intention to behavior, but not the reverse)—an assumption that does not accord with the well-established notion of constraint satisfaction as a mechanism underlying several social psychological phenomena (Read & Miller, 1998).

In summary, the work from the Rivera Lab is of interest because it brings an engineering/control systems perspective to health behavior modeling using a well-established psychological theory as its foundation. For the health behavior field, this effort supports the larger goal of developing intervention systems that, similar to a thermostat in a heating system, control behaviors related to health. To realize this goal, we suggest that the next steps in this work focus on strengthening the approach with respect to the criteria in Table 5.1.

## Modeling Health Behavior Using Artificial Neural Networks

The work of Lowe and colleagues (Lowe, Bennett, Walker, Milne, & Bozionelos, 2003) represents, to our knowledge, the earliest effort to integrate computational modeling with health behavior theory. This effort revolved around the question of whether a feed-forward pattern associator (a specific type of artificial neural network) could represent well the mapping between intention and a pattern of beliefs across a corpus of real human subjects' data. The empirical measures were designed in terms of the TPB.

Figure 5.2 shows the structure of the model. It was trained, successfully, to learn the mappings between each subject's set of beliefs and his or her intention. Lowe et al. (2003) used the hidden layer representation to classify subjects as more or less similar to each other. Using this information, the subjects were classified into three types of high-intenders, one type of moderate intender and two types of low-intenders. This was useful in that it provided a more nuanced analysis of the differences between subjects (or really, groups of subjects) that would be difficult to detect using more traditional statistical techniques.

Although this was an interesting and fruitful approach for understanding the given data in a novel way, it does not serve as an example of a dynamic computational model of health behavior. The manner in which the model was analyzed and interpreted makes it clear that their approach was a data-analytic approach that was designed to reveal different types of subjects (which it did successfully). This is an approach to the analysis of complex data that is commonly used in the machine learning and statistical learning literatures.

More recently, over the past few years, our lab has developed a dynamic constraint satisfaction model of the Theory of Reasoned Action (TRA) (Fishbein & Ajzen, 1975) that was strongly influenced by the criteria listed in Table 5.1 (Orr & Plaut, 2014; Orr, Thrush, & Plaut, 2013). The TRA, the precursor to the TPB, assumes that behavior is driven by one's intention to perform the behavior; intention is driven by norms, attitudes, and perceptions of behavioral control

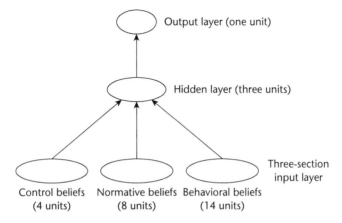

**FIGURE 5.2** A schematic structure of an artificial neural network (reproduced with permission from Lowe et al., 2003) that was used as a statistical learning approach for classifying types of subjects in a human subjects study. See text for details.

which are driven by beliefs related to the behavior. Our model's core innovation was that it represents the dynamics of what we call intention formation—a notion of how intention is generated on-the-fly (for the origin of this notion, see Conrey & Smith, 2007).

In our model, intention formation is dynamic in a particular way. It accounts for both what has been learned about a behavior (in terms of beliefs) by social learning from past experience and the immediate influence from the current social context, simultaneously. As an extreme analog, imagine this situation. A Democrat is at a cocktail party hosted by the Republican National Convention, and the topic of voting for the Democratic presidential candidate comes up in conversation. Our model attempts to capture the on-the-fly intention formation (to vote for the Democratic candidate) of the Democratic constituent given his/her past experiences and the current conversation at the cocktail party. In terms of health behavior, we can imagine other relevant examples, such as a college student studying abroad. The learned beliefs about a behavior might vary significantly across international borders.

Figure 5.3 depicts the formal structure of our model. A belief is represented as a set of memory units that are linked; one unit represents positive valence, and the other represents negative valence (e.g., two circles labeled with numeral 1 represent the positive and negative valence of one belief, and the fixed horizontal lines connecting these two units represent a bidirectional inhibitory function (called inter-bank connections in Figure 5.3). The coupling between valence units is, by design, inhibitory such that everything else equal, the activation of one valence will inhibit the potential for activation of the other valence within a belief. Conceptually, this is a reconceptualization of the belief structure proposed by the Theory of Reasoned Action in which a belief is represented as (using outcome beliefs as the example) $b^*e$, where $b$ is strength of the belief (the subjective probability that the outcome of performing a behavior will come true), and $e$ is the evaluation of the behavioral outcome (its valence). The inhibitory coupling within belief valence units in our model does not exclude the potential for both belief units having high activation simultaneously, but only attempts to reduce this possibility. Memory units are constrained to vary in activation from not active to fully active (represented as 0 and 1, respectively).

A key assumption of our model is that the memory units are activated (or cued) by exposure to belief valence analogs in social situations and contexts in which relevant belief are present—that is, these units are hypotheses that a belief and its associated valence is present or absent in a social situation or context. In the simulations described below, a social context is operationalized by clamping the relevant memory units that map onto the belief valences present in the social context. Once exposed to a social context, the system settles into a local equilibrium that is constrained by (1) the presence of the cued belief valences in the current social context, and (2) the set of connections between memory units. Formally, the equilibrium state defines the on-the-fly intention state as the multidimensional point in unit activation space. In the simulations that follow, we simplify this by aggregation of the activations at equilibrium of the positive and negative valence units separately. In doing so, intention is relative to which set of valences (positive or negative) has a higher average value.

The set of like-valenced units (either positive or negative) are fully connected by a set of modifiable connections that allow for encoding the patterns of belief structures in the social contexts across time (called the intra-bank connections in Figure 5.3). That is, the model has the ability to capture statistical regularities over a set of social contexts separated in time (e.g., the simplest regularity is frequency of exposure to a belief valence; a complex regularity would be a nonlinear combination such as the positive belief valence 1 occurs only when either the positive belief valence 2 or the positive belief valence 3 is present, but not when both are present). These connections are depicted in Figure 5.3 as the intra-bank connections, where the term "bank" refers to the grouping of units by valence.

It is important to realize that our modeling assumptions (the formal structure and processes) should not be thought of as a contradiction of the TRA, but instead as an attempt to flesh out some critical details when considering TRA as a dynamic theory (for details on this issue, see Orr & Plaut, 2014). The choices that dictated our model architecture were theoretical. We represented single beliefs as opposing valences, an idea we borrowed from prior work (Shultz & Lepper, 1996, 1998) and work on ambivalence of attitudes (De Liver, Van der Pligt, & Wigboldus, 2007; Thompson & Zanna, 1995). Moreover, our desire to capture the notion of an attitude being a state rather than a thing (borrowed from Conrey & Smith, 2007), naturally led to a recurrent (constraint satisfaction) network.

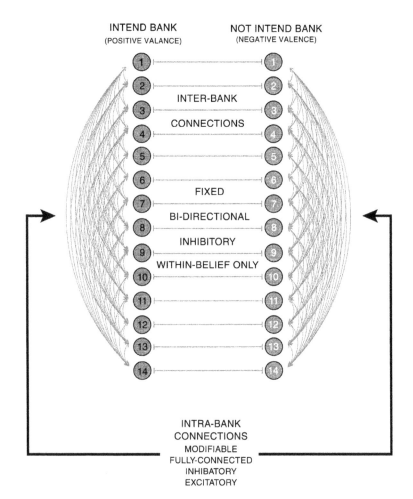

**FIGURE 5.3** A depiction of an artificial-neural network model of the Theory of Reasoned Action (Fishbein & Ajzen, 2010) (reproduced with permission from (Orr et al., 2013). Each belief (the numbered circles where number indexes belief) is composed of two processing units, one representing negative valence and the other representing positive valence. The constraints within each bank (depicted as curved arrows on the right and left of the rows of belief units) represent the relations among beliefs; learning operates by modifying these constraints. The constraints between the banks are fixed and reflect the theoretical commitment that beliefs are unidimensional (i.e., valence units within a belief should inhibit one another). Model operation starts with an exposure to beliefs from a social context (the external input) and ends in an intention state through the process of constraint satisfaction (the processing units are directly clamped by external input; the output of the processing units is directly taken as each unit's activation). See text for details.

Using this basic model, we addressed two separate issues that are of high relevance for health behavior theory. The first issue centers on a key driver of the heterogeneity in behavior across individuals with respect to intention formation (Orr & Plaut, 2014). The second issue deals with how a person mitigates the effects of past experience (what one has learned over time, e.g., from parents and peers) and the effects of his/her immediate social context ("immediate" is a relative term, but to mean something like within a few days) when forming health behavior intentions (Orr et al., 2013). In what follows, we summarize this prior work (for details, please consult the original works).

## Drivers of Heterogeneity in Health Behaviors

Health behavior theory explains heterogeneity within a population in a linear way. In terms of dynamics, this means, roughly, that changes in the inputs to a system will produce similarly scaled outputs. However, an alternative explanation was offered by so-called quantum behavior change theory—a characterization of health behavior as prone to sudden and dramatic shifts (e.g., quitting and re-uptake of cigarettes) (Resnicow & Page, 2008). Such sudden shifts are by nature very difficult to predict precisely because the drivers of behavior interact in a nonlinear, so-called quantum fashion. By this account, nonlinear processes may drive the heterogeneity across individuals. Our work, described next, puts forth the first formal computational model of this process and provides a set of simulations to serve as proof of concept (Orr & Plaut, 2014). The overarching goal of the simulations was to test whether our TRA neural network model would act characteristically as a nonlinear complex system. This is both a practical concern (How do we intervene when the system may act chaotically?) and a theoretical concern (a formalization of the notion of quantum behavior change put forth by Resnicow & Page, 2008 to include sensitivity to initial conditions, path dependence and tipping points).

The simulation was designed to capture, in the abstract, the dynamic nature of intention given a series of changing social contexts. (This was a theoretical exercise, so the model was not supposed to represent a particular behavior.) It is useful to imagine the time-course of intention states as a person goes through a significant period of time (this could be several weeks or months) during which each time point represents exposure to another social context. At every time point, the model computes an intention state using its intention state from the last time point mixed with the intention states in the immediate social context (similar to neighbors in a social network). In this simulation, the model was not "allowed" to learn because our interest was in whether the system, even without learning, would show complexity. In fact, we purposely set up the intra-bank connections such that all were positive; thus, small amounts of activation within a valence bank had the potential for rapidly increasing the activation of other units in the same valence bank during the settling process for a single exposure to a social context (see the original source for more details on the model structure: Orr & Plaut, 2014).

During a single simulation, on each of 600 time steps, the model was randomly exposed to one of three types of social contexts (biased towards intending, biased towards not intending, and ambivalent with respect to intention). Each of the three contexts was presented exactly 200 times. The biasing was formalized as inputs that activated all of the units within only one of the valence banks; ambivalence activated an equal number of units within both valence banks (40% of the inputs). During the process of the simulation, the activation levels of all belief valence units were recorded upon exposure to each social context, yielding a time series (length = 600) of the intention state of the model. That is, the state of the model at equilibrium after exposure to a social context was read out as the raw output of all of the units of the model individually; the valence of each output unit was tagged so that the overall valence could be seen graphically.

We ran 20 separate simulations; the difference between each was the ordering of the sequence of social contexts (each was a unique, random order). The purpose of running multiple simulations was to capture the variety of behaviors of the model under the condition that the only difference between the 20 simulations was the ordering of the inputs.

The operation of each simulation was as follows. The initial state of the model was driven by exposure to the first social context. For example, it may have been exposed to the ambivalent context. Subsequently, the model dynamics were driven by the series of social contexts. Importantly, for all of the simulation, except at the very beginning, the state of the model at any point in time was also dependent on its immediate ($t$-1) past intention state. This secondary feature forced the model to mitigate its very recent past with its current social context.

Figure 5.4 shows four of the 20 simulations. The key behaviors of the model were represented by four distinct dynamic profiles. The first profile, shown in panels A and B, shows the positive valence bank (to "intend") winning out early on, followed by maintenance of this state throughout the simulation; the negative valence bank (to "not intend") was reduced to zero activation. The second row shows the model rapidly changing from "intend" to "not intend." Row 3 exhibits a persistent ambivalence towards the behavior. Both the positive and negative valence banks were strongly activated throughout the simulation. The final row is characterized by switching between "not intend" and ambivalence.

Remember, the overarching purpose of this simulation effort was to judge to what degree our computational model exhibited complex, quantum-like behavior. The complex systems literature, including catastrophe theory, offers some well-established qualitative criteria for this purpose (Miller & Page, 2007; Witkiewitz & Masyn, 2008). Using these criteria, our model displayed key signatures of complex systems. First, the statistical signature of the different contexts (1/3 favored intend, 1/3 not intend, and 1/3 ambivalent), did not present in time series in the simulations—that is, we would expect to see 1/3 of the time series

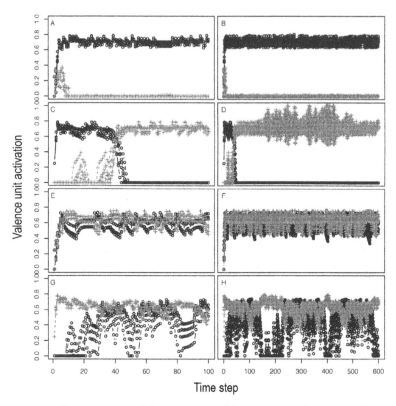

**FIGURE 5.4** The timecourse of the activation of the positive and negative valence units over four separate simulations, each represented by a row (reproduced with permission from Orr & Plaut, 2014). The first column represents the first 100 social contexts; the second column shows the full time series of social contexts (600 contexts). The positive valence units are depicted as black circles, the negative as gray crosses. See text for details on the simulation procedure.

show intention states of not intend, 1/3 intend, and 1/3 ambivalent, but this was not the case. This feature, that the output was not linearly related to the input, is a classic signature of complex systems. Panel B of Figure 5.4 illustrates this behavior in the extreme—the time series of intention states of the model did not show any indication of negative or ambivalent social contexts even though 2/3 of the input contexts were of this nature. Second, panels B, D, and F in Figure 5.4 clearly demonstrate path dependence, another signature of complex systems whereby the system remains in an attractor state. Third, in panel C, we see a bifurcation, probably driven by a self-organizing process, in which the system changes states rapidly—another clear signature of complex systems. Fourth, panels E and G show oscillatory behavior, something that is common in complex systems.

Also, our model shows some of the key qualitative properties of a catastrophic system, called "catastrophe flags" (Gilmore, 1981). For example, we see what are called *sudden jumps*—a rapid transition from one behavioral state to another (see Figure 5.4, panels C and H); we also see *multimodality*—having only a few pronounced behavioral states. The valence units were mostly either of an activation between 0.60 and 0.80 or of very low activation across the 20 simulations. Finally, we see what is called *inaccessibility*—behavioral states that were very unstable. The valence units did not have resting values other than near zero activation or between 0.60 and 0.80.

In summary, this modeling effort served as a proof of concept that our computational model of the TRA could exhibit behavior as if it were a complex system. Thus, we succeeded in unifying TRA, a traditional health behavior theory, with quantum health behavior theory via instantiation of a computational model. Furthermore, these results beg the question: What if quantum-like health behaviors were networked? We will address this question below, in the section "Emerging Work on Psychologically Plausible Social Systems."

## *Mitigating Past Experience with Immediate Social Context*

The second simulation explored the role of how learning from past experience can change the way current social context is interpreted. This simulation used human subjects data, on sexual behavior in a cohort of adolescents in a US school district, that were developed specifically with consideration of the measurement constructs of the Theory of Reasoned Action (these data are described in Gillmore et al., 2002). The simulation explored what happens when the model learns from a social context in which beliefs about having sex are less positive, and then, after learning is complete, switches to a context that is more positive. (The original work and the modeling details can be found in Orr et al., 2013.)

To this end, we first trained the model, using the generalized delta-rule, to learn a belief structure from exposure to the beliefs of 10th-grade females who never had sex. There were 105 10th-grade females in the data set, each of which was transformed into a binary vector; 200 epochs of the 105 inputs were used for training. Then we tested the model via exposure to 12th-grade females who had never had sex and 12th-grade females who had had sex. During testing, we constrained the model so that it could no longer learn. By this manipulation, the simulation probed the degree to which the formation of intention was constrained by both past (exposure to 10th-grade non-experienced females) and current contexts (sexually experienced females); please refer the section "Modeling Health Behavior Using Artificial Neural Networks" for a reminder of how constraint satisfaction works in the model. Simply put, we explored how the intention towards sexual behavior of a 10th-grade female virgin would emerge when she was put in a social situation with 12th-grade females.

(We did not choose the term "virgin," but simply follow the lead of the authors of the original empirical study: Gillmore et al., 2002. Please refer to the original work for further details.)

Figure 5.5 shows the key findings in terms of the mean activation of each of the sets of valence units (positive = intend; negative = not intend). From left to right, the first condition (F10V) illustrates that the model exhibits a strong negative response when tested against the same input that was used when it was learning. This makes sense given that the data for F10V were largely negative in terms of sexual behavior. This condition serves as a baseline for comparison to the other two conditions, F12V and F12NV, in which we see a decline in the activation of the negative valence units and a corresponding increase for the positive valence units. Also, notice that for the F12NV condition, the response of the model was still more negative than positive.

The remaining two conditions, P50 and P75, reflect purely simulated data, but provide further insight into the model's behavior during testing. The P50 condition represents completely neutral inputs. For this condition, we would expect the activation for both the positive and negative valence units to be equal if the prior training context did not bias the system. However, the negative valence units win out, reflecting the prior training context. The same bias was found for the P75 condition, which represents largely positive inputs. Although the positive valence wins out, it is highly dampened (we would expect greater activation in this condition without bias from past experience).

In summary, the current social context influenced but did not override what was learned from past experience. Specifically, exposure to relatively more positive beliefs about sexual behavior in the current social context did increase intention, but this tendency was dampened from the learning in prior social contexts with less positive beliefs about sexual behavior. In short, this notion is highly congruent with the needs of the health behavior field—a formal and explanatory account of how the present and the past are integrated to generate an intention state. We can imagine that the distribution of biases from past experience would greatly impact the spread of intention along a social network.

## Synopsis of the Neural Network Approach to Health Behavior

Our prior work presented above on the use of artificial neural networks and health behavior owes equally to prior work in both social cognition and social networks. In fact, we designed the model to serve as the vertices of a large-scale social network, and thus, by our estimation, it meets all of the criteria, by design, listed in Table 5.1.

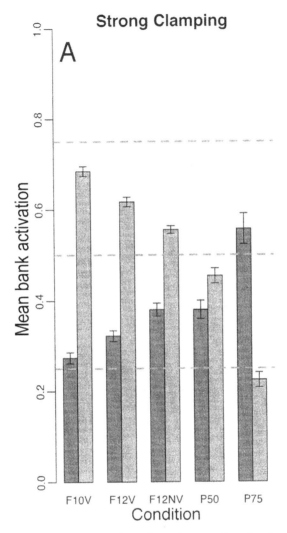

**FIGURE 5.5** Simulations of the interdependence between learning from past experience and the current social context on intention formation in the Theory of Reasoned Action (reproduced with permission from Orr et al., 2013). The x-axis represents the condition during testing (F10V = female 10th-grade virgins; F12V = female 12th-grade virgins; F12NV = female 12th-grade non-virgins). The other two conditions, P50 and P75, were highly structured, simulated data (P50 inputs were 50 percent positive; P75 inputs were 75 percent positive). The mean activation of the valence banks is represented on the y-axis (dark gray = positive; light gray = negative). The dashed horizontal lines show the mean bank activation of values 0.25, 0.50, and 0.75.

## Emerging Work on Psychologically Plausible Social Systems

Our prior work using artificial neural networks of health behavior, as described above, was designed in part for integration into the social networks framework. This idea, for us, originated from work on the dynamics of dyadic relations (Shoda et al., 2002): work that suggested, theoretically, that the mental state of an individual depended upon the presence of social interaction—without it, an individual ended up in state A; with it, the same individual, everything else equal, could end up in state B. This was intriguing from a psychological point of view because it put the person–context system in a formal computational model with an equal emphasis on both person and context. The preliminary work we present next was driven by a different but closely related question, one that is crucial for the health behavior field: To what extent would the dynamics of the diffusion of behavior in a social network depend on the parameters of the computational model of individuals' behavior?

Both of the simulations from our lab presented above are suggestive. Imagine a set of agents connected in a social network with the heterogeneity shown in Figure 5.4 (each of the rows in Figure 5.4 represents a separate individual). Would this heterogeneity persist if the individuals were influencing one another (e.g., the input of one individual would be the output of another)? Consider the notion that learning from past experience biases the relation between input to output (from Figure 5.5). Do such biases, at the individual level, have an effect on the diffusion of intention in a population? These and similar considerations led our lab to develop the Multi Agent Neural Network (MANN) platform, a new simulation platform designed to study the effects of different vertex architectures ("architecture" refers to the type of computational models used to represent individuals' behavior) on the diffusion of attitudes, beliefs, and behaviors on relatively large-scale social networks ($n = 10^3$). (For the link to the code base, see Chen & Orr, 2016.)

What is presented next is a proof of concept that variation in parameters of the vertex architecture does, in fact, affect the diffusion of intention on a social network even when the generating parameters of the social network are fixed. In general terms, the diffusion paradigm works as follows. First, it sets all vertices to one type of state (the simple case is "off"), then seeds a small fraction of the vertices to have a different state (the simple case is "on"). The seed vertices then spread the different states throughout the network in a way defined by assumptions about how the state can be transferred between vertices joined by a social network tie. A real-world analog is the spread of a virus in a school or community.

For this exercise, we based the vertex architecture on the neural network presented above from our prior work (Orr & Plaut, 2014). Our approach was to span the parameter space generated by the full factorial of two ranges of the inter- and intra-bank connections. (See Figure 5.3 and its description above for details of these two parameters.) For each cell of the factorial we ran approximately ten simulations using the diffusion paradigm to simulate the diffusion of intention. The work presented here is a replication of a similar parameter sweep that showed similar results using the MANN platform (Orr, Ziemer, & Chen, in press).

Each simulation began with the generating of a small-world social network (as specified in Watts & Strogatz, 1998), fixed with the following parameter values: 250 vertices, ten nearest neighbors, a 0.02 rewiring probability, and bidirectional edges). All vertices were initialized to have the same approximate values of the inter- and intra-bank connections. The diffusion process began by exposing five of the vertices to an input, randomly chosen, that reflected either strong intention, strong not intention, or ambivalence. Diffusion was allowed to progress for 100 time steps. Each time step updated all of the vertices, during which, roughly, each vertex was given one of its neighbors' intention state vector (its output) at t-1 as its input. The intention state of each vertex was calculated as the average value of the positive valence bank minus the average value of the negative valence bank. Figure 5.6 provides a comparison between the early diffusion process and its later stage in a single simulation.

Figure 5.7 shows the full results of the full factorial of the inter- and intra-bank connection parameters (20 levels of inter-bank connections and 30 levels of intra-bank connections for a total of 600 cells in the factorial). Each cell in Figure 5.7 represents the average value over approximately ten simulations. (So, in total, Figure 5.7 represents approximately 6000 separate diffusion simulations.) The measurement represented in Figure 5.7 is the assortativity with regard to

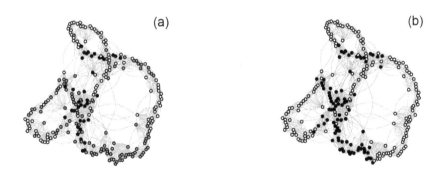

**FIGURE 5.6**   An example diffusion of intention simulation on a small-world social network (N = 250). The vertex architecture is a recurrent neural network that models intention formation per the Theory of Reasoned Action (Fishbein & Ajzen, 2010). Vertex states are represented by the gray scale; black is "not intending" and white is "intending." The plots show the diffusion process at (a) an early and (b) a late point in the simulation.

intention state at the end of each simulation—a measure that represents the amount of clustering of intention given the typology of the social network. For reference, Figure 5.6b depicts strong clustering with regard to intention and a high degree of assortativity.

These results provide clear evidence that, in the abstract, the parameters of the vertex architecture alone can have a dramatic effect on the social network diffusion process. Given the theoretical nature of these simulations, a natural set of questions arise with regard to the implications of an idea—the idea of

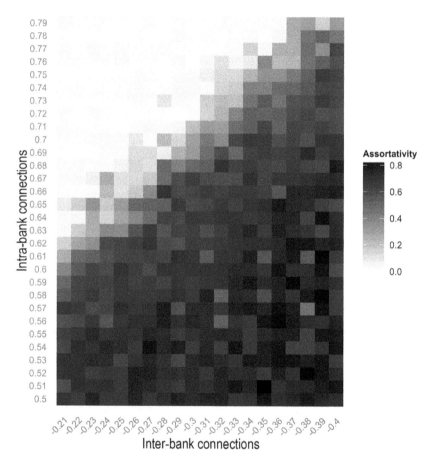

**FIGURE 5.7**  The average network assortativity across approximately ten diffusion of intention simulations (per cell). The two axes represent parameters of the recurrent neural network of the Theory of Reasoned Action (Fishbein & Ajzen, 2010) (20 levels of inter-bank connections and 30 levels of intra-bank connections for a total of 600 cells in the factorial). For all simulations, the generating parameters of the social network were identical. See text for further details.

embedding computational psychological models into social networks; this question is equally important for both psychology and the field of health behavior. (We co-opted the notion of thinking in terms of the implication of an idea with regard to the use of computational modeling for understanding cognitive processes from McClelland, 2009.) The primary implications, as we see it, are as follows. First, the link to applications in the practice of public health and health behavior is dependent on successfully bridging theory (presented above) that is closely grounded in data (not presented above) which can eventually drive interventions and prevention efforts in human populations by virtue of causal what-if scenario modeling. Public health, in particular, has had some success leveraging agent-based modeling for the purpose of intervention and prevention work that is tied to data and used to think about potential intervention/prevention efforts (e.g., Hashemian, Qian, Stanley, & Osgood, 2012; Hennessy et al., 2016), so there may be use in borrowing this approach. Another possibility may be the investigation of how the interaction between vertex architecture and social network topology drives how an agent's inputs vary over time and how inputs vary across agents within a system. Distribution of inputs, as a broad construct, is important for many psychological processes (e.g., learning, development, skill acquisition). A third, admittedly vague, implication is that there may be potential for gaining new insights into how cognitive processes have evolved in evolutionary time (see McLeod, Plunkett, & Rolls, 1998 for early work in this area in cognition, and also Goldberg & Holland, 1988 for information on the related work on genetic algorithms). A system like MANN allows for, in theory, manipulating environment (e.g., social network topology), cognitive mechanisms, and the interdependencies between both simultaneously. This seems, to a first approximation, minimally sufficient for beginning to study biological evolution related to cognition and social context. Although many challenges arise in these types of endeavors, something like the MANN platform should prove useful, at least as a starting point.

## Future Directions

The criteria in Table 5.1 lay out a good deal of the work that is needed over the next several years in order to work towards computational social systems of health behavior. The more difficult activities will be the iteration between model development, theory generation, and empirical grounding. In this vein, we think a fruitful approach will use a mixture of tightly controlled experiments and large-scale social experiments. For example, our lab is leading an NSF-funded project (with collaborators at Virginia Tech, Carnegie Mellon University, Sandia National Laboratory: NSF #1520359) that will soon run a controlled large-scale (N = 1000) online social experiment in which participants' social behavior (something like posting and reading tweets on Twitter) is collected over several weeks. In addition to this, we plan on capturing changes in attitudes at several points throughout the online experiment using an adaption of the evaluative priming experimental procedure (see Fazio & Olson, 2003). Thus, we will combine a loosely controlled social experiment with a tightly controlled attitude measurement procedure—ecological validity at the social level with high construct validity at the individual level.

A central issue for all of the modeling approaches we reviewed above, including those in the section "Emerging Work on Psychologically Plausible Social Systems," is that the models are of limited (or focused) scope. Our neural network of TRA is really just a dynamic model of attitude formation. The work by the Rivera Lab is similarly constrained in scope. Neither approach represents decision-making in the larger sense, something for which production systems—for example, ACT-R (Anderson, 2007; Anderson & Lebiere, 1998)—and other larger scoped cognitive architectures are designed. We think a fruitful and potentially necessary direction for the computational health behavior modeling field will lie in this direction.

## Note

1 The production of this chapter was supported in part by NSF Award #1520359.

## References

Ajzen, I. (1991). The theory of planned behavior. *Organizational behavior and human decision processes, 50*, 179–211.

Anderson, J. R. (2007). *How can the human mind occur in the physical universe?* Oxford: Oxford University Press.

Anderson, J. R., & Lebiere, C. (1998). *The atomic components of thought.* Mahwah, NJ: LEA.

Bandura, A. (1986). *Social foundations of thought and action: A social cognitive theory.* Englewood Cliffs, NJ: Prentice Hall.

Bhattacharyya, S., & Ohlsson, S. (2010). Social creativity as a function of agent cognition and network properties: A computer model. *Social Networks, 32*, 263–278.

Bohlin, T. (2006). *Practical grey-box process identification: Theory and applications.* London: Springer-Verlag.

Chen, D., & Orr, M. G. (2016). Multi Agent Neural Network (MANN). Retrieved from https://github.com/chendaniely/multi-agent-neural-network

Conrey, F. R., & Smith, E. R. (2007). Attitude representation: Attitudes as patterns in a distributed, connectionist representational system. *Social Cognition, 25*(5), 718–735.

De Liver, Y., Van der Pligt, J., & Wigboldus, D. (2007). Positive and negative associations underlying ambivalent attitudes. *Journal of Experimental Social Psychology, 43*, 319–326.

Fazio, R. H., & Olson, M. A. (2003). Implicit measures in social cognition research: Their meaning and use. *Annual Review of Psychology, 54*, 297–327.

Fishbein, M., & Ajzen, I. (1975). *Belief, attitude, intention and behaviour: An introduction to theory and research.* Reading, MA: Addison-Wesley.

Fishbein, M., & Ajzen, I. (2010). *Predicting and changing behavior: The reasoned action approach.* New York: Psychology Press.

Gillmore, M. R., Archibald, M. E., Morrison, D. M., Wilsdon, A., Wells, E. A., Hoppe, M. J., Nahom, D., & Murowchick, E. (2002). Teen sexual behavior: Applicability of the theory of reasoned action. *Journal of Marriage and the Family, 64*(4), 885–897.

Gilmore, R. (1981). *Catastrophe theory for scientists and engineers*. New York: Wiley.

Goldberg, D. E., & Holland, J. H. (1988). Genetic algorithms and machine learning. *Machine Learning, 3*, 95–99.

Hashemian, M., Qian, W., Stanley, K. G., & Osgood, N. D. (2012). Temporal aggregation impacts on epidemiological simulations employing microcontact data. *BMC Medical Informatics and Decision Making, 12*(132).

Hennessy, E., Ornstein, J. T., Economos, C. D., Herzog, J. B., Lynskey, V., Coffield, E., & Hammond, R. A. (2016). Designing an agent-based model for childhood obesity interventions: A case study of ChildObesity180. *Preventing Chronic Disease: Public Health Research, Practice, and Policy, 13*, 150414.

King, A. C., Hekler, E. B., Grieco, L. A., Winter, S. J., Sheats, J. L., Buman, M. P., Banerjee, B, Robinson, T. N, & Cirimele, J. (2013). Harnessing different motivational frames via mobile phones to promote daily physical activity and reduce sedentary behavior in aging adults. *PLoS One, 8*(4), e62613.

Ljung, L. (1999). *System identification: Theory for the user*. Englewood Cliffs, NJ: Prentice Hall.

Lowe, R., Bennett, P., Walker, I., Milne, S., & Bozionelos, G. (2003). A connectionist implementation of the theory of planned behavior: Association of beliefs with exercise intention. *Health Psychology, 22*(5), 464–470. doi:10.1037/0278-6133.22.5.464

Marsh, K. L., Richardson, M. J., & Schmidt, R. C. (2009). Social connection through joint action and interpersonal coordination. *Topics in Cognitive Science, 1*, 320–339.

Martin, C. A., Rivera, D. E., Riley, W. T., Hekler, E. B., Buman, M. P., Adams, M. A., & King, A. C. (2014). A dynamical systems model of social cognitive theory. Paper presented at the *2014 American Control Conference*, Portland, OR.

McClelland, J. L. (2009). The place of modeling in cognitive science. *Topics in Cognitive Science, 1*, 11–38.

McLeod, P., Plunkett, K., & Rolls, E. T. (1998). *Introduction to connectionist modelling of cognitive processes*. New York: Oxford University Press.

Miller, J. H., & Page, S. E. (2007). *Complex adaptive systems: An introduction to computational models of social life*. Princeton, NJ: Princeton University Press.

Mischel, W., & Shoda, Y. (1995). A cognitive-affective system theory of personality: Reconceptualizing situations, dispositions, dynamics and invariance in personality structure. *Psychological Review, 102*(2), 246–268.

Monroe, B. M., & Read, S. J. (2008). A general connectionist model of attitude structure and change: The ACS (Attitudes as Constraint Satisfaction) Model. *Psychological Review, 115*(3), 733–759.

Muchnik, L., Aral, S., & Taylor, S. J. (2013). Social influence bias: A randomized experiment. *Science, 341*(6146), 647–651.

Navarro-Barrientos, J. E., Rivera, D. E., & Collins, L. M. (2011). A dynamical model for describing behavioural intentions for weight loss and body composition change. *Mathematical and Computer Modelling of Dynamical Systems, 17*(2), 183–203.

Orr, M., & Plaut, D. C. (2014). Complex systems and health behavior change: Insights from cognitive science. *American Journal of Health Behavior, 38*, 404–413.

Orr, M. G., Thrush, R., & Plaut, D. C. (2013). The Theory of Reasoned Action as parallel constraint satisfaction: Towards a dynamic computational model of health behavior. *PLoS One, 8*(5), e62409.

Orr, M. G., Ziemer, K., & Chen, D. (in press). Systems of behavior and population health. In A. M. El-Sayed & S. G. Galea (Eds.), *Systems science and population health.* New York: Oxford University Press.

Read, S. J., & Miller, L. C. (Eds.). (1998). *Connectionist models of social reasoning and social behavior.* Mahwah, NJ: Lawrence Erlbaum.

Resnicow, K., & Page, S. E. (2008). Embracing chaos and complexity: A quantum change for public health. *American Journal of Public Health, 98*(8), 1382–1389. doi:10.2105/ajph.2007.129460

Schoner, G. (2008). Dynamical systems approaches to cognition. In R. Sun (Ed.), *The Cambridge handbook of computational psychology.* New York: Cambridge University Press.

Shoda, Y., LeeTiernan, S., & Mischel, W. (2002). Personality as a dynamical system: Emergence of stability and distinctiveness from intra- and interpersonal interactions. *Personality and Social Psychology Review, 6*(4), 316–325.

Shoda, Y., & Mischel, W. (1998). Personality as a stable cognitive-affective activation network: Characteristic patterns of behavior variation emerge from a stable personality structure. In S. J. Read & L. C. Miller (Eds.), *Connectionist models of social reasoning and social behavior* (pp. 175–208). Mahwah, NJ: Lawrence Erlbaum.

Shultz, T., & Lepper, M. (1996). Cognitive dissonance reduction as constraint satisfaction. *Psychological Review, 103*(2), 219–240.

Shultz, T., & Lepper, M. (1998). The consonance model of dissonance reduction. In S. J. Read & L. C. Miller (Eds.), *Connectionist models of social reasoning and social behavior.* Mahwah, NJ: Lawrence Erlbaum.

Smith, L. B., & Thelen, E. (1994). *A dynamic systems approach to the development of cognition and action.* Cambridge, MA: MIT Press.

Thompson, M. M., & Zanna, M. P. (1995). The conflicted individual: Personality-based and domain-specific antecedents of ambivalent social attitudes. *Journal of Personality and Social Psychology, 63*(2), 259–288.

Valente, T. W. (2010). *Social networks and health: Models, methods and applications.* New York: Oxford University Press.

Vallacher, R. R., Read, S. J., & Nowak, A. (2002). The dynamical perspective in personality and social psychology. *Personality and Social Psychological Review, 6,* 264–273.

Watts, D. J., & Strogatz, S. H. (1998). Collective dynamics of "small-world" networks. *Nature, 393*(6684), 440–442.

Wilensky, U., & Rand, B. (2015). *An introduction to agent-based modeling: Modeling natural, social and engineered complex systems with NetLogo.* Cambridge, MA: MIT Press.

Witkiewitz, K., & Masyn, K. E. (2008). Drinking trajectories following an initial lapse. *Psychology of Addictive Behaviors, 22*(2), 157–167. doi:10.1037/0893-164x.22.2.157

# PART II
# Interpersonal Dynamics

# 6

# INTERACTION-DOMINANT DYNAMICS, TIMESCALE ENSLAVEMENT, AND THE EMERGENCE OF SOCIAL BEHAVIOR

*Brian A. Eiler, Rachel W. Kallen, and Michael J. Richardson*

## Introduction

It is perhaps self-evident to say that the dynamics of human behavior are complex. This is particularly true for social behavior, in that social structures provide the prototypical example of a complex system. Yet it is this simple assertion that best defines the ways in which we may uncover stable patterns of social behavior, as well as investigate and understand why individuals behave the way they do—namely, using the theoretical principles and methodological tools of nonlinear dynamics and complexity science. It is troubling, therefore, that these tools and principles remain relatively marginalized within the field of social psychology, a field that instead concedes explanatory power to a more traditional, information processing, and non-dynamical social cognitive perspective. Accordingly, in this chapter we suggest how researchers may investigate social behavior from a complex systems perspective, and discuss the implications of adopting such a framework for social psychology more broadly.

A central theme throughout this chapter will be the degree to which the behavioral regularities (or irregularities) that characterize human social behavior and cognition are the result of *interaction-dominant dynamics* and, as such, naturally emerge from the reciprocally nested, multi–timescale interactions that exist between mind, body, and environment (Eiler, Kallen, Harrison & Richardson, 2013; Richardson, Dale & Marsh, 2014). Thus, we first briefly define what is meant by *interaction-dominant dynamics* and how stable patterns of behavior emerge in *interaction-dominant dynamical systems* (IDDS). We then describe a defining feature of IDDS, slow-to-fast timescale enslavement, which can be leveraged to identify theoretical arguments and test hypotheses about the emergence and self-organization of social behavior. In doing so, we review relevant and noteworthy examples from the psychological sciences that demonstrate the value of this approach, as well as providing a brief discussion of some of the methodological tools that can be employed to study and understand interaction-dominant, dynamical social systems.

## Interaction-Dominant Dynamical Systems

The easiest way to understand what an IDDS is, is to contrast it with a component dominant dynamical system, or CDDS. For a CDDS, stable behavior is defined by the linear addition or combination of the intrinsic dynamics of component processes (i.e., fixed, a priori defined modules). As such, the macroscopic behavior of a CDDS is rigidly defined (hard-molded), context-independent, and functionally closed. The canonical example of a CDDS is a pendulum clock, whereby individual components perform specifically defined functions in order to keep time. The functionality of each component and the system as a whole is fixed in that it can only behave in one way. Thus, a mechanical clock cannot spontaneously cook dinner, just as an oven cannot suddenly change its functionality and become a timekeeper. Of course, the opposite is true for most biological, non-mechanical, human perception–action systems. This is to say that a human adult can be both a timekeeper and a chef, even at the same time. It is for this very reason that human systems (including social systems), as well as other complex biological systems, are best conceptualized as interaction-dominant dynamical systems, in that the macroscopic behavior of an IDDS is *soft-molded*,[1] *highly context-dependent*, and *multi-functional*.

The soft-molded and context-dependent nature of an IDDS is due to the fact that the behavioral dynamics and functional organization exhibited by such systems are typically *self-organized* and result from the reciprocal interactions and couplings that exist *between* the components of a system, rather than the intrinsic dynamics of the components themselves (Van Orden, Hollis, & Wallot, 2012). In other words, the time-evolving, macroscopic, observable behavior of an IDDS is not determined by any single component process or by means of a single centralized (executive) control function, but rather emerges from the free interplay of system elements and component processes (Bak, 1996; Van Orden et al., 2012). In this way, emergence is the result of nonlinear interactions amongst components in which these nonlinearities give rise to non-obvious, or emergent behavioral phenomena (e.g., Bak, 1996; Chalmers, 2006; Kelso, 1995; Masataka, 1993). It is worth stating, however, that to say that the behavior of an IDDS is self-organized is not to say that the behavior of an IDDS is "uncontrolled" or "uncontrollable." On the contrary, the behavior of an IDDS is often highly controlled and well organized in relation to a specific set of environmental constraints or functional goals. What makes it different from the behavioral control inherent to a CDDS is that for an IDDS, behavioral control emerges in a circularly causal manner, whereby lower-level component interactions produce higher-order structural patterns of organization that then feed back to enslave, and often maintain, the behavioral order of those very same lower-level component relationships. In other words, *fast-timescale processes lead to slow-timescale processes that feed back to constrain the fast-timescale processes that gave rise to them.*

With the latter point in mind, it is important to appreciate that the interactive processes and spatial-temporal couplings that define the macroscopic behavior of an IDDS are not restricted to local spatial-temporal scales or component connections. Rather, these relationships exist across multiple spatial-temporal scales. Accordingly, for an IDDS, stable or persistent patterns of behavioral order and control arise from the structural asymmetries that emerge between processes at differing rates of change. The idea that control operates from slow to fast in an IDDS[2] is by no means new, and has been well articulated elsewhere (Anderson, Richardson, & Chemero, 2012; Kello, Beltz, Holden, & Van Orden, 2007; Bruineberg & Rietveld, 2014; Eiler et al., 2013; Friston, 2010; Karl, 2012; Haken, 1983, 2004; Haken & Tschacher, 2010; Van Orden, Kloos, & Wallot, 2011; Van Orden, 2010; Van Orden et al., 2012). One of the most profound and controversial implications of this idea is that the fast-timescale, neural process of the brain cannot be responsible for controlling the slower-timescale processes of perceptual-motor behavior alone (Van Orden et al., 2012). On the contrary, it is more likely that the slower timescale processes of perceptual-motor behavior (and the structured environment within which this behavior is situated) are what define and control the emergent neural activity and organizational structures inherent to central nervous system (CNS) functionality (Van Orden et al., 2012). As Jordan and colleagues have so eloquently stated, the structure of organisms, including the structures of the CNS and brain, are embodiments of the environmental and social context that they are thoroughly, relationally, consistently, and continuously embedded within (e.g., Jordan, 2008; Jordan, Bai, Cialdella, & Schloesser, 2015; Jordan & Heidenreich, 2010).

With regard to social behavior, the implication of control operating from slower to faster behavioral timescales is that although the fast-timescale behavior of individuals or small groups within a society can modulate or perturb slower societal dynamics, it is the slower-timescale dynamics of the society as a whole (i.e., culture) that constrain and control the dynamics of individuals and small groups. In a circularly causal manner, the dynamics of higher-order social and cultural processes both emerge from and enslave the dynamics of lower-order individual or small group processes (cf. Kitayama & Uskul, 2011). Accordingly, the social context that emerges from ongoing human social interaction provides the structure that controls and determines the dynamics of future human social behavior.

Unlike the arguments mentioned above with regard to CNS control, these latter statements are by no means controversial, and are intuitively accepted within the literature on social and cultural systems. As stated at the beginning of the chapter, classifying a social system as a complex IDDS is self-evident. Indeed, it would seem hard to argue against the notion that social and cultural behavior results from interaction-dominant, time-evolving processes, or that such behavior does not emerge from the reciprocal interactions that entail interpersonal, intragroup, and intergroup processes. Even if one accepts these points to be true, however, it is often difficult to see the ways in which researchers may experimentally examine and identify the complex dynamical processes that give rise to specific social processes or social cognitive phenomena, or how adopting an IDDS perspective might lead to a more concrete or pragmatic understanding (and explanation) of why individuals behave as they do given a social context. The barrier to answering these questions and investigating social psychological phenomenon from a self-organized, IDDS perspective more generally has been a lack of well-defined theoretical and methodological principles for determining when social phenomenon and behavioral stabilities are the result of interaction-dominant dynamics and for investigating how these interaction-dominant dynamical processes operate to shape the social phenomenon in question. However, much of these theoretical and methodological principles have been developed within the interdisciplinary field of complexity science. Thus, what follows is a brief overview of key theoretical and methodological principles and how they may be employed to investigate and understand social psychological phenomena. As already noted, we wish to place particular emphasis on the principle of slow-to-fast *timescale enslavement*, thus we begin with a more detailed explanation of this principle.

## Slow-to-Fast Timescale Enslavement

Timescale enslavement refers to the fact that more slowly changing processes emerge from, and yet disproportionately constrain, faster-timescale processes in an IDDS. This is not to say that fast-timescale processes cannot influence slower-timescale processes. For example, in a multistable system (i.e., when there is more than one possible stable state or mode of behavior the system can exhibit) small changes or perturbations associated with fast-timescale processes can sometimes lead to a qualitative change, or "switch," between macroscopic modes of behavioral organization. Such fluctuations can also amplify small asymmetries, leading to a preferential stable state (Kondepudi & Gao, 1987). Persistent perturbations can also operate to destabilize a slower-timescale dynamic by pushing a system towards a tipping point and a new stable state. In this case, the activity of a faster-timescale process works to modulate a system's control parameter that, when moved beyond a critical point, results in a bifurcation, or sudden change in the qualitative state of the system. As an example, take the recent legalization of same-sex marriage and the rapid increase in the positive national attitude towards gay marriage in the United States. This sudden shift in the attitudes of individual Americans could be conceptualized as the result of a bifurcation in US culture that resulted from the persistent activity (social perturbations) of the LGBTQA+ community and their allies (circular causality in operation again).

Additionally, soft-modeled, self-organized IDDS often sit near the precipice of instability, in that they exhibit stable behavior, but only critically. Synonymous with the phenomena of *self-organized criticality* (Bak, 1996) and meta-stable systems (Kelso, 2012), this means that the stable order exhibited by an IDDS at any point in time is not perpetual or immutable, but intermittent. In this way, an IDDS is a critical system in which multiple behavioral patterns can exist, but behavior manifests adaptively in response to changing contexts. As a relevant example, consider the multiple social roles that individuals must switch between during the course of the day. An individual might be a parent, a spouse, a friend, a coach, a mentor, an employee, and a boss at different times and in different social contexts. Here, each role corresponds to a critical or meta-stable state of behavior that an individual must be able to quickly and flexibly switch between in real time. These meta-stable states intermittently organize and control how individuals behave and interact with those around them. Yet this occurs only critically, such that fast-timescale fluctuations or sudden changes in social context can easily bring about adaptive changes to the slower identity dynamics, by switching between these meta-stable roles of behavioral control.

Note, however, that in all of the cases we just mentioned, the potentiality of the macroscopic behavioral organization that a system exhibits must already be structured in a meta-stable or self-critical way in order for faster-timescale processes to modulate those slower-order dynamics. Thus, even in instances in which faster-timescale processes functionally influence the higher-order behavioral organization of an IDDS, this is only possible if the structure of the higher-order states, collective-order parameters, or meta-state manifolds (i.e., set of meta-stable roles) have already emerged. Again, slower-timescale dynamics emerge from and then dominate the faster-timescale dynamics that gave rise to them.

Returning to our discussion of social behavior more generally, the implication of timescale enslavement is that more slowly changing social processes (e.g., social norms, fundamental belongingness needs, pervasive stereotypes, cultural differences) exert a disproportionate influence on the fast-timescale, moment-to-moment social behavior of individuals within groups and groups within societies (see Figure 6.1). In this way, long-timescale processes provide a dynamic structure that shapes and constrains the possible trajectory of moment-to-moment behavior. Take, for example, when co-actors are asked to cooperatively move wooden planks together from one location to another. Here, cooperation emerges as a function of the slow-timescale dynamics of interaction history among co-actors. In this way, participants who had previously been working together continued to do so even when the task could be accomplished successfully alone (Isenhower, Richardson, Carello, Baron, & Marsh, 2010). In this example, the stable macroscopic state of "co-action" that emerges between cooperating individuals over time is due to the extended action capabilities that such cooperative co-action is perceived to provide. This functional extension of the individuals' solo action capabilities then comes to dominate the moment-to-moment actions of the individuals' current and future behavior (for more details about this specific example, see Marsh, Chapter 9 in this volume). Similar effects define the perception of momentum during sport, whereby competitive goals and confidence during play are dependent on the history of momentum changes during a match (Gernigon, Briki, & Eykens, 2010).

It is important to note that the aforementioned slower-timescale effects on the trajectory of an individual's or group of individuals' moment-to-moment behavior are not simply an effect of history per se, but rather appear as history effects because changes in the higher-order stabilities that give rise to them operate at a much slower timescale This self-sustaining (i.e., auto-catalytic) persistence can, of course, have negative social consequences. For instance, the history of long-timescale discrimination in labor markets has been shown to have a negative

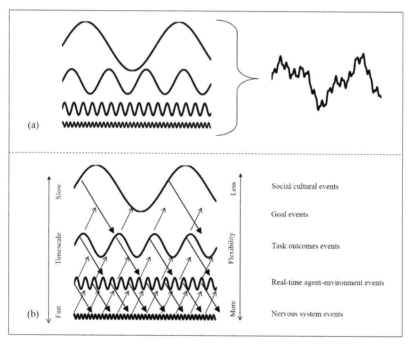

**FIGURE 6.1**  (a) An illustration of how different levels of organization or behavioral order are nested within a complex behavioral signal. (b) An illustration of the reciprocal and mutually defined system of interactional constraint that characterizes interaction-dominant dynamical systems. Note how the causal basis of behavioral order is circular, with the slower/larger-amplitude processes operating to enslave the micro-order of faster/smaller-amplitude processes, while at the same time the faster/smaller-amplitude processes operate to modulate or perturb the macro-order of the slower/larger-amplitude processes. Adapted from Eiler et al. (2013), with permission from the authors.

effect on learning ability and leads to situations of learned helplessness, which, in turn, perpetuates discrimination in the labor market (Elmslie & Sedo, 1996). In this way, such timescale enslavement effects reflect how prior social interactions and experience influence collective belief systems or stable social or interpersonal relationships that then constrain future social behavior in such a way that those collective belief systems or social relationships persist. In sum, the slow-timescale dynamics of social systems emerges from and enslaves the faster-timescale dynamics of those processes and individuals that gave rise to it.

## Examples of Interaction Dominant Dynamical Social Systems

In the sections that follow, we further unpack how timescale enslavement can be used to understand specific social phenomena. We situate this discussion with regard to three interaction-dominant phenomena: *synergistic social motor coordination*, *social networks*, and the *fractal nature of human cognitive and behavioral performance*.

### Synergistic Social Motor Coordination

Social motor coordination is defined as a stable, collective mode of dyadic or group-level motor behavior that emerges and persists due to informational or mechanical coupling. Common examples include the synchronized limb or body movements of individuals walking side-by-side (Harrison & Richardson, 2009; Van Ulzen, Lamoth, Daffertshofer, Semin, & Beek, 2008), rocking side-by-side in rocking chairs (e.g., Richardson, Marsh, Isenhower, Goodman, & Schmidt, 2007; Richardson, Garcia, Frank, Gregor, & Marsh, 2012), the coordinated postural and gestural movements of two or more individuals during a conversational interaction (e.g., Schmidt, Morr, Fitzpatrick & Richardson, 2012; Schmidt, Nie, Franco, & Richardson, 2014; Shockley, Santana, & Fowler, 2003), or while moving a large piece of furniture together (Richardson, Marsh & Baron, 2007). Such interpersonal coordination is argued to underlie many types of interpersonal and social activities and, moreover, is associated with behavior in pro-social, affiliative, and positive ways (e.g., Marsh, Richardson, & Schmidt, 2009; Miles, Griffiths, Richardson, & Macrae, 2010; Miles, Lumsden, Richardson, & Macrae, 2011; see also Marsh, Chapter 9 in this volume, for an excellent discussion). Of particular relevance here is that the stable patterns of social motor coordination that characterize everyday social interaction are by definition the result of interaction-dominant dynamical processes. That is, the stable patterns of social motor coordination emerge from the visual, auditory, haptic, and verbal interactions (couplings) that exist between two or more co-acting individuals. Moreover, these stable states of social motor coordination correspond to higher-order, collective organizations that enslave the behavioral order of the component limb or body movements of individuals involved in the interaction, including the neural activity inherent to an individual's limb and body movements (Anderson et al., 2012; Kelso, 1995).

Founded on interaction-dominant dynamical processes, stable patterns of social motor coordination are therefore soft-molded, context-dependent states of social organization. It is for these reasons that social motor coordination is also argued to be *synergistic* (Dale, Fusaroli, Duran, & Richardson, 2013; Marsh, Richardson, Baron, & Schmidt, 2006; Richardson, Marsh, & Schmidt, 2010). With regard to human motor coordination more generally, a synergy is a coalition of two or more degrees of freedom that are temporarily bound together to operate as a single functional system. This temporary assemblage of biomechanical elements are linked in such a way that (i) the number of component variables that need to be controlled during task performance is significantly reduced, so-called *dimensional compression*, and (ii) effective behavioral control is maintained in the presence of unforeseen environmental perturbations or system noise by the *reciprocal compensation* (mutual adaptation) of linked biomechanical elements (Riley, Richardson, Shockley, & Ramenzoni, 2011; Romero, Kallen, Riley, & Richardson, 2015). A social or interpersonal synergy is therefore a coalition of motor degrees of freedom across two or more individuals that result in (i) dimensional compression and (ii) reciprocal compensation (Riley et al., 2011). Note, of course, that the synergistic processes of dimensional compression and reciprocal compensation provide direct evidence of timescale enslavement, in that synergistic coordinative structures by definition represent slower-timescale stabilities that constrain and control the faster, moment-to-moment motor actions of individuals engaged in a particular social motor task.

Although there is now a growing body of literature to support the hypothesis that social motor coordination is synergistic and the result of IDDS processes (e.g., Black, Riley, & McCord, 2007; Dale et al., 2013; Riley et al., 2011, Ramenzoni, 2008), the most compelling evidence has come from a recent study by Romero and colleagues (2015), in which they investigated the limb coordination that occurred between two individuals performing an interpersonal targeting task (i.e., qualitatively similar to hand shaking). Utilizing an advanced mathematical modeling technique (the *uncontrolled manifold* technique) to identify the magnitude of dimensional compression and reciprocal compensation at both the intrapersonal and interpersonal levels, results demonstrated that behavioral control occurred at both levels, but that successful task performance was most strongly defined at the interpersonal level (Romero et al., 2015). Moreover, the synergistic control that occurred between co-actors emerged rapidly (within the first few trials), ensuring robust task performance across several hundred trial sessions.

Richardson and colleagues (2015) have also provided strong evidence that social motor coordination is synergistic. The authors investigated and modeled the task dynamics of an interpersonal collision avoidance targeting task. Of particular significance was the finding that the movement roles that emerged between co-actors were complementary—each actor moved in a different yet reciprocal manner between targets in order to ensure that task performance was both robust and energetically efficient. Moreover, once these task roles were established, they persisted across future task performance. Importantly, these roles were a self-organized consequence of the shared task goal and trial-by-trial performance outcomes (long-timescale dynamics), rather than a result of the faster dynamics of individuals' perceptual-motor organization. Indeed, the persistence with which participants adopted a specific task role within and across trials was a consequence of the real-time movement dynamics of each participant quickly becoming enslaved and collectively controlled by the slow-timescale dynamics of the complementary state of the interpersonal motor coordination that defined task success (Eiler et al., 2013).

Beyond human movement, Fusaroli and Tylén (2015) have demonstrated that synergetic properties of dialog are the best predictors of collective performance for joint action tasks performed by dyads (see also Fusaroli, Rączaszek-Leonardi, & Tylén, 2013). There is evidence to suggest that interpersonal synergies also exist at the level of brain-to-brain coupling, in which brains are reciprocally influential via motor coordination in a shared environment (Hasson, Ghazanfar, Galantucci, Garrod, & Keysers, 2012). It therefore seems likely that such synergistic coordination processes can be extended both more locally (cf. Di Paolo & De Jaegher, 2012) and more globally (cf. Eiler et al., 2013), in that synergistic control processes exist at all levels of human behavior (neural, perceptual-motor, interpersonal, social, etc.).

Key to demonstrating that a particular social coordination phenomenon is synergistic and has emerged from interaction-dominant dynamical processes and timescale enslavement, is to use methods that quantify the collective state of the interpersonal or group dynamics that defined the phenomena in question. For movement tasks that invite highly precise measurements of limb and body positions over time, measures of relative phase (Kelso, 1995), phase space methods (Richardson et al., 2015), and cross wavelet spectral analysis (Issartel, Marin, Gaillot, Bardainne, & Cadopi, 2006; Walton, Richardson, Langland-Hassan & Chemero 2015) are particularly useful to compare coordination across multiple timescales. For groups larger than two, cluster phase measures have been developed for measuring group synchrony (Frank & Richardson, 2010; Richardson et al., 2012). This allows for comparisons of short- and long-timescale coordination, in which an IDDS perspective would predict that stable patterns of coordination emerge over longer timescales to constrain the local movements of the individuals who make up the group. Recurrence and cross-recurrence quantification analyses (Webber & Zbilut, 2007) are also powerful tools for identifying the underlying dynamics of interpersonal interaction, and can be used to identify leader–follower relationships or other asymmetries (i.e., coupling strength), with regard to both categorical and continuous movement, and behavioral data (Coco & Dale, 2014; Richardson et al., 2015), and have been successfully employed for the analysis of other synergistic behavioral streams such as eye movement coordination (Richardson & Dale, 2005; Dale, Warlaumont, & Richardson, 2011), postural coordination and control (Shockley et al., 2003; Riley et al., 2011), and joint attention (Richardson, Dale, & Kirkham, 2007).

Finally, it is worth noting that synergistic social coordination is not modal-specific, but rather involves synergistic processes at the neural, physiological, motor, perceptual, and linguistic levels simultaneously. To date, however, very little research has been directed toward this cross-modal exploration (for exceptions see Dale et al., 2013; Gorman et al., 2016). Consistent with an IDDS perspective, therefore, researchers should be encouraged to devote more attention to uncovering how social synergies are established, maintained, and organized across time. It is likely that such research will not only lead to a better understanding of the interactive, self-organized processes that shape and constrain social interaction, but how perceptual, motor and cognitive aspects of human behavior are mutually and intrinsically related (i.e., provide greater insights into the embodied and embedded nature of human and social perception, action and cognition).

## Social Networks

Networks are, by definition, relational structures. Boccaletti and colleagues (Boccaletti, Latora, Moreno, Chavez, & Hwang, 2006) argue that the central issue for understanding any complex network is to graphically denote global system properties by modeling components, or nodes, as the dynamical units, and the links between them as representative of their interactions. Understood within the IDDS framework, nodes are therefore made interdependent by various types of connections, or ties (edges), that emerge over time to define the structural order of the network (and the behavior of the nodes themselves) in a circularly causal manner. Thus, it is the structural topology of the network that emerges from node linkages, which then feeds back to enslave the links between components in ways that give rise to emergent social phenomena (cf. Westaby, Pfaff, & Redding, 2014).

Although there are many examples of networks of differing composition (cells, the Internet, neurons in the brain, etc.), it is becoming increasingly clear that similar interaction-dominant dynamical principles underlie the formation of the complex structures that emerge in these different contexts (Albert & Barabási, 2002). It is also clear that networks exist at multiple temporal and physical scales in which they are both embedded within, and interact with, other networks. Accordingly, two complementary approaches have emerged with regard to research on human networks, which typically relate network structure either across disparate networks or across disparate processes. First, researchers have sought to relate network-level properties across distinct networks (e.g., human and orca whale societal structure; Hill, Bentley, & Dunbar, 2008) or seemingly unrelated phenomena (e.g., geographic movement patterns and friendship ties;

Cho, Myers, & Leskovec, 2011). This approach underscores the universality of timescale enslavement, in that each network system entails slower-timescale structures that emerge to constrain faster-timescale observable behavior. For example, with regard to social behavior, the network principle of homophily (that similarity underlies social connection at the network level) structures interactions as diverse as marriage, friendship, work, support, and information exchange, and seems to constrain social connections in ways that have drastic impact on information propagation, attitudes, and intergroup relations (e.g., McPherson, Smith-Lovin, & Cook, 2001). Indeed, this underlying dynamical principle generates social structures with geographic, socioeconomic, racial/ethnic, and attitudinal similarity that are irreducible to individual agents.

The underlying dynamical process of timescale enslavement operates to structure social networks in ways that demonstrate this principle across networks of differing composition. Consider healthcare networks, where slow-timescale emergent social infrastructure (the network structure of referral contacts for physical and mental health) has been related to accessibility for Latino immigrants in a non-traditional migration area and used to make targeted recommendations for reducing health disparities (Eiler, Bologna, Vaughn, & Jacquez, 2017). Here, referrals are passed between similar healthcare providers such that changes in policy or service provision (e.g., the absence of bilingual healthcare professionals) at individual locations constrains the entire network and subsequently leads to inadequate healthcare service delivery for Latinos. Similar enslavement effects have been observed with regard to smoking cessation, such that smokers tend to quit when their immediate social group quits, and this quitting behavior tends to spread through close individual ties initially and sparse connections between groups of smokers over time (Christakis & Fowler, 2008). Some social networks even tend to co-evolve in the case of organizational culture and individual knowledge transfer (Lin & Desouza, 2010), demonstrating how networks are both irreducible to individual dynamics and mutually structured by asymmetries across temporal scales.

The second approach to understanding networks considers network properties from an IDDS perspective more directly. In this way, researchers tend to explore how network structure at slow timescales relates to highly desirable properties at faster timescales across many social domains: how slower-timescale network behavior generates robust and highly effective faster-timescale behavior. In particular, how many networks, such as the nervous system of the *C. elegans*, collaborations between film actors, or the power grid in the United States (Watts & Strogatz, 1998), are topographically structured in a way that is neither completely random (random ties between components), nor completely regular (ties between components that follow a deterministic rule). In short, these and many other networks are what are called *small world* networks, which are characteristic of self-organized and self-sustaining systems that recruit or remove nodes or connections between nodes during development (Watts & Strogatz, 1998).

The significance of these small world networks is that they display efficient infor-mation propagation (i.e., attitudes, social norms), enhanced computational power (i.e., wisdom of crowds), and synchronization (i.e., propensity to coordinate) compared to other network types (cf. Watts & Strogatz, 1998). Small world networks comprised of humans are also self-regulating, whereby agents draw on various information sources distributed across the network such that a com-mon and flexible understanding of governance emerges (Folke, Hahn, Olsson, & Norberg, 2005). The self-regulating and information propagation properties of small world networks have also been identified in models that capture the dynamics of disease spread. For instance, Eubank and colleagues (2004) dem-onstrated that targeted vaccination in specific network hub locations, combined with early detection, can lead to herd immunity and containment in the case of an outbreak. Here, the local interactions among infected individuals give rise to a pattern of disease spread that then constrains the network in such a way as to provide an opportunity for targeted intervention in a circularly causal manner.

Overall, network research in psychological science is consistent with an IDDS approach, and can be used to demonstrate timescale enslavement and the self-organized nature of social behavior. Furthermore, Westaby and colleagues (2014) have developed a dynamic network perspective in which social networks influ-ence processes at interpersonal, faster timescales (i.e., goals). While some research exists that has modeled social network evolution and outcome (Snijders, Van de Bunt, & Steglich, 2010; Westaby & Shon, Chapter 11 in this volume), another interesting avenue for future research is the measurement of social networks over time. Such research would provide key insights about how to model and understand the dynamics of social network formation and change, and the role that such formation and change plays in defining social engagement or inter-action potentials. Teasing apart how asymmetries between interacting change processes (e.g., network topology and individual dynamics) permit stable behav-ior to emerge would also provide an opportunity for demonstrating how the behavior of individuals both emerges from and imparts structure on social and cultural processes (cf. Kitayama & Uskul, 2011). For example, women's under-representation in STEM (science, technology, engineering, and mathematics) at the faculty level might be conceptualized as emerging from networks in which cultural factors (i.e., departmental network structure) lead to isolation (i.e., fewer network ties for women faculty), which, in turn, perpetuate isolation and may limit opportunities for advancement or persistence.

### *Fractal Scaling of Human Performance*

Researchers in psychology typically collapse multiple measurements into sum-mary variables (i.e., mean, standard deviation) and assume that the variance observed across multiple measurements is random and normally distributed. For dynamic behavior, however, this is not typically the case, with behavioral patterns over time often structured in a self-similar, fractal or scale-free manner (e.g., Van Orden, Holden, & Turvey, 2003; Van Orden et al., 2011, see Figure 6.2). In simple terms, this means that the temporal variability observed in human behavior and performance is correlated over time, with the structure of smaller-scale fluctuations being statistically similar to the structure of larger-scale fluctuations. Analogous to geometric fractals, this nested statistical structure is characterized by an inverse relationship between the power and the frequency of the observed variability in performance data over time. More specifically, the relationship between the power of a specific change or fluctuation in a behavioral measurement and how often that specific change in measurement is observed (the frequency, $f$, with which a behavioral measurement is observed) follows an inverse power-law function. Often referred to as $1/f$ or "pink" noise due to this power–frequency relationship, such behavioral variation is the result of reciprocally defined inter-component interactions that propagate perturbations that occur at one level of a system across all other system levels (Wang, Kádár, Jung, & Showalter, 1999; Bak, Tang, & Wiesenfeld, 1987, 1988); hence the self-similarity of behavioral variability across small and large scales of analysis.

With respect to our discussion of the IDDS approach to social behavior, what is important here is that fractal behavior is a clear sign of nonlinearity, meta-stability and self-organized criticality (Van Orden, Holden, & Turvey, 2003). Thus, $1/f$ scaling has become a benchmark signature of IDDS (Eiler et al., 2013;

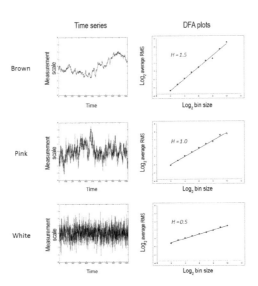

**FIGURE 6.2** Examples of simulated time series data (left column) and detrended fluctuation analysis plots and Hurst ($H$) values (right column) for brown, pink, and white signals.

Van Orden et al., 2003; Ihlen & Vereijken, 2010; Bak, 1996). It is for this reason that the presence of fractal or pink noise ($1/f$ scaling with an exponent $\approx 1$) has been argued to provide evidence that mind and body are intrinsically linked, and that human behavior emerges from self-organized, interaction-dominant dynamical processes (Van Orden et al., 2003). Indeed, the fractal nature of human behavior and performance variability over time has been studied quite extensively over the last few decades (e.g., Kello et al., 2007; Kello et al., 2010; West, 2010; Dixon, Holden, Mirman, & Stephen, 2012), with this research consistently demonstrating how stable human neural, perceptual-motor, and cognitive behavior result from interaction-dominant dynamical processes.

Of particular significance here is the research that has demonstrated that time-scale enslavement typically manifests, fractal, $1/f$ scaling. For example, functional magnetic resonance imaging studies have demonstrated endogenous activity (characterized by a fractal, $1/f$ structure) to be dominated by slow-timescale dynamics, even in the absence of other experimental effects (e.g., Bullmore et al., 2001). Perhaps the most compelling evidence comes from a wealth of research that has consistently demonstrated how human cognitive performance is characterized by fractal performance variability (e.g., Gilden, 2001; Ihlen & Vereijken, 2010; Kello et al., 2007; Van Orden et al., 2005), with this type of long-range correlation being due to distributed neural processes that interact along multiple scales, rather than due to simple feedback loops or other mechanisms typically associated with modular approaches to cognition (Chen, Ding, & Kelso, 2001).

Beyond intrapersonal behavior and cognition, interpersonal and group behaviors have also been demonstrated to display fractal structure. For instance, the collective reaction time variability of co-actors performing a Simon task is fractal rather than random in nature (Malone, Castillo, Kloos, Holden, & Richardson, 2014). The fractal scaling of co-actors' behavior also tends to become matched over the course of an interaction (Marmelat & Delignières, 2012). Such *complexity matching* appears to optimize information flow between coupled systems, thereby enhancing the overall quality and flexibility of the social exchange. This type of complex entrainment between co-acting individuals has also been observed in verbal and conversational interaction (Abney, Paxton, Dale, & Kello, 2014; Kello, Anderson, Holden, & Van Orden, 2008), interpersonal movement coordination (Marmelat & Delignières, 2012; Fine, Likens, Amazeen, & Amazeen, 2015), neural networks (Mafahim, Lambert, Zare, & Grigolini, 2015), and during anticipatory control (Washburn, Kallen, Coey, Shockley, & Richardson, 2015). Furthermore, Rigoli and colleagues (Rigoli, Holman, Spivey, & Kello, 2014) have argued that complexity matching formalizes multi-scale coordination as fundamental to both individual behavior and interaction more generally. This idea is consistent with the general IDDS approach to social behavior, in that group processes enslave individual processes in order to enact socially and functionally relevant behavior. Moreover, complexity matching may increase informational coupling across nervous systems that support shared goal states (cf. Mafahim et al., 2015).

Fundamental social processes also display fractal structure. For instance, individual social processes such as self-esteem exhibit fractal scaling (Delignières, Fortes, & Ninot, 2004) indicating that our global view of ourselves is dynamic and only critically stable, self-sustained via interaction-dominant dynamical processes. Changes in collective and synergistic emotional arousal and valence are also associated with differential fractal structure (Tadić, Gligorijević, Mitrović, & Šuvakov, 2013). Humans also tend to form social groups in discrete scale-invariant ways, with group sizes that mimic herding behavior in financial markets (Zhou, Sornette, Hill, & Dunbar, 2005). Moreover, robust (small world) social networks in general possess a fractal topology and demonstrate scale-invariant statistical structure over time (e.g., Hamilton, Milne, Walker, Burger, & Brown, 2007). Indeed, fractal self-similarity pervades social processes at all levels of individual, small group and cultural behavior, leading some to argue that fractal social systems are not only a fundamental class of social organization (De Florio, Bakhouya, Coronato, & Di Marzo, 2013), but typify the self-organized and interaction-dominant nature of social behavior (Bradbury & Vehrencamp, 2014).

## Conclusion

Here we have detailed a theory of social behavioral organization founded on a key tenet of interaction-dominant dynamical systems, namely timescale enslavement. Our goal was to explicate how IDDS theory and timescale enslavement fit within the field of social psychology more broadly. As stated at the beginning of this chapter, we do not view these principles of behavioral organization as controversial or contrary to an intuitive understanding of how social behavior emerges over time. Similar dynamical ideas, such as conceptualizing life spaces as vector fields of attracting and repelling social forces (Lewin, Lippitt, & White, 1939) or coordinated action as a means for social inclusion (Asch, 1952), have been theorized since the middle of the last century. Moreover, stating that interactions between individuals are fundamental to the structure of human social behavior is theoretically inherent to the field of social psychology.

Yet, if the principles of interaction dominance and timescale enslavement are taken seriously, then how we understand and investigate social behavior becomes somewhat different from that traditionally hypothesized within the field of social psychology. Indeed, to take interaction dominance seriously means that one should be committed to the idea of circular causality and self-referential, self-sustainable processes of emergence—that the faster-timescale interactions of individuals give rise to the historical constraints and macroscopic stabilities of the social systems that those same individuals then find themselves embedded within. This implies that the goal for social psychology should be to uncover how societal and cultural processes are self-organized, emerge from, and enslave the behavioral dynamics of the individuals embedded within those slower-timescale societal and cultural processes.

To some extent, this requires a complete reconsideration of how we define socially situated behavior. This is to say that social behavior is a contextually constrained property of a complex and dynamic agent–environment system, rather than a property inherent to or possessed by individuals. That is, to be social is not to be in the mere presence of another, but in fact to be defined by others and to define others through ourselves. Moreover, social context is not simply the addition of individuals into an objective reality, but an objective reality defined by the social interactions that individuals are generatively embedded within. Importantly, this grounds human behavior in principles that pervade science at the broadest levels. For social psychologists, this means sociality is fundamental to behavior—an idea that has long eluded traditional cognitive scientists that typically subjugate our behavior as the mere product of brain signaling. Most importantly, this approach allows us to address deep questions in social psychology from a strong empirical position in which the answers that emerge will demonstrate how the stable micro- and macroscopic patterns of human social behavior emerge from the same IDDS principles that shape the stable micro- and macroscopic patterns of behavior of other complex biological systems.

## Notes

1 The term "soft-molded" refers to stable yet temporary behavioral patterns or functional organization. Such behavioral patterns or functional organization are non-fixed, highly flexible and can be created, re-organized, and destroyed in response to changes in environmental context.
2 In this chapter, we have chosen to use the term "timescale enslavement" to refer to the circular causality principle in which slower-timescale processes or dynamic stabilities enslave faster-timescale processes or dynamic stabilities. It is worth nothing that this principle is referred to as the *slaving principle* in synergetics (e.g., Haken, 1983, 2004).

## References

Abney, D. H., Paxton, A., Dale, R., & Kello, C. T. (2014). Complexity matching in dyadic conversation. *Journal of Experimental Psychology: General, 143*(6), 2304–2315. doi:10.1037/xge0000021

Albert, R., & Barabási, A.-L. (2002). Statistical mechanics of complex networks. *Reviews of Modern Physics, 74*(1), 47–97. doi:10.1103/RevModPhys.74.47

Anderson, M. L., Richardson, M. J., & Chemero, A. (2012). Eroding the boundaries of cognition: Implications of embodiment. *Topics in Cognitive Science, 4*(4), 717–730. doi:10.1111/j.1756-8765.2012.01211.x

Asch, S. (1952). *Social psychology.* New York: Prentice Hall.

Bak, P. (1996). *How nature works: The science of self-organized criticality.* New York: Springer-Verlag.

Bak, P., Tang, C., & Wiesenfeld, K. (1987). Self-organized criticality: An explanation of $1/f$ noise. *Physical Review Letters, 59*(4), 381–384. doi:10.1103/PhysRevLett.59.381

Bak, P., Tang, C., & Wiesenfeld, K. (1988). Self-organized criticality. *Physical Review A, 38*(1), 364–374. doi:10.1103/PhysRevA.38.364

Black, D. P., Riley, M. A., & McCord, C. K. (2007). Synergies in intra- and interpersonal interlimb rhythmic coordination. *Motor Control*, *11*(4), 348–373.

Boccaletti, S., Latora, V., Moreno, Y., Chavez, M., & Hwang, D.-U. (2006). Complex networks: Structure and dynamics. *Physics Reports*, *424*(4–5), 175–308. doi:10.1016/j.physrep.2005.10.009

Bradbury, J. W., & Vehrencamp, S. L. (2014). Complexity and behavioral ecology. *Behavioral Ecology*, *25*(3), 435–442. doi:10.1093/beheco/aru014

Bruineberg, J., & Rietveld, E. (2014). Self-organization, free energy minimization, and optimal grip on a field of affordances. *Frontiers in Human Neuroscience*, *8*, 599. doi:10.3389/fnhum.2014.00599

Bullmore, E., Long, C., Suckling, J., Fadili, J., Calvert, G., Zelaya, F., Carpenter, T. A., & Brammer, M. (2001). Colored noise and computational inference in neurophysiological (fMRI) time series analysis: Resampling methods in time and wavelet domains. *Human Brain Mapping*, *12*(2), 61–78. doi:10.1002/1097-0193(200102)12:2<61::AID-HBM1004>3.0.CO;2-W

Chalmers, D. J. (2006). Strong and weak emergence. In P. Clayton & P. Davies (Eds.), *The re-emergence of emergence*. Oxford: Oxford University Press.

Chen, Y, Ding, M., & Kelso, J. A. S. (2001). Origins of timing errors in human sensorimotor coordination. *Journal of Motor Behavior*, *33*(1), 3–8. doi:10.1080/00222890109601897

Cho, E., Myers, S. A., & Leskovec, J. (2011). Friendship and mobility: User movement in location-based social networks. In *Proceedings of the ACM SIGKDD International Conference on Knowledge Discovery and Data Mining*, San Diego, CA, August 21–24, 2011 (pp. 1082–1090). New York: ACM. doi:10.1145/2020408.2020579

Christakis, N. A., & Fowler, J. H. (2008). The collective dynamics of smoking in a large social network. *New England Journal of Medicine*, *358*(21), 2249–2258. doi:10.1056/NEJMsa0706154

Coco, M. I., & Dale, R. (2014). Cross-recurrence quantification analysis of categorical and continuous time series: An R package. *Frontiers in Psychology*, *5*, 1–14. doi:10.3389/fpsyg.2014.00510

Dale, R., Fusaroli, R., Duran, N. D., & Richardson, D. C. (2013). The self-organization of human interaction. In B. H. Ross (Ed.), *The psychology of learning and motivation*. New York: Elsevier.

Dale, R., Warlaumont, A. S., & Richardson, D. C. (2011). Nominal cross recurrence as a generalized lag sequential analysis for behavioral streams. *International Journal of Bifurcation and Chaos*, *21*, 1153–1161. doi:10.1142/S0218127411028970

De Florio, V., Bakhouya, M., Coronato, A., & Di Marzo, G. (2013). Models and concepts for socio-technical complex systems: Towards fractal social organizations. *Systems Research and Behavioral Science*, *30*(6), 750–772. doi:10.1002/sres.2242

Delignières, D., Fortes, M., & Ninot, G. (2004). The fractal dynamics of self-esteem and the physical self. *Nonlinear Dynamics, Psychology, and Life Sciences*, *8*(4), 479–510.

Di Paolo, E., & De Jaegher, H. (2012). The interactive brain hypothesis. *Frontiers in Human Neuroscience*, *6*(1), 1–16. doi:10.3389/fnhum.2012.00163

Dixon, J. A., Holden, J. G., Mirman, D., & Stephen, D. G. (2012). Multifractal dynamics in the emergence of cognitive structure. *Topics in Cognitive Science*, *4*(1), 51–62. doi:10.1111/j.1756-8765.2011.01162.x

Eiler, B.A., Bologna, D., Jacquez, F., & Vaughn, L. (2017). A social network approach to understanding community partnerships in a non-traditional destination for Latinos. *Journal of Community Psychology*, *45*(2), 178–192. doi:10.1002/jcop.21841

Eiler, B. A., Kallen, R. W., Harrison, S. J., & Richardson, M. J. (2013). Origins of order in joint activity and social behavior. *Ecological Psychology, 25*(3), 316–326. doi:10.1080/10407413.2013.810107

Elmslie, B., & Sedo, S. (1996). Discrimination, social psychology, and hysteresis in labor markets. *Journal of Economic Psychology, 17*(4), 465–478. doi:10.1016/0167-4870(96)00021-9

Eubank, S., Guclu, H., Kumar, V. S. A., Marathe, M. V., Srinivasan, A., Toroczkai, Z., & Wang, N. (2004). Modelling disease outbreaks in realistic urban social networks. *Nature, 429*(6988), 180–184. doi:10.1038/nature02541

Fine, J. M., Likens, A. D., Amazeen, E. L., & Amazeen, P. G. (2015). Emergent complexity matching in interpersonal coordination: Local dynamics and global variability. *Journal of Experimental Psychology: Human Perception and Performance, 41*(3), 723–737. doi:10.1037/xhp0000046

Folke, C., Hahn, T., Olsson, P., & Norberg, J. (2005). Adaptive governance of social-ecological systems. *Annual Review of Environment and Resources, 30*, 441–473. doi:10.1146/annurev.energy.30.050504.144511

Frank, T. D., & Richardson, M. J. (2010). On a test statistic for the Kuramoto order parameter of synchronization: An illustration for group synchronization during rocking chairs. *Physica D, 239*(23–24), 2084–2092. doi:10.1016/j.physd.2010.07.015

Friston, K. (2010). The free-energy principle: A unified brain theory? *Nature Reviews Neuroscience, 11*(2), 127–138. doi:10.1038/nrn2787

Fusaroli, R., Rączaszek-Leonardi, J., & Tylén, K. (2013). Dialog as interpersonal synergy. *New Ideas in Psychology, 32*(1), 147–157. doi:10.1016/j.newideapsych.2013.03.005

Fusaroli, R., & Tylén, K. (2015). Investigating conversational dynamics: Interactive alignment, interpersonal synergy, and collective task performance. *Cognitive Science, 40*(1), 145–171. doi:10.1111/cogs.12251

Gernigon, C., Briki, W., & Eykens, K. (2010). The dynamics of psychological momentum in sport: The role of ongoing history of performance patterns. *Journal of Sport and Exercise Psychology, 32*(3), 377–400.

Gilden, D. L. (2001). Cognitive emissions of $1/f$ noise. *Psychological Review, 108*(1), 33–56. doi:10.1037//0033-295X.108.1.33

Gorman, J. C., Martin, M. J., Dunbar, T. A., Stevens, R. H., Galloway, T. L., Amazeen, P. G., & Likens, A. D. (2016). Cross-level effects between neurophysiology and communication during team training. *Human Factors, 58*(1), 181–199. doi:10.1177/0018720815602575

Haken, H. (1983). *Synergetics, an introduction: Nonequilibrium phase transitions and self-organization in physics, chemistry, and biology.* New York: Academic Press.

Haken, H. (2004). *Synergetics: Introduction and advanced topics.* Berlin: Springer-Verlag. doi:10.1007/978-3-662-10184-1

Haken, H., & Tschacher, W. (2010). A theoretical model of intentionality with an application to neural dynamics. *Mind and Matter, 8*(1), 7–18.

Hamilton, M. J., Milne, B. T., Walker, R. S., Burger, O., & Brown, J. H. (2007). The complex structure of hunter-gatherer social networks. *Proceedings of the Royal Society B: Biological Sciences, 274*(1622), 2195–2202. doi:10.1098/rspb.2007.0564

Harrison, S. J., & Richardson, M. J. (2009). Horsing around: Spontaneous four-legged coordination. *Journal of Motor Behavior, 41*(6), 519–524. doi:10.3200/35-08-014

Hasson, U., Ghazanfar, A. A., Galantucci, B., Garrod, S., & Keysers, C. (2012). Brain-to-brain coupling: A mechanism for creating and sharing a social world. *Trends in Cognitive Sciences, 16*(2), 114–121. doi:10.1016/j.tics.2011.12.007

Hill, R. A., Bentley, R. A., & Dunbar, R. I. M. (2008). Network scaling reveals consistent fractal pattern in hierarchical mammalian societies. *Biology Letters, 4*(6), 748–751. doi:10.1098/rsbl.2008.0393

Ihlen, E. A., & Vereijken, B. (2010). Interaction-dominant dynamics in human cognition: Beyond $1/f^\alpha$ scaling. *Journal of Experimental Psychology: General, 139*(3), 436–463. doi:10.1037/a0019098

Isenhower, R. W., Richardson, M. J., Carello, C., Baron, R. M., & Marsh, K. L. (2010). Affording cooperation: Embodied constraints, dynamics, and action-scaled invariance in joint lifting. *Psychonomic Bulletin & Review, 17*(3), 342–347. doi:10.3758/PBR.17.3.342

Issartel, J., Marin, L., Gaillot, P., Bardainne, T., & Cadopi, M. (2006). A practical guide to time-frequency analysis in the study of human motor behavior: The contribution of wavelet transform. *Journal of Motor Behavior, 38*(2), 139–159. doi:10.3200/JMBR.38.2.139-159

Jordan, J. S. (2008). Wild agency: Nested intentionalities in cognitive neuroscience and archaeology. *Philosophical Transactions of the Royal Society B: Biological Sciences, 363*(1499), 1981–1991. doi:10.1098/rstb.2008.0009

Jordan, J. S., Bai, J., Cialdella, V., & Schloesser, D. (2015). Foregrounding the background. In E. Dzhafarov, J. S. Jordan, R. Zhang, & V. Cervantes (Eds.), *Contextuality from quantum physics to psychology*. Hackensack, NJ: World Scientific Publishing.

Jordan, J. S., & Heidenreich, B. A. (2010). The intentional nature of self-sustaining systems. *Mind and Matter, 8*(1), 45–62.

Karl, F. (2012). A free energy principle for biological systems. *Entropy, 14*(11), 2100–2121. doi:10.3390/e14112100

Kello, C. T., Anderson, G. G., Holden, J. G., & Van Orden, G. C. (2008). The pervasiveness of $1/f$ scaling in speech reflects the metastable basis of cognition. *Cognitive Science, 32*(7), 1217–1231. doi:10.1080/03640210801944898

Kello, C. T., Beltz, B. C., Holden, J. G., & Van Orden, G. C. (2007). The emergent coordination of cognitive function. *Journal of Experimental Psychology: General, 136*(4), 551–568. doi:10.1037/0096-3445.136.4.551

Kello, C. T., Brown, G. D. A., Ferrer-i-Cancho, R., Holden, J. G., Linkenkaer-Hansen, K., Rhodes, T., & Van Orden, G. C. (2010). Scaling laws in cognitive sciences. *Trends in Cognitive Sciences, 14*(5), 223–232. doi:10.1016/j.tics.2010.02.005

Kelso, J. A. S. (1995). *Dynamic patterns: The self-organization of brain and behavior*. Cambridge, MA: MIT Press.

Kelso, J. A. S. (2012). Multistability and metastability: Understanding dynamic coordination in the brain. *Philosophical Transactions of the Royal Society B: Biological Sciences, 367*(1591), 906–918. doi:10.1098/rstb.2011.0351

Kitayama, S., & Uskul, A. K. (2011). Culture, mind, and the brain: Current evidence and future directions. *Annual Review of Psychology, 62*(10), 419–449. doi:10.1146/annurev-psych-120709-145357

Kondepudi, D. K., & Gao, M.-J. (1987). Passages through the critical point and the process of state selection in symmetry-breaking transitions. *Physical Review A, 35*(1), 340–348. doi:10.1103/PhysRevA.35.340

Lewin, K., Lippitt, R., & White, R. K. (1939). Patterns of aggressive behavior in experimentally created "social climates." *Journal of Social Psychology, 10*, 271–299.

Lin, Y. & Desouza, K. C. (2010). Co-evolution of organizational network and individual behavior: An agent-based model of interpersonal knowledge transfer. *ICIS Proceedings, 153*. Retrieved from http://aisel.aisnet.org/icis2010_submissions/153

Mafahim, J. U., Lambert, D., Zare, M., & Grigolini, P. (2015). Complexity matching in neural networks. *New Journal of Physics, 17*(015003), 1–17. doi:10.1088/1367-2630/17/1/015003

Malone, M., Castillo, R. D., Kloos, H., Holden, J. G., & Richardson, M. J. (2014). Dynamic structure of joint-action stimulus–response activity. *PLoS One, 9*(2), e89032. doi:10.1371/journal.pone.0089032

Marmelat, V., & Delignières, D. (2012). Strong anticipation: Complexity matching in interpersonal coordination. *Experimental Brain Research, 222*(1–2), 137–148. doi:10.1007/s00221-012-3202-9

Marsh, K. L., Richardson, M. J., Baron, R. M., & Schmidt, R. C. (2006). Contrasting approaches to perceiving and acting with others. *Ecological Psychology, 18*(1), 1–38. doi:10.1207/s15326969eco1801_1

Marsh, K. L., Richardson, M. J., & Schmidt, R. C. (2009). Social connection through joint action and interpersonal coordination. *Topics in Cognitive Science, 1,* 320–339. doi:10.1111/j.1756-8765.2009.01022.x

Masataka, N. (1993). Effects of experience with live insects on the development of fear of snakes in squirrel monkeys, *Saimiri sciureus. Animal Behavior, 46*(4), 741–746. doi:10.1006/anbe.1993.1251

McPherson, M., Smith-Lovin, L., & Cook, J. M. (2001). Birds of a feather: Homophily in social networks. *Annual Review of Sociology, 27,* 415–444. doi:10.1146/annurev.soc.27.1.415

Miles, L. K., Griffiths, J. L., Richardson, M. J., & Macrae, C. N. (2010). Too late to coordinate: Contextual influences on behavioral synchrony. *European Journal of Social Psychology, 40*(1), 52–60. doi:10.1002/ejsp.721

Miles, L. K., Lumsden, J., Richardson, M. J., & Macrae, C. N. (2011). Do birds of a feather move together? Group membership and behavioral synchrony. *Experimental Brain Research, 211*(3–4), 495–503. doi:10.1007/s00221-011-2641-z

Ramenzoni, V. C. (2008). *Effects of joint task performance on interpersonal postural coordination* Doctoral dissertation. Retrieved from ProQuest Information & Learning (AAI3323881).

Richardson, D. C., & Dale, R. (2005). Looking to understand: The coupling between speakers' and listeners' eye movements and its relationship to discourse comprehension. *Cognitive Science, 29*(6), 1045–1060. doi:10.1207/s15516709cog0000_29

Richardson, D. C., Dale, R., & Kirkham, N. Z. (2007). The art of conversation is coordination: Common ground and the coupling of eye movements during dialogue. *Psychological Science, 18*(5), 407–413. doi:10.1111/j.1467-9280.2007.01914.x

Richardson, M. J., Dale, R., & Marsh, K. L. (2014). Complex dynamical systems in social and personality psychology: Theory, modeling and analysis. In H. T. Reis & C. M. Judd (Eds.), *Handbook of research methods in social and personality psychology* (2nd ed.). Cambridge: Cambridge University Press.

Richardson, M. J., Garcia, R. L., Frank, T. D., Gergor, M., & Marsh, K. L. (2012). Measuring group synchrony: A cluster-phase method for analyzing multivariate movement time-series. *Frontiers in Physiology, 3,* 1–10. doi:10.3389/fphys.2012.00405

Richardson, M. J., Harrison, S. J., Kallen, R. W., Walton, A., Eiler, B. A., Saltzman, E., & Schmidt, R. C. (2015). Self-organized complementary joint action: Behavioral dynamics of an interpersonal collision-avoidance task. *Journal of Experimental Psychology: Human Perception and Performance, 41*(3), 665–679. doi:10.1037/xhp0000041

Richardson, M. J., Marsh, K. L., & Baron, R. M. (2007). Judging and actualizing intrapersonal and interpersonal affordances. *Journal of Experimental Psychology: Human Perception and Performance, 33*(4), 845–859. doi:10.1037/0096-1523.33.4.845

Richardson, M. J., Marsh, K. L., Isenhower, R. W., Goodman, J. R. L., & Schmidt, R. C. (2007). Rocking together: Dynamics of intentional and unintentional interpersonal coordination. *Human Movement Science, 26*, 867–891, doi:10.1016/j.humov.2007.07.002

Richardson, M. J., Marsh, K. L., & Schmidt, R. C. (2010). Challenging egocentric notions of perceiving, acting, and knowing. In L. F. Barrett, B. Mesquita, & E. Smith (Eds.), *The mind in context* (pp. 307–333). New York: Guilford Press.

Rigoli, L. M., Holman, D., Spivey, M. J., & Kello, C. T. (2014). Spectral convergence in tapping and physiological fluctuations: Coupling and independence of $1/f$ noise in the central and autonomic nervous systems. *Frontiers in Human Neuroscience, 8*, 1–10. doi:10.3389/fnhum.2014.00713

Riley, M. A., Richardson, M. J., Shockley, K., & Ramenzoni, V. C. (2011). Interpersonal synergies. *Frontiers in Psychology, 2*(38), 1–7. doi:10.3389/fpsyg.2011.00038

Romero, V., Kallen, R. W., Riley, M. A., & Richardson, M. J. (2015). Can discrete joint action be synergistic? Studying the stabilization of interpersonal hand coordination. *Journal of Experimental Psychology: Human Perception and Performance, 41*(5), 1223–1235. doi:10.1037/xhp0000083

Schmidt, R. C., Morr, S., Fitzpatrick, P., & Richardson, M. J. (2012). Measuring the dynamics of interactional synchrony. *Journal of Nonverbal Behavior, 36*(4), 263–279. doi:10.1007/s10919-012-0138-5

Schmidt, R. C., Nie, L., Franco, A., & Richardson, M. J. (2014). Bodily synchronization underlying joke telling. *Frontiers in Human Neuroscience, 8*, 633. doi:10.3389/fnhum.2014.00633

Shockley, K., Santana, M., & Fowler, C. A. (2003). Mutual interpersonal postural constraints are involved in cooperative conversation. *Journal of Experimental Psychology: Human Perception and Performance, 29*(2), 326–332. doi:10.1037//0096-1523.29.2.326

Snijders, T. A. B., Van de Bunt, G. G., & Steglich, C. E. G. (2010). Introduction to stochastic actor-based models for network dynamics. *Social Networks, 32*(1), 44–60. doi:10.1016/j.socnet.2009.02.004

Tadić, B., Gligorijević, V., Mitrović, M., & Šuvakov, M. (2013). Co-evolutionary mechanisms of emotional bursts in online social dynamics and networks. *Entropy, 15*(12), 5084–5120. doi:10.3390/e15125084

Van Orden, G. C. (2010). Voluntary performance. *Medicina (Kaunas), 46*(9), 581–594.

Van Orden, G. C., Holden, J. G., & Turvey, M. T. (2003). Self-organization of cognitive performance. *Journal of Experimental Psychology: General, 132*(3), 331–350. doi:10.1037/0096-3445.132.3.331

Van Orden, G. C., Holden, J. G., & Turvey, M. T. (2005). Human cognition and $1/f$ scaling. *Journal of Experimental Psychology: General, 134*(1), 117–123. doi:10.1037/0096-3445.134.1.117

Van Orden, G. C., Hollis, G., & Wallot, S. (2012). The blue-collar brain. *Frontiers in Psychology, 3*, 1–12. doi:10.3389/fphys.2012.00207

Van Orden, G. C., Kloos, H., & Wallot, S. (2011). Living in the pink. Intentionality, well-being, and complexity. In C. Hooker (Ed.), *Philosophy of complex systems* (pp. 629–672). Oxford: Elsevier B.V.

Van Ulzen, N. R., Lamoth, C. J. C., Daffertshofer, A., Semin, G. R., & Beek, P. J. (2008). Characteristics of instructed and uninstructed interpersonal coordination while walking side-by-side. *Neuroscience Letters, 432*(2), 88–93. doi:10.1016/j.neulet.2007.11.070

Walton, A. E., Richardson, M. J., Langland-Hassan, P., & Chemero, A. (2015). Improvisation and the self-organization of multiple musical bodies. *Frontiers in Psychology, 6*, 313. doi:10.3389/fpsyg.2015.00313

Wang, J., Kádár, S., Jung, P., & Showalter, K. (1999). Noise driven avalanche behavior in subexcitable media. *Physical Review Letters, 82*(4), 855–858. doi:10.1103/PhysRev Lett.82.855

Washburn, A., Kallen, R. W., Coey, C. A., Shockley, K., & Richardson, M. J. (2015). Harmony from chaos? Perceptual-motor delays enhance behavioral anticipation in social interaction. *Journal of Experimental Psychology: Human Perception and Performance, 41*(4), 1166–1177. doi:10.1037/xhp0000080

Watts, D. J., & Strogatz, S. H. (1998). Collective dynamics of "small-world" networks. *Nature, 393*(6684), 440–442. doi:10.1038/30918

Webber, Jr., C. L., & Zbilut, J. P. (2007). Recurrence quantifications: Feature extractions from recurrence plots. *International Journal of Bifurcation and Chaos, 17*(10), 3467–3475. doi:10.1142/S0218127407019226

West, B. J. (2010). Fractal physiology and the fractional calculus: A perspective. *Frontiers in Physiology, 1*, 12. doi:10.3389/fphys.2010.00012

Westaby, J. D., Pfaff, D. L., & Redding, N. (2014). Psychology and social networks: A dynamic network theory perspective. *American Psychologist, 69*(3), 269–284. doi:10.1037/a0036106

Zhou, W.-X., Sornette, D., Hill, R. A., & Dunbar, R. I. M. (2005). Discrete hierarchical organization of social group sizes. *Proceedings of the Royal Society B: Biological Sciences, 272*(1561), 439–444. doi:10.1098/rspb.2004.2970

# 7

# COMPUTATIONAL TEMPORAL INTERPERSONAL EMOTION SYSTEMS

*Emily A. Butler, Jinyan Guan, Andrew Predoehl, Ernesto Brau, Kyle Simek, and Kobus Barnard[1]*

Emotions motivate and guide most complex human behavior (Frijda, 1986; Gross, 1999; Izard, 1977). If we could mathematically model emotions with enough accuracy to predict emotional responding, we could intervene in a broad array of domains, ranging across (but not limited to) close relationships, education, parenting, business management, consumer behavior, work performance, health behaviors, conflict resolution, and political negotiations. Most contemporary models frame emotion as an *intrapersonal* dynamic system comprised of subcomponents such as appraisals, experience, expressive behaviors, and autonomic physiology that interact over time to give rise to emotional states (Boker & Nesselroade, 2002; Butner, Amazeen, & Mulvey, 2005; Hoeksma, Oosterlaan, Schipper, & Koot, 2007; Kuppens, Allen, & Sheeber, 2010; Lewis, 2005; Lodewyckx, Tuerlinckx, Kuppens, Allen, & Sheeber, 2010). An important extension of these models acknowledges that many emotional episodes, if not most, occur in the context of social interactions or ongoing relationships. When this occurs, an *interpersonal* emotion system is formed, in which the subcomponents of emotion interact not only within the individual, but across the partners as well (Boker & Laurenceau, 2007; Butler, 2011; Butner, Diamond, & Hicks, 2007; Chow, Ram, Boker, Fujita, & Clore, 2005; Ferrer & Nesselroade, 2003; Granic & Hollenstein, 2003; Hsieh, Ferrer, Chen, & Chow, 2010; Lodewyckx et al., 2010). Predicting and intervening in these temporal interpersonal emotion systems (TIES) requires statistical models that represent complex, dynamic interdependencies across emotional subcomponents over time, both within individuals and between partners in an emotional transaction.

## Modeling TIES

Several aspects of TIES need to be considered when choosing a mathematical model to represent them, all of which can be seen in Figure 7.1, which depicts typical emotional data appropriate for studying TIES (e.g., time series observations of emotional experience, behavior or physiology from interacting pairs of people). First, emotions are oscillatory (Boker & Nesselroade, 2002; Butner et al., 2007; Chow et al., 2005; Pettersson, Boker, Watson, Clark, & Tellegen, 2013). Like a thermostat, people have their own individual emotional set points that they tend to return to after being perturbed (Chow et al., 2005; Pettersson et al., 2013). External stimulation provokes emotional responses, but well-functioning people adapt to these experiences, both automatically and via purposeful emotion regulation, and stabilize back to their homeostatic set point. This combination of perturbations and self-regulation results in an oscillating pattern of emotions across a range of time spans (e.g., from minutes to days) (Chow et al., 2005; Helm, Sbarra, & Ferrer, 2012; Pettersson et al., 2013).

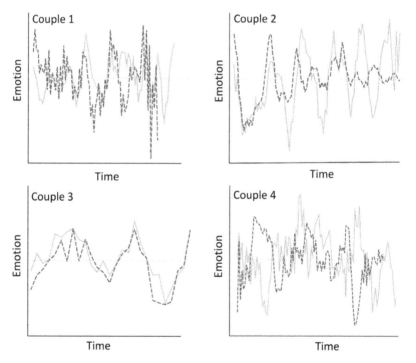

FIGURE 7.1  Prototypical emotional data appropriate for studying TIES (e.g., time series observations of emotional experience, behavior, or physiology from interacting pairs of people). Some measure of emotion is on the y-axis, and time is on the x-axis. Dashed lines represent one partner, and solid lines represent the other. Several features of interpersonal emotions can be seen, including oscillations at different frequencies, damping/amplification, and both in-phase and anti-phase between-partner coupling.

A second feature of emotions is that they may dampen or amplify over time. Regulating emotions involves both negative feedback loops (e.g., A produces B, which in turn inhibits A), and positive feedback loops (e.g., A produces B, which produces more of A). Negative feedback dampens emotional oscillations, while positive feedback amplifies them. Damping and amplification are most relevant when examined in the context of a single regulatory process evolving over time. For example, we may be more likely to observe damping or amplification in laboratory-based studies that focus on specific regulatory tasks (e.g., resolving a conflict with a partner), as opposed to daily diary studies that likely assess numerous regulatory events over time. Thus, a dynamic model of emotions designed to capture regulatory processes should allow for damping back to a homeostatic set point, or amplification away from it.

A third feature is that partners' emotions typically become interconnected, due to both automatic and conscious mechanisms, including shared stimuli, contagion, or being a stimulus for each other (Butler, 2011). Additionally, partners may explicitly attempt to regulate each other's emotions, whereby one partner is motivated to change the other's affective state (Diamond & Aspinwall, 2003; Zaki & Williams, 2013). Therefore, partners' oscillating emotions can become coupled, meaning that some aspect of one partner's emotional dynamics is influencing some aspect of the other partner's dynamics. For example, partners may be pulled into or out of synchrony with each other, or have mutually damping or amplifying effects on each other (Boker & Laurenceau, 2006; Butner et al., 2005; Butner et al., 2007; Ferrer & Helm, 2012; Steele & Ferrer, 2011). Thus a dynamic model of emotions in interpersonal contexts should allow for coupling to exist between social partners.

A growing body of research guided by a dynamic systems perspective suggests that conceptualizing relationships as dynamic interpersonal emotion systems provides a unifying theoretical framework (Butler, 2011). Although metaphors taken from a dynamic systems framework are often invoked in research on emotion and relationships, access to analytic tools to turn those metaphors into empirical outcomes has lagged behind (Boker & Laurenceau, 2007; Chow, Ferrer, & Nesselroade, 2007; Granic & Hollenstein, 2006). As a result, social scientists are typically limited to what is available in standard software packages, producing the risk that the software package ends up dictating the models, rather than theoretical considerations about the phenomenon of interest. We are at risk of TIES researchers looking where the light is, rather than where TIES processes are actually occurring. For example, if emotional oscillations are relevant to the research question, then classic approaches such as repeated measures regression, temporal multilevel models, growth modeling, latent change models, or sequential analyses are inadequate (Boker & Nesselroade, 2002; Butner et al., 2005; Hessler, Finan, & Amazeen, 2013). Such methods can assess the general emotional tone of an interaction, trajectories of change across time, or within- and between-person concurrent associations (synchrony) and time-lagged associations (transmission)

(Butler, 2011; Randall, Post, Reed, & Butler, 2013; Reed, Randall, Post, & Butler, 2013). However, such methods do not allow for an oscillatory pattern or damping/amplification, both of which may arise due to regulatory dynamics. Furthermore, virtually all methods available in off-the-shelf software are dependent upon distributional assumptions, the most important for TIES research being the assumption of stationarity, meaning that the statistical properties of a time series (e.g., mean and variance) do not change over time (Hsieh et al., 2010). This is untenable when considering emotional interaction data, given that emotions rise and fall, as well as fluctuate more or less, across time.

## Mindful Modeling

Cross-disciplinary collaboration is our proposed solution for making appropriate models available for TIES research. Our team includes social and computational scientists working together to represent TIES theory in the form of testable mathematical models, a process we call "mindful modeling."[2] The social scientists provide a theory about some aspect of TIES, along with relevant data, and the computational scientists provide a Bayesian generative model that embodies the key aspects of that theory, along with the ability to estimate the parameters of the model. A Bayesian generative model is a specification for the combined (joint) probability distribution of: (1) observed data, (2) parameters of a mathematical model, and (3) latent variables (Gelman, Carlin, Stern, & Rubin, 2004; Jordan, 2004; Koller & Friedman, 2009; Murphy, 2012). Prior knowledge, such as established estimates for some of the model parameters based on prior research, is encoded by distributions over parameters. One strength of generative models is that they are conducive to having the parameters represent theoretical constructs. This supports a top-down approach, whereby theory dictates the model. A key philosophical point in applying our mindful modeling approach is separating theoretical/mathematical modeling from inference. Inference refers to the process of estimating model parameters given data, which is what statistics packages do behind the scenes in order to return estimates of parameters such as the intercept and slopes for a regression model. So, in other words, we do not allow our modeling choices to be constrained by the inference options that are readily available, but rather focus on the theory of interest to guide our decisions. This can lead to challenging inference problems, but this is precisely the research domain of many computational scientists, and they have developed extensive methods and tools for addressing such problems.

A second key aspect of our approach is that we develop and test our models based on their ability to predict held-out data (e.g., cross-validation) (Geisser, 1975; Mosier, 1951). In other words, some portion of the data is used to develop the model and estimate the parameters; then we test the ability of that model with those parameter values to predict new observations. We prefer models that predict better in a new data set. In contrast, typical model selection and development procedures used in the social sciences, such as model fit indices and significance testing, are known to over-fit the data, which means they capitalize on chance idiosyncrasies present in any given data set. Thus every time we include a predictor in a regression model because it increases R-squared, or free a path in a structural equation model because it improves the fit indices, we are likely reducing the chance that the model will predict new data well. The problem becomes increasingly serious as we move away from strict a priori hypothesis testing towards more exploratory or post hoc analyses. This is a critical limitation, and is likely contributing to the replication crisis in social psychology. These facts were noted in social science publications as early as the 1950s, but appear to have been largely forgotten (Cureton, 1950; Kurtz, 1948; Mosier, 1951). Further, ultimately we would like our models to be able to predict outcomes either in the future or in different circumstances for specific people in particular relationships, not simply provide an estimate of a group mean or average effect in one data set. Without the ideographic prediction provided by cross-validation, our theories have little hope of achieving wide ranging applied relevance.

## An Example: Moderated and Drifting Linear Dynamical Systems

As an example we present an investigation of TIES processes using self-reported emotional data from interacting romantic partners (for details, see Guan et al., 2015; Reed, Barnard, & Butler, 2015). Committed heterosexual couples engaged in a conversation about their health-relevant lifestyle choices in the laboratory (39 couples; average conversation length = 10.8 minutes). Following the conversation, the participants watched the videotape of their own interaction and used a rating dial which turned through 180 degrees, with anchors of "negative," "neutral," and "positive," to indicate how they remembered feeling during the conversation. This produced second-by-second continuous self-reports of emotional experience ranging from -2 to +2 (see Figure 7.1 for typical data). The study was focused on health processes in couples, and participants had been recruited based on their dyadic weight status (e.g., both partners healthy weight, both partners overweight, or mixed-weight). We hypothesized that in this context, the partners' relative body mass index (BMI) would contribute to the emotional dynamics of the conversations.

Linear dynamical systems (LDS) provide a particularly useful class of models for studying TIES because they can represent complex oscillatory patterns of interconnected time series (e.g., the dynamics of two persons' emotions over time). LDS refer to models in which the subsequent states of a set of variables are linear functions of their current states. For this example, we focus on a particular subset of linear dynamical systems often called coupled oscillator models (see Guan et al., 2015 for additional mathematical and technical details for all aspects of this section). Coupled linear oscillators (CLO) are a particular version of LDS in which the accelerations of a pair of oscillators are a linear function of their velocities and positions. CLO models have been fairly extensively used to represent TIES processes because they model both intrapersonal and interpersonal characteristics, including frequency, damping, and coupling (Boker & Laurenceau, 2006, 2007; Butner et al., 2007; Ferrer & Steele, 2014; Helm et al., 2012; Reed et al., 2015; Steele & Ferrer, 2011; Steele, Ferrer, & Nesselroade, 2014). They are also useful for distinguishing between qualitatively different TIES processes such as coregulation and codysregulation (Butler & Randall, 2013; Reed et al., 2015).

Specifically, if we let $x_t^w$ and $x_t^M$ be the positions of two oscillators at time $t$, with the first oscillator representing a woman's emotional state and the second being her male partner's, then their joint emotional dynamics are defined by the second-order differential equation

$$\ddot{x}_t^W = f^W x_t^W + d^W \dot{x}_t^W + c^W \left( x_t^M - x_t^W \right) \tag{7.1}$$

$$\ddot{x}_t^M = f^M x_t^M + d^M \dot{x}_t^M + c^M \left( x_t^W - x_t^M \right) \tag{7.2}$$

Here, $\ddot{x}_t$ denotes the second derivative of the emotional observations (e.g., emotional acceleration) and $\dot{x}_t$ denotes their first derivative (e.g., emotional velocity), $f^w$ and $f^M$ can be translated into emotional oscillation frequencies for the woman and man respectively, $d^w$ and $d^M$ represent damping parameters for each partner, and $c^w$ and $c^M$ represent the coupling between the two partners.

One way to fit a CLO model to data is to use multilevel regression (for an example and references, see Reed et al., 2015). To do so, one estimates first and second derivatives from the observed emotional time series data and then uses the original observed data ($x_t^w$ and $x_t^M$), along with the estimated first and second derivatives, as predictor and outcome variables in a multilevel regression model. This approach has the advantage that most social scientists with training in graduate statistics will be able to implement it without needing to collaborate with computational scientists. It also has many limitations, however, and although ignoring any particular item in the following list is probably not problematic, ignoring many or all of them will likely result in spurious results. First, estimating derivatives directly from data is inherently noisy and introduces additional error into the process. Second, we are usually not interested in emotional acceleration at each time point per se, but rather the entire dynamic pattern of interconnected partner's emotions. Despite this, in the regression approach it is specifically acceleration that is predicted. As a result, the prediction errors that are minimized in the fitting process are not directly related to what we actually want to predict. Third, the regression approach does not include a representation of initial states, but dynamic systems are highly sensitive to start values, meaning that very different dynamic patterns could arise from the same CLO model, given different emotional starting points for the partners. Fourth, extending the model to include multivariate emotional observations (e.g., observed emotional experience and physiology from both partners, not just experience) is unwieldy, yet in theory emotion is a multivariate system comprised of several components, and ideally this would be represented by the model. Finally, the regression approach assumes stationarity, which in this case means that the CLO parameters do not change over time—an assumption which is likely violated in many interpersonal emotional interactions. Further, in theory we expect partners' emotional dynamics to change over time, not remain stationary, so an optimal model should include that possibility for substantive reasons, not simply to avoid violating statistical assumptions.

To address all these limitations, we take a Bayesian generative modeling approach. A generative model posits that the observed data is a random sample from a (typically) complex probability distribution that includes probabilities for both model parameters and observable data. In other words, the model prescribes a combined distribution of model parameters and observables, potentially informed by knowledge gained from prior research such as likely estimates for some parameters. Thus, given the model parameters, we can generate samples that should have similar characteristics to our observed data. Likewise, given a set of parameter estimates or an observed data point, we can calculate the likelihood that it came from the prescribed joint distribution. One thing this allows us to do is search for likely parameter sets for complex models (e.g., the inference process). Although the details of the procedure are often challenging, developing such inference algorithms using sampling methods is an area of expertise for our computational team. Another thing this allows us to do is evaluate models based on how likely the data is given a set of parameters, or even more important, how likely a new sample of data is, thus avoiding the over-fitting problem inherent in traditional statistical procedures that was discussed above.

Generative models can include a lot of complexity. For example, at one extreme we could specify that all the model parameters and observed data are completely inter-correlated (e.g., everything is correlated with everything), but such a model would be both impractical and scientifically useless, since it does not simplify the world. We need to set some constraints, ideally driven by theory, which is done by specifying conditional independencies. What this means in the specific case of the observed data is that all the variables become independent (e.g., there would be no remaining correlations among any of the variables), conditioned on the model. In other words, if the model is accurate, then it accounts for the observed correlation patterns in the data. In our example, we model a latent dyadic emotional state that evolves following the dynamics of a coupled oscillator. The observed emotional self-reports at each time point for each person are posited to be independent, conditioned on their latent dyadic emotional state. Specifically, if we knew each dyad's true latent emotional states at every time point, we theorize that it would account for all observed correlations within and between partners' emotions over time.

Our model can be broken into two parts for the purpose of description. First, we use a state-space model to represent a CLO. The latent states in this model can account for any number of observed variables, thus easily allowing for multivariate extensions, although in this example we limit ourselves to the univariate version where we consider only emotional self-reports. In addition, the parameters of this model (e.g., the frequency, damping, and coupling parameters for each partner) can either be stable across time or allowed to drift, thus accommodating non-stationarity. The parameters can be different for each couple, but allowing them to be completely free leads to over-fitting. Instead, in the second part of the model we constrain the parameters for each couple to come from a common distribution, with the means for each parameter potentially being a function of moderators (here, BMI). This allows variability of the CLO parameters across couples, and hence variability in their emotional dynamics, but also provides a test of theoretical factors that may lead to similarities between couples (e.g., BMI).

### State-Space Representation

Any system that is defined by a set of differential equations, such as a CLO, can be represented in state space, which refers to all the possible configurations of a multivariate system. Concretely, each variable in a model provides one dimension, so a model with five variables has five dimensions. Each possible combination of those five variables represents a state of the whole five-dimensional system. The general equations for a continuous-time LDS state-space model are

$$\dot{x}_t = \mathbf{A}x_t + \mathbf{B}u_t + \delta_t \tag{7.3}$$

$$y_t = \mathbf{C}x_t + \mathbf{D}u_t + \varepsilon_t \tag{7.4}$$

Here $x_t$ is a vector containing the system's latent state variables at time $t$ (note that these are latent states, not observed ones). In our example, we are modeling the joint emotional state of each male–female dyad, and so conceptually,[3] $x_t$ contains a two-dimensional state representing the true emotional state at time $t$ for each pair of people (e.g., one latent score for the male and one for the female). These latent emotional states evolve over time and generate the emotional observations. In our example, we focus on self-reported experience, but the latent states could also generate both partners' physiology or behavior, thus easily making it a multivariate model if desired.

In Equation 7.3, $\dot{x}$ is the first derivative of the state variables, so this equation represents the process by which the states transition from one time point to the next. The matrix $\mathbf{A}$ defines the dynamics by which the states transition, so in our example $\mathbf{A}$ contains equations defining a CLO (e.g., similar to Equations 7.1 and 7.2 above). Obviously, this matrix could contain different equations defining a different dynamic process, making the model very versatile. In addition, the components of **A** can be allowed to vary over time, thus modeling a non-stationary process. In other words, the quality of the dynamics can change across time. The optional vector $u$ represents any measured external variables that influence the dynamic process, and the matrix **B** determines how it affects the system. We do not include these components in our example (e.g., **B**$u$ is set to zero), but they could be used to represent something like noise in the room if we thought that emotional dynamics might be perturbed by noise levels. For example, partners' emotions may follow a CLO pattern quite well when they can hear each other, but noise may interrupt that pattern if it disrupts their communication. The optional $\delta_t$ represents stochastic fluctuations (e.g., unmeasured random errors) in the way the system transitions between latent states at time $t$. We again set this component to zero in our example, so that all random variance is accounted for either by observation noise (e.g., measurement error) or smoothly changing parameter drift.

Equation 7.4 defines how the observed variables, $y_t$, are related to the latent state variables at time $t$. In the univariate case of our example, matrix **C** has a particularly simple form that models the observed data as the latent state together with observation noise, but more complex forms are possible. In the multivariate case, for example, it could encode different measurement units for the observed variables (e.g., different physiological variables might be recorded with different scales and have different offsets—intercepts). Finally, the optional matrix **D** specifies how the vector $u$ affects the observations. For example, noise in the room may impact the measurement quality of some variables (voice intonation) and not others (physiology). This component is again set to zero in our example. Finally, $\varepsilon_t$ represents observation noise at time $t$, which we specify to be normally distributed with mean zero and unknown variance.

## Bayesian Hierarchical Model

Recall that a generative model prescribes a combined probability distribution of model parameters and observables, potentially informed by prior knowledge such as likely estimates for some parameters. Graphical models are a tool to visualize the conditional dependence structure among a set of random variables, and are useful for representing the set of independence relationships specified by a generative model. Figure 7.2 shows the graphical model for our example, omitting parameter drift (e.g., the CLO parameters for the model depicted in the figure stay the same across time). Nodes represent all the components of the model, including observed variables ($y_{it}$), latent states ($x_{it}$), and model parameters (all other nodes). Arrows represent dependencies, and a lack of arrows represents independence. For example, the observed variables are dependent on the latent states (e.g., the arrows go from the latent state to the observed variable) and are conditionally independent of each other conditioned on those latent states (e.g., the observed variables are not linked to each other by arrows because their inter-correlations are accounted for by the latent states).

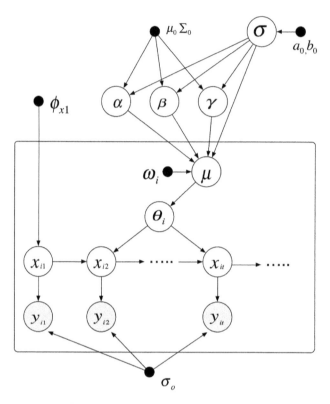

**FIGURE 7.2** A graphical model of the state-space model with BMI-dependent Gaussian prior. Open circles represent the random variables of the model, including observed variables ($y$) (shaded by convention), latent states ($x$), and other model parameters. Small circles denote constants which might be known, set by hand, or learned from data. Arrows depict dependencies, and lack of arrows represents independence. By convention, we describe how the model generates the data top-down (this is called *ancestral sampling*). To begin, the shared BMI-coefficients and the standard deviation, $\sigma$, come from (are generated by) a joint Normal-Inverse-Gamma prior distribution. These, together with BMI, $\omega_i$, determine the means, $\mu$, of a distribution over CLO parameters. This generates the CLO parameter set for a couple $i$, denoted by $\theta_i$. To use a CLO to specify latent state values, we need a starting point, and these initial values, $x_{t1}$, are generated from a normal distribution with mean zero and variance one (depicted by $\Phi_{x1}$). Given these initial values and the CLO parameters, the rest of the values of the latent states are determined in sequence. The latent states then generate the observed values, $y_{it}$. In the particular case of this example, this amounts to the latent state values being used as the means of normal distributions with shared standard deviation $\sigma_0$. These distributions then generate the observed $y_{it}$.

As shown in Figure 7.2, the pair of observed variables (e.g., both partners' self-reported emotional experience) for couple $i$ at time $t$, $y_{it}$, depend on the latent state for couple $i$ at time $t$, $x_{it}$. Specifically, $x_{it}$ provides the means of a normal distribution for each partner's observations (e.g., one distribution for men and one for women) with shared standard deviations $\sigma_0$. The first latent state for couple $i$ in turn comes from a prior distribution of emotional start values, $\Phi_{x1}$, specified to be normal with mean zero and variance one. Each subsequent state depends on the prior state and a set of six CLO parameters for that couple, $\theta_i$ (e.g., both partners' frequency, damping, and coupling). Those parameters are generated from normal distributions with means and standard deviations for each CLO parameter specified by vectors $\mu$ and $\sigma_\mu$ respectively.

Up until here, the model represents a CLO in which each dyad could have its own CLO parameters and hence unique emotional dynamics. Such a model is very powerful, and will fit the data extremely well (see "Results" on pp. 139), but would do so by over-fitting random noise and would have poor ability to predict new data or speak to theoretical factors expected to influence emotional processes. In particular, in the context of discussing health and lifestyle choices, we expected body mass index to impact emotional dynamics in systematic ways. For example, we expected that healthy-weight couples would be relatively unemotional compared to overweight couples where health was a source of concern. Similarly, we expected health to be a particularly contentious issue for mixed-weight couples where one partner was overweight but the other was healthy. Thus we let the means of the distribution of CLO parameters depend upon a linear function of both partners' BMI. Specifically, in Figure 7.2, $\omega_i$ is a vector with couple $i$'s average BMI (male BMI plus female BMI/2) and the difference between the partners' BMI (male BMI minus female BMI), $\alpha$ represents the offset (intercept) for each of the six CLO parameters, $\beta$ is the linear coefficient for BMI-average predicting each CLO parameter, and $\gamma$ is the linear coefficient for BMI-difference. Thus each couple's parameter set, $\theta_i$ (e.g., the six CLO parameters for couple $i$), depends on their joint BMI status in a way that is similar across couples with similar BMI values. Finally, the couple-shared BMI-coefficients, $\alpha$, $\beta$, and $\gamma$, and shared standard deviation $\sigma$ are random variables generated from a joint Normal-Inverse-Gamma prior distribution (e.g., represented in Figure 7.2 by $\mu_0$, $\Sigma_0$, $a_0$, $b_0$).

## Inference and Evaluation

Typically, inference proceeds by maximizing a function representing the probability of the model parameters given the observed data. For simple problems, there might be a closed form solution, such as least squares for multiple regression. For complex problems, however, this is not the case, and typically the approach becomes a search in the parameter space for values that make the probability of the parameters conditioned on the data most likely. This can be accomplished by various forms of Markov-Chain Monte Carlo (MCMC) sampling. Inference in the case of our model includes: (1) using sampling methods to find good estimates for the parameters that are shared across couples, such as the BMI coefficients (a process called *learning*), and (2) given good estimates of the shared parameters, using those to get good estimates for couple-specific parameters (a process called *fitting*). In our example, we use the couple-shared parameters to estimate couple-specific emotional trajectories into the future.

We combine learning and fitting in a multi-stage model evaluation process whereby we learn the shared model parameters in one subset of the data and then use those learned estimates to predict the observed data in a different subset. Specifically, we use ninefold cross-validation, which means we start by dividing the couples into nine groups. We get estimates of the shared parameters using the data from the couples in eight of the groups (learning groups). We then use those shared parameters to estimate couple-specific parameters for the first 80% of the conversation time for the held-out ninth group of couples (testing group). Finally, we predict the remaining 20% of the time points for each held-out testing couple by taking their estimated CLO parameters and evolving the process into the future (e.g., predicting values for the future based on the CLO parameters obtained from the past). We then repeat these steps eight more times, using each group in turn as the testing group. We record the root mean squared error (RMSE) of prediction for each testing couple for the first 80% of the conversation (fitting error based on the same data used to estimate that couple's parameters) and for the last 20% of the conversation (prediction error based on new data that was not used in any stage of parameter estimation). Models with low prediction error are less likely to be capitalizing on chance and are more likely to be representing robust processes that gave rise to the data, or in other words, real-world processes of substantive interest such as emotional dynamics taking the form of coupled oscillators.

Our multi-stage cross-validation approach can be contrasted with the use of fit statistics such as the AIC, DIC, or WAIC. Such fit measures will only work if the assumptions used to derive them are met. For models as complex as the ones we are implementing, it is hard to know what those assumptions should be, and we have generally found that fit statistics do not concur with cross-validation for our applications. Further, the gold standard for developing and validating model fit statistics is to compare their results against cross-validation and the only argument for using them is to avoid the computational cost of conducting actual cross-validation (Gelman, Hwang, & Vehtari, 2014; Vehtari, Gelman, & Gabry, 2016; Vehtari, Mononen, Tolvanen, Sivula, & Winther, 2014).

## Results

Table 7.1 presents mean RMSEs and their 95% confidence intervals across couples for both fitting and prediction for a sequence of models (since these are error estimates, smaller values imply a better-fitting model). Non-overlapping confidence intervals for any pair of RMSEs indicate that the estimates are significantly different, with p < .05. In general, one would prefer the model(s) with the lowest prediction errors. The first model (Average), estimates each person's mean emotional ratings for the first 80% of the conversation and simply predicts that mean will continue into the future 20%. The second model (Linear), estimates each person's intercept and slope for the first 80%, then predicts it will continue on that trajectory into the future 20%. Notice that although the fitting error is smaller for the Linear model than the Average, the reverse is true for the prediction error, suggesting that any apparent benefit for the Linear model is being driven by over-fitting. The third model (Couple-Specific CLO) estimates a unique CLO model for each couple based on the first 80% of their conversation, then predicts that dynamic pattern will continue into the future 20%. Here the presence of over-fitting is highly apparent, with very low fitting errors, but very high prediction error. The fourth model (Couple-Shared CLO) estimates a CLO model for the first 80% of the conversation in which all couple's parameters come from a shared distribution (e.g., all couples share the same mean of the CLO parameters). This shared dynamic pattern is then predicted to continue into the future 20%. Although this model does not fit quite as well as the Couple-Specific model, it has the lowest prediction error so far, suggesting that CLO dynamics are a fairly good characterization for the emotional self-reports obtained in this context. Finally, the fifth model (BMI-CLO) estimates a CLO model for the first 80% of the conversation in which the distribution of CLO parameters depends on the couple's BMI average and difference. Thus couples who are similar to each other in their joint BMI (e.g., both healthy weight, both overweight, mixed-weight) are predicted to show similar dynamics. This model has the lowest prediction error, suggesting that a couple's joint BMI has an influence on emotional dynamics in this context (although the confidence interval overlaps slightly with the Couple-Shared CLO, suggesting a statistically marginal improvement). To visualize this influence, Figure 7.3 shows the model-predicted emotional trajectories for a couple in which the woman is heavier than the man, as compared to the reverse. We can see that couples in which the woman is heavier than the man may be emotionally disconnected and the woman may show increasingly volatile emotional responses. This could contribute to poorly modulated emotion responses when discussing health and lifestyle choice.

**TABLE 7.1** Mean root mean squared errors and their 95% confidence intervals across couples for fitting and prediction for a sequence of models.

| Model | Fitting | Predicting |
| --- | --- | --- |
| Average | 0.52 (0.49–0.55) | 0.70 (0.65–0.80) |
| Linear | 0.47 (0.44–0.50) | 0.76 (0.68–0.84) |
| Couple-Specific CLO | 0.39 (0.36–0.42) | 1.10 (0.91–1.29) |
| Couple-Shared CLO | 0.44 (0.41–0.47) | 0.68 (0.62–0.74) |
| BMI-CLO | 0.41 (0.39–0.43) | 0.59 (0.54–0.64) |

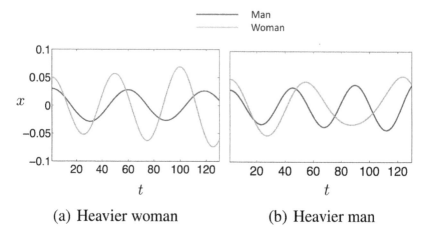

FIGURE 7.3 Model-predicted emotional states over time, with the same initial emotional start values but differing BMI moderator values. Black lines are the emotional state for the male partner, and gray lines are for the female partner. (a) The predicted emotional state for couples in which the woman is heavier than the man. (b) The predicted emotional state for couples in which the man is heavier than the woman.

## Future Directions

One trivial extension of our model, similar to making it multivariate, is to represent social units including more than two members. Doing so simply involves including variables for as many people as desired (e.g., three-person families, six-person work groups, etc.) as indicative of the latent states (as values in the vector $x_i$ of the state-space model). Of course, this implies that there is some meaningful emotional pattern at the level of the social unit, such as hypothesized by family systems (e.g., polarization or escalation) or theories about team functioning (e.g., group-think or synergy), but these theories could be tested using such a model. A second extension we are working on is to allow qualitative shifts in emotional dynamics across time using regime switching, which allows distinct state changes across time. In our model so far, we have allowed the CLO parameters to drift smoothly across time, which accommodates non-stationary emotional processes and improves prediction. It does not, however, lend itself to substantive interpretation. In contrast, regime switching can be used to model distinct shifts in emotional dynamic states, which can be visualized and related to substantive theory. Such states can either be specified a priori, or learned from the data. In the latter exploratory case, cross-validation is particularly critical to avoid overfitting, and ideally the learned states would then be tested in an a priori fashion on new data. For example, it may be common for couples to go through phases of highly oscillatory emotional functioning, well characterized by a CLO pattern, but spend time in relatively quiescent and disconnected phases in between, when the couple are less emotional or less involved with each other. Qualitative shifts may be particularly relevant when studying longer periods of time, so this extension is likely to be especially helpful for modeling emotional dynamics over days, weeks, or even longer periods. Finally, we are working to make our methods available for other researchers via Web services (Predoehl, Guan, Butler, & Barnard, 2015). Soon, you will be able to use our interface to upload your data, choose model settings, and receive back a table of results similar to those reported in this chapter. We encourage you to try it out (as of writing, we are in the testing phase) and hope this service will support extensive, exciting, and cumulative future research on TIES.

## Notes

1  This research was supported in part by Grant 1R21HL109746-01A1 from the National Heart, Lung, and Blood Institute awarded to the first author, and by Grant BCS-1322940 from the National Science Foundation awarded to the first and last authors.
2  We are also working to make all our modeling tools available to other researchers via Web services. At the time of writing, we are in the testing phase and hope to have the service fully functional soon at www.compties.org/software.html.
3  We say "conceptually" because, in practice, the CLO model includes second derivatives as well as first, which leads to a slightly different set of equations (see Guan et al., 2015). In particular, $x_t$ includes both the emotional state for each partner and their first derivatives, but for the purpose of intuitive explanation, we ignore that detail here.

## References

Boker, S. M., & Laurenceau, J. P. (2006). Dynamical systems modeling: An application to the regulation of intimacy and disclosure in marriage. In T. A. Walls & J. L. Schafer (Eds.), *Models for intensive longitudinal data* (pp. 195–218). New York: Oxford University Press.
Boker, S. M., & Laurenceau, J. P. (2007). Coupled dynamics and mutually adaptive context. In T. D. Little, J. A. Bovaird, & N. A. Card (Eds.), *Modeling contextual effects in longitudinal studies* (pp. 299–324). Mahwah, NJ: Lawrence Erlbaum.
Boker, S. M., & Nesselroade, J. R. (2002). A method for modeling the intrinsic dynamics of intraindividual variability: Recovering parameters of simulated oscillators in multiwave panel data. *Multivariate Behavioral Research, 37*(1), 127–160.
Butler, E. A. (2011). Temporal interpersonal emotion systems: The "TIES" that form relationships. *Personality and Social Psychology Review, 15,* 367–393. doi:10.1177/1088868311411164
Butler, E. A., & Randall, A. K. (2013). Emotional coregulation in close relationships. *Emotion Review, 5,* 202–210.
Butner, J., Amazeen, P. G., & Mulvey, G. M. (2005). Multilevel modeling of two cyclical processes: Extending differential structural equation modeling to nonlinear coupled systems. *Psychological Methods, 10*(2), 159–177.
Butner, J., Diamond, L. M., & Hicks, A. M. (2007). Attachment style and two forms of affect coregulation between romantic partners. *Personal Relationships, 14,* 431–455.
Chow, S., Ferrer, E., & Nesselroade, J. R. (2007). An unscented Kalman filter approach to the estimation of nonlinear dynamical systems models. *Multivariate Behavioral Research, 42*(2), 283–321.

Chow, S., Ram, N., Boker, S. M., Fujita, F., & Clore, G. (2005). Emotion as a thermostat: Representing emotion regulation using a damped oscillator model. *Emotion, 5*(2), 208–225.

Cureton, E. E. (1950). Validity, reliability and baloney. *Educational and Psychological Measurement, 10*(1), 94–96.

Diamond, L. M., & Aspinwall, L. G. (2003). Emotion regulation across the life-span: An integrative perspective emphasizing self-regulation, positive affect, and dyadic processes. *Motivation and Emotion, 27*(2), 125–156.

Ferrer, E., & Helm, J. L. (2012). Dynamical systems modeling of physiological coregulation in dyadic interactions. *International Journal of Psychophysiology, 88*(3), 296–308.

Ferrer, E., & Nesselroade, J. R. (2003). Modeling affective processes in dyadic relations via dynamic factor analysis. *Emotion, 3*(4), 344–360.

Ferrer, E., & Steele, J. S. (2014). Differential equations for evaluating theoretical models of dyadic interactions. In P. C. M. Molenaar, K. M. Newell, & R. M. Lerner (Eds.), *Handbook of developmental systems theory and methodology* (pp. 345–368). New York: Guilford Press.

Frijda, N. H. (1986). *The emotions*. Cambridge: Cambridge University Press.

Geisser, S. (1975). The predictive sample reuse method with applications. *Journal of the American Statistical Association, 70*(350), 320–328.

Gelman, A., Carlin, J. B., Stern, H. S., & Rubin, D. B. (2004). *Bayesian data analysis* (2nd ed.). London: Chapman & Hall.

Gelman, A., Hwang, J., & Vehtari, A. (2014). Understanding predictive information criteria for Bayesian models. *Statistics and Computing, 24*(6), 997–1016.

Granic, I., & Hollenstein, T. (2003). Dynamic systems methods for models of developmental psychopathology. *Development and Psychopathology, 15*, 641–669.

Granic, I., & Hollenstein, T. (2006). A survey of dynamic systems methods for developmental psychopathology. In D. Cicchetti & D. J. Cohen (Eds.), *Developmental psychopathology. Vol. 1: Theory and method* (2nd ed.). New York: John Wiley & Sons.

Gross, J. J. (1999). Emotion and emotion regulation. In L. A. Pervin & O. P. John (Eds.), *Handbook of personality: Theory and research* (2nd ed., pp. 525–552). New York: Guilford Press.

Guan, J., Simek, K., Brau, E., Morrison, C. T., Butler, E. A., & Barnard, K. (2015). Moderated and drifting linear dynamical systems. In *Proceedings of the 32nd International Conference on Machine Learning* (Vol. 3, pp. 2463–2472). Stroudsburg, PA: International Machine Learning Society.

Helm, J. L., Sbarra, D., & Ferrer, U. (2012). Assessing cross-partner associations in physiological responses via coupled oscillator models. *Emotion, 12*(4), 748–762.

Hessler, E. E., Finan, P. H., & Amazeen, P. G. (2013). Psychological rhythmicities. In J. P. Sturmberg & C. M. Martin (Eds.), *Handbook of systems and complexity in health*. New York: Springer Science+Business Media.

Hoeksma, J. B., Oosterlaan, J., Schipper, E. M., & Koot, H. (2007). Finding the attractor of anger: Bridging the gap between dynamic concepts and empirical data. *Emotion, 7*(3), 638–648.

Hsieh, F., Ferrer, E., Chen, S., & Chow, S. (2010). Exploring the dynamics of dyadic interactions via hierarchical segmentation. *Psychometrika, 75*(2), 351–372.

Izard, C. E. (1977). *Human emotions*. New York: Plenum.

Jordan, M. I. (2004). Graphical models. *Statistical Science* (special issue on Bayesian statistics), *19*, 140–155.

Koller, D., & Friedman, N. (2009). *Probabilistic graphical models*. Cambridge, MA: MIT Press.

Kuppens, P., Allen, N. B., & Sheeber, L. (2010). Emotional inertia and psychological adjustment. *Psychological Science, 21,* 984–991.

Kurtz, A. K. (1948). A research test of the Rorschach test. *Personnel Psychology, 1*(1), 41–51. doi:10.1111/j.1744-6570.1948.tb01292.x

Lewis, M. D. (2005). Bridging emotion theory and neurobiology through dynamic systems modeling. *Behavioral and Brain Sciences, 28,* 169–245.

Lodewyckx, T., Tuerlinckx, F., Kuppens, P., Allen, N. B., & Sheeber, L. (2010). A hierarchical state space approach to affective dynamics. *Journal of Mathematical Psychology, 55,* 68–83.

Mosier, C. I. (1951). The need and means of cross validation. I: Problems and designs of cross-validation. *Educational and Psychological Measurement, 11,* 5–11.

Murphy, K. (2012). *Machine learning: A probabilistic perspective*. Cambridge, MA: MIT Press.

Pettersson, E., Boker, S. M., Watson, D., Clark, L. A., & Tellegen, A. (2013). Modeling daily variation in affective circumplex: A dynamical systems approach. *Journal of Research in Personality, 47,* 57–69. doi:10.1016/j.jrp.2012.10.003

Predoehl, A., Guan, J., Butler, E. A., & Barnard, K. (2015). *CompTIES Web App*. Retrieved from www.compties.org/COM.html

Randall, A. K., Post, J. H., Reed, R. G., & Butler, E. A. (2013). Cooperating with your romantic partner: Associations with interpersonal emotion coordination. *Journal of Social and Personal Relationships, 30*(8), 1072–1095.

Reed, R. G., Barnard, K., & Butler, E. A. (2015). Distinguishing emotional co-regulation from co-dysregulation: An investigation of emotional dynamics and body-weight in romantic couples. *Emotion, 15,* 45–60. http://dx.doi.org/10.1037/a0038561

Reed, R. G., Randall, A. K., Post, J. H., & Butler, E. A. (2013). Partner influence and in-phase versus anti-phase physiological linkage in romantic couples. *International Journal of Psychophysiology, 88,* 309–316.

Steele, J. S., & Ferrer, E. (2011). Latent differential equation modeling of self-regulatory and coregulatory affective processes. *Multivariate Behavioral Research, 46*(6), 956–984.

Steele, J. S., Ferrer, E., & Nesselroade, J. R. (2014). An idiographic approach to estimating models of dyadic interactions with differential equations. *Psychometrika, 79*(4), 675–700. https://doi.org/10.1007/s11336-013-9366-9

Vehtari, A., Gelman, A., & Gabry, J. (2016). Practical Bayesian model evaluation using leave-one-out cross-validation and WAIC. *Journal of Statistics and Computing,* 1–20.

Vehtari, A., Mononen, T., Tolvanen, V., Sivula, T. & Winther, O. (2014). Bayesian leave-one-out cross-validation approximations for Gaussian latent variable models. *Journal of Machine Learning Research, 17*(103), 1–38.

Zaki, J., & Williams, W. C. (2013). Interpersonal emotion regulation. *Emotion, 13*(5), 803–810. doi:10.1037/a0033839

# 8

# MAPPING CO-REGULATION IN SOCIAL RELATIONS THROUGH EXPLORATORY TOPOLOGY ANALYSIS

*Jonathan E. Butner, Arwen A. Behrends, and Brian R. Baucom*

> The family. We were a strange little band of characters trudging through life sharing diseases and toothpaste, coveting one another's desserts, hiding shampoo, borrowing money, locking each other out of our rooms, inflicting pain and kissing to heal it in the same instant, loving, laughing, defending, and trying to figure out the common thread that bound us all together.
>
> *(Bombeck, 1987, p. 11)*

## Introduction

Social relationships are inherently complex, with that complexity arising from many sources and taking many forms. For example, individuals in relationships are inherently interdependent on many levels (e.g., behavior, emotions, cognition; Lansing & Berg, 2014). These interdependent relationships have led to a revolution in the study of dyads, with the conclusion that dyads should not merely be studied as a pair of individuals (Gottman, Murray, Swanson, Tyson, & Swanson, 2002). Their relationships are adaptive, changing through time, showing both stable and varying qualities. Recent work that considers the full range of these possibilities demonstrates the potential advantages of this perspective relative to traditional methods of analysis (e.g., Baucom et al., 2015). This suggests that the complexity of social relationships is difficult to depict from a reductionist point of view.

In this chapter, we advance a simple premise: social relationships are better understood through flexible statistical methods that are capable of modeling complex, interdependent processes that evolve and emerge over time rather than reducing their inherent complexity. We believe modeling with methods designed for complex, interdependent processes can actually describe social relationships in a more tractable fashion (Nowak, 2004; Nowak & Lewenstein, 1994). One class of modeling techniques that is especially well suited to this task is dynamical systems models (DSMs). Dynamical systems models are a family of time series techniques that aim to depict data through differential equations or difference equations. As a whole, DSMs are very flexible modeling techniques that can be used to capture patterns of change and, in this case, we will capitalize on the link between two or more variables over time to represent the social relationship context. In this chapter, we focus on the application of DSMs for modeling co-regulation in romantic relationships. We begin by defining the concept of co-regulation and describing how theoretical constructs in co-regulation can be conceptualized from a dynamical systems perspective. We then provide an example application of a DSM to modeling co-regulation in ambulatory heart rate in a married couple. We close with a discussion of important issues to consider when applying DSMs to modeling co-regulation and other complex forms of interdependence in social relationships.

## Co-Regulation: What It Is in Romantic Relationships

Co-regulation is a concept that is receiving rapidly growing attention in relationship science. Though it has been variously defined and operationalized (for a review, see Butler & Randall, 2013), the term "co-regulation" most commonly refers to a linkage between romantic partners' affective states that promotes affective homeostasis within each partner (e.g., Sbarra & Hazan, 2008). That is, co-regulation is the extent to which partners assist one another in maintaining affective states. This assistance may be active or passive, but is in direct contrast to the affective qualities one would observe if the partner were not in the romantic relationship. Healthy, well-functioning relationships where partners feel safe and are securely attached to one another are thought to promote co-regulation, and recent research provides initial empirical support for this supposition (e.g., Butner, Diamond, & Hicks, 2007; Helm, Sbarra, & Ferrer, 2012; Helm, Sbarra, & Ferrer, 2014). However, co-regulation can also be adverse, in that partners can assist one another in maintaining poor affective states.

   This definition suggests that there are several processes involved in co-regulation and that a comprehensive statistical model of co-regulation should be able to capture, describe, and distinguish each of these processes. First, this definition makes a distinction between homeostatic processes that occur within an individual partner and those that occur between partners. One way to illustrate this key idea is to consider the emotional reactions of two romantic partners during an argument. For example, suppose that Sam and Jordan disagree about whether or not to let their son go to a party. Both Sam and Jordan are upset by the argument, and their different responses to one another's emotional reactions illustrate the differences between intrapersonal homeostatic mechanisms and interpersonal homeostatic mechanisms. When Sam expresses frustration, Jordan is responsive to what Sam is saying, but Sam's frustration does not impact Jordan's distress above and beyond the distress that Jordan was already feeling. In contrast, Sam is very sensitive to Jordan's distress such that the higher Jordan's distress, the higher Sam's frustration in addition to the impact of the frustration that Sam was already feeling. In this example, Jordan's reactions are governed by intrapersonal homeostatic mechanisms while Sam's are governed by both intrapersonal and interpersonal (i.e., co-regulatory) mechanisms.

A second implication of this definition of co-regulation is that co-regulation occurs over time and can only be observed when there is temporal variability in both partners' affective states. This statement may seem obvious, but it raises subtle yet crucial conceptual issues that are difficult to translate from theory to statistical model. Because co-regulation is so strongly tied to the idea of homeostasis, variability cannot be measured with regard to any particular point. Rather, it should be measured with regard to a homeostatic set point, and many of the situations that provoke emotional responses in social relationships can also obscure homeostatic set points. For example, consider Figure 8.1, which plots Jordan and Sam's emotional responses during their argument about whether or not to let their son go to a party. Jordan's responses clearly vary about a single point, but Sam's responses vary about a parabola that initially increases, but ultimately decreases over time. While it would be possible to calculate both partners' variability about his/her mean affective state or affective state at the beginning of the argument, it is less clear that either approach would represent the same affective construct (i.e., variability about a homeostatic set point) for both partners.

## Conceptualizing Co-Regulation from a Dynamical Systems Perspective

Numerous strategies could be used in considering the multitude of options for translating these theoretical notions of what co-regulation is as a psychological phenomenon into a statistical model. Consistent with our premise that social relationships are better understood by examining the higher-order patterning,

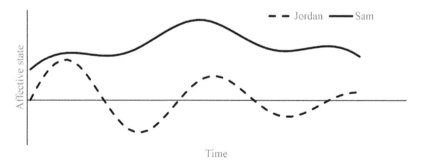

**FIGURE 8.1** Affective responses over time.

we propose that one valuable approach to this task is to consider the degree to which the theoretical assumptions about a psychological phenomenon, such as co-regulation, are consistent with the theoretical assumptions underlying the statistical models. This proposition is not meant to suggest that processes in social relationships cannot be accurately characterized using relatively simple statistical models. Much to the contrary, we recommend using the simplest possible model that is consistent with the theoretical underpinnings of the psychological phenomenon. In the remainder of this section, we illustrate how DSMs satisfy these criteria for modeling co-regulation.

DSMs are a class of modeling techniques that utilize differential equations or difference equations to characterize change processes over time. DSMs are based in dynamical systems theory, in that they inherently describe temporal patterns in ways consistent with how systems theory assumes temporal processes function. Dynamical systems theory is primarily concerned with understanding patterns of change over time, under the assumption that these temporal patterns are a byproduct of the interactions of many higher- and lower-order processes known as *emergence*. Due to this assumption, systems theory makes several important assumptions about the nature of change over time. First, dynamical system theory assumes that the characteristics of a system can be observed by measuring the behavior of the variables involved in the system. Applied to co-regulation, this idea implies that it is possible to understand a relational process, such as co-regulation, by observing the behavior of the individuals involved in the relationship.[1] This idea is commonly referred to as "emergence" in the dynamical systems literature, and suggests that the "how" is a much more difficult question to assess, if not impossible, and instead a researcher's focus should be on what emerges. Second, dynamical systems theory assumes that the ways a system changes over time are best understood in terms of patterns (what emerges), which means that variables tend to change over time in a predictable fashion or fashions (e.g., oscillating about a single point, escalating over time, etc.). Applied to co-regulation, this idea suggests that co-regulation can be described as partners' typical responses to each other's behavior (e.g., when Jordan is more distressed, what is Sam's most likely response, and vice versa?). Third, dynamical system theory assumes that some patterns of change over time are more likely to occur than others. Applied to co-regulation, this idea implies that even though partners may have typical ways of responding to one another, it is also possible, though less likely, for them to deviate from their typical response. Fourth, these patterns differ in their inherent stability, and many of the patterns are, in fact, defined by reactions to outside forces generating temporary divergences from the pattern. Applied to co-regulation, this idea implies that our description of a typical response is really the degree to which the typical response is able to be maintained despite constant forces that could lead to diverging from that response pattern.

Patterns that emerge under systems theory and that are applied to co-regulation include both how changes in one partner's affect are related to changes in the other partner's affect as well as the point about which those changes occur. The point about which changes occur is commonly called the *set point* in the dynamical systems literature. In dynamical systems theory, a set point that a system is drawn towards is called an *attractor* and a set point that a system is pushed away from is called a *repeller*. Attractors are analogous to the idea of a homeostatic set point—when the variables in a system move away from an attractor, they show a pattern of returning to that set point. This pattern of change over time is similar to the idea of homeostasis as representing a pattern of change where a person returns to a preferred affective state after being perturbed from that state. In contrast, repellers represent a set point that is unlikely to occur or that the system avoids. A system can have one or more attractors, one or more repellers, or some combination of the two. This quality of dynamical systems theory provides an elegant solution to the ambiguity of defining homeostatic set points—rather than defining them a priori, homeostatic set points (i.e., attractors) can be quantified by observing the likelihood of patterns of change over time. The advantage of this approach is that it allows for characterizing the system in terms of behavior as it unfolds over time, which is what is of primary interest in studying co-regulation.

## Modeling Social Relations

We illustrate how to construct a dynamical systems model of two romantic partners' data utilizing data from a single married couple where both the husband and wife wore ambulatory heart monitors. These data are from a larger study where couples completed seven days of ambulatory data collection after participating in a thorough laboratory assessment. This particular couple was in the clinically distressed range of relationship satisfaction, based on an average score of 12 between the spouses on the four-item version of the Couple Satisfaction Index (Funk & Rogge, 2007). We present results for a single day totaling 16 hours of heart rate data. Heart rate, measured in beats per minute (BPM), was continuously measured during all waking hours using an Actiheart biosensor (CamNTech); their data were recorded at 128 Hz sampling rate and aggregated to one-minute epochs prior to analysis. Heart rate values greater than 130 BPM were omitted from analyses as they were likely artifacts, resulting in a total of 973 minutes of data for the couple. Continuous GPS data were also recorded during the seven days of ambulatory data collection; these data were used to determine if the couple was together (within 250 feet of one another) or apart (greater than 250 feet apart from one another) for any given reading.

Here we chose to restrict our analysis to a single dyad on a single day to keep the example relatively simple. However, it is reasonable to analyze all couples on all days simultaneously with the procedure we outline. Under this circumstance, the assumption would be that individuals all function within the same dynamic system and that there is equivalency in the heart rate metrics across couples. Centering techniques akin to multilevel modeling can be applied to help differentiate some of these issues, but would complicate our example. Alternatively, analyzing a single couple and even on a single day has been promoted as a way to help seek ergodic solutions (Molenaar & Campbell, 2009). Ergodicity is a notion from physics that has been extrapolated to the social sciences as having the same model both within and between individuals. As is true of virtually all statistical approaches that can be used with nested data (i.e., data sets with repeated observations nested within higher-order groups; in the example in this chapter, repeated measurements of BPM are nested within individuals and individuals are nested within couples), results from dynamical systems models estimated on one group (i.e., one couple on one day) cannot be assumed to apply to all couples on all days. This idea is consistent with the systems theory concept of intrinsic dynamics—that the system for individuals (and in this case, across days) could be quite different (Vallacher & Nowak, 1997). A seminal example of intrinsic dynamics is seen in Molenaar's illustration of how the Big Five has a different factor structure within people in comparison to across people. The implication of intrinsic dynamics for beginning dynamic systems modelers is that ergodicity cannot be assumed to hold for results based on a case example and, if one wishes to make interpretations about ergodicity, the consistency of results within and between higher-order groups must be directly tested with approaches that decompose within- and between-group variance and covariance, such as multilevel modeling and multilevel structural equation modeling.

## Covariation

Probably the hardest part of computational modeling under a dynamical systems logic is knowing where to begin. Here we start with the singularly most common examination, that of same-time covariation. To illustrate covariation, Figure 8.2 is a scatterplot of the husband BPM (on the y-axis) and wife BPM (on the x-axis), with a loess smoother (a graphical line that is sensitive to data nonlinearities) and best fitting straight line overlaid. The best fitting straight line directly represents the covariation itself—the extent to which we observe highs and lows together (positive relationship), or when one is high, the other being low (a negative relationship). As can be seen in Figure 8.2, there is some correspondence of points. The correlation is 0.25 (95% confidence interval [CI]: $0.19 < 0.25 < 0.31$), indicating that when wives have higher heart rates, husbands also tend to have higher heart rates. Interestingly, this correlation is substantially higher when together (95% CI: $0.34 < 0.45 < 0.55$) than when apart (95% CI: $0.13 < 0.20 < 0.27$). This result would commonly be interpreted as some simple evidence of there being some sort of co-regulation.

The single biggest problem with a covariation approach to understanding systems is that covariation only tells us about the existence of value correspondence. That is, when wives have higher heart rates, do husbands also have higher heart rates (or lower, for a negative correlation)? There are many circumstances in

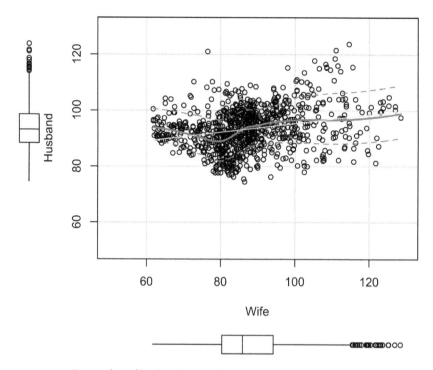

**FIGURE 8.2** Scatterplot of husband and wife BPM.

systems that can create correspondence of values and many that will not generate correspondence. Some might call aspects from both "co-regulation." As a hypothetical example, consider husbands and wives hovering around a homeostatic value alone coming just from intraindividual dynamics. Whenever the husband or wife encounters various environmental situations, his or her heart rate changes and, over time, moves back towards the homeostatic value—the attractor mentioned earlier. Notice that these events might only influence the husband or the wife, and thus the return pattern over time can actually be counter to covariation.

However, the homeostatic pattern itself is one of covariation, in that husbands and wives are converging towards the same value over time, and if they are sitting at that value, it will generate consistency of that single point. If there exist two such homeostatic values and the couple switches between these two stable locales, one can then imagine a very strong degree of covariation due to the relative placement of the homeostatic values to one another (e.g., do they fall on a nice diagonal?). It would be difficult to argue that such regime switching was co-regulation. We need a much more nuanced examination to know.

To better understand this issue of correspondence, Figure 8.3 is a two-dimensional kernel density plot of husband (on the y-axis) and wife (on the x-axis) BPM data. This plot is a graphical way to estimate the probability density function (PDF), where the frequency of data points are represented topographically (a hill is many points) and points that occur with greater probability are represented by taller hills. Notice that there are two or three peaks (the third is at lower husband BPM). That is, our covariation difference may well be this second scenario described above. Each peak could be a homeostatic point in the combination of husband and wife BPM, where regime switching between the two could be driving the existence of covariation.

## Dynamical Systems as Maps

Topography is the drawing of maps, and topology is the math behind them. It just so happens that topology is also the math behind dynamical systems (Butner, Gagnon, Geuss, Lessard, & Story, 2014). So there is a direct correspondence between the way maps function and our understanding of systems theory. In systems terms, the two-dimensional kernel density plot (Figure 8.3) also corresponds to something known as the *phase portrait*—a map of where data converges over time (Abraham and Shaw, 1992). The phase portrait is merely a scaled inverse of the PDF (a hill on the PDF is a valley on a phase portrait; Guastello, 2011). From our perspective, this map (the PDF or phase portrait) shows where BPM values

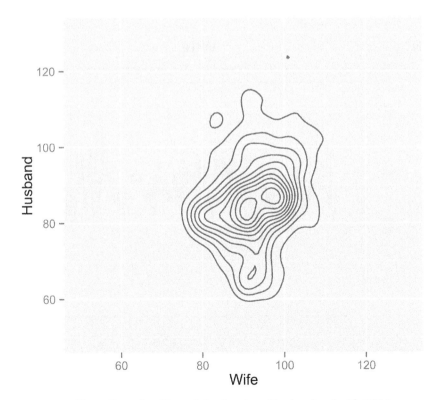

**FIGURE 8.3** Two-dimensional kernel density plot of husband and wife BPM.

are converging through time (i.e., the peaks). It allows us to start to understand what covariation is capitalizing upon.

However, dynamical systems are about the time evolution of processes, thus this also inherently highlights the ignorance of time in covariation. We can think of this as one extreme treatment of our data—where time is ignored. Figure 8.3 just shows us where data coalesces. The other extreme is where time is explicit. Common treatments of explicit time-based models are growth modeling and forms of time series analyses like ARIMA models, in all their various forms. Figure 8.4 shows a pair of time series plots for each heart rate—the graphical equivalent to an explicit time representation. To generate a systems understanding, we need to live between these two extremes. Time must be taken into account, but we will do so implicitly rather than explicitly. That is, we will need to link the evolution in Figure 8.4 with the map features in Figure 8.3.

It is helpful to consider the potential contributors to variation over time from a systems perspective, and there are three potential contributors to the values we observe (Riley & Turvey, 2002). In map terms, there are basins of attraction where all activity in a topographical region is related (e.g., combinations of BPM where husband and wife tend to reside as a function of constraints; e.g., stress at work and home, common coping methods). In the case of an attractor, these

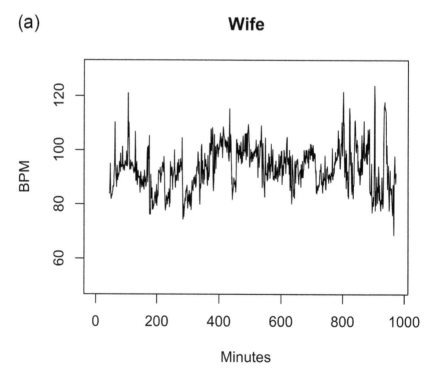

FIGURE 8.4 Time series plots of (a) wife BPM by time and (b) husband BPM by time.

(b)

# Husband

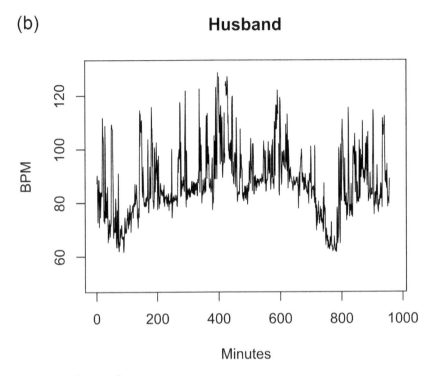

FIGURE 8.4 *(continued)*

tend to be regions that all function around a single set point. However, a basin of attraction expands beyond the logic of just an attractor. For example cycles are attractive looped trails (not unlike Gottman et. al.'s chain of negativity; Gottman et al., 2002), and more complicated trails are possible.

The second contributors to the values we observe, from a systems perspective, are perturbations. Modern systems theory uses mathematical techniques based on the recognition that our examination is only part of the system, that the system is open (Prigogine, 1977). The other parts of the system that are not being directly examined still contribute to the variation observed in values through time as constant changes to the values. Observing basins of attraction in the data (locations or trails) is thus despite perturbations. Perturbations can then be thought of as a stochastic element that helps define the stability of the attractive features—for example, how strong the attractor is where stronger attractors are able to resist larger perturbations.

The final contributor is measurement error, though this is much more limited in scope once perturbations are taken into account in comparison to notions of error in classical test theory. Specifically, error may just be a representation of measurement imprecision. For example, under classical test theory, the impact of the lighting in a room during a test would be measurement error on test performance.

From a systems perspective, the lighting is part of the system itself, and thus constitutes a perturbation instead. Techniques differ greatly on their ability to distinguish perturbations from error. For example, a growth model makes no distinction. However, systems-based techniques can be built to account for this difference if they are able to distinguish the stability of a pattern. If we assume perturbations always exist, then pattern stability inherently is in reaction to those perturbations. The technique we will use will include notions of stability by estimating perturbation resistance, but will not generate a specific perturbation term.

To begin to understand the role of time evolution, it helps to see how an observed time series translates into trails instead of the map itself; a pair of time series represent a series of vectors on the map. Figure 8.5 shows the logic. Specifically, we can imagine a time series of northness and a time series of eastness. The corresponding values represent a vector or series of vectors in northness/eastness space. In our circumstance, the time series for the husband and wife from Figure 8.4 correspond to a series of vectors in the husband/wife space, illustrated in Figure 8.5d. Given the density of the data, it is difficult to see a clear trail (we proportionally shortened the arrows to help distinguish all the vectors), and it is possible that this represents multiple trails rather than just one (e.g., the couple is switching between different trails).

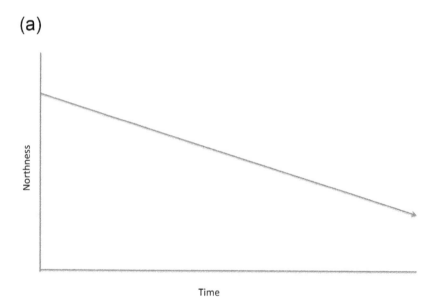

**(a)**

Northness

Time

**FIGURE 8.5**  Vector plot of husband and wife BPM.

(b)

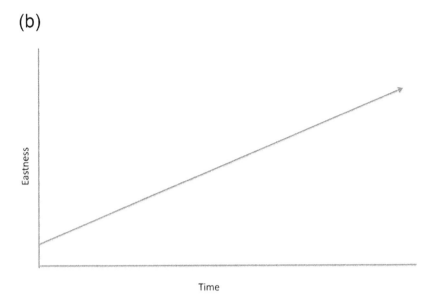

(C)

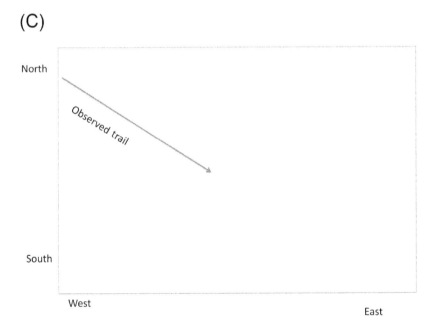

**FIGURE 8.5** *(continued)*

(d)

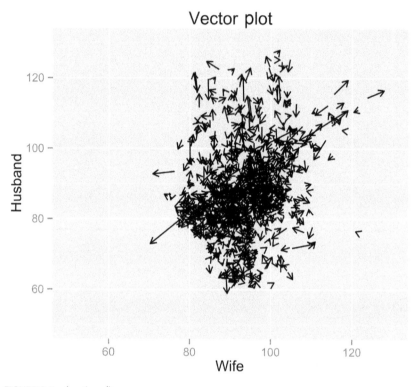

FIGURE 8.5 *(continued)*

## The Inferred Map

One common comment about dynamical systems is that it is a descriptive technique. So far, that is exactly what we have done—described the patterns of the data through time. However, computational modeling approaches are inferential ones. Within the context of our example, we want to generate the population-level equations that depict the changes of heart rate through time. We want to come to an understanding of the higher-order patterns within the data and how these patterns connect to the ideas of co-regulation. Graphically, this corresponds to generating an inferential version of Figure 8.5d. That is, we can extract an inferred map from the data by using equations that conform to the types of topographical features.

From an inferential viewpoint, there are four common stable topographical features we can observe from two first-order equations (more on this shortly) with the addition of some interesting combinations (Abraham & Shaw, 1992; Butner et al., 2014; Kugler & Turvey, 1987). This includes the two already depicted (attractor and repeller), but now in two-dimensional logic (husband

and wife simultaneously). An attractor is the shared homeostatic combination of BPMs the couple would congregate at in time. This is one possible description for the peaks we observe in the PDF (or a valley in the phase portrait, since the PDF and phase portraits are inverses of one another), with the steepness as an indication of how quickly one moves towards the homeostatic point, but also the stability of the homeostatic value as it is assumed to constantly be undergoing perturbations (Figure 8.6a).

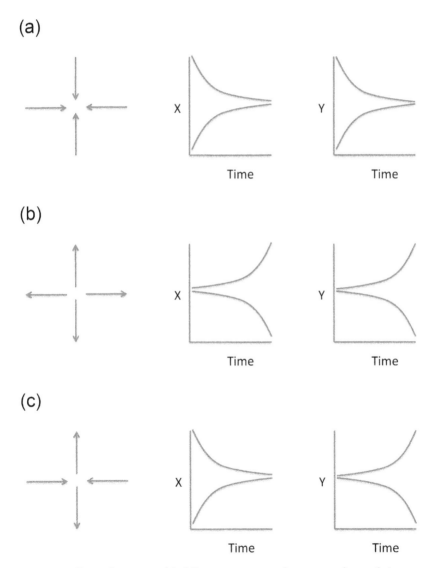

**FIGURE 8.6** Example topographical features represented as vector plots and time series.

(d)

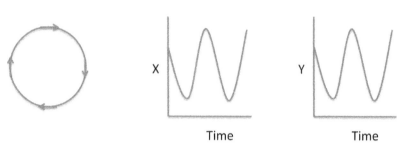

FIGURE 8.6   *(continued)*

A repeller is a case where there is a combination of heart rate values from which the couple moves away in time (Figure 8.6b). It is a hill in a phase portrait or the lack of data in a PDF, and thus would be represented by a lack of values at or around it. Repellers are actually a case of instability rather than stability, as they have a shared point where the couple can hypothetically sit. However, the moment there is a perturbation, the couple will move away from that point in time. The steepness of the repeller represents the speed at which one would move away.

A saddle is a repeller in one direction and an attractor in another. In topographical terms, it is a ridgeline with the combinatory point of BPMs being the location of the equivalent of the mountain pass (Figure 8.6c). Saddles often depict the separation of different basins of attraction, where being on one side of the saddle depicts a tendency to go to one attractive feature, while being on the other side depicts going to a different one.

The last common topographical feature is known in systems theory as the limit cycle (Figure 8.6d). It represents oscillations or, in map terminology, a looped trail. Limit cycles capture the angular motion around a combination of BPM values.

It is also possible to combine angular motion with the other various topographical features. For instance, one can have a cyclical attractor where there is a homeostatic value the couple moves towards in time, but in a cyclical manner. This angular motion is of particular interest for investigating social relations, as it represents the coupling influence between partners—the notion of coupling itself. Thus, cyclical properties suggest a push-pull relationship that emerges. This push-pull relationship is the idea of interpersonal co-regulation.

### Estimating the Map

A combination of several statistical techniques can be used to describe these push-pull relationships. First and foremost, it is necessary to quantify change over time. There are several methods for achieving this aim (e.g., McArdle, 2009); here we propose the use of a simple difference score that is calculated by subtracting the previous value of the time series from the current value of the time series. If this quantity is positive, the time series has gone up in absolute value, and conversely, if the quantity is negative, the time series has gone down in absolute value. Second, we want to describe the associations between change from one measurement point to the next (the difference score) and the absolute value of the previous time point. As with quantifying change, there are numerous methods for modeling this association (e.g., Butner, Berg, Baucom, & Wiebe, 2014); here we propose using Structural Equation Modeling (SEM), because SEM allows us to specify equations for both members of the couple simultaneously and in a straightforward fashion. Finally, we want to allow for the possibility that the system may be best described by one topographic feature or a set of topographic features (e.g., two attractors and a repeller). We propose that mixture modeling can be used to conduct an empirical test for the existence of qualitatively different features, as described by the equations for both members of the couple that are parameterized using SEM. Qualitatively different topographic features emerge as different latent classes in a mixture modeling approach. Below we provide a detailed discussion of how to accomplish each of these modeling steps.

All of the features described thus far require a pair of first-order coupled equations. By "first-order," we mean that the equations capture some notion of the first derivatives within them. In this particular case, we will build two first-order difference equations where the differences are the change in BPM over time for the husband and wife respectively. Husband and wife values of BPM are then allowed to predict both differences. There are some distinctions between building two first-order difference equations versus two first-order differential equations. Furthermore, many approaches focus on second-order equations instead (where the second derivatives are also included). These alternative cases are discussed near the end of the chapter.

Attractors, repellers, saddles, limit cycles, and combinations of these can all be directly extrapolated by a pair of first-order difference/differential equations.

$$(BPM_{Ht+\tau} - BPM_{Ht}) = b_0 + b_1 BPM_{Ht} + b_2 BPM_{Wt} + e_{Ht}$$

$$(BPM_{Wt+\tau} - BPM_{Wt}) = b_3 + b_4 BPM_{Ht} + b_5 BPM_{Wt} + e_{Wt} \qquad (8.1)$$

Tau ($\tau$) is some fixed distance in time. Let us focus on $b_1$ and $b_5$ respectively. They represent the homeostatic nature of the topographical feature in Husband/Wife space. To understand why this is the case, let us first consider a single equation and its graphical equivalent.

$$(BPM_{Ht+\tau} - BPM_{Ht}) = b_0 + b_1 BPM_{Ht} + e_{Ht} \qquad (8.2)$$

Equation 8.2 represents a one-predictor linear regression where change is the out-come and the value of what constitutes that change is the only predictor. Graphically, we can think about this as a scatterplot with change on the y-axis and BPM on the x-axis, as illustrated in Figure 8.7. Negative coefficients like the one in Figure 8.7 are indicative of attractors. To understand why this is, we must identify the set point and then ask what changes we would expect in BPM if one were currently above the set point (to the right of the set point on the x-axis) as opposed to below the set point (to the left of the set point on the x-axis). The set point is the point at which change would be zero, where our regression slope crosses the horizontal axis in Figure 8.7. When BPM is higher than the set point (to the right), the regression pre-dicts negative change—a decline in BPM. When BPM is lower than the set point (to the left), the regression predicts positive change—an increase in BPM. Since time is implicit here, we can start to imagine what would happen as our BPM is constantly being updated. We converge on the set point. This is the behavior of an attractor.

Returning to Equation 8.1, this kind of relationship is occurring for both husband and wife BPM simultaneously through $b_1$ and $b_5$. If both are negative, then both represent attraction towards a shared set point. Two positive coef-ficients indicate a repeller where, over time, one would diverge from the shared set point. One positive and one negative indicate a saddle.

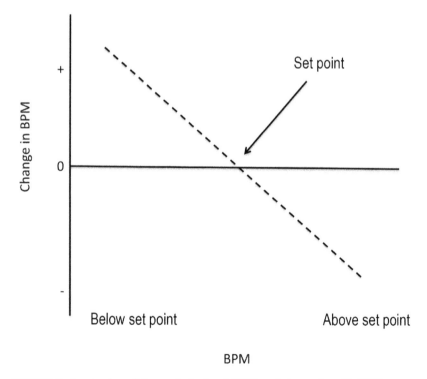

FIGURE 8.7 Scatterplot of change in husband BPM and change in wife BPM.

$B_2$ and $b_4$ are the coupling coefficients. They represent how previous values of the partner predict the other partner's future changes. Thus, they capture the swirling patterns within the couple. A true limit cycle will result in $b_1$ and $b_5$ being zero with substantial coupling relationships. That is, a true limit cycle never moves closer to the set point which would be captured by $b_1$ and $b_5$. It merely moves around it. Finding a limit cycle would be akin to saying that all detectable co-regulation was interpersonal.

Latent Change Score (LCS) Modeling (McArdle, 2009) is a method in SEM for estimating a pair of simultaneous difference score equations. LCS consists of a series of dummy latent variables with constrained parameters so that all that is estimated are the parameters that correspond to Equation 8.1. To see how this works, consider a regression where earlier values in BPM are allowed to predict future values of BPM with an intercept of zero and a regression slope of 1. The residual from this regression ends up being the difference of the future value (the observed value) minus the previous value (the predicted value). LCS constrains these parameters and then uses a latent variable to capture the residual, representing a discrete change. Additional relationships are then estimated, treating the discrete change latent variables as the outcomes from the earlier values, in our case capturing Equation 8.1. LCS models can be expanded to include some degree of data smoothing, and can be applied to panel data, but also used as a time series approach, as we will do so here.

To convert LCS into a time series approach, one must structure the data into what has been called a Toeplitz or time delay data structure. We illustrate this in Table 8.1 such that the data are converted into a current and lead value for husband and wife simultaneously ($\tau$ is fixed to 1 here). To smooth the data, one need merely create additional lead and lag variables using the same value of $\tau$ and extend the model equating like parameters over time.

The equations in Equation 8.1 are only capable of capturing a single topographical feature. However, the PDF implies that there could be several topographical features in the data, different locations of data density. Equation 8.1 is known as a linear dynamic model, in that the predictors depict a linear association with change (the outcomes). To capture more than one topographical feature or changing topographical features, one must instead use nonlinear equation forms. There are several ways to do this, including polynomials and interactions. Here we utilize mixture modeling.

**TABLE 8.1** Toeplitz data structure for husband and wife BPM.

| Husband at T | Husband at T+1 | Wife at T | Wife at T+1 |
|---|---|---|---|
| $BPM_{H1}$ | $BPM_{H2}$ | $BPM_{W1}$ | $BPM_{W2}$ |
| $BPM_{H2}$ | $BPM_{H3}$ | $BPM_{W2}$ | $BPM_{W3}$ |
| $BPM_{H3}$ | $BPM_{H4}$ | $BPM_{W3}$ | $BPM_{W4}$ |
| $BPM_{H4}$ | $BPM_{H5}$ | $BPM_{W4}$ | $BPM_{W5}$ |

Mixture modeling is an analytic procedure where the PDF is estimated as the cumulative function of a series of equations, rather than just one. That is, we will estimate a series of equations, where the set of equations as a whole, weighted by their commonality (i.e., the degree of consistency across the equations), reproduce the entire PDF. Bauer (2007) criticized mixture modeling as only really being able to reconstruct the PDF, and therefore being based on flawed assumptions for common statistical goals. Given the relationship between the PDF, the phase portrait, and the change equations we are utilizing, this criticism is a strength here, in that the approach specifically focuses on the topographical features of the data.

Mixture modeling can be used as an exploratory or confirmatory technique, and has been incorporated into current versions of Mplus (Lanza, Flaherty, & Collins, 2003). Fit indices, for example, can be used to determine the number of latent classes (or groups of data vectors described by different equations, in our case). Simulation work has shown that the Bayesian Information Criterion (BIC) tends to minimize at the proper number of classes (Nylund, Asparouhov, & Muthén, 2007). Furthermore, the Vuong Lo Mendell Rubin Likelihood ratio (VLMR), Lo Mendell Rubin adjusted Likelihood ratio (aVLMR—better in small samples), and the bootstrapped Likelihood ratio (BLRT) all test to see if the current number of classes adds something above and beyond having one less class (Henson, Reise, & Kim, 2007). Thus one can determine the number of classes by iteratively increasing the number of classes until no gain in prediction has been identified and settling on one less class (in the case of the fit index approach).

Metaphorically, mixture modeling can be thought of as both a categorical latent variable and a multiple group analysis where assignment to group is unknown. Thus, anything that can be allowed to differ across groups or in relation to a latent construct in SEM can be used to distinguish the different classes. In this case, we only allow parameters that would distinguish different types of topographical features that differ across classes (i.e., different strengths of those features and different locations of the features on the map). Figure 8.8 shows a complete path diagram of the model, with all the parameters allowed to vary across classes in black. Code for this procedure can be found in the appendix to this chapter.

## Results

The combination of fit indices all indicated that three classes was an improvement over two classes (VLMR = 48.499, $p$ = .02; aVLMR=172.588, $p$ = .02), but four classes did not improve data description over three classes (VLMR = 26.947, $p$ = .11; aVLMR = 103.898, $p$ = .11). We therefore report the three-class solution. Figures 8.9a, 8.9b, and 8.9c show three inferred vector plots generated in the Apple Inc. program *Grapher*.

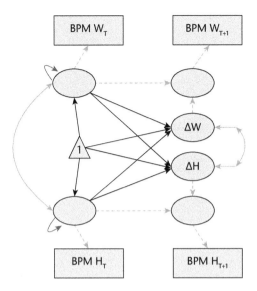

**FIGURE 8.8** Path model diagram of the bivariate LCS model of husband and wife BPM. Dashed arrows indicate that a parameter is fixed to 1, and black arrows indicate that a parameter was allowed to differ across groups.

(a)

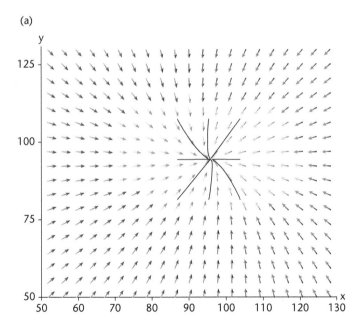

**FIGURE 8.9** Separate vector plots of the three class solution. Heat map scaling is used to represent the rate of change. Darker shading (e.g., black) indicate a faster rate of change, while lighter shading (e.g., grey) indicate a slower rate of change.

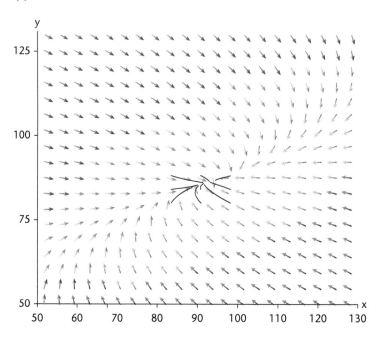

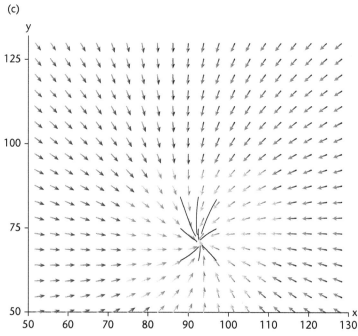

**FIGURE 8.9** *(continued)*

In addition, each figure includes trajectories inferred by the equations. Since each class estimates a unique mean and standard deviation (variance) for husband and wife BPM, we generated predicted trajectories extrapolating from simple slopes logic from regression: one trajectory for each combination of means and standard deviations above and below the means in BPM. We then used the Runge-Kutta fourth-order algorithm for estimating the expected values several steps into the future (all done within *Grapher*). This approach is particularly useful in that it is able to also identify issues of nonstationarity. For example, if we observe an attractor, what should normally occur under this procedure is that we see the various starting points all converging on the attractor inside the cloud of starting values. Under nonstationarity, the coefficients can indicate an attractor, but when following this graphing procedure, the points will converge towards a set point that is outside of the cloud of start values—essentially a series of growth patterns. Figure 8.10 shows all three sets of inferred trajectories. Notice that we have rebuilt the phase portrait, now with inferred trails.

Table 8.2 shows the table of coefficients (and 95% confidence intervals) for the three different classes. Each of three topographical features are quite different in terms of the coregulatory dynamics. The first feature accounts for 46% of vectors. It is an attractor in that both of the coefficients of BPM predicting its own changes were negative with 95% confidence intervals, excluding zero.

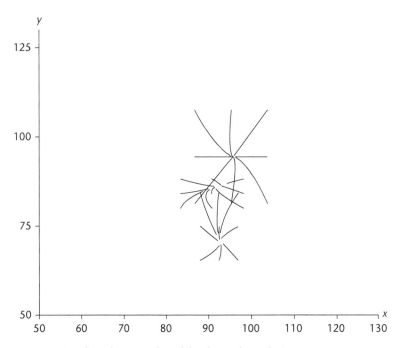

**FIGURE 8.10**  Combined vector plot of the three–class solution.

Also notable, though, is that the coupling/crossover influences included zero within the confidence intervals, suggesting that while the couple tended to converge on a shared combination of heart rates, it was a pattern of intraindividual regulation rather than interindividual. A better description was one of an emergent dynamic of elevated heart rate for both individuals, such that both husband and wife maintained their own elevated level.

The second topographical feature accounted for 35% of vectors. It represents a lower combination of heart rates for the husband and wife, homeostatically. It also includes non-zero coupling, in that the husband's heart rate predicts positive changes in the wife's heart rate. This coupling relationship is consistent with an interindividual relationship of co-regulation. Previous values of the husband predict the changes we observe in the wife, and thus she seems sensitive to both her own intraindividual pattern and the husband's pattern. Notice in Figure 8.10 that this coupling relationship is what generates the swirling pattern in the topographical representation.

The third topographical feature accounted for 18% of vectors. Most interesting is that only the wife's own intraindividual effect excluded zero from the confidence interval. The pattern of results suggested an attractor. But inferentially, this is more a description of dysregulation where there did not tend to be homeostatic responses, just a tendency for lower heart rates for the husband, but not the wife.

We assessed the extent to which being together or apart was able to predict class assignment. A dummy code was added to the mixture model to predict class membership. However, adding this new variable can result in changing

**TABLE 8.2** Parameter estimates and 95% CI for the three-class solution.

| Class | 1: High husband and wife BPM | 2: Mid heart rates | 3: Low husband BPM |
|---|---|---|---|
| Husband intercept | $20.78 < 35.26^* < 49.74$ | $5.48 < 14.48^* < 23.48$ | $-26.42 < 9.19 < 44.81$ |
| Husband own | $-0.48 < -0.38^* < -0.28$ | $-0.33 < -0.20^* < -0.08$ | $-0.37 < -0.17 < 0.03$ |
| Husband < wife | $-0.12 < 0.007 < 0.14$ | $-0.02 < 0.03 < 0.08$ | $-0.25 < 0.03 < 0.32$ |
| Wife intercept | $23.54 < 33.01^* < 42.48$ | $-12.79 < -0.07 < 12.64$ | $8.15 < 21.70^* < 35.25$ |
| Wife own | $-0.39 < -0.30^* < -0.21$ | $-0.27 < -0.18^* < -0.10$ | $-0.34 < -0.21^* < -0.08$ |
| Wife < husband | $-0.09 < -0.04 < 0.00$ | $0.021 < 0.20^* < 0.37$ | $-0.11 < -0.03 < 0.06$ |

Note: $^* p < 0.05$.

the observed results for the three topographical features. To ensure we were predicting the three original classes, we included the posterior probabilities of class assignment for each data point as training data in the new model that then included the dummy code as a predictor of class assignment. This method ensured replication of the original results while allowing for proper assessment of the togetherness effect.

Togetherness only differentiated the third topographical feature from the other two (1 from 2, $Z = 1.566$, $p = .117$; 1 from 3, $Z = 2.655$, $p = .008$; 2 from 3, $Z = 3.334$, $p = .001$), in that being together decreased the likelihood of being in the dysregulatory topographical feature. In essence, intrapersonal dysregulation and interpersonal disconnection only occurred for the couple when they were apart. When they were together, both the high-high attractor and the mid-mid spiral attractor existed, possibly in a multistable arrangement where the couple could switch between the two. Note that the couple were apart much more frequently than being together, and thus all three states could be observed sometimes when they were apart.

## Discussion

What does all this mean? Within a single couple in a single day, we see the full range of co-regulatory patterns. When the spouses were together, their heart rates tended to display one of two patterns. In this first pattern, change in each spouse's heart rate was governed by his or her own previous heart rate; this pattern is consistent with intrapersonal regulation. In the second pattern, change in each spouse's heart rate was governed by his or her own previous heart rate, and change in wife's heart rate was also significantly associated with husband's previous heart rate. This pattern is consistent with both intrapersonal regulation (both spouses) and wife-to-husband co-regulation. Finally, when spouses were apart, they were more likely to display a third pattern where change in wife's heart rate were associated with her own previous heart rate (intrapersonal regulation) and change in husband's heart rate was not significantly associated with his own (dysregulation) or wife's previous heart rate (disconnection).

While these findings must be interpreted with caution given that they are exploratory and based on one day of heart rate data for one couple, several aspects of the findings are consistent with existing research and substantive theory. First, the differences in set points across the three patterns are consistent with findings that spouses in distressed relationships show elevations in heart rate when interacting with one another relative to when apart (e.g., Denton, Burleson, Hobbs, Von Stein, & Rodriguez, 2001; Levenson & Gottman, 1985; Nealey-Moore, Smith, Uchino, Hawkins, & Olson-Cerny, 2007; Smith et al., 2009). More specifically, both spouses' set point in the third class, which was more likely to occur when spouses were separate, was lower than their set points in the other two classes. To the best of our knowledge, these findings are the first evidence of this effect in daily life. Second, the variability in within- and cross-partner associations between the two spouses and across the three classes is consistent with a small but growing body of work demonstrating that intrapersonal and co-regulatory patterns change depending on circumstance (e.g., Helm et al., 2012; Helm et al., 2014). Lastly, the nature of the co-regulatory effect in the second pattern is consistent with clinical theory. The positive sign of the association between husband's previous heart rate and wife's change in heart rate combined with the negative sign of the association between wife's previous heart rate and wife's change in heart rate indicates a compensatory influence of the two spouses' previous heart rates on wife's change in heart rate. More specifically, wife's heart rate returns to her set point more slowly to the extent that husband's heart rate is further away from his own set point. Similar findings emerged in work examining treatment-seeking, distressed spouses' vocally encoded emotional arousal during relationship conflict. Prior to receiving couple therapy, to the extent that husbands were more aroused, wives returned to their set points more slowly. However, after receiving couple therapy, wives' rates of return to their set points was unrelated to husbands' levels of arousal (Baucom & Atkins, 2012). These findings are all consistent with numerous theoretical models of romantic relationships, which posit that relationship distress tends to co-occur with increased difficulty with emotion regulation (for a review, see Baucom et al., 2015).

## Issues to Consider within a Dynamical Systems Approach

We set out to illustrate an approach that embraced the complexity of co-regulation while also aiming for as simple a description as we thought necessary for the phenomena. This required several considerations along the way. Some of these decisions may be different for other co-regulatory phenomena. We therefore explicitly address these considerations in the following section.

### Linear and Nonlinear Equations

In the broader literature of DSM, the distinction between linear and nonlinear dynamics is paramount. One aspect of the distinction that warrants careful examination is that linear dynamic models are capable of describing nonlinear patterns through time (Butner et al., 2014; Boker & Laurenceau, 2006). So we specifically stipulate that a nonlinear dynamic model includes nonlinear terms such as polynomials and interactions on the predictor side of the equation, or some approach like the mixture modeling one presented here, which uses multiple linear terms to reconstruct the nonlinear. The addition of these terms allows the equation to capture multiple set points. This addition also allows for differences in change rates across individuals—something that is not feasible in linear models.

Linear dynamic models are able to capture just one set point, and assume that the rate of change is constant. The benefit of using linear models is that they can be easier to test and interpret. However, it is probably safe to assume that most systems, including co-regulatory systems, are not linear. These models, for example, are not sensitive to initial conditions (where a particular individual starts out), and require that every person have the same set point. Thus, they lack the descriptive and predictive power of nonlinear models.

There are multiple ways to create nonlinear models (Butner et al., 2014). Our use of mixture modeling did exactly that by capitalizing on the notion that even in nonlinear models, they are locally linear. That is, near the set points, system dynamics can be captured by a linear dynamic model. The mixture modeling approach then allowed for multiple linear dynamic models that then combine together to reconstruct the nonlinear form. This approach has the added benefit of the ease of interpretation from linear dynamic models while also allowing for the additional descriptive precision and flexibility of nonlinear models.

Another method of using nonlinear terms is to add polynomials and/or other interactions to the predictor side of the equations. This approach creates nonlinear dynamic models that are capable of capturing multiple topographical features (as stated above). The number of features that are captured in these models is a function of the polynomial form included in the model. For example, a squared predictor is capable of capturing two set points. A cubic predictor is capable of capturing one to three set points. A quadratic predictor is capable of capturing four set points.

Importantly, nonlinear models allow for multistability (the ability to have multiple change patterns), differences in topographical feature stability (the likelihood of being in one topographical features versus another one), and the ability to model control parameters (variables that alter the topographical features). Importantly, one of the losses from using this mixture modeling approach is in our ability to distinguish when a system is multistable as opposed to being subject to different dynamics under different levels of a control parameter. This issue is discussed in more detail later in this chapter.

## Orders of Equations

As mentioned earlier, DSMs can be constructed with either first- or second-order equations. Our example case utilized two first-order coupled difference equations. A first-order difference equation models a form of velocity of a variable (the change in position from one time point to the next; in this case, a difference in consecutive values). In the example case, the regression equation outcome was husband and wife's change in heart rate (velocity). First-order equations can typically only capture attractors, repellers, and saddles. Due to the coupling link in Equation 8.1 ($b_2$ and $b_4$), the equation can also capture swirling patterns in the state space (such as a spiral attractor or repeller).

Second-order equations model acceleration, or the change in velocity. While a pair of first-order models is capable of generating oscillations through limit cycles (a function of the coupling relationships; the swirling pattern), second-order equations assume oscillations exist. Coupling can still exist among two second-order equations, but the coupling is about how two oscillatory patterns push and pull one another rather than two values.

Consider the hypothetical couple Sam and Jordan from the beginning of the chapter. It is possible that once a particular physiological threshold is reached, Sam's distress level increases much more rapidly than it was increasing before. Similarly, the rate of change in Sam's distress level could suddenly decrease once a particular threshold is reached. Each of these changes in velocities could be a function of intrapersonal dynamics. That is, Sam fluctuates irrespective of Jordan. Jordan's influence then may be in terms of where in the cycle Sam currently exists, rather than whether Sam is currently higher or lower at a particular moment.

The decision of whether to use first- or second-order equations should be guided by theory. Under an expectation of oscillations, the question is whether you expect the interaction between Sam and Jordan to generate the oscillations, or if Sam and Jordan would oscillate anyway and their relationship is reflected in the linkages between the oscillations. In the first case, first-order modeling is most appropriate because it constructs the oscillations as a function of their interactions. In the second, each is expected to oscillate even if they never influence one another, and second-order models are therefore most appropriate.

### Time

Time is implicit within dynamical systems modeling (Butner et al., 2014). The focus in DSM is not as much on an individual's linear movement from point a to point b, but rather the dynamics of how the system as a whole evolves over time. What DSM seeks to identify are the shifting patterns and points of transition within a system. In other words, knowing where an individual would end up if they were placed on a random location on a topographical map. Rather than using time as a predictor of change, DSMs use time to describe the change.

When utilizing DSMs, it is important to understand the difference between discrete and continuous conceptualizations of time. A discrete conceptualization requires that time be divisible, but really only in the division we observe. In this sense, it is possible to break up time into meaningful individual segments while allowing for the possibility that other temporal segments might generate different dynamics. This is the approach used in our example analyses. Under the continuous conceptualization of time, any segment is plausible. That is, the timing of the measurements themselves is essentially arbitrary, and can be meaningfully thought of as representing a temporal sequence where the segments between measurements are infinitely small (the definition of a derivative is a difference in the observed variable when the segment of time elapsed, in this case, approaches zero). This distinction is important to understand in order to avoid confusion regarding measurement periods and the actual unfolding of the phenomenon.

Issues related to time also crop up at several other points while constructing a DSM. In the earlier stages, it is critical to identify the time scale at which the phenomenon of interest is operating. This identification will inform your measurement period. If a shorter time scale than the actual phenomenon is measured, the local dynamics are likely to be overemphasized and the larger scaled patterning could be difficult to observe. For example, if a particular variable repeats a particular pattern every five days and measurement is only collected for five days, then all that could be observed is a stable value. It would be difficult to see that it actually is repeating over time. In this case, the local dynamics are obscuring the larger, emergent dynamics. When a phenomenon's time scale is unknown, it is preferable to oversample than to undersample. This dense scale of measurement is unlikely to affect our results, and it would still be possible to observe the larger-scale dynamics.

This logic can be extended to the co-regulation models. If measurement only occurs while couples are together, the coupling link may be over- or underemphasized. It is necessary to identify where an individual's homeostatic set point is located when together and apart from their partner in order to properly observe the coupling phenomenon.

Time is also important when constructing leads and lags (Butner et al., 2014). This process is also referred to as creating a *time delayed embedding space* (Boker & Laurenceau, 2006). The smallest plausible lag should be selected, because longer lags could obscure shorter-term dynamics. The example case used a lag of 1, which is typically used in DSMs. Longer lag values can be problematic with missing data, as each missing data point will generate several additional missing points. However, longer lags can be beneficial, in that two consecutive measures can be highly correlated (autocorrelated) because not enough time has passed to observe change. This form of autocorrelation can mask the system dynamics and tends to linearize system models overall. Thus, we want a small lag, but the smallest plausible one where change will be observed, rather than just the smallest.

## Moderation and Multistability

Under DSMs, control parameters can be conceptualized as moderators (Butner et al., 2014; Thelen & Smith, 2008). Control parameters are variables that change the existing topology. In the example case, the together/apart dummy code was a control parameter. This is simply a variable that moves individuals through a phase transition (changing from one set point to another). Without this variable, it would not be possible to determine when the trajectories were more strongly associated with each of the three attractors.

Consider the three attractors found in our example couple. The presence of the high-high attractor and mid-mid spiral attractor indicate the possibility that multistability is present. In this scenario, individuals can switch between these two features. However, when the couple were together, we were more likely to observe the third attractor (and decrease the probability of being in the dsyregulatory feature).

It is important to note that control parameters are not considered to be causal variables (Thelen & Smith, 2008). Instead, they are the points of transition from one particular pattern to another. The goal of identifying a control parameter is to explain how, when, and why people move between different states (such as elevated heart rate). Essentially, you are looking for variables that predict the system's attractors. In our analysis, we would not claim that the couple being together prevented the individuals from dysregulation, but rather this physical proximity increases the likelihood of transitioning to another stable pattern (the third attractor).

In co-regulation, DSMs also have to allow for differences in homeostatic set points and strength of the coupling link. Each individual is a separate system. Co-regulation arises from these systems being coupled together in some way. However, this coupling link may not affect each partner the same way. It may exert more force on one partner than the other. Recall the hypothetical couple, Sam and Jordan. In their argument, Sam is more affected by Jordan's distress than Jordan is affected by Sam's distress. Thus the link between the two systems is stronger for Sam than for Jordan.

## Conclusion

The need for ways to approach complexity that both embrace the complexity but also keep the description relatively simple is paramount. As co-regulation continues to gain growing attention and social scientists increase their ability to collect rich time-dependent data, approaches like the one described here are going to be in demand. DSM models, under thoughtful application, can do just that. And when that careful consideration allows for nonlinear systems approaches that clearly map onto theory, they elevate the science. Ultimately, they provide a step towards a new stage of social sciences.

## Appendix

```
TITLE: Mixture Model of Bivariate Latent Change BPM

DATA:

    ! enter the name of the data set
    FILE = couple6 day2.csv;
```

```
VARIABLE:

   ! enter the names of the variables in the data set
   NAMES = bpm_w1 bpm_w2 bpm_h1 bpm_h2 together;
   usevariables = bpm_w1 bpm_w2 bpm_h1 bpm_h2;
   missing is all.;
   classes = node(3);
!Auxiliary with r3step specifies to use training data without
togetherness
!   auxiliary = together(R3STEP);
!   idvariable is time;

Analysis:

Type is Mixture;
!Random start values to help ensure solution is not just
local maxima
starts = 2500 500;
processors=4;

!optseed overrides random starts to only run the solution
with this seed
   !value, recommend identify ideal seed value and then add
in the tech11
   !and tech14 commands
!optseed = 907342;!for one node;
!optseed = 469158;!for two nodes;
optseed = 496016;!for three nodes;
!optseed = 346843;!for four nodes;

MODEL:

%Overall%
!Construct a latent representation of each variable
Lbpm_w2 by bpm_w2@1;
Lbpm_w1 by bpm_w1@1;
Lbpm_h2 by bpm_h2@1;
Lbpm_h1 by bpm_h1@1;

!Fix intercepts and variances of observed variables to zero
!Note that when building with more leads and lags & smooth-
ing, can estimate
   !variances as error variances (usually equated)
bpm_w1@0 bpm_h1@0 bpm_w2@0 bpm_h2@0;
[bpm_w1@0 bpm_h1@0 bpm_w2@0 bpm_h2@0];
```

```
!Perfect regression of Future = Past at a slope of 1 and
intercept of zero
Lbpm_w2 on Lbpm_w1@1;
Lbpm_h2 on Lbpm_h1@1;
Dbpm_w by Lbpm_w2@1;
Dbpm_h by Lbpm_h2@1;
lbpm_w2@0 lbpm_h2@0;
[lbpm_w2@0 lbpm_h2@0];

!Build our change variables grabbing what remains
Dbpm_w on lbpm_h1 lbpm_w1;
Dbpm_h on lbpm_h1 lbpm_w1;

Dbpm_w Dbpm_h;
[Dbpm_w Dbpm_h];
lbpm_w1 lbpm_h1;
[lbpm_w1 lbpm_h1];

%Node#1%
!Regression slopes
Dbpm_w on lbpm_h1 lbpm_w1;
Dbpm_h on lbpm_h1 lbpm_w1;

!Variances and means of BPM by class
Dbpm_w Dbpm_h;
[Dbpm_w Dbpm_h];
lbpm_w1 lbpm_h1;
[lbpm_w1 lbpm_h1];

%Node#2%
Dbpm_w on lbpm_h1 lbpm_w1;
Dbpm_h on lbpm_h1 lbpm_w1;

Dbpm_w Dbpm_h;
[Dbpm_w Dbpm_h];
lbpm_w1 lbpm_h1;
[lbpm_w1 lbpm_h1];

%Node#3%
Dbpm_w on lbpm_h1 lbpm_w1;
Dbpm_h on lbpm_h1 lbpm_w1;

Dbpm_w Dbpm_h;
[Dbpm_w Dbpm_h];
```

```
lbpm_w1 lbpm_h1;
[lbpm_w1 lbpm_h1];

!%Node#4%
!Dbpm_w on lbpm_h1 lbpm_w1;
!Dbpm_h on lbpm_h1 lbpm_w1;

!Dbpm_w Dbpm_h;
![Dbpm_w Dbpm_h];
!lbpm_w1 lbpm_h1;
![lbpm_w1 lbpm_h1];

!tech11 for the vlmr and tech14 for the BLRT, both are com-
puter intensive and
    !recommend identifying solution first
!Output:cinterval tech11; !tech14;

!Can output the posterior probabilities for each data vec-
tor for further
    !examination

!Savedata:
!save=Cprob;
!file = 'cprobc5d4.txt';
```

## Note

1 Dynamical systems theory provides ways in which a couple-level phenomenon such as co-regulation could be examined from a single individual. This is a direct extrapolation of Takens' (1981) theorem into a measurement perspective.

## References

Abraham, R. H., & Shaw, C. D. (1992). *Dynamics: The geometry of behavior*. Boston, MA: Addison-Wesley.

Baucom, B. R., & Atkins, D. C. (2012). Polarization in marriage. In M. Fine and F. Fincham (Eds.), *Families theories: A content-based approach* (pp. 145–166). New York: Routledge.

Baucom, B. R., Dickenson, J. A., Atkins, D. C., Baucom, D. H., Fischer, M.S., Weusthoff, S., Hahlweg, K., & Zimmermann, T. (2015). The interpersonal process model of demand/withdraw behavior. *Journal of Family Psychology*, *29*, 80–90.

Baucom, B. R., Sheng, E., Christensen, A., Georgiou, P. G., Narayanan, S. S., & Atkins, D. C. (2015). Behaviorally-based couple therapies reduce emotional arousal during couple conflict. *Behaviour Research and Therapy*, *72*, 49–55.

Bauer, D. J. (2007). Observations on the use of growth mixture models in psychological research. *Multivariate Behavioral Research*, *42*, 757–786.

Boker, S. M., & Laurenceau, J. P. (2006). Dynamical systems modeling: An application to the regulation of intimacy and disclosure in marriage. In T. A. Walls & J. L. Schafer (Eds.), *Models for intensive longitudinal data* (pp. 195–218). New York: Oxford University Press.

Bombeck, E. (1987). *Family: The ties that bind . . . and gag.* New York: Random House.

Butler, E. A., & Randall, A. K. (2013). Emotional coregulation in close relationships. *Emotion Review, 5,* 202–210.

Butner, J. E., Berg, C. A., Baucom, B. R., & Wiebe, D. J. (2014). Modeling coordination in multiple simultaneous latent difference scores. *Multivariate Behavioral Research, 49*(6), 554–570.

Butner, J., Diamond, L., & Hicks, A. (2007). Attachment style and two forms of emotion co-regulation between romantic partners. *Personal Relationships, 14,* 431–455.

Butner, J., Gagnon, K. T., Geuss, M. N., Lessard, D. A., & Story, T. N. (2014). Using topology to generate and test theories of change. *Psychological Methods, 20,* 1–25.

Denton, W. H., Burleson, B. R., Hobbs, B. V., Von Stein, M., & Rodriguez, C. P. (2001). Cardiovascular reactivity and initiate/avoid patterns of marital communication: A test of Gottman's psychophysiologic model of marital interaction. *Journal of Behavioral Medicine, 24,* 401–421.

Funk, J. L., & Rogge, R. D. (2007). Testing the ruler with item response theory: Increasing precision of measurement for relationship satisfaction with the Couples Satisfaction Index. *Journal of Family Psychology, 21,* 572.

Gottman, J. M., Murray, J. D., Swanson, C. C., Tyson, R., & Swanson, K. R. (2002). *The mathematics of marriage.* Cambridge, MA: MIT Press.

Guastello, S. J. (2011). Discontinuities: SETAR and catastrophe models with polynomial regression. In S. J. Guastello & R. A. M. Gregson (Eds.), *Nonlinear dynamical systems analysis for the behavioral sciences using real data* (pp. 251–280). Boca Raton, FL: CRC Press.

Helm, J. L., Sbarra, D., & Ferrer, E. (2012). Assessing cross-partner associations in physiological responses via coupled oscillator models. *Emotion, 12,* 748.

Helm, J. L., Sbarra, D. A., & Ferrer, E. (2014). Coregulation of respiratory sinus arrhythmia in adult romantic partners. *Emotion, 14,* 522.

Henson, J. M, Reise, S. P., & Kim, K. H. (2007). Detecting mixtures from structural model differences using latent variable mixture modeling: A comparison of relative model fit statistics. *Structural Equation Modeling, 14,* 202–226.

Kugler, P. N., & Turvey, M. T. (1987). *Information, natural law and the self-assembly of rhythmic movement: Theoretical and experimental investigations.* Hillsdale, NJ: Lawrence Erlbaum.

Lansing, A. H., & Berg, C. A. (2014). Topical review: Adolescent self-regulation as a foundation for chronic illness self-management. *Journal of Pediatric Psychology, 39*(10): 1091–1096.

Lanza, S. T., Flaherty, B. P., & Collins, L. M. (2003). Latent class and latent transition analysis. In J. Schinka, W. Velicer, & I. Weiner (Eds.), *Handbook of Psychology* (Vol. 2, pp. 319–325). Hoboken, NJ: John Wiley & Sons.

Levenson, R. W., & Gottman, J. M. (1985). Physiological and affective predictors of change in relationship satisfaction. *Journal of Personality and Social Psychology, 49,* 85.

McArdle, J. J. (2009). Latent variable modeling of longitudinal data. *Annual Review of Psychology, 60,* 577–605.

Molenaar, P. C., & Campbell, C. G. (2009). The new person-specific paradigm in psychology. *Current Directions in Psychological Science*, *18*(2), 112–117.

Nealey-Moore, J. B., Smith, T. W., Uchino, B. N., Hawkins, M. W., & Olson-Cerny, C. (2007). Cardiovascular reactivity during positive and negative marital interactions. *Journal of Behavioral Medicine*, *30*, 505–519. doi:10.1007/s10865-007-9124-5

Nowak, A. (2004). Dynamical minimalism: Why less is more in psychology. *Personality and Social Psychology Review*, *8*(2), 183–192.

Nowak, A., & Lewenstein, M. (1994). *Dynamical systems: A tool for social psychology?* In R. R. Vallacher & A. Nowak, (Eds.), *Dynamical systems in social psychology*. San Diego, CA: Academic Press.

Nylund, K. L., Asparouhov, T., & Muthén, B. O. (2007). Deciding on the number of classes in latent class analysis and growth mixture modeling: A Monte Carlo simulation study. *Structural Equation Modeling*, *14*(4), 535–569.

Prigogine, I. N. G. (1977). *Self-organization in nonequilibrium systems*. Hoboken, NJ: John Wiley & Sons.

Riley, M. A., & Turvey, M. T. (2002). Variability and determinism in motor behavior. *Journal of Motor Behavior*, *34*, 99–125.

Sbarra, D. A., & Hazan, C. (2008). Coregulation, dysregulation, self-regulation: An integrative analysis and empirical agenda for understanding adult attachment, separation, loss, and recovery. *Personality and Social Psychology Review*, *12*, 141–167.

Smith, T. W., Uchino, B. N., Berg, C. A., Florsheim, P., Pearce, G., Hawkins, M., Henry, N. J. M., Beveridge, R. M., Skinner, M. A., Ko, K. J., & Olsen-Cerny, C. (2009). Conflict and collaboration in middle-aged and older couples. II: Cardiovascular reactivity during marital interaction. *Psychology and Aging*, *24*(2), 274–286.

Takens, F. (1981). Detecting strange attractors in turbulence. In D. A. Rand and L.-S. Young (Eds.), *Dynamical systems and turbulence (lecture notes in mathematics)* (vol. 898, pp. 366–381). New York: Springer-Verlag.

Thelen, E., & Smith, L. B. (2008). Dynamic systems theories. In R. M. Lerner (Ed.), *Handbook of Child Psychology, Vol. 1: Theoretical models of human development* (5th ed., pp. 563–634). Hoboken, NJ: John Wiley & Sons.

Vallacher, R. R., & Nowak, A. (1997). The emergence of dynamical social psychology. *Psychological Inquiry*, *8*(2), 73–99.

# 9

# DYNAMICS OF SYNCHRONY AND JOINT ACTION

*Kerry L. Marsh*[1]

This chapter is concerned with social connection as it is manifested in unity states that individuals form with others, as a consequence of each responding to the other's perceptuo-motoric behavior. How do coordinated social units rapidly come into being, operate for some time—brief or relatively lasting—and dissolve as rapidly? How does responsiveness to others who are nearby yield coordinated states, even when there is no overt goal? When there *is* a goal, how do people cooperate to complete an action? This chapter presents an embodied account in which coordination and cooperation are defined not by between-person harmony in verbal or cognitive processes—something that could play out via asynchronous media communication, for instance. Rather, they are approached as states that involve harmony at a physical level—something that could occur on the football pitch, for instance. In this view, coordination and cooperation involve congruencies in physical movement states: synchronous movement, or other coordinated or complementary movements among people who have visual systems and other senses, are in continual motion over time, and are co-present in some shared physical setting. The assumption in this chapter is that progress toward a computational and dynamical social psychology not only requires that social psychologists substantially rethink data collection and data analytic approaches, but make substantial theoretical advances as well.

The more traditional view of social connection phenomena views unity states as operating in opposition to individual autonomy, as involving individual sacrifice *in order* to be a part of a whole. The challenge from that view is understanding why/when individuals choose to cooperate rather than engage in competition or self-interested action. Such strategic processes can be entirely virtual; they do not necessarily involve physical movement or physical co-presence. They are also defined by cognitive activity, and they require the heavy mental machinations of active "mind reading." Researchers taking such a perspective are considerably benefitted by the fact that social cognitive psychology has an excellent understanding of the science of mind reading. From the attribution era onward, we have five decades of knowledge about how people make inferences about others' intent and decide whether to trust that others will be cooperative or will instead choose immediate self-interest, "defecting" from cooperation. We have well-developed and nicely tested economic theoretic approaches to "playing such games" that require sophisticated, high-level mentalizing processes so essential for this kind of approach to cooperation and coordination.

I suggest in this chapter an alternative view to understanding cooperation and the pull to connect and be a social unit with others: one that does not require competition as the backdrop for cooperation, and thus does not posit that mind reading is crucial. One danger of an account that is almost exclusively grounded on mentalizing processes is that it leads to neglecting the surround, that which is outside our brains (Mace, 1977; Richardson, Marsh, & Schmidt, 2010), in determining sociality and connection processes. It neglects to consider the influence of the social world we evolved in, the physical environmental context that provided the embedding context for evolving humans. We are not merely attribution-computing devices, but animate and intentional creatures who respond to other animals *within a shared grounding context*. This primal context includes the co-presence of other conspecifics in situations that unfold and change over time and make pressing situational demands on us. We are equipped by evolution to handle such demands—not solely because we can step back from it and mentally analyze it. Rather, we are on the ground, actively engaged from a first-person perspective in exploring that environment and those in it, by moving our eyes, engaging other sensory systems, and moving our bodies. The premise of this chapter is that understanding social connection in its most basic and diverse forms requires a theoretical approach that is social-ecological[2]—grounded in the social, physical and objectively real environments that surround behavior, and is dynamic—involving ongoing regulation of behavior in response to the unfolding information detected from our social world. Such a dynamic account will necessarily require data that preserve rich temporal information, and analytic strategies that can handle the more entangled, nonlinear nature of underlying causal forces at operation (Richardson, Dale, & Marsh, 2014). This chapter, however, focuses on advancing theory.

The first section of this chapter, "Minimalist Social Connection: The Emergence of 'Form' or Synergies," focuses on emergence of basic units, where the *game*'s ultimate purpose is not the economic outcome, but the playing of the game (the mere engagement with another individual), if you will. The underlying theoretical issues about causality essential for understanding these processes are described in the subsection "Theoretical Underpinnings: Self-Organization." The subsection "Empirical: Interpersonal Synchrony" discusses research that illustrates these principles—namely, experiments on interpersonal synchrony.

These subsections of the chapter examine sociality in terms of the minimal conditions necessary for the emergence of the merest of social unity states.

The second section, "Connecting through Cooperation," addresses social connection emergence in the context of goal-directed action, specifically joint action. Before discussing an empirical way to study joint action from an embodied and ecological framework, here too, considerable theoretical groundwork is needed because the principles are widely unfamiliar or the terms widely misunderstood.[3] The subsection "Perceptual Processes" discusses perceptual principles in depth, particularly the concept of affordances (i.e., what opportunities for agency an environment provides). The subsection "Empirical Work on Affording Cooperation" then discusses application of these principles in research on goal-directed cooperative action.

Finally, the section "Future Directions: Affordances of Behavior Settings" addresses the most neglected factor in understanding the emergence of social connection states: the role of the physical setting.

## Minimalist Social Connection: The Emergence of "Form" or Synergies

A fundamental principle that underlies this approach is dynamic emergence of social unity states. In the dynamic pickup of information from a rich environment, new phenomena, basic sociality, emerges. In this first section, I focus on simple causal principles that are essential for understanding interpersonal synchrony: dynamical principles of self-organization. In this section, I suggest that by understanding the dynamics of how lower-level physical movements spontaneously capture the motions of others in our physical spaces, apparently trivial mutual influences of incidental movement can create spontaneous interpersonal synchrony.

### *Theoretical Underpinnings: Self-Organization*

This subsection and the next address how to look at the most fundamental means of social interaction that allow for social connection, given evidence that synchrony is a cause and a consequence of affiliative needs (e.g., Hove & Risen, 2009; Lumsden, Miles, Richardson, Smith, & Macrae, 2012). Research on synchrony illustrates how an approach that is not based on mind reading can proceed. To explain how synchrony naturally emerges due to the dynamics of social perception-action processes requires discussing three interrelated issues. First, causality understood via self-organization principles is discussed. Second is a discussion of how to conceptualize emergent structures when they come about as a consequence of the first principle. This is essential for understanding emergence of social units (dyad or group) created through self-organization—what can be called a social "synergy." Third is a discussion of what new predictions come about from such an approach, describing the unique features of nonlinear dynamical systems.

## Causality

Self-organization means that coherent higher-order states of an overall system emerge in a bottom-up fashion as a consequence of the individual elements engaged in mutual adjustment to each other (Vallacher, Van Geert, & Nowak, 2015). Such a view suggests that states can evolve because of internal mechanics of a system. No external operator drives the process, and there is no central internal director that has particular responsibility for other processes unfolding.

When looking for a causal explanation, cognitive science commonly looks for a controller that directs the action—DNA, intervention of others who train us, or internal mental processes—that offer an explanation. Certain parts of the brain light up during certain social cognitive processes, so *that* then becomes viewed as the cause. This is oversimplified, of course; for example, modern evolutionary views are epigenetic, and understand that mechanistic explanations require gene X environment accounts. But it is not far wrong to say that an assumption that the brain must re-present the world, simulate action of others, and make other transformations of the outside world that bring it into the brain is viewed as the primary causal principle underlying most areas of cognitive science.

It is easy to understand why that is so. When we see complicated behavior, such as an individual's highly coordinated movement of a large range of muscles and joints in completing an action, we assume that such complexity must require some plan—a motor program, for instance.[4] We assume that complicated behaviors must involve skilled mental calculation or must have developed through simple associative learning principles involving extraordinarily long chains of associations. In this way, our brains have either built-in or developed through experience a complex mental structure that directs sophisticated actions. Note that an assumption is that contact with the external environment requires that it be translated into our heads, re-presented, in order for us to plan our actions. The assumption is that we rely on internal simulations of the outside world inside our heads in order to be able to predict and respond to it.

An alternative view is to recognize phenomena such as brain activity during a task, for instance, as an inextricable part of a system rather than the cause or director of the activity. To call the brain the cause, Järvilehto (1998) believes, is analogous to putting in the last puzzle piece to complete a jigsaw puzzle and thinking that the piece is the cause of the depicted image (Järvilehto, 1998). Even phenomena so readily viewed as brain-based, or at least localized in the individual, such as emotion, he argues, cannot be localized in the brain, but reside at the level of the dynamic living system, the organism environment system (Järvilehto, 2001).

If one takes a radical system-oriented perspective, it yields the notion that the causality principle is self-organization. Multiple components become *collectively organized*, new states and new actions are achieved, without an executive system directing the individual components (Turvey, 1990). Self-organization relies on certain assumptions about the underlying relations of the particular components that make up the system. If components of a system have strong interdependencies and particular connections, linkages among components can yield incredibly complicated coordination patterns. Phenomena can emerge based merely on the interaction of the components, and in response to constraints, press, or demands on the system from without. A biological system is not like a mechanical one that can be deconstructed into isolatable parts that still remain parts when deconstructed, such as separating a bicycle into a wheel, chain, seat, and so forth. Although the meaning of what a wheel does within a bicycle might not be entirely clear without knowing the whole of which it is a part, it still has a relatedness to the other components that is highly different from the *context dependencies* of components in biosocial-environmental systems (Juarerro, 2002). A context dependent mechanical system might yield the astounding result that, when pulling a wheel off a bicycle and inserting it into a different machine, it morphs into an entirely different thing—unidentifiable any longer as a bicycle wheel.

## Structure

The kinds of structures that emerge from self-organization are dramatically different than structures that an external controller would create. The human skeletal system, for instance, entirely violates traditional principles of construction that an architect would follow—it is neither heavy, rigid, nor sturdy enough to pass muster as a load-bearing structure. But if we consider the entire biomechanical system of the body, made up of components such as the muscles, bones, fascia, and ligaments, it is clear that the system is unexpectedly strong, efficient, and responsive because the body's structure operates on a principle of biotensegrity.

*Tensegrity* is the principle that underlies the (very strong) geodesic structures that Buckminster Fuller was famous for promoting. Within the body, *biotensegrity* means that muscle/tendons/bones are linked in such a way that there is a continual balance of compression (by some elements) occurring within a context of linkages that provide continual pull (tension) throughout the system (Ingber, 2008; Turvey, 2007; Turvey & Fonseca, 2014). The linkages between multiple components allow them to function as a whole, a "synergy" or coordinative structure, without something in charge of controlling the action of these components. The very high-dimensional system of innumerable muscles and tendons would make untenable computational demands for a motor program that must compute current states and predict future states. Coordinated behavior is instead more parsimoniously explained by the low-dimensional operation of coordinative structures or synergies. In sum, this approach indicates that in the body, qualitatively different states involving highly ordered, complex coordination can come about as a result of demands of the environment.

Once a synergy emerges, it has a reality that then constrains the components comprising the whole. Forces exerted on the system, for example by situational demands, yield one of two phenomena: resilience of the whole to temporary perturbation (a tendency to bounce back to its current, stable state), but also qualitatively new patterns of organization upon reaching some crucial amount of press on the system. Causality in such a system resides at the level of interaction, as a result of how the system is structured, and what forces are impinging on it (Eiler, Kallen, & Richardson, Chapter 6 in this volume). Thus, putting pressure on one part of the resilient system results in changes in other parts of the system. Twisted in a person's hand, a toy geodesic-type orb changes into a qualitatively different shape, while maintaining its integrity in other ways.

## Features of Nonlinear Dynamical Systems

Transient synergies, whether mechanically or biologically based states of coordination, obey these two principles of resilience and change as well. Two identically built pendulum clocks hanging near each other on a wall become mechanically coupled through vibrations in the wall that influence each of them. As a result, the clocks' pendulums will come to move in a synchronized pattern. A coupled oscillator dynamic (Haken, Kelso, & Bunz, 1985) similarly describes biomechanical phenomena. The way components of the body are linked means that one can hold identical weighted sticks ("pendulums") in each hand and easily swing the pendulums at a comfortable speed moving in precisely opposite directions for a long time. Such a pattern of *anti-phase* synchrony is a fairly strong attractor—in fact, it is impossible to swing each pendulum at a rhythm entirely independent of the other. During anti-phase swinging, if pressure is exerted on the system—for instance, if one must speed up—then at some critical speed, an even stronger, more stable attractor pulls the system to a new state of order. The nature of the interrelation of the limbs' movements would change, with the arms shifting to swing the pendulums in an *in-phase* synchrony state, in which the pendulums are both swinging backward and both swinging forward at the exact same time.

This last example also illustrates an important phenomenon in nonlinear dynamical systems—namely, abrupt discontinuities. Nonlinear systems are ones that are not well described by common regression equations. Rather, linear increases in a variable across some range of values results in a non-commensurate degree of change in another variable (Nowak & Vallacher, 1998; Richardson et al., 2014; Vallacher & Nowak, 1994; Vallacher, Read, & Nowak, 2002). Increasing the pendulum speed or experiencing a subtle perturbation would have minimal effect on anti-phase synchrony up to a certain increase in speed, but at some critical point of increased speed, there is an abrupt change in the state of the system. The system becomes briefly disordered (with temporarily increased fluctuations), and then stabilizes into a new state: in-phase synchrony.

Another crucial feature of such a system is that the present state cannot be considered ahistorically—that is, it cannot be examined without considering the immediate trajectory by which one got to that point; how one got "here" matters. The quality of *hysteresis* means that there is a lack of symmetry in reaching one state from different directions (e.g., reaching the current state from a state of decreasing pressure versus increasing pressure on the system) in terms of its consequences for future states. In other words, events could not be reversed in sequence and get the outcome implied by their obverse. If one starts from a state of in-phase behavior, a change in speed (e.g., decrease) does not shift one spontaneously to anti-phase behavior, despite the fact that speeding up in anti-phase leads spontaneously to in-phase behavior.

The implications of a synergistic account for a single biological system may seem easy to accept. Any child trying to pat their head and rub their tummy learns the interdependence of apparently independent body components, as does a novice drummer trying to simultaneously beat unrelated rhythms with two drumsticks. It is a big conceptual leap, however, to imagine that two strangers who lack any direct biomechanical connection could be coupled in a way that would obey laws similar to those which coordinate the limbs of one's body.

## *Empirical: Interpersonal Synchrony*

Despite the implausibility that two strangers with no direct physical connection are pulled to spontaneous states of coordination in their incidental movement, research suggests that even fairly minimalistic interaction between two people— e.g., happening to rock in a rocking chair alongside another person—can lead to their becoming linked in a way such that they could be described as a *social* "synergy" (Fusaroli, Rączaszek-Leonardi, & Tylén, 2013; Marsh, Richardson, Baron, & Schmidt, 2006; Riley, Richardson, Shockley, & Ramenzoni, 2011). When individuals are engaged in some kind of rhythmic movement such as swinging their legs while seated or swinging a pendulum, or moving in a rocking chair alongside another person doing the same, strangers can readily synchronize their movements with each other when instructed to do so. Moreover, the conditions under which they could readily do this, the types of synchrony patterns that were possible, which patterns were more stable than others, and the deviations away from perfect synchrony closely follow the predictions of bidirectional coupled oscillator models (Richardson, Marsh, Isenhower, Goodman, & Schmidt, 2007; Schmidt, Bienvenu, Fitzpatrick, & Amazeen, 1998; Schmidt, Carello, & Turvey, 1990a, 1990b; Schmidt, Christianson, Carello, & Baron, 1994).

We suggested that being mutually pulled into synchrony with another person *spontaneously* might be the basis for a rudimentary social connection with others (Marsh, 2010, 2013; Marsh et al., 2006; Marsh, Richardson, & Schmidt, 2009). If the predictions of a dynamical model hold for unintentional synchrony, it would lead to predictions that could not be anticipated by current perspectives that dominate explanations of mimicry and joint action, namely embodied simulation accounts (e.g., Chartrand & Bargh, 1999; Sebanz, Knoblich, & Prinz, 2005). We viewed interpersonal synchrony not as a cognitively mediated process such as priming (Bargh, Chen, & Burrows, 1996), but as the result of a field of forces, a view more compatible with a field theory metaphor (Lewin, Lippitt, & White, 1939). More concretely, we view synchrony as something that could be a consequence of thermodynamic principles applied to the emergence of form or new "atomisms"— new synergies (Iberall, 1987; Iberall & Soodak, 1987; Iberall, Wilkinson, & White, 1993; Soodak & Iberall, 1987).

Being pulled inadvertently into a synchrony state through one's incidental, idle, and non-goal-directed movements we likened to being swept into another person's orbit. The synergy of two people coupled in this way is like a social eddy, analogous to a whirlpool of movement (Marsh et al., 2006). In the ocean, a whirlpool has a real, forceful existence, and yet the entity only exists in the relatedness that creates the force. It has a characteristic, visualizable form resulting from the interrelatedness of molecules flowing through it temporarily. The particular molecules do not define the whirlpool, only the patterned force does. The social eddy has no other real existence except in its temporal dynamics: its harnessing of energy and creation of form.

From a social physics or thermodynamic perspective, social synergies or social "eddies" can be understood as energy and dissipation processes occurring in a *near-equilibrium* system (Iberall, 1987). Energy is either kinetic or potential energy (i.e., conserved in bonds). When a system is at equilibrium, there is no motion, no flow of energy. At near equilibrium, however, there are gradient differences (differences in knowledge, social power, or for the case of concrete movement, merely differences in energy of one individual's movement) and as a result of these gradient differences, flows of energies occur. Flows can be transient—the mere capturing of another's movement into a synchronous state, for instance. Small fluctuations in arousal (presence of others) can be dissipated, or they can be amplified and stabilized, leading to the emergence of form. Critical levels of stress are achieved by reaching a certain level of physiological arousal, with touch, close proximity, and language likely to induce such energy. Temporary eddies of movement—emergent, temporary structured patterns in which two or more people move as a unit—emerge when stress criticality is reached.

For more stable structures to form (a bond rather than transient sync), stronger energy is required; this then becomes bound up in the relationship. Because individuals will always be buffeted by other sources of attractions—other potential eddies that could form—the binding energy between two people must be stronger than the energy that exists between the components and external agents. Iberall's social focus was on the implications of such an approach at a higher level of analysis. Thus he discussed the development of civilizations and economic activity in terms of the flow of variables between regions where there are gradient differences (e.g., economic activity of transporting wares and money between cities).

But at the interpersonal scale that this chapter is concerned with, what would be transported interpersonally might be informational products. Gradients would lead to conversation, transmission of information, or orders given.

A final prediction of thermodynamic principles is with regard to dissolution of bonds. When a given atomism, whether only temporary form (a social eddy) or a stable structure (a relationship), is disrupted, energy is released. Energy flows out of an interaction when synchrony dissipates, for instance. When more stable structures are broken (relationships), substantially more energy is released.

Although most of these higher-order predictions extrapolated from the thermodynamics of energy flow and arousal have not yet been tested (e.g., using physiological measures), the basic underlying dynamical model that predicts how people become spontaneously synchronized when engaged in rhythmic movement (e.g., the Haken-Kelso-Bunz model of bidirectional coupled oscillators: Haken et al., 1985) has been supported. From an ecological perspective, the means by which people are pulled into another's orbit is *informational*. Whereas mechanical and biological systems have physical direct linkages between components, individuals are coupled by visual information about the other person's movements, or auditory information about the other person's movements. The key predictions of the model have been tested using a variety of methods such as walking, swinging pendulums, moving in rocking chairs, moving arms rhythmically, and shaking maracas, while using motion sensors to track movement (Demos et al., 2012; Richardson, Garcia, Frank, Gregor, & Marsh, 2012; Richardson, Marsh, & Baron, 2007; Richardson, Marsh, & Isenhower et al., 2007; Richardson, Marsh, & Schmidt, 2005; Schmidt & O'Brien, 1997; Schmidt & Richardson, 2008; Van Ulzen, Lamoth, Daffertshofer, Semin, & Beek, 2008). Motion sensors allow for continuously and precisely tracking synchrony in a way that does not rely on more global and subjective assessments by coders viewing videotapes. Coordination of even highly stochastic, nonsinusoidal (wave-like) movements such as postural sway have been tracked, using force plates or Wii technologies (Fowler, Richardson, Marsh, & Shockley, 2008; Shockley, Richardson, & Dale, 2009; Shockley, Santana, & Fowler, 2003). Moreover, new automated video analysis techniques allow for analysis of synchrony in terms of ebbs and flows of total amounts of movement, or coordination of *behavior waves* (Schmidt, Fitzpatrick, Caron, & Mergeche, 2011; Schmidt, Morr, Fitzpatrick, & Richardson, 2012; cf. Newtson, 1994, 1998). As predicted, seeing the movement of another person's rocking chair or hearing the movement is sufficient to lead individuals to coordinate their movements without instruction (Demos et al., 2012; Richardson, Marsh, Isenhower et al., 2007). (Indeed, coordination of movement has been found to occur even when people actively attempt to not be affected by the others' movements: Issartel, Marin, & Cadopi, 2007.) Unlike intrapersonal coordination of limbs, spontaneous synchrony involves *relative* coordination. People shift into coordination for some period before falling out for a while, then becoming coordinated again. Synchrony seems to be particularly important in early phases of forming a connection, such as when being co-present with strangers or when interacting with someone different in significant ways from oneself but with whom a connection is desired (Miles, Griffiths, Richardson, & Macrae et al., 2010; Miles, Lumsden, Richardson, & Macrae, 2011). Moreover, a variety of predictions based on dynamic models have been confirmed including how weaker versus stronger coupling (by changing the amount of visual information available) affects synchrony, and the link between having similar natural frequencies of movement and better coordination (see Marsh, Johnston, Richardson, & Schmidt, 2009).

In particular, dynamical principles suggest that individuals with different underlying perceptual-motor systems may be less likely to mutually influence each other, leading to less synchrony. Some studies that focus on groups that have perceptual-motor systems that are distinctively associated with dysfunction have supported this prediction. One example is from a study of children who were on the autism spectrum (and thus were diagnosed with significant perceptual-motor deficits as well as social connection problems). They not only had more difficulty doing basic drumming tasks alone (Isenhower et al., 2012), but they also showed less spontaneous synchrony with their caregiver in the rocking chair paradigm than did typically developing children (Marsh et al., 2013).

One prediction of the synergistic approach (Marsh et al., 2009) that has received minimal support is the *mooring* hypothesis. The hypothesis is focused on individuals who are either overly variable in their movement, or in other ways perceptually and motorically not well grounded in the rhythms of their physical world. This would mean they would be less resonant to the natural pacing of temporal events, or even to the auditory information conveyed in speech or music. Such individuals might benefit from the mutual influence of being present with another individual in motion. The more stable or skilled individual might provide an anchor onto whom less adaptively anchored individuals could tether themselves. An alternative is that individuals who have more highly honed senses to the rhythms of the world and are more responsive to those rhythms will change *their* movement more to adjust to the other person in creating synchrony rather than vice versa. To date, unpublished studies provide more evidence for the latter hypothesis than for mooring effects, but forming clear conclusions would be premature at this point.

A related hypothesis of anchoring also remains to be tested more thoroughly. One assumption of a dynamical approach is that new modes of action (e.g., a social synergy emerging from interactions of two initially independent actors) emerge because they are lower energy states. Thus the gait patterns of a horse change (between a trot, canter, or gallop) when the increased speed of movement makes a different coordination of limbs easier and quantifiably more energy-efficient than the previous mode of locomotion. Based on this logic, a social synergy is predicted to be more energy-conserving for the individual if they are operating as a part of an easily coordinated ensemble. That teams of workers at hard labor chant or sing together to coordinate their movement relies on this principle (McNeil, 1995). It may be more efficient to hike a mountain by being able to perceptually entrain to the rhythms of others' footsteps in one's visual field. Mere visual attention to a rhythmic stimulus has been found to lead to unintentionally matching the external rhythm (Lopresti-Goodman, Richardson, Silva, & Schmidt, 2009). Thus, it may be less effortful to do difficult movement tasks (Nie, Caban, & Marsh, 2015) if someone else is in sync with us. Intriguingly, rowers have a higher pain tolerance after rowing with teammates than after rowing alone (Cohen, Ejsmond-Frey, Knight, & Dunbar, 2010). Our belief is that the mechanism is not an explicit motivational boost from shared experience. Instead, our assumption is that some states (e.g., in-phase synchrony) are so readily achievable and promote cognitive and perceptual fluency such that more perceptual and executive function resources are available for other tasks. Such benefits should be apparent across a wide range of outcomes, from pain tolerance to cognitive tasks (e.g., memory; for indirect evidence, see Macrae, Duffy, Miles, & Lawrence, 2008 and Richardson et al., 2005).

Understanding the most fundamental emergence of social connection with others via quite trivial movements of individuals suggests the potential power of a dynamical, ecological perception-based approach for understanding social psychological phenomena. Research has strongly confirmed our suggestions that synchrony is a fundamental basis for sociality. In the decade prior to the first interpersonal synchrony studies that used dynamic, precise and objective measures of synchrony, video coding observation studies suggested a link between rapport and affiliation for dyads of interacting adults, and for infant–parent bonding pairs as well (Bernieri, 1988; Bernieri, Reznick, & Rosenthal, 1988; Bernieri, Davis, Rosenthal, & Knee, 1994; Condon & Sander, 1974; LaFrance, 1979). In the time since Schmidt first studied interpersonal synchrony using motion sensors two decades ago (for a review, see Schmidt & Richardson, 2008), research has proliferated that uses interpersonal synchrony as an independent variable to induce social connection (e.g., Wiltermuth & Health, 2009; Valdesolo, Ouyang, & DeSteno, 2010), or as an outcome measure to assess sociality (e.g., Paxton & Dale, 2013). As a whole,[5] increased interpersonal synchrony is linked in the short term as a cause or consequence of increased liking, stronger sense of team/group cohesion, perceived smoothness, rapport, affiliation, and satisfaction with emotional support (Bernieri, 1988; Bernieri et al., 1994; LaFrance, 1979; Hove & Risen, 2009; McNeil, 1995; Miles, Nind, & Macrae, 2009; Vacharkulksemsuk & Fredrickson, 2012; for a review, see Vicaria & Dickens, 2016). Over the long term, repeated experience with synchronization could have a defining effect on a person's psychological tendencies and have consequences for subsequent interaction behavior (Novak, Vallacher, & Zochowski, 2005).

## Connecting through Cooperation

In the previous section, the scope of social connection phenomena was limited to interpersonal synchrony. Understanding joint action, where two people must coordinate to complete some action, might intuitively seem to *require* reading the mind of the other in order to be able to coordinate. What would an ecological, dynamical account require beyond the principles discussed in the previous section to explain goal-directed action? Most other accounts rely on the individual internally modeling or mentally simulating the other's actions to do the heavy lifting of crossing the gulf between other and self to engage in joint action (Sebanz, Bekkering, & Knoblich, 2006). A social synergistic account requires more in-depth understanding of the relatedness of the person to the environment, and the dynamic interdependence of action on perceptual flow. These perceptual processes are discussed here in depth, focusing particularly on affordance perception. Being able to cooperate with others means not only detecting one's own functional fit to the environment and what opportunities for solo agency are available and when they are not, but also requires the ability to detect what others have to offer, particularly when solo person–environment fit is deficient (Marsh & Meagher, 2016). The next subsection, "Perceptual Processes," describes the underlying principles, and the subsection after that, "Empirical Work on Affording Cooperation," describes empirical work testing, such an account of joint action.

### *Perceptual Processes*

Traditional perspectives view perception in the following way. Sensation, as a consequence of light hitting the retina, for instance, is viewed as occurring prior to perception, which requires mental processes in order for the perceiver to be able to piece together what those stimulations mean.[6] The challenge, called the *binding problem*, is understanding how static two-dimensional images on the retina become bound together in order to construct a three-dimensional understanding of the objects we feel we are seeing. Within any individual static retinal image, the entirety of a three-dimensional object is never depicted, only some sides or parts of sides. Thus our brains have to fill in the missing parts and bind them into coherent images. Each retinal image provides insufficient information to specify where one object ends and another begins, and where in space things are—what parts of the image are in the foreground or behind other objects, and how far away things are. The mind must home in on particular cues that it has learned through past experience in order to imperfectly infer these properties. The fundamental problem is that the two-dimensional projection of the world onto our retina is intractably nonspecific; any number of different situations of the world could produce the same flat retinal image. The challenge for the mind is deducing which state of the world has greater probability of producing the image.

However, Gibson's theory of perception (Gibson, 1979) fundamentally rejects such a perspective, suggesting that "the optical support for vision . . . is not ambiguous, is not impoverished, and, therefore, not intractable" (Gibson, 1979, p. 103; Turvey & Shaw, 1999). Gibson believed that because animals co-evolved with their environment, they would have evolved perceptual systems that were capable of using the various forms of energy distributions of their environment to gain veridical knowledge of the world. Humans and many other animals, for instance, evolved in a world that is filled with ambient light during the daytime. Light reflects off every surface that reaches our eyes. Gibson posited that there may be information in the optic array that veridically specifies what object is in front of another object, and the continuity versus the ending (edges) of objects, for instance—*provided that perceiver is in motion*. Across the transformations that occur in the optic array as a person merely moves their head, there is structural persistence in aspects of the optic array, and we are sensitive to these invariants. As we move, we correctly *see* where the edges of objects are because texture accumulates at that leading edge. We see what is behind and in front by the occlusion and revealing of textures in the world when we move our head. Similar invariants veridically specify distance of objects. No inferential process is required, only motion, so that information is specified via what persists across the optic array over time.

## Affordance Perception

Even more radically, Gibson (1977, 1979) hypothesized that if animals' ecological niches persisted over a sufficient numbers of generations, then there might be information in the energy distributions that is specifically relevant to the actions a given species needs to engage in for survival, beyond just information that specifies the edges of objects, and how large, small, or distant they are. If visual information can specify the edge of a chair, and haptic and other information convey body awareness, attunement to information regarding more complex constellations of features that specifies functionality of this special edge with regard to one's own body is not that far of a leap. Assume that information can specify the edges of things. Assume as well that animals evolved to be highly fitted to their world, and responsive with their bodies to the world they move through. It is not a far leap from those assumptions that animals would have the perceptual equipment to be able to immediately grasp the relatedness of things to themselves, and be able to discern, with proper attunement,[7] what surfaces have the proper array of qualities that allow the surface to be sit-on-able-for-me. Gibson (1977, 1979) coined the term "affordances" to indicate the useful aspects of a world that provide action opportunities for a given species. The term captures an objective feature of the world, but one that is inherently relational—depending on certain fittedness, certain capabilities, of a given species. Thus, whereas a level ground affords easy transport of the body for a land animal via walking, it does not afford walking for a fish. The surface of water can afford walking-on for small insects, but not for creatures that are of different size and weight.

Critically, researchers have defined perceiving affordances as being about *agency* specifically, not the usefulness of objects more generally, nor about others' agency. Thus, saying an "apple affords nutrition" is incorrect (Michaels, 2003); rather, an apple has the affordances of being holdable-in-one's-hand, throwable, and bite-into-able. Note, however, that we only talk about such affordances *with respect to* an animal that has certain "ways of life," reflecting the particular aspects in one's environment that are relevant—that is, our ecological *niche* (Rietveld & Kiverstein, 2014). Living things that occupy the same plot of land, whether bugs, earthworms, or mammals, may occupy different ecological niches.

Evidence that animals are able to perceive affordances is provided by experiments that systematically vary information provided to an animal that specifies affordances, and showing "empirical evidence of *differential behavior* tied to differential information availability" (Reed, 1996, p. 96). Reed (1996) discussed experiments conducted with spiders and cats in which their behavior reveals a sensitivity to distance, body-scaled to their capabilities. They were highly successful at knowing whether a distance was leapable for them, suggesting that some information covaried with their differential behavior. In addition, Reed discussed studies Darwin conducted with earthworms that demonstrated that earthworms had awareness of the usefulness of leaves for plugging up their burrows and also demonstrated selectivity in the materials they used. Behavioral discrimination was revealed, for instance, by pulling a given leaf differently into the burrow depending on its features (e.g., shape). In the research, trial and error could not explain behavior, and concepts such as instincts, reflexes, or fixed action patterns were inadequate to the task of explaining the rich flexibility and adaptability of the earthworms' behavior because they carried these tasks out even with materials not normally found in that environment. The most parsimonious explanation for these animals' behaviors is that something—namely, *information that can be objectively quantified and manipulated by a scientist*—specifies affordances that animals use to regulate their behaviors in an environment.

Gibson (1979) suggested that animals would also be sensitive to what other conspecifics afford them, something that McArthur and Baron elaborated on in an influential paper several years later (McArthur & Baron, 1983). Reviews of the social perception and affordance literature suggest that people are highly sensitive to dynamic perceptual information that specifies significant features of individuals such as gender and age, and more complex features as well (Marsh & Meagher, 2016; Marsh et al., 2006; McArthur & Baron, 1983; Johnson, 2013; Johnston, 2013; Johnston, Hudson, Richardson, Gunns, & Garner, 2004). Intriguing research suggests superficial cues such as hair, clothing, or wrinkles on a face are not required to detect social features, but rather that there is something in the temporal dynamics of moving form that specifies features such as age and gender (Berry, Kean, Misovich, & Baron, 1991; Runeson & Frykholm, 1983). Researchers studying the *kinematic specification of dynamics* (KSD) put reflective dots on key joints of an individual in motion, and film this under minimal light such that the only information available to a perceiver is moving points of light when the video plays. Not only can people detect what action someone is doing, such as walking, dancing, or picking up a heavy box, they can also detect whether a heavy or light object is being lifted, even when the actors are pretending to lift something heavier. Static images of the point lights do not allow for such detection. Most critically, perceivers also detect what opportunities for their own actions are afforded by the presence of that individual—namely, social affordances. Observers can detect when a dyad is cooperating or competing (Kean, 2000), or whether a person is carrying a child rather than rubbish (Hodges & Lindhiem, 2006). Other KSD studies found that criminals can use the dynamics of a person's movement to determine the individual's "muggability" (Johnston, 2013; Johnston et al., 2004).

In one sense, it is not that drastic a leap from the notion of direct perception of an edge to the notion of direct perception of a unique constellation of features (edges and the like) that are specifically relevant to how one's action system can make use of those features. But, in another sense, it is quite radical. With the concept of affordances, the meaning of even quite abstract things, such as a physical space, is not an arbitrary social construction. Instead, the environment declares to us its meaning. This yields the hypothesis that our feelings and emotional responses to places can be a consequence of our ability to rapidly see what affordances are in a situation, even if the setting and features of the environment are entirely new to us. Such responses should be detectable, albeit imperfectly, by the words we use to describe environments. Somewhere between objective fact ("What is the square footage of this room?") and purely aesthetic evaluations ("Do you like this room?") are judgments that have both a functional and valenced flavor, such as how spacious or cozy a room feels (Meagher & Marsh, 2015). These reactions to space, expressed in words and in deeds, should be particularly apparent when the affordances of a space are *most* self-relevant—for example, the dorm room or work space is our own territory rather than someone else's (Meagher, 2014).

Finally, an affordance-based perspective suggests that meaning is relational—it is partly determined by what an individual is, in terms of their capabilities, as well as what they *could* be, given the degree to which the physical and social environment completes us, by fitting an unmet need or untapped capability. Crucially, meaning emerges out of dynamic interaction with the environment—new possibilities are encountered and created, with the new possibilities that come into being with the presence of others being most significant of all.

In the following subsection, we first discuss affordances at the more immediate level, involving dyadic interaction. A decade ago, we began to explore the question of how the presence of others holds out the promise of allowing us to become a more capable entity, by studying cooperation. The final section of the chapter, "Future Directions: Affordances of Behavior Settings," will discuss the role of the broader situation in affording opportunities for social connection.

## *Empirical Work on Affording Cooperation*

Inspired by solo perception-action research, my colleagues and I hypothesized that cooperative action, such as moving an object together, might be approached from an affordance-based perspective rather than from an economic game theory approach. One hallmark of an affordance-based approach is that there is information in a situation about the task demands, and the other persons as well. Cooperation would not be an abstract symbolic choice made with a person who was not physically present, as is often the case in studies based on game theory, but it would be examined as a behavior that involved physical actions. A social synergistic perspective would view two individuals in cooperation as a new entity, a *social* perception-action system in which the perceptions and actions of each member of the ensemble were tightly responsive in real time to that of the others.

Asch, for instance, talked about the example of two boys moving a log together as creating a performance that was a wholly "new product, strictly unlike the sum of [each boy's] separate exertions" (Asch, 1952, pp. 173–174). A similar take on embodied cooperation was offered by the philosopher Margaret Gilbert (1996, 2014). She viewed cooperative actions such as deciding to take a walk together as being a situation in which actors simultaneously jointly commit to being as a *plural subject* of action, with the attendant obligations and benefits to complete the action as a social entity, much like Asch described.

If an affordance account is suitable for describing the emergence of cooperative action, two key predictions from solo affordance research should hold. First, cooperation should be predicted as a new "mode of action" that emerges from solo action, with this mode of action precisely predictable by quantifying the capabilities of individuals, and the demands of the task, taken with respect to each other. This is the *pi number* prediction. A pi number is a body-scaled assessment of the person–environment relation in which some quantity of an individual and the environment are each assessed (e.g., in centimeters), and divided. It is called a "pi number" because it is a dimensionless number, just as pi is. At crucial values of a *pi number*, the system should shift from one action mode (e.g., solo action or joint action) into the other mode. The second key prediction reflects dynamical principles. Shifts between solo and joint action modes should have characteristic dynamic features that previously have been found in the solo affordance research upon shifting between *solo* action modes. For example, the system should display features of a nonlinear dynamical system rather than a linear system, with abrupt shifts in action modes.

The task that we developed to examine cooperative action was similar to one well studied in solo action: moving objects of different sizes. Previous research had examined how children, for instance, will choose to pick up objects using a one-handed grip versus a two-handed grip (Cesari & Newell, 1999; Van der Kamp, Savelsbergh, & Davis, 1998). We thought the shifts between one actor moving an object using a two-handed grip (a solo action mode) to a *two-person* action mode (joint action) should obey similar principles to that of the solo perception-action research. In our studies, we used narrow planks of wood of a wide range of sizes, which were presented in a continuous sequence. Each plank was painted red on the ends, and participants were told they could move the planks however they chose, with the restriction that they could only touch the ends of the planks, as if their middles had wet paint on them.

## Pi Number Hypothesis

Research on a variety of actions such as passing through apertures (doorways), climbing stairs, and moving objects supports the notion that these behaviors (and perceptual judgments as well) are precisely predicted by pi numbers. For example, Warren (1984) studied the affordance of stairs being climbable by normal means—that is, upright, with only one foot resting on a step while the next leg smoothly begins to move the other foot to the next step. He demonstrated that when stairs cease to be comfortably climbable in this mode was *not* merely a function of riser height, nor a function of how tall the different climbers were. Rather, shifts between modes were entirely determined by a relational measure. He calculated a body-scaled ratio of leg length to riser height, and found that a consistent value of the pi number determined comfortable stair climbing across individuals. By varying riser height as well, he could determine the pi number value at which normal stair climbing became consistently challenging for all individuals. Similarly, children's natural tendencies to pick up objects using one hand or two are precisely predicted by a calculation that quantifies the relation between hand size and object size: a pi number (Cesari & Newell, 1999; Van der Kamp et al., 1998).

We first replicated the pi number prediction in an experiment in which solo actors were asked to report how they would move planks of wood presented to them—where their choices were using one hand, two hands, or an axe handle with a claw-like end that would extend their arm span. In another experiment, solo participants' actual behaviors (using one hand, two hands, or the tool) were assessed. These experiments supported the pi number prediction for solo actors, where pi numbers were calculated as the relation between hand size and plank size (for shifts between one- and two-handed grips) or as the relation between arm span and plank size (for shifts between two hands and tool use).

In a joint action experiment (where pairs of participants took planks off a conveyor belt, moving them either alone or together), we also found support for the pi number hypothesis. Key values of the pi number determined the boundaries between engaging in solo action and joint action (Richardson, Marsh, & Baron, 2007). A comparable experiment examined only perceptual *judgments*, and replicated the results. In subsequent studies that more systematically varied the height of participants, shifts between action modes were determined by the value of the pi number for both tall dyads and short dyads (Isenhower, Richardson, Carello, Baron, & Marsh, 2010).

## Dynamical Hypotheses

Thus, emergence of a cooperative social unit occurred naturally in response to the task becoming more challenging: cooperation was an emergent adaptation to the situation. We also expected that the dynamics of cooperation's emergence and subsidence would display features of other nonlinear dynamical systems, including abrupt shifts between action modes, and also the characteristic behavior of *hysteresis*.

To allow us to look at dynamical features, another feature of our joint action (or perception) experiment was that the sequencing of planks was varied, and presented in a steady sequence with moderate pacing. Three planks of one length were presented before the next length. In one condition, the planks were presented in order of ascending length; in another, they were in descending order. For comparison, a random order of plank trios was presented. As predicted, when the crucial pi number values occurred, the shift to a new mode of action was relatively abrupt. That is, once the dyads shifted to a new mode of action, this action mode was stable and the subsequent actions stayed in that new mode. Moreover, the action experiments displayed hysteresis. The precise boundary between joint action and solo action modes was shifted somewhat as a function of the past trajectory of action. This pattern indicated that the system had *multistability*— that is, regions where both solo action and joint action are stable attractors. Hysteresis occurred in the ascending versus descending conditions, reflecting a "stickiness" of past action. That is, the current mode persisted somewhat beyond the pi value at which, in the random condition, behavior would have switched. To clarify, in the descending lengths condition, where participants by necessity start off in cooperative action, cooperation persisted into the multistable region. Thus, slightly shorter planks were carried cooperatively in this condition, in contrast to the ascending condition, where planks of those lengths would have still been carried alone. Interestingly, the opposite dynamical characteristic occurred in the perception experiments; perception was anticipatory, or forward-looking. As soon as the multistable region was reached, people's judgments abruptly shifted to the next action mode in that region.

The limits of these sets of experiments are that they focused solely on actions in which another person extends one's action possibilities in a quantitative manner, where each lower action mode (one hand, two hand) is nested within a higher-order mode (two hands, two people). One assumption of a dynamical approach, however, is that there will also be *qualitatively* new possibilities for action that the presence of others provides for the individual. Emergence of new "atomisms"—for example, a social synergy, should yield novel properties unique to that atomism. In the plank moving experiments, we found the somewhat surprising result that the precise pi numbers that determined action boundaries between solo and joint action closely matched that of boundaries between one- to two-hand action modes, suggesting, perhaps, close parallels in what constrains the solo perception-action system and the social perception-action system.

However, as social ecological research moves into domains where there are added complexities of affordances in the joint action domain, processes will differ in important ways from results of solo perception-action experiments. A series of recent perception studies examining how anticipated assistance carrying a heavy weight affected perceived distance illustrates the challenge. Whereas some experiments found results that mapped precisely onto what solo perception-action experiments would predict—namely, distances would seem shorter because a heavy weight will be easier to carry (Doerrfeld, Sebanz, & Shiffrar, 2012)—other studies found the opposite (Meagher & Marsh, 2014). These differences were presumed to occur because the presence of another person provides not only possibilities for action that lighten a load, but also negative interpersonal possibilities. One might fear that one could let the other person down if one was unable to do one's part, for instance. Such interpersonal concerns change the equation in significant ways.

## *"Perception-Based" Inaccuracies*

The veridical perceptions involved in coordination and cooperation may seem hard to reconcile with extensive evidence that judgments of social environments are distorted by desire (Balcetis & Dunning, 2006; Balcetis & Lassiter, 2010). Note, however, that perceptual judgmental processes will be expected to be veridical only to the extent to which a scientist is able to objectively assess that there is information *available* that specifies an affordance; only limited experimental research on cooperative action to date has taken an explicitly social affordance perspective (for a review, see Marsh & Meagher, 2016).

In social judgment tasks, accuracy will increasingly decline to the degree to which judgments are based not on perceiving affordances per se (detecting action possibilities for oneself), but determining whether a situation provides possibilities for another's actions—whether a high shelf is reachable for them, for instance. Although strong evidence is lacking, some recent research provides indirect evidence for the hypotheses that (1) impoverished information as well as impoverished experience with others' capabilities is associated with greater inaccuracies, and (2) perceptual attunements are constrained by social roles, groups, recent experience, and repeated experiences inculcated through culture

(Eiler et al., Chapter 6 in this volume; Marsh & Meagher, 2016; Meagher & Kang, 2013; Ye, Cardwell, & Mark, 2009).

In many situations involving observing others' interactions, where the situation involves multiple actors, the situation is more complex in that it involves two or more agentic beings, and there are multiple possibilities for action present for each agent. What response one has to such a situation will be highly affected by attentional focus. Take, for instance, a situation of high potential conflict and ambiguity, where one is making judgments as to whether a police officer's use of force is justified. Social processes bias the judgments by causing one to focus on different aspects of the situation (Granot, Balcetis, & Schneider, 2014). Group identification with one individual or the other will make some action possibilities more salient via its redirection of visual attention to opportunities for agency (or lack of agency) for one person rather than agentic possibilities for the other (Granot et al., 2014). In general, the degree to which stimuli are impoverished and the perceiver is focused on seeing a situation "for" another person rather than with regard to one's own capabilities, the more that motivated inferential processes will dominate judgmental outcomes (Balcetis & Dunning, 2006; Balcetis & Lassiter, 2010) rather than veridical, affordance-based detection. Even in motivation-distorting, highly inferential process-based situations (Granot et al., 2014), however, attentional measures (what part of a visual display one focuses on) should be in support of inferential processes that follow.

Indeed, exploring the detection and enactment of affordances in rich and complex social environments is a neglected area of research for social ecological psychologists. However, there has been a flurry of interesting research on social affordance detection and action in the sport psychology arena (e.g., Araújo, Ramos, & Lopes, 2016; Silva, Garganta, Araújo, Davids, & Aguiar, 2013; Silva et al., 2015)—albeit very little of it conducted by social psychologists. Research from a social-ecological perspective has focused on emergent transient synergies such as interpersonal synchrony, or on detection of social affordances, or emergence of cooperative action. Little research has illuminated the *environment* side of social affordances that is relevant to coordination and cooperation. In the final section, we turn to this issue.

## Future Directions: Affordances of Behavior Settings

The terms "environment," "setting," and "situation" have all been used in multiple and overlapping ways. Social psychology currently favors the term *situation*, and sometimes uses it when assessing the kinds of activities people are engaged in, in a particular location and time (Guillaume et al., 2016). Most often, the term is currently used to categorize what is happening around a person in terms of high-level interpersonal processes or the psychological reality of a setting, rather than its spatiotemporal reality (e.g., Edwards & Templeton, 2005; Cantor, Mischel, & Schwartz, 1982; Reiss, 2008; Ten Berge & De Raad, 2002). From an ecological and dynamical account, however, the only reasonable starting point for a taxonomy of situations is one that focuses on the degree to which a situation allows an individual to fulfill relevant goals, as Yang, Read, and Miller (2009) proposed in their comprehensive review of situation taxonomies. What would a research program look like that takes the situation's opportunities for various forms of agency as its starting point? Unpacking an affordance-based account implies a wide range of questions that social psychology has simply not pursued in any depth, with the exception of some environmental psychology research, which did not have the benefit of Gibson's concepts to allow a principled (rather than purely descriptive) approach to pursue those issues.

First, an affordance-based account implies certain assumptions about situations: that they should be conveyed by information available for pickup, not that they are mere cultural constructions, or that because of habit, or experience, one believes the situation allows certain opportunities for action. That a situation tells us certain actions are possible here must be in some way conveyed by information available to an active perceiver. But almost no research has pursued these questions: What is it *in* a situation that allows it opportunities for certain manifestations of agency, and restrains others? And from the perspective of the goals of this chapter in particular, what aspects of a situation provide opportunities or close down opportunities for social connection? To what extent do the opportunities of the environment universally evoke certain behaviors (e.g., with young enough children, when encountering an unusually bouncy surface, nearly all will jump up and down)? To what extent do the social affordances for connection in a setting interact with individual traits (Yang et al., 2014) or need states to predict environmental responses (Meagher & Marsh, 2017)?

The social ecological perspective cares about a physical environment, one which has a "durable existence"—a spatial and temporal reality (Barker, 1968; Schoggen, 1989), and is not merely the *construal* of an environment, or a subjective representation of an environment. Roger Barker developed an area of research focused on ecological environments, and more specifically, developed the notion of *behavior settings* which provides direction for a way forward (Heft, 2001). A behavior setting is a part of the ecological environment that has definable temporal and spatial boundaries—one can know that the setting will be in existence at particular times (it might be advertised, for instance), and a perceiver, entering a behavior setting unexpectedly would be able to detect where the boundary is. Behavior settings cease existence during the times when they do not occur (e.g., when a basketball game is not occurring, or when music class is not being held), even though aspects of the milieu (e.g., basketballs, court, music stands) may continue to exist. Important aspects of what defines a behavior setting are objective, observable "standing patterns of behavior by people—that is, specific sequences of people's behavior that regularly occur within particular settings" (Schoggen, 1989, pp. 2–3).

Importantly, there is an interdependency of participants in the setting, but the existence of the behavior setting is not dependent on a particular individual's behavior. Thus a standing pattern of behavior "has unique and stable character-istics that persist even when current inhabitants of the setting are replaced by others" (Schoggen, 1989, p. 31). If one player or referee is injured or unavailable, another person fills that role, and the standing pattern of playing or refereeing remains intact. An important aspect of the behavior setting is therefore the "*dynamic, on-going pattern of relationships among individuals*" (Heft, 2007, p. 97). Barker discovered behavior settings by starting out to focus on individual dif-ferences in children's behavior—dispositional differences— and finding instead that children's behaviors varied less *across children* than they varied *across settings*. Knowing what behavior setting a child was in substantially predicted aspects of their behavior, much more so than knowing the particular behavioral tendencies of the child (Barker, 1978; Barker & Wright, 1954; Barker, Wright, Barker, & Schoggen, 1961).

Barker's rich and extremely detailed observations of the behavior of members of behavior settings within a small Midwestern US town and a small British town (Barker & Schoggen, 1973; Barker & Wright, 1951) illustrated how strong the possibilities and constraints of our environments are for social behavior. Barker's perspective provides a fertile starting point for research determining the informational and dynamical features that define situations, considered from an affordance-based perspective (Yang et al., 2009). However, only a few hypotheses Barker developed about behavior settings have been tested using rigorous experi-mental (or even correlational) methodologies (e.g., Heft, Hoch, Edmunds, & Weeks, 2014). For a field that has been calling for a more situated, embodied, behavioral and *situation*-focused approach (e.g., Agnew, Carlston, Graziano, & Kelly, 2009; Baumeister, Vohs, & Funder, 2007; Rauthmann, Sherman, & Funder, 2015; Rauthmann, Sherman, Nave, & Funder, 2015; Reiss, 2008; Smith & Semin, 2004), this offers an excellent way forward to understanding the environment-based features that provide a grounding for social coordination and cooperation.

## Conclusion

In this chapter, I have suggested that an approach to social psychology that reaches into its evolutionary roots to focus on the local interactions between co-present actors in a local environmental niche provides a substantially new approach to understanding the nature and emergence of sociality phenomena such as interper-sonal synchrony and joint action. Dynamical principles explain how self-organizing principles can provide the causal mechanism for social connection's emergence, and active perceptual exploration processes are essential as well. The approach sug-gests a way for the field to become unstuck from its all too common focus on the individual (or at best, the dyad) as the unit of analysis for study.

## Notes

1 This work was completed while the author was serving at the National Science Foundation. The views expressed in this chapter are solely those of the author and do not necessarily represent those of the NSF. The author thanks Harry Heft, Stephen Read, Brian Eiler, and Andrzej Nowak for comments on an earlier version of this chapter.

2 The term "ecological psychology" is inherently problematic, as this term has been claimed by a wide-range of individuals such as population biologists, behavioral ecologists, and cognitive, clinical, evolutionary, and developmental psychologists and anthropologists who have a traditional cognitivist bent, but wish to signal a concern with situated or evolutionary influences. Typical concerns for "ecology," for instance, might include using levels of explanations that are mindful of how the studied behavior would normally occur in natural, real-world contexts, or would normally be situated in important community contexts (families, cultures). Here I use the term more narrowly, to include ecological psychologists who view humans as first and foremost animals, and who focus on environments in a substantial way in their research—specifically, the ecological niche in which a species evolved, and not merely an animal's general habitat or a human's interpersonal or cultural context. More specifically, my account focuses on the work of those whose theoretical concepts derive from Gibson's (1977, 1979) theory of perception, a theory that provided an alternative to classical constructivist approaches to perception (Marr, 1982).

3 For example, the term "affordance" was widely popularized by publication of Norman's otherwise excellent book on the design of everyday objects (Norman, 1988). Unfortunately, his inaccurate use of the term (as he acknowledges) was not corrected until the book was revised (Norman, 2002).

4 This section liberally paraphrases what my collaborators and I have explained elsewhere (Marsh, Johnston, Richardson, & Schmidt, 2009, p. 1220).

5 A caution to readers that the size of the relationships between synchrony and self-reported liking, affiliation, and self-other connection appear overstated by the published literature, not surprisingly (Open Science Collaboration, 2015). Correspondence with other researchers and the author's own experience suggest that at least in minimal interaction paradigms, effects using any particular self-report measures are not always replicable, much like analogous effects in the mimicry literature.

6 See Marsh (2015) for further elaboration about these issues surrounding perceptual processes.

7 This is not to say that experience has no role. With new capabilities, for instance (a child learning to crawl, or someone wearing shoes with high blocks attached; Mark, 1987), experience is needed in order to develop perceptual attunement to information that specifies affordances. Perceptual cliff experiments with crawling infants indicate that ability to detect a falling-off place is not instantaneously perceived by an infant; it requires some crawling experience in order to learn what information to attend to in the environment (Gibson & Walk, 1960).

## References

Agnew, C. R., Carlston, D. E., Graziano, W. G., & Kelly, J. R. (Eds.) (2009). *Then a miracle occurs: Focusing on behavior in social psychology theory and research.* New York: Oxford University Press.

Araújo, D., Ramos, J. P., & Lopes, R. J. (2016). Shared affordances guide interpersonal synergies in sports teams. In N. P. Passos, K. Davids, & J. Y. Chow (Eds.), *Interpersonal coordination and performance in social systems* (pp. 165–178). London: Routledge.

Asch, S. (1952). *Social psychology.* New York: Prentice Hall.

Balcetis, E., & Dunning, D. (2006). See what you want to see: Motivational influences on visual perception. *Journal of Personality and Social Psychology, 91,* 612–625.

Balcetis, E., & Lassiter, G. D. (Eds.) (2010). *The social psychology of visual perception.* New York: Psychology Press.

Bargh, J. A., Chen, M., & Burrows, L. (1996). Automaticity of social behavior: Direct effects of trait construct and stereotype activation on action. *Journal of Personality and Social Psychology, 71,* 230–244.

Barker, R. G. (1978). Need for an eco-behavioral science. In R. G. Barker et al., *Habitats, environments, and human behavior* (pp. 36–48). San Francisco, CA: Jossey-Bass.

Barker, R. G., & Schoggen, P. (1973). *Qualities of community life: Methods of measuring environment and behavior applied to an American and an English town.* San Francisco, CA: Jossey-Bass.

Barker, R. G., & Wright, H. F. (1951). *One boy's day: A specimen record of behavior.* New York: Harper.

Barker, R. G., & Wright, H. F. (1954). *Midwest and its children: The psychological ecology of an American town.* New York: Row, Peterson, & Co.

Barker, R. G., Wright, H. F., Barker, L. S., & Schoggen, M. (1961). *Specimen records of American and English children.* Oxford: University of Kansas Publications.

Baumeister, R., Vohs, K. D., & Funder, D. C. (2007). Psychology as the science of self-reports and finger movements: Whatever happened to actual behavior? *Perspectives on Psychological Science, 2,* 396–403.

Bernieri, F. J. (1988). Coordinated movement and rapport in teacher–student interactions. *Journal of Nonverbal Behavior, 12,* 120–138.

Bernieri, F. J., Davis, J. M., Rosenthal, R., & Knee, C. R. (1994). Interactional synchrony and rapport: Measuring synchrony in displays devoid of sound and facial affect. *Personality and Social Psychology Bulletin, 20,* 303–311.

Bernieri, F. J., Reznick, J. S., & Rosenthal, R. (1988). Synchrony, pseudosynchrony, and dissynchrony: Measuring the entrainment process in mother–infant interactions. *Journal of Personality and Social Psychology, 54,* 243–253.

Berry, D. S., Kean, K. J., Misovich, S. J., & Baron, R. M. (1991). Quantized displays of human movement: A methodological alternative to the point-light display. *Journal of Nonverbal Behavior, 15,* 81–97.

Cantor, N., Mischel, W., & Schwartz, J. C. (1982). A prototype analysis of psychological situations. *Cognitive Psychology, 14,* 45–77.

Cesari, P., & Newell, K. M. (1999). The scaling of human grip configurations. *Journal of Experimental Psychology: Human Perception and Performance, 25,* 927–935.

Chartrand, T. L., & Bargh, J. A. (1999). The chameleon effect: The perception–behavior link and social interaction. *Journal of Personality and Social Psychology, 76,* 893–910.

Cohen, E. E., Ejsmond-Frey, R., Knight, N., & Dunbar, R. I. (2010). Rowers' high: Behavioural synchrony is correlated with elevated pain thresholds. *Biology Letters, 6,* 106–108.

Condon, W. S., & Sander, L. W. (1974). Synchrony demonstrated between movements of the neonate and adult speech. *Child Development, 45,* 456–462.

Demos, A. P., Chaffin, R., Lewis, A., Begosh, K. T., Daniels, J. R., & Marsh, K. L. (2012). Rocking to the beat: Effect of music and partner's movements on spontaneous interpersonal coordination. *Journal of Experimental Psychology: General, 141,* 49–53.

Doerrfeld, A., Sebanz, N., & Shiffrar, M. (2012). Expecting to lift a box together makes the load look lighter. *Psychological Research, 76,* 467–475.

Edwards, J. A., & Templeton, A. (2005). The structure of perceived qualities of situations. *European Journal of Social Psychology, 35,* 705–723.

Fowler, C. A., Richardson, M. J., Marsh, K. L., & Shockley, K. (2008). Language use, coordination, and the emergence of cooperative action. In A. Fuchs & V. K. Jirsa (Eds.), *Coordination: Neural, behavioral and social dynamics* (pp. 261–279). Berlin: Springer-Verlag.

Fusaroli, R., Rączaszek-Leonardi, J., & Tylén, K. (2013). Dialog as interpersonal synergy. *New Ideas in Psychology, 32,* 147–157.

Gibson, E. J., & Walk, R. D. (1960). The "visual cliff." *Scientific American, 202,* 67–71.

Gibson, J. J. (1977). The theory of affordances. In R. Shaw & J. Bransford (Eds.), *Perceiving, acting, and knowing: Toward an ecological psychology* (pp. 67–82). Hillsdale, NJ: Lawrence Erlbaum.

Gibson, J. J. (1979). *The ecological approach to visual perception.* Boston, MA: Houghton Mifflin.

Gilbert, M. (1996). *Living together: Rationality, sociality, and obligation.* New York: Rowman & Littlefield.

Gilbert, M. (2014). *Joint commitment: How we make the social world.* New York: Oxford University Press.

Granot, Y., Balcetis, E., & Schneider, K. E. (2014). Justice is not blind: Visual attention exaggerates effects of group identification on legal punishment. *Journal of Experimental Psychology: General, 143,* 2196–2208.

Guillaume, E., Baranski, E., Todd, E., Bastian, B., Bronin, I., Ivanova, C., et al. (2016). The world at 7:00: Comparing the experience of situations across 20 countries. *Journal of Personality, 84,* 493–509.

Haken, H., Kelso, J. A. S., & Bunz, H. (1985). A theoretical model of phase transitions in human hand movements. *Biological Cybernetics, 51,* 347–356.

Heft, H. (2001). *Ecological psychology in context: James Gibson, Roger Barker, and the legacy of William James's radical empiricism.* Mahwah, NJ: Lawrence Erlbaum.

Heft, H. (2007). The social constitution of perceiver-environment reciprocity. *Ecological Psychology, 19,* 85–105.

Heft, H., Hoch, J., Edmunds, T., & Weeks, J. (2014). Can the identity of a behavior setting be perceived through patterns of joint action? An investigation of place perception. *Behavioral Sciences, 4,* 371–393.

Hodges, B. H., & Lindhiem, O. (2006). Carrying babies and groceries: The effect of moral and social weight on caring. *Ecological Psychology, 18,* 93–111.

Hove, M. J. & Risen, J. L. (2009). It's all in the timing: Interpersonal synchrony increases affiliation. *Social Cognition, 27,* 949–960.

Iberall, A. S. (1987). A physics for study of civilizations. In F. E. Yates (Ed.), *Self-organizing systems: The emergence of order* (pp. 521–540). New York: Plenum.

Iberall, A. S., & Soodak, H. (1987). A physics for complex systems. In F. E. Yates (Ed.), *Self-organizing systems: The emergence of order* (pp. 499–520). New York: Plenum.

Iberall, A. S., Wilkinson, D., & White, D. (1993). *Foundations for social and biological evolution: Progress toward a physical theory of civilization and of speciation.* Laguna Hills, CA: Cri-de-Coeur Press.

Ingber, D. E. (2008). Tensegrity and mechanotransduction. *Journal of Bodywork & Movement Therapies, 12,* 198–200.

Isenhower, R. W., Marsh, K. L., Richardson, M. J., Helt, M., Schmidt, R. C., & Fein, D. (2012). Rhythmic bimanual coordination is impaired in young children with Autism Spectrum Disorder. *Research in Autism Spectrum Disorders, 6,* 25–31.

Isenhower, R. W., Richardson, M. J., Carello, C., Baron, R. M., & Marsh, K. L. (2010). Affording cooperation: Embodied constraints, dynamics, and action-scaled invariance in joint lifting. *Psychonomic Bulletin and Review, 17*, 342–347.

Issartel, J., Marin, L., & Cadopi, M. (2007). Unintended interpersonal co-ordination: "Can we march to the beat of our own drum?" *Neuroscience Letters, 411*, 174–179.

Järvilehto, T. (1998). The theory of the organism–environment system. I: Description of the theory. *Integrative Physiological & Behavioral Science, 33*, 321–334.

Järvilehto, T. (2001). Feeling as knowing, Part II: Emotion, consciousness and brain activity. *Consciousness & Emotion, 2*, 75–102.

Johnson, K. L. (2013). Social constraints on perceiving biological motion. In K. L. Johnson & M. Shiffrar (Eds.), *Visual perception of the human body in motion: Findings, theory, and practice*. New York: Oxford University Press.

Johnston, L. (2013). Kinematics and vulnerability perception. In K. L. Johnson & M. Shiffrar (Eds.), *Visual perception of the human body in motion: Findings, theory, and practice*. New York: Oxford University Press.

Johnston, L., Hudson, S. M., Richardson, M. J., Gunns, R. E., & Garner, M. (2004). Changing kinematics as a means of reducing vulnerability to attack. *Journal of Applied Social Psychology, 34*, 514–537.

Juarerro, A. (2002). *Dynamics in action: Intentional behavior as a complex system*. Cambridge, MA: MIT Press.

Kean, K. J. (2000). An investigation into the interpersonal kinematics of cooperation and competition. *Dissertation Abstracts International, Section B: The Sciences and Engineering, 60*, 4965.

LaFrance, M. (1979). Nonverbal synchrony and rapport: Analysis by the cross-lag panel technique. *Social Psychology Quarterly, 42*, 66–70.

Lewin, K., Lippitt, R., & White, R. K. (1939). Patterns of aggressive behavior in experimentally created "social climates." *Journal of Social Psychology, 10*, 271–299.

Lopresti-Goodman, S. M., Richardson, M. J., Silva, P. L., & Schmidt, R. C. (2009). Period basin of entrainment for unintentional visual coordination. *Journal of Motor Behavior, 40*, 3–10.

Lumsden, J., Miles, L. K., Richardson, M. J., Smith, C. A., & Macrae, C. (2012). Who syncs? Social motives and interpersonal coordination. *Journal of Experimental Social Psychology, 48*, 746–751.

Mace, W. M. (1977). James J. Gibson's strategy for perceiving: Ask not what's inside your head, but what your head's inside of. In R. Shaw & J. Bransford (Eds.), *Perceiving, acting, and knowing: Toward an ecological psychology* (pp. 43–65). Hillsdale, NJ: Lawrence Erlbaum.

Macrae, C. N., Duffy, O. K., Miles, L. K., & Lawrence, J. (2008). A case of hand waving: Action synchrony and person perception. *Cognition, 109*(1), 152–156.

Marr, D. (1982). *Vision*. San Francisco, CA: W. N. Freeman.

Marsh, K. L. (2010). Sociality from an ecological, dynamical perspective. In G. R. Semin & G. Echterhoff (Eds.), *Grounding sociality: Neurons, minds, and culture* (pp. 43–71). London: Psychology Press.

Marsh, K. L. (2013). Coordinating social beings in motion. In K. L. Johnson & M. Shiffrar (Eds.), *People watching: Social, perceptual, and neurophysiological studies of body perception* (pp. 236–257). New York: Oxford University Press.

Marsh, K. L. (2015). Social ecological context of conversing. *Ecological Psychology, 27*(4), 310–334. doi:10.1080/10407413.2015.1086229

Marsh, K. L., Isenhower, R. W., Richardson, M. J., Helt, M., Verbalis, A. D., Schmidt, R. C., & Fein, D. (2013). Autistic and social disconnection in interpersonal rocking. *Frontiers in Integrative Neuroscience, 7*(4), 1–8. doi:10.3389/fnint.2013.00004

Marsh, K. L., Johnston, L., Richardson, M. J., & Schmidt, R. C. (2009). Toward a radically embodied, embedded social psychology. *European Journal of Social Psychology, 39,* 1217–1225.

Marsh, K. L., & Meagher, B. R. (2016). Affordances and interpersonal coordination. In P. Passos, K. Davids, & J. Y. Chow (Eds.), *Interpersonal coordination and performance in social systems* (pp. 245–258). London: Routledge.

Marsh, K. L., Richardson, M. J., Baron, R. M., & Schmidt, R. C. (2006). Contrasting approaches to perceiving and acting with others. *Ecological Psychology, 18,* 1–37.

Marsh, K. L., Richardson, M. J., & Schmidt, R. C. (2009). Social connection through joint action and interpersonal coordination. *Topics in Cognitive Science, 1,* 320–339.

Mark, L. S. (1987). Eyeheight-scaled information about affordances: A study of sitting and stair climbing. *Journal of Experimental Psychology: Human Perception and Performance, 13,* 361–370.

McArthur, L. Z., & Baron, R. M. (1983). Toward an ecological theory of social perception. *Psychological Review, 90,* 215–238.

McNeill, W. H. (1995). *Keeping together in time: Dance and drill in human history.* Cambridge, MA: Harvard University Press.

Meagher, B. M. (2014). The emergence of home advantage from differential perceptual activity. Unpublished doctoral dissertation, University of Connecticut, Storrs, CT.

Meagher, B. R., & Kang, J. J. (2013). Gender identification as a constraint on detecting multiple affordances. In T. Davis, P. Passos, M. Dicks, & J. A. Weast-Knapp (Eds.), *Studies in perception and action XII: Seventeenth International Conference on Perception and Action* (pp. 106–109). New York: Psychology Press.

Meagher, B. R., & Marsh, K. L. (2014). The costs of cooperation: Action-specific perception in the context of joint action. *Journal of Experimental Psychology: Human Perception and Performance, 40,* 429–444.

Meagher, B. R., & Marsh, K. L. (2015). Testing an ecological account of spaciousness in real and virtual environments. *Environment and Behavior, 7,* 782–815.

Meagher, B. R., & Marsh, K. L. (2017). Seeking the safety of sociofugal space: Environmental design preferences following social ostracism. *Journal of Experimental Social Psychology, 68,* 192–199.

Michaels, C. F. (2003). Affordances: Four points of debate. *Ecological Psychology, 15,* 135–148.

Miles, L. K., Griffiths, J. L., Richardson, M. J., & Macrae, C. (2010). Too late to coordinate: Contextual influences on behavioral synchrony. *European Journal of Social Psychology, 40,* 52–60.

Miles, L. K., Lumsden, J., Richardson, M. J., & Macrae, C. (2011). Do birds of a feather move together? Group membership and behavioral synchrony. *Experimental Brain Research, 211,* 495–503.

Miles, L. K., Nind, L. K., & Macrae, C. N. (2009). The rhythm of rapport: Interpersonal synchrony and social perception. *Journal of Experimental Social Psychology, 45,* 585–589.

Newtson, D. (1994). The perception and coupling of behavior waves. In R. R. Vallacher & A. Nowak (Eds.), *Dynamical systems in social psychology* (pp. 139–167). New York: Academic Press.

Newtson, D. (1998). Dynamical systems and the structure of behavior. In K. M. Newell (Ed.), *Applications of nonlinear dynamics to developmental process modeling* (pp. 199–220). Mahwah, NJ: Lawrence Erlbaum.

Nie, L., Caban, J., & Marsh, K. L. (2015). Comparing solo and joint syncopation shows dyadic facilitation. In J. A. Weast-Knapp, M. L. Malone, & D. H. Abney (Eds.), *Studies in perception and action XIII: Eighteenth International Conference on Perception and Action* (pp. 69–72). New York: Psychology Press.

Norman, D. (1988). *The psychology of everyday things.* New York: Basic Books.

Norman, D. (2002). *The design of everyday things* (revised and expanded ed.). New York: Basic Books.

Nowak, A., & Vallacher, R. R. (1998). *Dynamical social psychology.* New York: Guilford Press.

Nowak, A., Vallacher, R. R., & Zochowski, M. (2005). The emergence of personality: Dynamic foundations of individual variation. *Developmental Review, 25*, 351–385.

Open Science Collaboration (2015). Estimating the reproducibility of psychological science. *Science, 349*(6251), aac4716.

Paxton, A. & Dale, R. (2013). Argument disrupts interpersonal synchrony. *Quarterly Journal of Experimental Psychology, 66*, 2092–2102.

Rauthmann, J. F., Sherman, R. A., & Funder, D. C. (2015). Principles of situation research: Towards a better understanding of psychological situations. *European Journal of Personality, 29*, 363–381.

Rauthmann, J. F., Sherman, R. A., Nave, C. N., & Funder, D. C. (2015). Personality-driven situation experience, contact, and construal: How people's personality traits predict characteristics of their situations in daily life. *Journal of Research in Personality, 55*, 98–111.

Reed, E. S. (1996). *Encountering the world: Toward an ecological psychology.* New York: Oxford University Press.

Reiss, H. T. (2008). Reinvigorating the concept of the situation in social psychology. *Personality and Social Psychology Review, 12*, 311–329.

Richardson, M. J., Dale, R., & Marsh, K. L. (2014). Complex dynamical systems in social and personality psychology: Theory, modeling and analysis. In H. T. Reis & C. M. Judd (Eds.), *Handbook of research methods in social and personality psychology* (2nd ed., pp. 251–280). New York: Cambridge University Press.

Richardson, M. J., Garcia, R. L., Frank, T. D., Gregor, M., & Marsh, K. L. (2012). Measuring group synchrony: A cluster-phase method for analyzing multivariate movement time-series. *Frontiers in Fractal Physiology, 3*, 405. doi:10.3389/fphys.2012.00405

Richardson, M. J., Marsh, K. L., & Baron, R. M. (2007). Judging and actualizing intrapersonal and interpersonal affordances. *Journal of Experimental Psychology: Human Perception and Performance, 33*, 845–859.

Richardson, M. J., Marsh, K. L., Isenhower, R. W., Goodman, J. R. L., & Schmidt, R. C. (2007). Rocking together: Dynamics of unintentional and intentional interpersonal coordination. *Human Movement Science, 26*, 867–891.

Richardson, M. J., Marsh, K. L., & Schmidt, R. C. (2005). Effects of visual and verbal couplings on unintentional interpersonal coordination. *Journal of Experimental Psychology: Human Perception and Performance, 31*, 62–79.

Richardson, M. J., Marsh, K. L., & Schmidt, R. C. (2010). Challenging the egocentric view of coordinated perceiving, acting and knowing. In L. F. Barrett, B. Mesquita, & E. R. Smith (Eds.), *Mind in context* (pp. 307–333). New York: Guilford Press.

Rietveld, E., & Kiverstein, J. (2014). A rich landscape of affordances. *Ecological Psychology, 26,* 325–352.

Riley, M. A., Richardson, M. J., Shockley, K., & Ramenzoni, V. C. (2011). Interpersonal synergies. *Frontiers in Psychology, 2,* 38. doi:10.3389/fpsyg.2011.00038

Runeson, S., & Frykholm, G. (1983). Kinematic specification of dynamics as an informational basis for person-and-action perception: Expectation, gender recognition, and deceptive intention. *Journal of Experimental Psychology: General, 112,* 585–615.

Schmidt, R. C., Bienvenu, M., Fitzpatrick, P. A., & Amazeen, P. G. (1998). A comparison of intra- and interpersonal interlimb coordination: Coordination breakdowns and coupling strength. *Journal of Experimental Psychology: Human Perception and Performance, 24,* 884–900.

Schmidt, R. C., Carello, C., & Turvey, M. T. (1990a). Critical fluctuations and non-equilibrium phase transitions in the coordination between two people. *Journal of Experimental Psychology: Human Perception and Performance, 16,* 227–247.

Schmidt, R. C., Carello, C., & Turvey, M. T. (1990b). Phase transitions and critical fluctuations in the visual coordination of rhythmic movements between people. *Journal of Experimental Psychology: Human Perception and Performance, 16,* 227–247.

Schmidt, R. C., Christianson, N., Carello, C., & Baron, R. (1994). Effects of social and physical variables on between-person visual coordination. *Ecological Psychology, 6,* 159–183.

Schmidt, R. C., & O'Brien, B. (1997). Evaluating the dynamics of unintended interpersonal coordination. *Ecological Psychology, 9,* 189–206.

Schmidt, R. C., Fitzpatrick, P., Caron, R., & Mergeche, J. (2011). Understanding social motor coordination. *Human Movement Science, 30,* 834–845.

Schmidt, R. C., Morr, S., Fitzpatrick, P., & Richardson, M. J. (2012). Measuring the dynamics of interpersonal synchrony. *Journal of Nonverbal Behavior, 36,* 263–279.

Schmidt, R. C., & Richardson, M. J. (2008). Dynamics of interpersonal coordination. In A. Fuchs & V. K. Jirsa (Eds.), *Coordination: Neural, behavioral and social dynamics* (pp. 281–307). Berlin: Springer-Verlag.

Schoggen, P. (1989). *Behavioral settings: A revision and extension of Roger G. Barker's Ecological Psychology.* Stanford, CA: Stanford University Press.

Sebanz, N., Bekkering, H., & Knoblich, G. (2006). Joint action: Bodies and minds moving together. *Trends in Cognitive Sciences, 10,* 71–76.

Sebanz, N., Knoblich, G., & Prinz, W. (2005). How two share a task: Corepresenting stimulus–response mappings. *Journal of Experimental Psychology: Human Perception and Performance, 31*(6), 1234–1246.

Shockley, K., Richardson, D. C., & Dale, R. (2009). Conversation and coordinative structures. *Topics in Cognitive Science, 1,* 305–319.

Shockley, K., Santana, M. V., & Fowler, C. A. (2003). Mutual interpersonal postural constraints are involved in cooperative conversation. *Journal of Experimental Psychology: Human Perception and Performance, 29,* 326–332.

Silva, P., Esteves, P., Correia, V., Davids, K., Araújo, D., & Garganta, J. (2015). Effects of manipulating player numbers vs. field dimensions on inter-individual coordination during youth football small-sided games. *International Journal of Performance Analysis of Sport, 15,* 641–659.

Silva, P., Garganta, J., Araújo, D., Davids, K., & Aguiar, P. (2013). Shared knowledge or shared affordances? Insights from an ecological dynamics approach to team coordination in sports. *Sports Medicine, 43,* 765–772.

Smith, E. R., & Semin, G. R. (2004). Socially situated cognition: Cognition in its social context. In M. P. Zanna (Ed.), *Advances in experimental social psychology* (Vol. 36, pp. 53–117). San Diego, CA: Elsevier Academic Press.

Soodak, H., & Iberall, A. S. (1987). Thermodynamics and complex systems. In F. E. Yates (Ed.), *Self-organizing systems: The emergence of order* (pp. 460–469). New York: Plenum.

Ten Berge, M. A., & De Raad, G. (2002). The structure of situations from a personality perspective. *European Journal of Personality, 16,* 81–102.

Turvey, M. T. (1990). Coordination. *American Psychologist, 45,* 938–953.

Turvey, M. T. (2007). Action and perception at the level of synergies. *Human Movement Science, 26,* 657–697.

Turvey, M. T., & Fonseca, S. (2014). The medium of haptic perception: A tensegrity hypothesis. *Journal of Motor Behavior, 46,* 143–187.

Turvey, M. T., & Shaw, R. (1999). Ecological foundations of cognition. I: Symmetry and specificity of animal–environment systems. *Journal of Consciousness Studies, 6,* 85–110.

Vacharkulksemsuk, T., & Frederickson, B. L. (2012). Strangers in sync: Achieving embodied rapport through shared movements. *Journal of Experimental Social Psychology, 48,* 399–402.

Valdesolo, P., Ouyang, J., & DeSteno, D. (2010). The rhythm of joint action: Synchrony promotes cooperative ability. *Journal of Experimental Social Psychology, 46,* 693–695.

Vallacher, R. R., & Nowak, A. (Eds.) (1994). *Dynamical systems in social psychology.* San Diego, CA: Academic Press.

Vallacher, R. R., Read, S. J., & Nowak, A. (2002). The dynamical perspective in personality and social psychology. *Personality and Social Psychology Review, 6,* 264–273.

Vallacher, R. R., Van Geert, P., & Nowak, A. (2015). The intrinsic dynamics of psychological process. *Current Directions in Psychological Science, 24,* 58–64.

Van der Kamp, J., Savelsbergh, G. J. P., & Davis, W. E. (1998). Body-scaled ratio as a control parameter for prehension in 5- to 9-year-old children. *Developmental Psychobiology, 33,* 351–361.

Van Ulzen, N. R., Lamoth, C. J. C., Daffertshofer, A., Semin, G. R., & Beek, P. J. (2008). Characteristics of instructed and uninstructed interpersonal coordination while walking side-by-side. *Neuroscience Letters, 432,* 88–93.

Vicaria, I. M., & Dickens, L. (2016). Meta-analyses of the outcomes of interpersonal coordination. *Journal of Nonverbal Behavior, 40,* 335–361.

Warren, W. H. (1984). Perceiving affordances: Visual guidance of stair climbing. *Journal of Experimental Psychology: Human Perception and Performance, 10,* 683–703.

Wiltermuth, S. S. & Heath, C. (2009). Synchrony and cooperation. *Psychological Science, 20,* 1–5.

Yang, Y., Read, S. J., Denson, T. F., Xu, Y., Zhang, J., & Pedersen, W. C. (2014). The key ingredients of personality traits: Situations, behaviors, and explanations. *Personality and Social Psychology Bulletin, 40,* 79–91.

Yang, Y, Read, S. J., & Miller, L. C. (2009). The concept of situations. *Social and Personality Psychology Compass, 3,* 1018–1037.

Ye, L., Cardwell, W., & Mark, L. S. (2009). Perceiving multiple affordances for objects. *Ecological Psychology, 21,* 185–217.

# 10

# FROM INTERACTION TO SYNCHRONIZATION IN SOCIAL RELATIONS

*Robin R. Vallacher and Andrzej Nowak*[1]

Interpersonal relations are established through social interactions. This connection is obvious, of course, but the means by which a complex relationship can develop from simple interaction is not as clear. One could argue that the exchange of compliments and agreed-upon attitudes in social interaction is the key to establishing a bond between people (e.g., Byrne, 1971; Swann, 1990; Thibaut & Kelley, 1959). But relationships are not limited to individuals who encounter each other already inclined to think, feel, and act the same way, nor to individuals who feel rapport at first sight. Relationships, like other social processes, evolve in time, and do so in a manner that promotes change in both individuals. We suggest that the development of interpersonal relationships can be understood by framing social interaction in terms of *synchronization*, a process that characterizes coupled dynamical systems (Kaneko, 1993; Shinbrot, 1994). The central idea is that interacting individuals are not static entities, maintaining fixed thoughts and action tendencies, but instead represent separate systems capable of displaying rich dynamics, and that the synchronization of their respective dynamics produces a higher-order system—the dyadic relationship—with its own dynamic properties. In this chapter, we document the role of synchronization in close relationships and present a formal model, implemented in computer simulations, that illustrates how synchronization develops in interpersonal contexts.

People in their daily lives clearly recognize the importance of synchronization in their social relationships. Thus, two individuals comprising a positive relationship are said to "be on the same wavelength" or to "resonate with one another," suggesting that their internal states and overt behaviors are coordinated on some timescale. As the relationship develops, their spontaneous reactions to events become increasingly similar and their moment-to-moment thoughts and feelings when in one another's presence rise and fall in tandem. Individuals in problematic relationships, in contrast, are described as "being out of synch with each other," with their respective reactions and feelings following different temporal trajectories. They may display the same pattern of thought and behavior when exposed to strong and unambiguous stimuli—a traumatic event or a celebratory occasion, for example—but when the stimuli diminish, the individuals fall back into their respective idiosyncratic patterns that evolve independently.

Despite the centrality of interpersonal synchronization in people's intuitive understanding of relationships, this construct has received sparse attention in social psychology. For the most part, theorists and researchers have conceptualized both short-term interactions and long-term relationships in terms of global variables that characterize the interaction or relationship as a whole. The interactions between individuals or among members of a group, for example, are commonly investigated in terms of constructs such as cooperation versus competition, compatibility of motives and goals, and the structure of norms and roles (e.g., Biddle & Thomas, 1966; Dawes, 1980; Levine & Moreland, 1998; Berkowitz & Walster, 1976; Wish, Deutsch, & Kaplan, 1976). In some approaches, the temporal aspects of social interaction are emphasized, but the focus is usually restricted to the development of strategies for achieving personal or shared goals (e.g., Axelrod, 1984; Messick & Liebrand, 1995; Thibaut & Kelley, 1959).

Synchronization between individuals takes on a different and more precise meaning when viewed from the perspective of nonlinear dynamical systems. In the dynamical account, two (or more) people are synchronized to the extent that the actions, thoughts, and feelings of one person are related over time to the actions, thoughts, and feelings of the other person or persons (cf. Marsh, Richardson, & Schmidt, 2009; Nowak & Vallacher, 1998; Nowak, Vallacher, & Zochowski, 2002). Because the temporal pattern of a person's phenomenal experience and overt behavior can be quite complex and hard to predict (Vallacher & Nowak, 1997), assessing the synchronization of two (or more) such patterns poses a daunting task. Fortunately, methods and tools have been developed to characterize temporal coordination in physical systems, including those capable of highly complex and chaotic behavior (e.g., Shinbrot, 1994). We suggest that this approach, based on principles of nonlinear dynamical systems, can be adapted to the investigation of synchronization in interpersonal systems. In particular, we employ coupled logistic equations—the simplest dynamical systems capable of chaotic behavior—to investigate synchronization dynamics.

## The Coordination of Behavior

The most basic and ubiquitous form of synchronization is the correlation over time between individuals with respect to some parameter. This phenomenon has been investigated extensively in the context of movement coordination (e.g., Beek & Hopkins, 1992; Bernieri, Reznick, & Rosenthal, 1988; Delaherche et al., 2012; Hove & Risen, 2009; Macrae, Duffy, & Lawrence, 2008; Marsh,

Richardson, & Schmidt, 2009; Miles, Griffiths, Richardson, & Macrae, 2010; Miles, Nind, Henderson, & Macrae, 2010; Miles, Nind, & Macrae, 2009; Newtson, 1994; Pelose, 1987; Schmidt, Beek, Treffner, & Turvey, 1991; Schmidt & Richardson, 2008; Shockley, Santana, & Fowler, 2003; Turvey, 1990). For example, a person is asked to swing his or her legs in time to a metronome and the other person is asked to match those movements. Two forms of coordination are typically observed: *in-phase* synchronization (the individuals swinging their legs in unison) and *anti-phase* synchronization (the individuals swinging their legs with the same frequency, but in the opposite direction). In a variation of this approach, the individuals are asked to synchronize out-of-phase. Up to a certain rate of movement, people can follow these instructions successfully. But beyond a certain tempo, the individuals cannot maintain this form of synchronization, and switch spontaneously to in-phase synchronization. Hysteresis—a signature feature of nonlinear dynamical systems—is also commonly observed in this research (cf. Kelso, 1995). Thus, when the tempo is decreased to some value, the individuals can re-establish anti-phase coordination, but this tempo is significantly lower than the point at which they originally started to coordinate in-phase.

In-phase coordination, then, is the easiest form to achieve and maintain, and it may be the only form that can be sustained as coordination becomes more difficult (e.g., as the tempo of behavior is increased). This constraint on coordination may find expression in more involving social situations. Under conditions conducive to high stress, for example, people may find it impossible to coordinate their behavior in any form other than in-phase. In a crowded club or auditorium that suddenly bursts into flames, taking turns in exiting through the doors is the only form of coordination that would make evacuation possible, yet the occupants are typically unable to do so. In similar fashion, when the level of emotionality reaches a critical point in a conversation, the individuals may find it impossible to take turns speaking.

In recent years, psychologists have investigated the role of behavioral synchronization in social relations, with particular emphasis on affect and liking. Much of this research has focused on behavioral mimicry, commonly referred to as the *chameleon effect* (e.g., Chartrand & Bargh, 1999; Dijksterhuis & Bargh, 2001). Mimicry is ubiquitous in interpersonal life, occurring in about a third of ordinary social interactions, and it typically unfolds with little or no conscious awareness on the part of interacting individuals (e.g., Chartrand & Bargh, 1999; Lakin & Chartrand, 2003). People's unconscious tendency to mimic one another occurs in multiple channels, including facial expressions, mannerisms, physical gestures, and posture (e.g., Dijksterhuis, 2005). Mimicry appears essential to empathy, rapport, and liking in social interaction. Even something as seemingly trivial as two people rubbing their respective faces in unison functions as "social glue" that binds people together (e.g., Bernieri, 1988; Chartrand & Bargh, 1999; Chartrand, Maddux, & Lakin, 2005; Dijksterhuis, 2005; Gueguen, 2004; LaFrance, 1979;

Lakin & Chartrand, 2003; Lakin, Jefferis, Cheng, & Chartrand, 2003; Maurer & Tindall, 1983; Stel, Van Baaren, & Vonk, 2008; Stel & Vonk, 2010; Van Baaren, Holland, Kawakami, & Van Knippenberg, 2004). But recent research suggests that synchronization rather than mimicry may be responsible for this effect. People who synchronize their respective finger movements to a metronome rather than to one another's movements, for example, tend to like one another (Hove & Risen, 2009).

## The Synchronization of Internal States

The synchronization of overt behavior is clearly an important component of interpersonal relations, but the synchronization of people's internal states—their thoughts and feelings—has broader significance for social relations (e.g., Nowak et al., 2002; Tickle-Degnen & Rosenthal, 1987). Internal states represent a broad category, ranging from states that operate on short timescales, such as mood or arousal, to features that reflect fairly enduring properties of a person that operate on considerably longer timescales, such as personality traits, values, goals, and temperament. A concern with synchronization of internal states is salient for people even in simple social interaction. In preparing for an interaction with a stranger, for example, people tend to change their mood to match the anticipated affective state of the stranger, even if this means toning down a positive mood in favor of a more subdued mood (e.g., Erber, Wegner, & Thierrault, 1996).

The quality of a relationship is signaled by the degree to which individuals coordinate in-phase with respect to their respective internal states (e.g., Baron, Amazeen, & Beek, 1994; Butler & Randall, 2013; McGrath & Kelly, 1986; Nowak, Vallacher, & Zochowski, 2005; Guastello, Pincus, & Gunderson, 2006; Sbarra & Hazan, 2008; Tickle-Degnen & Rosenthal, 1987). Indeed, the synchronized ebb and flow of moods, emotional reactions, and judgments may convey deeper insight into the nature of a relationship than might global properties such as the average sentiment, the amount of information exchanged, or the summary judgments reached. In essence, synchronization binds individuals in a relationship into a higher-order functional unit that has its own dynamic properties. In a close romantic relationship, for example, the synchronized flow of thoughts, feelings, and actions cannot be reduced to the individuals' personal dynamics. We speak of the "couple" as if it, rather than the separate individuals, constituted the relevant unit of analysis. The emergence of higher-order functional units through synchronization can be used to characterize other enduring and meaningful relationships, including long-term friendships, tight-knit groups, and successful work and sports teams.

To capture the essence of interpersonal synchronization and explore its relevance and generality, we propose a formal model that depicts the emergence of synchronization of both overt behavior and internal states in social relationships. The key assumptions of the model are tested in computer simulations of the emergence of synchronization in a dyad as the individuals develop a progressively closer relationship. Based on the simulation results, we discuss the implications of synchronization dynamics for topics and issues of interest in the study of social experience.

## Humans as Nonlinear Dynamical Systems

The backdrop and rationale for the model are derived from the study of nonlinear dynamical systems (e.g., Haken, 1978; Holland, 1995; Schuster, 1984; Strogatz, 2003; Weisbuch, 1992). In its most basic sense, a dynamical system is a set of interconnected elements that evolve in time, with the elements influencing, or adjusting, to each other to achieve a coordinated state that characterizes the system as a whole. Because of the influence arising within the system, the system may display a pattern of change in some system-level property in the absence of external influence. Depending on the topic, elements can represent anything from atoms to animals and planets. The task of dynamical systems theory is to specify how the elements interact with each other over time to promote global properties and behavior characterizing the system as a whole. In physics, the issue is how subatomic particles interact to produce visible matter and forces; in ecology, the focus is how animals interact to generate and maintain a balance between predator and prey; in cosmology, a central concern is how planets and other celestial bodies influence each other to produce stable orbits.

Nonlinear systems are noteworthy for their tendency to demonstrate *emergence*. This simply means that the higher-order property or behavior that results from the mutual influence among elements cannot be reduced to the properties of the elements. The stable pattern of planetary orbits, for example, depends on the mutual gravitational influences among the planets, not on the properties of the planets in isolation. Rather than being imposed on the system by outside forces, in other words, the higher-level properties and behaviors emerge from the internal workings of the system itself. For this reason, the process responsible for emergence is referred to as *self-organization*.

Once a higher-level property or behavior emerges in a dynamical system, it constrains the behavior of the elements that give rise to it, and can capture the behavior of new elements that enter the system. When a stable orbit emerges in a planetary system, for example, it constrains the orbits of each planet and can capture the orbit of passing asteroids and comets. Because it functions to "attract" the behavior of both existing and new elements, the system-level property is referred to as an *attractor*. A system's attractor actively resists change due to outside influences, and thus serves to stabilize the system. If system-level change occurs, it is because the mutual influences among the elements are weakened, so that they evolve independently of one another, which undermines the attracting power of the system's higher-order property or behavior. From this disassembled state of affairs, however, the system is primed for self-organization and emergence to a new higher-order state that provides a different configuration of the lower-level elements. A dynamical system, in other words, tends to display periods of stability and resistance to disruption and change, punctuated by periods of disassembly that set the stage for a new round of self-organization and emergence.

Because humans display change over time, and often do so in the absence of external influence, they can be conceptualized—and presumably investigated—as dynamical systems (Vallacher, Van Geert, & Nowak, 2015). Every domain of human functioning reflects the complementary tendencies of stability and change due to the mutual influence among the elements comprising the domain. The mind is in constant motion, generating an endless flow of momentary thoughts and feelings, but it also demonstrates strong attractor tendencies that provide coherence and stability in social judgment. Social interactions, meanwhile, demonstrate a continuous flow of words and gestures that is never replicated exactly, yet they admit to regularities and patterns that qualify as attractors. And social relationships are characterized by the evolution of roles and sentiments, with the emergence of scripts and agendas that function as attractors for the actions and thoughts of the partners. In recognition of the complex, dynamic, and emergent nature of human experience, the approach of nonlinear dynamical systems has emerged in recent years as an integrative model for the topical landscape of social psychology (cf. Boker & Wenger, 2007; Butner, Gagnon, Geuss, Lessard, & Story, 2014; Guastello, Koopmans, & Pincus, 2009; Nowak & Vallacher, 1998; Vallacher, Read, & Nowak, 2002; Vallacher & Nowak, 1994, 1997, 2007).

A psychological system may have more than one attractor, each representing a different global system-level property that provides stability and coherence for the system. Which attractor governs a system's dynamics at a given point in time depends on the initial states or starting values of the system's elements. The set of initial states that converge on each attractor represents the *basin of attraction* for that attractor. For a person or a group characterized by multiple attractors, then, the process in question can display different equilibrium tendencies, each associated with a distinct basin of attraction. Within each basin, different initial states will follow a trajectory that eventually converges on the same stable value. Even a slight change in the system's initial state, however, will promote a large change in the system's trajectory if this change represents a state that falls just outside the original basin of attraction and within the basin for an alternative attractor. The potential for multiple attractors in a psychological system captures the intuition that people can have different or even mutually contradictory patterns of thought, feeling, and action.

The attractor landscape (e.g., single versus multiple) that characterizes a dynamical system depends in part on the value of one or more *control parameters* that influence the mutual interactions among the elements of the system. In the research on synchronization of leg swinging, for example, the tempo of leg swinging is the relevant control parameter. When the value of this parameter (i.e., tempo) increases and reaches a threshold, the form of synchronization changes (e.g., from anti-phase to in-phase). The relevant control parameters for various psychological systems have yet to be identified, but likely candidates include stress, arousal, subjective importance, rate of information intake, task or judgment difficulty, and perceived control (Vallacher & Nowak, 2007). Changes in the values of these factors can shape the manner in which momentary thoughts, feelings, and actions self-organize to promote the emergence of attractors for the system. Depending on the value of a system's control parameter, the system may evolve in very different ways, including convergence on a single attractor, the generation of two (or more) attractors, and very complex patterns of evolution resembling randomness (i.e., deterministic chaos). Mild stress or arousal, for example, may promote a flow of thought and feeling that converges on a single attractor for judgment and global affect, whereas more intense stress or arousal may promote a flow of thought and feeling that results in conflicting attractors for judgment and affect. A particularly intense level of stress or arousal, meanwhile, might change the interactions of momentary thoughts and feelings, such that the person's global judgment or affect is characterized by chaos rather than by attractors with fixed values.

Dynamical systems come in many forms, but the simplest system capable of complex behavior is the *logistic equation* (Feigenbaum, 1978). The logistic equation involves repeated iteration, so that the output value representing the system's state ($x$) at one step ($n$) becomes the input value for the equation at the next step ($n+1$). The current value of the system's state (which varies between 0 and 1), in other words, depends on the state's previous value—that is, $x_{n+1} = f(x_n)$. This dependency has two opposing components. First, the *higher* the previous value, the *higher* the current value; specifically, $x_{n+1}$ equals $x_n$ multiplied by the value of the system's control parameter, represented as $r$. Second, the *higher* the previous value, the *lower* the current value; specifically, $x_{n+1}$ equals $(1-x_n)$ multiplied by the value of $r$. The combined effect of these competing tendencies is expressed as $x_{n+1} = rx_n(1-x_n)$. Depending on the value of $r$, repeated iteration of the logistic equation can display qualitatively different patterns of behavior (pattern of changes in $x$), including the convergence on a single value (i.e., attractor), oscillatory (periodic) changes between two or more values, and very complex patterns of behavior resembling randomness (i.e., deterministic chaos).

We suggest that the logistic equation provides a useful way of conceptualizing human dynamics (cf. Nowak & Vallacher, 1998; Nowak et al., 2002). In this approach, $x$ represents a person's behavior, and changes in $x$ represent variations in the intensity of the behavior. The control parameter, $r$, corresponds to internal states (e.g., moods, arousal levels, traits, values) that shape the person's pattern of behavior (changes in $x$ over time). The opposing forces expressed by the logistic equation capture the idea of conflict, which is a key concept in many psychological theories. In classic research on motivational conflict (Miller, 1944), for example, movement toward a goal increases both approach and avoid tendencies. Research on achievement motivation (e.g., Atkinson, 1964), in turn, has identified two concerns, the desire for success and the fear of failure, that combine in different ways to produce resultant motivation. Research on thought suppression, meanwhile, suggests that attempts at suppression activate an ironic process that works at cross-purposes with the attempted suppression (cf. Wegner, 1994). More generally, the assumption that conflicting forces or tendencies are central to human experience is common to most issues of psychological interest (e.g., short-term versus long-term self-interest, impulse versus self-control, autonomy versus social identity, egoism versus altruism).

## Social Interaction as the Coupling of Nonlinear Dynamical Systems

If an individual can be represented as a dynamical system, then social interaction can be conceptualized and investigated as the coupling or synchronization of two (or more) dynamical systems. Accordingly, we have employed coupled logistic equations, which have a successful track record in modeling the synchronization of physical systems (e.g., Shinbrot, 1994), to model the synchronization of interacting individuals. The basic idea is that when the value of the behavior $(x)$ for one person (i.e., equation) depends not only on its previous value but also to some degree on the value of $x$ for the other equation, the two equations tend to become synchronized over time. This idea is easy to appreciate in the context of human interaction: the behavior of each person depends not only on his or her preceding behavior, but also on the preceding behavior of the other person. In formal terms, this influence or coupling is operationalized according to the following equations:

$$x_1(t+1) = \frac{r_1 x_1(t)(1-x_1(t)) + \alpha r_2 x_2(t)(1-x_2(t))}{1+\alpha} \tag{10.1}$$

$$x_2(t+1) = \frac{r_2 x_2(t)(1-x_2(t)) + \alpha r_1 x_1(t)(1-x_1(t))}{1+\alpha} \tag{10.2}$$

To the value of the dynamical variable representing one person's behavior $(x_1)$, one adds a fraction, denoted by $(alpha)$, of the value of the dynamical variable representing the behavior of the other person $(x_2)$. The size of *alpha* represents the strength of coupling and reflects the mutual influence or interdependency of the interacting individuals. When the fraction is 0, there is no coupling on the behavior level, whereas a value of 1.0 signifies that each person's behavior is determined equally by his or her preceding behavior and the preceding behavior of the other person. Intermediate values of *alpha* represent intermediate values of coupling.

## Modeling the Synchronization of Behavior

When the control parameters $(r)$ of each person have the same value, the dependence between their respective behaviors causes the systems to synchronize completely, with the temporal changes in $x_1$ and $x_2$ becoming identical (e.g., Kaneko, 1984). In the real world, of course, the respective control parameters of two individuals are rarely (if ever) identical, nor does the same degree of mutual influence or interdependence characterize all relationships. In an initial set of computer simulations, therefore, we investigated how the coordination of dynamical variables (corresponding to individuals' behavior) depends on the similarity of control parameters (corresponding to individuals' internal states) and the strength of coupling (corresponding to the strength of influence between individuals).

We began each simulation with a random value of the dynamical variables for each person, drawn from a uniform distribution that varied from 0 to 1. We assume that individuals often tend to display complex temporal patterns that can be difficult to identify and may seem unpredictable. Accordingly, the control parameter for one system (one person) was held constant at a value of 3.67, which corresponds to low levels of chaotic behavior. We systematically varied the value of the control parameter for the other person between values of 3.6 and 4.0, which corresponds to the highest value of the chaotic regime. We let the simulations run for 300 steps, so that each system had a chance to come close to its pattern of intrinsic dynamics (i.e., pattern of changes in $x$) and both systems had a chance to synchronize. For the next 500 simulation steps, we recorded the values of the dynamical variables (behavior) for each system and measured the degree of synchronization (i.e., the difference between the dynamical variables).

The primary results reflected the intuitions expressed earlier. The degree of synchronization tended to increase both with increases in *alpha* (mutual influence) and with increasing similarity in *r*. This suggests that mutual influence and similarity in internal states can compensate for one another in achieving a particular level of synchronization in social interaction. Thus, despite relatively weak mutual influence, two people can achieve a high degree of synchronization if their respective internal states are similar. If the individuals have different internal states, however, high mutual influence—for example, constant monitoring, communication, or mutual reinforcement—is necessary to maintain the same level of synchronization.

The simulation results also revealed less straightforward, but interesting effects for behavior coordination due to variation in *alpha*. For very high values of *alpha*, the predominant mode of coordination was in-phase synchronization. But for low values of *alpha*, the simulation results revealed different modes of coordination. In addition to in-phase synchronization, the coupled systems displayed anti-phase synchronization (analogous to turn-taking in behavior), independence in behavior, and yet more complex forms of coordination. This suggests that when mutual influence is relatively weak, a richer repertoire of modes of coordination is available. There was also a tendency for the systems to stabilize each other under relatively weak coupling, so that each system behaved in a more regular (e.g., less chaotic) manner than it would have without the weak influence (cf. Ott, Grebogi, & York, 1990). Considered together, these results suggest that for high levels of mutual influence and control (e.g., constant monitoring and control), the behavior of one person largely tends to mirror the behavior of the other partner. For relatively weak mutual influence, in contrast, behavior coordination can be manifest in more complex and less obvious forms. The complex and nonlinear nature of coordination in this case suggests that observers may find it difficult to note or understand the ways in which the behaviors of the individuals are synchronized.

These results imply that mutual influence in close relationships (cf. Thibaut & Kelley, 1959) may be a mixed blessing. To be sure, if two individuals have very dissimilar internal states, they may nonetheless achieve a fair degree of coordination by directly influencing one another's behavior. But at the same time, this scenario creates the potential for instability in the relationship because the dynamics of the two people will immediately diverge as soon as the influence is weakened. In contrast, a high level of similarity in the setting of control parameters can maintain synchronization for a considerable period of time when mutual influence is broken. Even if the individuals' behaviors do not synchronize in time, the overall form of their respective dynamics will remain similar, making the reestablishment of coordination at a later time relatively easy. In couples characterized by similarity in their respective internal states, then, relatively little influence or communication is required to maintain coordination and thus maintain the relationship. Couples characterized by weak similarity in their internal states, in contrast, may be able to maintain coordination in their behavior, but only through strong and sustained attempts at mutual influence. Because such couples thus are at heightened risk for a breakdown in coordination, they may engage in events together that induce a common mood and also bring about coordination on a behavioral level. Activities that are affectively positive (e.g., dancing, entertainment, sexual relations) can clearly have this effect, but so can negatively toned events, such as witnessing a tragic event or having a heated argument.

## Modeling the Synchronization of Internal States

Modeling the synchronization of internal states (i.e., the similarity of control parameters) is straightforward, at least in principle. One need only assume that on each simulation step, the values of each person's control parameter drifts in the direction of the value of the other person's control parameter. How quickly the control parameters begin to converge is determined by the rate of this drift and the size of the initial discrepancy between the values of the respective control parameters. This mechanism works fine if one can assume that both individuals can directly observe or estimate the settings of one another's control parameters. However, direct observation of the internal states of an interaction partner may be difficult, or even impossible in some cases. People engage in considerable effort when communicating or attempting to infer one another's dispositional qualities and other internal states (cf. Jones & Davis, 1965; Kunda, 1999; Nisbett & Ross, 1980; Wegner & Vallacher, 1977). Despite the multiplicity of cognitive means available to people, the precise nature of a person's momentary state or relevant chronic disposition may be opaque to others—or wildly misperceived.

Interacting individuals may lack insight or clear inferences into one another's internal states, but they may nonetheless achieve similarity in these states by means of behavioral coordination. This possibility follows from several lines of social psychological research. Research on *facial feedback* (e.g., Strack, Martin, & Stepper, 1988), for example, has demonstrated that when people are induced to mechanically adopt a specific facial configuration linked to a particular affective state (e.g., disgust), they tend to experience that affective state. The matching of one's internal states to one's overt behavior has also been demonstrated for behavior that is interpersonal in nature. Even role-playing, in which a person follows a scripted set of actions *vis-à-vis* another person, often produces noteworthy changes in the role-player's attitudes and values to match his or her overt actions (e.g., Zimbardo, 1970).

To simulate this mechanism in our model, we allowed each system (i.e., person) to modify the value of its own control parameter in order to match the other system's pattern of behavior. So although the exact value of the other person's control parameter is invisible to the person, he or she remembers the partner's most recent set of behaviors (i.e., the most recent values of $x$), as well as his or her own most recent behaviors. The person compares the other person's pattern with his or her own, and adjusts his or her own control parameter until the two behavior patterns match (Zochowski & Liebovitch, 1997). If the other person's observed behavior pattern is more complex (e.g., more chaotic) than the person's own behavior pattern, he or she adjusts (increases) the value of his or her own control parameter (internal state) until similarity in their respective behavior patterns is achieved. But if the other person's behavior is less complex than the person's own behavior, the person decreases slightly the value of his or her own control parameter. In effect, interacting individuals can "discover" the internal state of one another by monitoring and matching the dynamics of one another's behavior.

Figure 10.1 displays the progressive similarity of internal states in accordance with this scenario under relatively weak coupling (*alpha* = 0.25). Time in simulation steps is represented on the $x$-axis, and the difference between the two systems in their respective control parameters (thick gray line) and in their dynamical variables (thin black line) is portrayed on the $y$-axis. The figure shows that the two systems become progressively similar in the values of their control parameters and perfectly synchronized in their behavior over time. These results suggest that attempting behavioral synchronization under relatively weak levels of mutual control over one another's behavior facilitates the matching of one another's internal state.

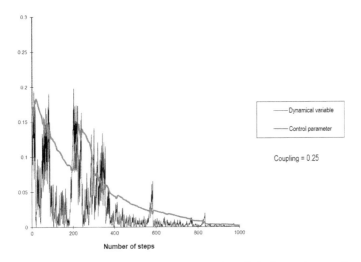

**FIGURE 10.1**  Development of synchronization under relatively weak mutual influence. From A. Nowak, R. R. Vallacher, & M. Zochowski (2002). The emergence of personality: Personal stability through interpersonal synchronization. In D. Cervone & W. Mischel (Eds.), *Advances in personality science* (Figure 1, p. 305). New York: Guilford Press. Reprinted with permission of Guilford Press.

Figure 10.2 displays very different results when the simulations were performed with a relatively high value of coupling (*alpha* = 0.7). Although virtually perfect synchronization in behavior develops almost immediately, the control parameters of the two systems fail to converge completely, even after many interaction opportunities (1000 simulation steps). Strong mutual influence causes full synchronization of behavior, even for systems with very different values of their respective control parameters. Even though full synchronization is achieved, the two individuals do not have a clue that their control parameters are different. If the coupling were suddenly removed, the dynamics of the two individuals would immediately diverge. This suggests that although very strong influence promotes behavioral coordination, it is likely to hinder synchronization at a deeper level.

The simulation results have interesting implications for interpersonal dynamics. They suggest, first of all, that there is an optimal level of influence and control over behavior in social relationships. If influence is too weak, synchronization may fail to develop at all. On the other hand, very strong influence is likely to prevent the development of a relationship based on mutual understanding, emotional similarity, and empathy. Partners who monitor and control one another may fully synchronize their behavior, but they are unlikely to adopt the internal states necessary to maintain such behavior in the absence of such monitoring and control. And as noted earlier, high values of coupling restrict the

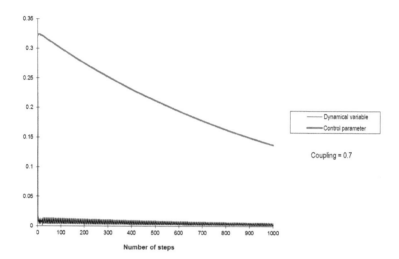

**FIGURE 10.2**  Development of synchronization under relatively strong mutual influence. From A. Nowak A. Nowak, R. R. Vallacher, & M. Zochowski (2002). The emergence of personality: Personal stability through interpersonal synchronization. In D. Cervone & W. Mischel (Eds.), *Advances in personality science* (Figure 2, p. 306). New York: Guilford Press. Reprinted with permission of Guilford Press.

range of possible modes of coordination in a relationship. Mutual influence that is too strong may therefore result in a relationship that is experienced as highly predictable and potentially boring. On balance, the optimal degree of coupling is one that enables effective coordination, but does so without directly influencing the behavior of the relationship partners. In effect, moderate coupling allows for the internalization of common internal states in a relationship. And under such conditions, relationships may develop rich dynamics and the potential to switch between different modes of coordination. The optimal degree of coupling, in sum, is the minimal amount necessary to achieve synchronization.

## Synchronization and Personality

It is widely assumed in psychology that personality plays an important role in social interaction and the formation of interpersonal relationships. Indeed, no one would quibble with the suggestion that people's stable characteristics (e.g., traits, values, temperament) bias the choice of interaction partners and influence the likelihood of success in establishing meaningful and enduring relationships with those who are chosen. An extraverted person, for example, seeks out a variety of other people for social interaction and is likely to form a fairly extensive network of friends and acquaintances. A shy person, on the other hand, approaches social interaction in a considerably more tentative fashion, interacts with far fewer individuals, and tends to have a relatively limited circle of friends and acquaintances.

One can look at the process in reverse, however, and consider how social interactions shape personality. After all, a person's personality comes from somewhere. The synchronization dynamics model implies that a person's history of social interactions plays a crucial role in personality development. In interacting with someone, the individual develops internal states that facilitate synchronization, provided the interactions proceed with moderate rather than strong mutual influence. Particularly if interactions with someone are sustained over time, the emergent internal states become engraved in the person's cognitive-affective system as attractors. The resultant attractors operate as ready-made parameters for subsequent interactions, and thus promote efficiency in the person's social relations. A person who has repeated interactions with someone whose behavior is characterized by high energy, for example, is likely to develop an internal setting for energetic behavior that shapes how he or she interacts with others.

Synchronization dynamics also account for personality complexity and explain why some people have a wider repertoire of stable internal states than do others. As noted earlier, nonlinear dynamical systems are often characterized by multistability, with more than one attractor shaping the system's dynamics. The emergence of multiple attractors characterizes human systems as well (e.g., Nowak & Vallacher, 1998; Vallacher, Van Geert, & Nowak, 2015). It is easy to appreciate the emergence of multistability in personality from this perspective. With increasing diversity among the people with whom one interacts and forms relationships, one is likely to develop a corresponding proliferation of stable internal states—attractors for cognitive, affective, and behavioral tendencies—for interpersonal encounters. Even a social recluse is bound to interact with a variety of people and is certain to have more than one more or less enduring relationship. For those who are more socially inclined—no doubt the majority of people, given humans' strong belongingness concerns (Baumeister & Leary, 1995)—many social relationships are likely to develop over a lifetime, with each one holding potential for establishing a different internal setting for behavior. People with extensive and diverse social relations are especially capable of acting in diverse fashion, with each mode representing control by a different internal state. In effect, each person has as many personality tendencies as he or she has different types of relationships.

In principle, some people may lack any stable attractors with respect to any internal state relevant to social relationships. This possibility follows from research on individual variation in action identification, which has shown that people differ in the extent to which they think about their behavior across numerous domains in relatively low-level, mechanistic terms as opposed to higher-level, comprehensive terms reflecting effects, consequences, and self-evaluative implications (Vallacher & Wegner, 1989). Because they focus on the granular aspects of their behavior, "low-level agents" tend to be unclear about what they are like with respect to broad personality traits, making them more open to social feedback regarding these personal qualities than are "high-level agents." It is noteworthy that low-level agents are more likely than their higher-level counterparts to have experienced environmental and interpersonal instability during childhood (Vallacher & Wegner, 1989). This finding is consistent with the synchronization dynamics model since sustained interaction with specific individuals is essential for engraving attractors for internal states.

The synchronization dynamics model also provides insight regarding a somewhat puzzling conclusion regarding the relative impact of parents and peers on children's personality development (e.g., Dunn & Plomin, 1990; Harris, 1995; Scarr, 1992). Children spend far more time with their parents than with any single peer when they are very young and thus highly impressionable, yet research suggests that they develop personality traits that are more similar to those of their peers than to those of their parents. Though controversial, this conclusion is consistent with the synchronization model and the results of its associated computer simulations. Because the parent–child relationship is characterized by strong coupling (monitoring and control), children have little need to internalize the settings of their parents' control parameters in order to achieve and maintain behavioral coordination with them. In monitoring a child's behavior, praising it when it is considered appropriate and providing discipline when it is less so, parents are exerting fairly constant and strong influence over what the child does. To the extent that the child is aware of the parents' behavior control, it learns to act in accordance with the relevant reinforcement contingencies, rules, expectations, and so forth.

Of course, children internalize important lessons from these experiences, and thus may develop control parameters that resemble their parents'. But children's need to adopt their parents' internal states pales in comparison to the strategic value of matching the internal states of their peers. Unlike parents, peers are not in a position to monitor or control a child's behavior on a daily basis. Beyond that, peers are considerably less faithful interaction partners, and the surface structure of their behavior tends to be more erratic as well. Because of these characteristics of peer relations—relatively weak coupling, relationship instability, and potential for unpredictable behavior—there is practical value in learning the internal bases for peers' behavior. Then, too, it is simply easier to resonate with the interests, moods, and thoughts of someone who is similar to oneself in age, power, experiences, and competencies. Children certainly love, admire, and appreciate their parents, but they are less likely to empathize and identify with them than they are with their peers. In short, because synchronization with peers has all the ingredients for convergence on common control parameters, it is more influential in establishing children's characteristic ways of thinking and acting.

## Caveats and Conclusions

The dynamical systems perspective on close relations resonates with lay intuition. In both cases, a close relationship is tantamount to the achievement and maintenance of behavioral and mental synchronization between two people. So although coupled non-linear dynamical systems were originally developed in mathematics and the physical sciences, they provide important insight into the dynamics of close relationships. Computer simulations confirm that synchronization occurs both with respect to dynamical variables, representing overt behavior, and control parameters, representing internal states (e.g., moods, values, personality traits, attitudes). These forms of synchronization are intimately related. In the simulations, a feedback loop exists such that each system changes its own control parameter to match the level of complexity in the dynamical variable of the other system. The model also acknowledges that the strength of mutual influence is an important factor in close relationships. This factor, represented by the strength of coupling (*alpha*), captures the essence of various social processes, including direct communication, promises of reward or threats of punishment, or other forms of control.

The computer simulations revealed that the synchronization of internal states in a relationship facilitates the synchronization of behavior. Interestingly, difficulty experienced in achieving behavioral synchronization may be used as a guide for achieving synchronization with respect to internal states. By the same token, very strong behavioral synchronization resulting from strong mutual influence (i.e., very high values of *alpha*) tends to hinder rather than facilitate the development of similarity in people's internal states. So, for a close relationship to develop and endure, the partners' control over one another's behavior must not be too strong. Although intuitively appealing, the synchronization model—and the dynamical systems perspective generally—is relatively new to psychology, so caution should be exercised when generalizing the results we have described to human relationships. There are important differences between physical systems and psychological systems, and it is an open question whether certain unique features of human thought and action (e.g., consciousness, intentionality) can be meaningfully reframed in terms of formal properties that are common to dynamical systems in other areas of science. This question, fortunately, has become an empirical question because of the rigorous methods and tools that have been developed in recent years (e.g., Boker & Wenger, 2007; Butner et al., 2014; Guastello et al., 2009; Nowak & Vallacher, 1998; Vallacher et al., 2015).

Although the logistic equation captures important features of human systems (e.g., conflicting forces), it is not clear at this early stage which synchronization phenomena are specific to the coupling of logistic equations and which reflect coupled nonlinear systems generally. The use of the logistic equation was motivated in part by the philosophy of dynamical minimalism (Nowak, 2004). The key point in this approach is that the simplest set of rules should be employed when attempting to model a real-world issue. As noted at the outset, the logistic equation is the simplest dynamical system capable of demonstrating chaotic (highly complex and unpredictable) behavior, which presumably captures the complex dynamism of human thought and behavior. Nonetheless, the robustness of the results we have observed to this point will ultimately depend on their generality across different models of dynamical systems.

At this stage in its development, the synchronization model cannot capture the complexity of human behavior and people's internal (psychological) states. Overt behavior can take a variety of forms, not all of which are likely to synchronize equally readily or in the same fashion. Internal states, for their part, are multidimensional (e.g., emotions, values, plans, temperaments) and it is not clear whether each manifestation functions in the same way as a control parameter for interpersonal synchronization. Finally, certain synchronization phenomena may be unique to humans, reflecting the influence of social and cultural norms, or perhaps expressing the unique biological properties of humans (e.g., sophisticated brains capable of self-awareness). So, although the synchronization model may provide insight into the nature of generic phenomena, empirical research with humans is critical for determining how these processes play out in the various domains of human interpersonal experience.

These caveats notwithstanding, the synchronization model and its implementation with computer simulations point to striking parallels between the dynamics of coupled logistic equations and the dynamics of close relationships. The simulation results showing that strong influence can compensate for differences in people's internal states, for example, resonates with intuitions regarding control in close relationships. The results are also consistent with research demonstrating that psychological changes obtained under relatively weak (and subtle) influence tends to be more enduring than are the more rapid changes obtained through excessive (rewarding and aversive) control (cf. Vallacher, Nowak, & Miller, 2003). In sum, framing human interpersonal dynamics in terms of synchronization dynamics prevalent in the natural world provides a conceptual and methodological bridge between psychological intuitions and the precision afforded by physical science.

## Note

1 Andrzej Nowak acknowledges the support of a grant from the Polish Committee for Scientific Research [DEC-2011/02/A/HS6/00231].

## References

Atkinson, J. W. (1964). *An introduction to motivation.* Princeton, NJ: Van Nostrand.

Axelrod, R. (1984). *The evolution of cooperation.* New York: Basic Books.

Baron, R. M., Amazeen, P. G., & Beek, P. J. (1994). Local and global dynamics of social relations. In R. R. Vallacher & A. Nowak (Eds.), *Dynamical systems in social psychology* (pp. 111–138). San Diego, CA: Academic Press.

Baumeister, R. F., & Leary, M. R. (1995). The need to belong: Desire for interpersonal attachments as a fundamental human motivation. *Psychological Bulletin, 117,* 497–529.

Beek, P. J., & Hopkins, B. (1992). Four requirements for a dynamical systems approach to the development of social coordination. *Human Movement Science, 11*, 425–442.

Berkowitz, L., & Walster, E. (Eds.) (1976). *Advances in experimental social psychology* (Vol. 9). New York: Academic Press.

Bernieri, F. J. (1988). Coordinated movement and rapport in teacher–student interactions. *Journal of Nonverbal behavior, 12*, 120–138.

Bernieri, F. J., Reznick, J. S., & Rosenthal, R. (1988). Synchrony, pseudosynchrony, and dissynchrony: Measuring the entrainment process in mother-infant interactions. *Journal of Personality and Social Psychology, 54*, 243.

Biddle, B. S., & Thomas, E. J. (Eds.) (1966). *Role theory: Concepts and research*. New York: Wiley.

Boker, S. M., & Wenger, M. J. (2007). *Data analytic techniques for dynamical systems in the social and behavioral sciences*. Mahwah, NJ: Lawrence Erlbaum.

Butler, E. A., & Randall, A. K. (2013). Emotional coregulation in close relationships. *Emotion Review, 5*, 202–210.

Butner, J., Gagnon, K. T., Geuss, M. N., Lessard, D. A., & Story, T. N. (2014). Using topology to generate and test theories of change. *Psychological Methods, 20*, 1–25.

Byrne, D. (1971). *The attraction paradigm*. New York: Academic Press.

Chartrand, T. L., & Bargh, J. A. (1999). The chameleon effect: The perception–behavior link and social interaction. *Journal of Personality and Social Psychology, 76, 6*, 893–910.

Chartrand, T. L., Maddux, W., & Lakin, J. (2005). Beyond the perception–behavior link: The ubiquitous utility and motivational moderators of nonconscious mimicry. In R. Hassin, J. Uleman, & J. A. Bargh (Eds.), *The new unconscious* (pp. 334–361). New York: Oxford University Press.

Dawes, R. M. (1980). Social dilemmas. *Annual Review of Psychology, 31*, 169–193.

Delaherche, E., Chetouani, M., Mahdhaoui, A., Saint-Georges, C., Viaux, S., & Cohen, D. (2012). Interpersonal synchrony: A survey of evaluation methods across disciplines. *IEEE Transactions on Affective Computing, 3*, 349–365.

Dijksterhuis, A. (2005). Why we are social animals: The high road to imitation as social glue. In S. Hurley & N. Chater (Eds.), *Perspectives of imitation: From cognitive neuroscience to social science* (Vol. 2, pp. 207–220). Cambridge, MA: MIT Press.

Dijksterhuis, A., & Bargh, J. A. (2001). The perception–behavior expressway: Automatic effects of social perception on social behavior. In M. P. Zanna (Ed.), *Advances in experimental social psychology* (Vol. 33, pp. 1–40). San Diego, CA: Academic Press.

Dunn, J., & Plomin, R. (1990). *Separate lives: Why siblings are so different*. New York: Basic Books.

Erber, R., Wegner, D. M., & Thierrault, N. (1996). On being cool and collected: Mood regulation in anticipation of social interaction. *Journal of Personality and Social Psychology, 70*, 757–766.

Feigenbaum, M. J. (1978). Quantitative universality for a class of nonlinear transformations. *Journal of Statistical Physics, 19*, 25–52.

Guastello, S. J., Koopmans, M., & Pincus, D. (Eds.) (2009). *Chaos and complexity in psychology: The theory of nonlinear dynamical systems*. New York: Cambridge University Press.

Guastello, S. J., Pincus, D., & Gunderson, P. R. (2006). Electrodermal arousal between participants in a conversation: Nonlinear dynamics and linkage effects. *Nonlinear Dynamics, Psychology, and Life Sciences, 10*, 365–399.

Gueguen, N. (2004). Mimicry and seduction: An evaluation in a courtship context. *Social Influence, 4*, 249–255.

Haken, H. (1978). *Synergetics*. Berlin: Springer.

Holland, J. H. (1995). *Emergence: From chaos to order*. Reading, MA: Addison-Wesley.

Harris, J. R. (1995). Where is the child's environment? A group socialization theory of development. *Psychological Review, 102*, 458–589.

Hove, M. J., & Risen, J. L. (2009). It's all in the timing: Interpersonal synchrony increases affiliation. *Social Cognition, 27*(6), 949–960.

Jones, E. E., & Davis, K. E. (1965). From acts to dispositions: The attribution process in person perception. In L. Berkowitz (Ed.), *Advances in experimental social psychology* (Vol. 2, pp. 220–266). New York: Academic Press.

Kaneko, K. (1984). Like structures and spatiotemporal intermittency of coupled logistic lattice: Toward a field theory of chaos. *Progress in Theoretical Physics, 72*, 480.

Kaneko, K. (Ed.) (1993). *Theory and applications of coupled map lattices*. Singapore: World Scientific.

Kelso, J. A. S. (1995). *Dynamic patterns: The self-organization of brain and behavior*. Cambridge, MA: MIT Press.

Kunda, Z. (1999). *Social cognition: Making sense of people*. Cambridge, MA: MIT Press.

LaFrance, M. (1979). Nonverbal synchrony and rapport: Analysis by the cross-lag panel technique. *Social Psychology Quarterly, 42*, 66–70.

Lakin, J. L., & Chartrand, T. L. (2003). Using nonconscious behavioral mimicry to create affiliation and rapport. *Psychological Science, 14*, 334–339.

Lakin, J. L., Jefferis, V. E., Cheng, C. M., & Chartrand, T. L. (2003). The chameleon effect as social glue: Evidence for the evolutionary significance of nonconscious mimicry. *Journal of Nonverbal Behavior, 27*, 145–162.

Levine, J. M., & Moreland, R. L. (1998). Small groups. In D. T. Gilbert, S. T. Fiske, & G. Lindzey (Eds.), *The handbook of social psychology* (4th ed., Vol. 2, pp. 415–469). New York: McGraw-Hill.

Macrae, C. N., Duffy, O. K., & Lawrence, J. (2008). A case of hand waving: Action synchrony and person perception. *Cognition, 109*, 152–156.

Marsh, K. L., Richardson, M. J. & Schmidt, R. C. (2009). Social connection through joint action and interpersonal coordination. *Topics in Cognitive Science, 1*, 320-339.

Maurer, R. E., & Tindall, J. H. (1983). Effects of postural congruence on client's perception of counselor empathy. *Journal of Counseling Psychology, 30*, 158–163.

McGrath, J. E., & Kelley, J. R. (1986). *Time and human interaction: Toward a psychology of time*. New York: Guilford Press.

Messick, D. M., & Liebrand, V. B. G. (1995). Individual heuristics and the dynamics of cooperation in large groups. *Psychological Review, 102*, 131–145.

Miles, L. K., Griffiths, J. L., Richardson, M. J., & Macrae, C. N. (2010). Too late to coordinate: Contextual influences on behavioral synchrony. *European Journal of Social Psychology, 40*, 52–60.

Miles, L. K., Nind, L. K., Henderson, Z., & Macrae, C. N. (2010). Moving memories: Behavioral synchrony and memory for self and others. *Journal of Experimental Social Psychology, 46*, 457–460.

Miles, L. K., Nind, L. K., & Macrae, C. N. (2009). The rhythm of rapport: Interpersonal synchrony and social perception. *Journal of Experimental Social Psychology, 45*, 585–589.

Miller, N. E. (1944). Experimental studies of conflict. In J. M. Hunt (Ed.), *Personality and the behavior disorders* (pp. 431–465). New York: Ronald.

Nisbett, R., & Ross, L. (1980). *Human inference: Strategies and shortcomings of social judgment*. Englewood Cliffs, NJ: Prentice Hall.

Newtson, D. (1994). The perception and coupling of behavior waves. In R. R. Vallacher & A. Nowak (Eds.), *Dynamical systems in social psychology* (pp. 139–167). San Diego, CA: Academic Press.

Nowak, A. (2004). Dynamical minimalism: Why less is more in psychology. *Personality and Social Psychology Review, 8,* 183–192.

Nowak, A., & Vallacher, R. R. (1998). *Dynamical Social Psychology*. New York: Guilford Press.

Nowak, A., Vallacher, R. R., & Zochowski, M. (2002). The emergence of personality: Personal stability through interpersonal synchronization. In D. Cervone & W. Mischel (Eds.), *Advances in personality science* (pp. 292–331). New York: Guilford Press.

Nowak, A., Vallacher, R. R., & Zochowski, M. (2005). The emergence of personality: Dynamic foundations of individual variation. *Developmental Review, 25,* 351–385.

Ott, E., Grebogi, C., & York, J. A. (1990). Controlling chaos. *Physics Review Letters, 64,* 1196–1199.

Pelose, G. C. (1987). The functions of behavioral synchrony and speech rhythm in conversation. *Research on Language and Social Interaction, 20,* 171–220.

Sbarra, D. A., & Hazan, C. (2008). Coregulation, dysregulation, self-regulation: An integrative analysis and empirical agenda for understanding adult attachment, separation, loss, and recovery. *Personality and Social Psychology Review, 12,* 141–167.

Scarr, S. (1992). Developmental theories for the 1990s: Development and individual differences. *Child Development, 63,* 1–19.

Schmidt, R. C., Beek, P. J., Treffner, P. J., & Turvey, M. T. (1991). Dynamical substructure of coordinated rhythmic movements. *Journal of Experimental Psychology: Human Perception and Performance, 17,* 635–651.

Schmidt, R. C., & Richardson, M. J. (2008). Dynamics of interpersonal coordination. In W. A. Fuchs & V. K. Jirsa (Eds.), *Coordination: Neural, behavioral and social dynamics* (pp. 281–307). Berlin: Springer-Verlag.

Schuster, H. G. (1984). *Deterministic chaos*. Vienna: Physik Verlag.

Shinbrot, T. (1994). Synchronization of coupled maps and stable windows. *Physics Review E, 50,* 3230–3233.

Shockley, K., Santana, M., & Fowler, C. A. (2003). Mutual interpersonal postural constraints are involved in cooperative conversation. *Journal of Experimental Psychology: Human Perception and Performance, 29,* 326–332.

Stel, M., Van Baaren, R. B., & Vonk, R. (2008). Effects of mimicking: Acting prosocially by being emotionally moved. *European Journal of Social Psychology, 38,* 965–976.

Stel, M., & Vonk, R. (2010). Mimicry in social interaction: Benefits for mimickers, mimickees, and their interaction. *British Journal of Psychology, 101,* 311–323.

Strack, F., Martin, L. L., & Stepper, S. (1988). Inhibiting and facilitating conditions of the human smile: A nonobtrusive test of the facial feedback hypothesis. *Journal of Personality and Social Psychology, 54,* 768–777.

Strogatz, S. (2003). *Sync: The emerging science of spontaneous order*. New York: Hyperion Books.

Swann, W. B., Jr. (1990). To be adored or to be known? The interplay of self-enhancement and self-verification. In E. T. Higgins & R. M. Sorrentino (Eds.), *Handbook of motivation and cognition* (Vol. 2, pp. 404–448). New York: Guilford Press.

Thibaut, J. W., & Kelley, H. H. (1959). *The social psychology of groups*. New York: Wiley.

Tickle-Degnen, L., & Rosenthal, R. (1987). Group rapport and nonverbal behavior. *Review of Personality and Social Psychology, 9,* 113–136.

Turvey, M. T. (1990). Coordination. *American Psychologist, 4,* 938–953.

Vallacher, R. R., & Nowak, A. (Eds.) (1994). *Dynamical systems in social psychology.* San Diego, CA: Academic Press.

Vallacher, R. R., & Nowak, A. (1997). The emergence of dynamical social psychology. *Psychological Inquiry, 8,* 73–79.

Vallacher, R. R., & Nowak, A. (2007). Dynamical social psychology: Finding order in the flow of human experience. In A. W. Kruglanski & E. T. Higgins (Eds.), *Social psychology: Handbook of basic principles* (2nd ed., pp. 734–758). New York: Guilford Press.

Vallacher, R. R., Nowak, A., & Miller, M. E. (2003). Social influence and group dynamics. In I. Weiner (Series Ed.) & T. Millon & M. J. Lerner (Vol. Eds.), *Handbook of psychology, Vol. 5: Personality and social psychology* (pp. 383–417). New York: Wiley.

Vallacher, R. R., Read, S. J., & Nowak, A. (2002). The dynamical perspective in personality and social psychology. *Personality and Social Psychology Review, 6,* 264–273.

Vallacher, R. R., Van Geert, P., & Nowak, A. (2015). The intrinsic dynamics of psychological process. *Current Directions in Psychological Science, 24,* 58–64.

Vallacher, R. R., & Wegner, D. M. (1989). Levels of personal agency: Individual variation in action identification. *Journal of Personality and Social Psychology, 57,* 660–671.

Van Baaren, R. B., Holland, R. W., Kawakami, K., & Van Knippenberg, A. (2004). Mimicry and prosocial behavior. *Psychological Science, 15,* 71–74.

Wegner, D. M. (1994). Ironic processes of mental control. *Psychological Review, 101,* 34–52.

Wegner, D. M., & Vallacher, R. R. (1977). *Implicit psychology.* New York: Oxford University Press.

Weisbuch, G. (1992). *Complex system dynamics.* Redwood City, CA: Addison-Wesley.

Wish, M., Deutsch, M., & Kaplan, S. J. (1976). Perceived dimensions of interpersonal relations. *Journal of Personality and Social Psychology, 33,* 409–420.

Zimbardo, P. G. (1970). The human choice: Individuation, reason, and order versus deindividuation. In W. J. Arnold & D. Levine (Eds.), *Nebraska Symposium on Motivation* (Vol. 17, pp. 237–307). Lincoln, NB: University of Nebraska Press.

Zochowski, M., & Liebovitch, L. (1997). Synchronization of trajectory as a way to control the dynamics of the coupled system. *Physical Review E, 56,* 3701.

# PART III

# Collective Dynamics

# 11

# SIMULATING THE SOCIAL NETWORKS IN HUMAN GOAL STRIVING

*James D. Westaby and DaHee Shon*

## Introduction

Describing, predicting, and explaining the complexities of human goal pursuit and behavior over extended periods of time is an ambitious pursuit for psychologists and social scientists. Relying upon conventional methods, unfortunately, is often limited because they have considerable difficulty navigating the various contingencies that humans face over time, the uncertain social environments into which they traverse, and the various events that can change at any probabilistic moment. Fortunately, computational modeling and computer simulations can allow researchers to apply and extend parameters from contemporary theories of psychology to navigate these more complex environments and make predictions about emergent system outcomes, such as goal achievement, performance, and emotional contagion.

According to Harrison and colleagues (Harrison, Lin, Carroll, & Carley, 2007), a variety of simulations can be created, such as (1) *agent-based models*, which examine how factors of interest can impact individuals simulated in a computer, (2) *systems dynamics models*, which model "the behavior of the system as a whole" (Harrison et al., p. 1238), and (3) *cellular automata models*, which examine how actors are influenced by the characteristics of neighboring cells. Simulations can not only address important linear and non-linear dynamics over time, they also allow researchers to arbitrarily change parameters of interest to see their impact on long-term system outcomes (Smith & Conrey, 2007). In contrast to the volume of computational research applied in the hard sciences, there is relatively less simulation research in the social sciences, despite its relevance to a wide variety of research topics examining dynamical issues (Richetin et al., 2010; Vallacher, Read, & Nowak, 2002; Weinhardt & Vancouver, 2012). And even less work has examined how social networks are motivationally involved in goal pursuits, despite the exponential growth of social network research (Borgatti, Mehra,

Brass, & Labianca, 2009). In response, this chapter explores how simulations can be used to model the complex ways in which social networks influence emergent goal striving processes and system outcomes. To traverse this new domain, a dynamic network theory perspective will be used to guide our thinking (Westaby, Pfaff, & Redding, 2014). This line of theorizing adds value over traditional goal striving research in psychology, because it comprehensively examines how social networks influence goal striving processes. Our approach is tangentially related to some of Castelfranchi, Cesta, Conte, and Miceli's (1993) computational theorizing on the interdependence of goals in social systems, although our approach systematically connects goal striving to explicit social network roles. The theory also adds value over traditional social network approaches in sociology and organizational science, because it is the first to systematically infuse goal nodes into social networks. *Goal nodes* represent potential stimuli that entities may be wanting, desiring, or pursuing (or not). Traditional network research has focused on structural links between entities alone (e.g., individuals, groups, or other collective units), and not on how those entities may be connected to specific goal pursuit nodes (e.g., how person X is supporting person Y who is striving for goal Z). Figure 11.1 illustrates these contrasts, as discussed below.

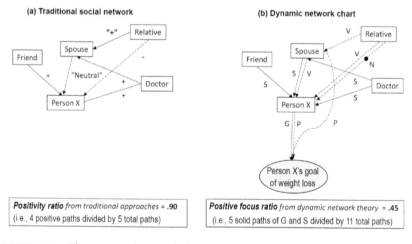

Positivity ratio *from traditional approaches* = .90 (i.e., 4 positive paths divided by 5 total paths)

Positive focus ratio *from dynamic network theory* = .45 (i.e., 5 solid paths of G and S divided by 11 total paths)

FIGURE 11.1   Chart comparisons. + indicates positive link. − indicates negative link. Quotation marks illustrate links in the traditional social network approach that have different motivational orientations in the dynamic network chart (e.g., "+" link between Spouse and Relative is actually a supportive resistance (V) link working against Person X's weight loss goal. Neutral path is not included in the positivity ratio, given ambiguity about positive or negative direction. G = goal striving. S = system supporting. P = goal preventing. V = supportive resisting. N = system negating. System reacting (R), interacting (I), and observing (O) are not illustrated, for simplicity. All manifest links are scored 1 for strength in both approaches.

The structure of the chapter is as follows. First, we review some basic network concepts. Second, we provide an overview of dynamic network theory and how it is different from traditional network theories. Third, given the importance of emergent phenomena (Nowak, Vallacher, & Zochowski, 2005; Vallacher & Nowak, 1997), we demonstrate how a rudimentary computational model can be derived from concepts in the theory to simulate emergent network power in a person's goal striving, which represents strong social networks mobilized to assist in dynamic goal pursuit. We assume in this chapter that "dynamic" means processes and outcomes changing in time. Third, we introduce *network goal graphing*, which sets the stage to create computational simulations to forecast and visualize the ways in which social networks dynamically impact emergent outcomes in real-world goal striving. In all, such network goal analysis has applications across social, organizational, and counseling psychology, as well as in conflict resolution, coaching, and consulting.

## Traditional Social Network Frameworks

Researchers have made enormous strides in describing network structures and processes in numerous domains, such as physics, technology, and the social and organizational sciences. There are several key concepts to keep in mind when thinking about networks. The first is that a network often represents how various entities (also known as vertices or nodes) are interconnected via links, edges, or ties (Burt, Kilduff, & Tasselli, 2013). For example, in highway systems, one may be interested in understanding how various cities (nodes) are connected by highways or rail (links). Or a social network researcher may be interested in how various individuals on a social networking platform are connected with one another. Once a network structure is identified or plotted, researchers can start examining a number of useful metrics to describe the system (Borgatti et al., 2009; Wasserman & Faust, 1994). For example, *network density* represents the degree to which the network is saturated with linkages, ranging from no connections to complete connections between all entities. Another powerful concept is related to the level of centrality in the system. Generally speaking, this represents the extent to which information or resources are flowing through key entities in the network. When centrality is high, certain entities in the network are receiving (or mediating) a greater amount of information or resources than others, which in turn may give them advantage by controlling the flow of information or resources in the system (Burt et al., 2013).[1] Other system-level concepts of interest to research include network size and network diversity.

From a psychological perspective, one can also examine the overall level of positivity or negativity in a system through linkages with positive or negative valence, such as friendship (positive) and foe (negative) networks. In Figure 11.1a, we illustrate such linkages in the context of a network involved in a person's goal pursuit of losing weight. Here, we see that four of the five individuals are positively linked, which gives a positivity ratio of .90. This is derived by dividing the total number of unambiguous positive paths by total number of positive and negative paths. The strength of manifest links are scored 1 in this simple illustration. As demonstrated later, results from dynamic network theory will suggest that this system has much more conflict than implied by the traditional approach. Although traditional network research has added enormous capacities to analyze complex social systems, it has not sufficiently drawn upon psychology to explain how network entities may be dynamically striving for their specific goals, wishes, and desires. Dynamic network theory attempts to fill this gap.

## Dynamic Network Theory

In dynamic network theory (Westaby et al., 2014), implicit or explicit judgment and decision-making processes are presumed to trigger the activation of one of eight types of social network role behaviors (or their multiplex combinations). The eight roles include goal striving, system supporting, goal preventing, supportive resisting, system negating, system reacting, interacting, and observing. Each role is summarized in Table 11.1, and then illustrated graphically.

**TABLE 11.1** The eight social network roles in dynamic network theory.

| Social network role | Label | Meaning | Examples |
|---|---|---|---|
| 1. Goal striving | G | Direct motivation toward a goal. | Wants, desires, intentions, wishes, or motivated states directed toward goal nodes of interest (e.g., I want to get a new job). |
| 2. System supporting | S | Providing support to others in a network in their pursuits. | Helping, supporting, assisting, aiding, advising, or backing up another's efforts to advance a goal pursuit (e.g., my friend in my network is trying to help me get a new job). |
| 3. Goal preventing | P | Direct motivation against someone's goal. | Preventing, hindering, thwarting, or attempting to stop a given goal (e.g., my boss is trying to prevent my quitting). |
| 4. Supportive resisting | V | Providing support to network entities that are showing resistance or negativity about a given goal pursuit. | Helping, supporting, assisting, aiding, advising, promoting, and backing up another's resistance or negativity toward another's goal (e.g., the company VP is supporting my boss's efforts at trying to prevent my quitting by offering me a raise). |

| | | | |
|---|---|---|---|
| 5. System negating | N | Having negative orientations toward others in their goal pursuit. | Negative attitude, feeling, affect, or disagreement directed at another's goal striving (e.g., my coworker is angry about my potential leaving, because there will be no replacement). |
| 6. System reacting | R | Having negative reactions toward others that are resisting another's pursuit. | Negative attitude, feeling, affect, or disagreement directed at another's resistance or negativity about a goal pursuit (e.g., my spouse is upset by my coworker's anger toward me). |
| 7. Interacting | I | Entities in the vicinity of another's pursuit. | Those near others in their pursuits, but not necessarily paying attention to what's going on. |
| 8. Observing | O | Entities only observing or simply being aware of another's pursuits. | Bystanders, observers, and curious entities that are attending to what's going on in a goal or behavior, but not helping or hurting others in the efforts (e.g., some customers are observing whether I will quit the company, simply out of curiosity). |

*Example system-level concepts*

| | | |
|---|---|---|
| Goal pursuit links (also known as network motivation) | The amount of goal striving and system supporting forces that fuel a goal pursuit. | In Figure 11.1: 1 G link from Person X to the goal plus 1 S link from the Friend to Person X plus 1 S link from the Spouse to Person X plus 1 S link from Doctor to Person X, and 1 S link from Doctor to Spouse (i.e., 1 G + 4 S's = 5). |
| Network resistance | The amount of goal prevention and supportive resistance in system. | In Figure 11.1: 1 P link from Person X to goal plus 1 P link from Spouse to goal plus 1 V link from Spouse to Person X plus 1 V link from Relative to Person X, and 1 V link from Relative to the Spouse (i.e., 2 P's + 3 V's = 5). |
| Positive focus ratio | The relative level of functional forces in a social system around a given goal. | Goal pursuit links (G and S) divided by all goal pursuit, network resistance, and negativity links (i.e., in Figure 11.1: $5/(5 + 6) = .45$). |

## The Eight Social Network Roles

Because goal nodes are systematically inserted into network structures, the theory can explain how networks are pivoting around goal striving processes (or not). It does so through the eight social network roles. First, the *goal striving* (G) role illustrates individuals in a network trying to pursue a given goal, aspiration, or behavior under study. Goal striving subsumes a variety of important psychological antecedents of behavior, such as the wants, dreams, wishes or desires toward a goal node (Austin & Vancouver, 1996). It also accounts for the importance of behavioral intention, one of the best predictors of human behavior (Ajzen, 1991; Fishbein & Ajzen, 2010; Westaby, 2005; Westaby, Probst, & Lee, 2010; Westaby, Versenyi, & Hausmann, 2005). Second, *system supporting* (S) represents those entities helping those in goal pursuit or encouraging those not pursuing a goal to start doing so, thereby accounting for powerful support processes on behavior (Rhoades & Eisenberger, 2002). These network forces are predicted to facilitate emergent goal achievement and performance in complex systems, especially when entities have system competency concerning the goal, such as objective skill or high self-efficacy (Stajkovic & Luthans, 1998).[2] Third, going beyond past approaches that have addressed negative interpersonal links in networks (Labianca, Brass, & Gray, 1998), to account for direct network resistance to a focal goal, *goal preventing* (P) represents entities more directly preventing, obstructing, or hindering the goal pursuit node, explicitly or implicitly. Fourth, *supportive resistance* (V) represents those indirectly supporting others in resistance efforts. The above two forces are predicted to inhibit emergent performance of those pursuing a target goal in ego-centric systems.

Fifth, as for negative interpersonal emotions, *system negating* (N) represents negative orientations to those working toward a goal. Sixth, in contrast, *system reactance* (R) represents those negatively reacting to those showing negativity or resistance to a given goal, such as when your friend gets upset with another who has intentionally obstructed your goal pursuit. While the former is negativity toward those pursuing the goal, the latter is negativity toward those resisting the goal pursuit. Hence, system reactance represents a form of negativity or arousal that is affirming the goal pursuit. Ironically, it could therefore be a *positive force*, often defending those in goal pursuit against those resisting it.

In contrast to the above factors that reflect strong motivational or emotional linkages to goal nodes or to others, the last two roles represent more peripheral ones that can inadvertently impact goal pursuits. Seventh, the *interacting role* (I), in its exclusive form, represents individuals simply interacting around others involved in a goal pursuit without necessarily paying attention to another's pursuits. This can affect performance in some settings, such as an individual trying to walk to work quickly, who becomes slowed by the density of people on a crowded sidewalk (Westaby, 2012a); those interactants that emerge in the network around a given goal pursuit are neither trying to help nor hinder the person—they have simply emerged around the person's own goal pursuit. Eighth, and lastly, those engaged exclusively in *observing* role behavior (O) represent those observing, watching, or learning about a person's goal pursuit, but not intentionally helping or hurting the process. These roles can affect performance in some cases as well, such as when experienced goal strivers increase performance when being observed, hence accounting for classic social facilitation effects in social psychology (Geen, 1991). More broadly, it is important to note that individuals can express multiplex combinations of the eight roles, which allows the theory to account for vastly different ways that individuals may demonstrate motivational, emotional, and peripheral linkages to others and their goals.[3]

## Charts, Metrics, and Conceptual Differences

In contrast to purely verbal theories, a distinct advantage of dynamic network theory for computational simulation research is its utilization of dynamic network charts to characterize and metricize complex human systems. Dynamic network charts show how social network entities are helping, hurting, or just peripherally involved in specific cases of goal pursuit. All paths in the charts are based on the finite set of roles proposed in the theory. These charts take the form of directed graphs (Snijders, Van de Bunt, & Steglich, 2010), but with the unique inclusion of a goal node. Goals play a special role in these networks because they allow researchers to examine how the entities in the network are involved in the given goal pursuit, such as a friend and coworker being supportive of one's new career plans (i.e., two system supporter links to one's career goal striving). Hence, we can now visualize and quantify how social network entities and their role linkages are pivoting around the goal node(s). This helps us theoretically explain (not just describe) how social networks are interpersonally and motivationally working for or against a given goal or behavior, instead of merely examining how interpersonal linkages alone may be influential.

However, this does not mean to imply that focusing on interpersonal connections exclusively is without merit. This has tremendous value, and its intuitive nature has been helpful in launching the network perspective to study a vast array of social, organizational, biological, technological, and physical systems (Westaby et al., 2014). However, to better predict and explain human behavior, we believe that incorporating goal nodes and corresponding social network roles is a critical next step to advance theory and scientific method.

Dynamic network charts can be focused in different ways. For example, an ego-centric version can show how entities in a network are behaviorally involved in (1) a focal person's overall goal pursuit, or (2) the person's goal pursuit at specific snapshots in time. We first illustrate the overall format in the context of Person X's attempts at trying to lose weight. We will illustrate the latter format in subsequent sections. In contrast to the traditional network approach shown in Figure 11.1a, the goal node is directly inserted into the dynamic network chart as shown in Figure 11.1b (i.e., "Person X's goal of weight loss"). Here we can see how entities and their motivated role linkages are connected to Person X's goal pursuit (or not). For simplicity, we focus on strong links here, although future research can examine weak links as well, given their potential importance in securing advantage (Granovetter, 1973). In the dynamic network charts below, the strength of manifest paths are scored 1. See Westaby (2012a) for additional ways to scale path strength, such as accounting for intensity levels.

In Figure 11.1b, we can see that Person X has often tried hard to lose weight (G path), but has also knowingly binge-eaten at times (P path); hence, a multiplex role combination path to the goal node exists in the chart (i.e., coming from the G and P paths). Person X's Friend and Spouse have also supported (S) Person X's weight loss attempt, although Person X's Spouse has worked directly against it at times by bringing home fattening food (P) and encouraging Person X to enjoy it (V path). Hence, the Spouse can manifest a complex set of non-linear behaviors that can differentially impact Person X over time. Further, Person X's Relative, who is extremely overweight, has shown supportive resistance to Person X by encouraging overeating during their dinner parties (V path).

From an emotional linkage perspective, the Relative also becomes upset when Person X does not eat a lot of food during dinner parties (N dashed path, where the black dot on path symbolizes de-affirmation against goal and visually distinguishes the path from V). This negativity is the same as the negativity seen in the traditional network approach. However, Person X does not react with negative emotions to this resistance, given that Person X realizes that the Relative is rather overweight and likely biased.[4] Lastly, a doctor has provided strong support and encouragement (S) for Person X's dieting goal as well as supportive discussions directed at the Spouse to help encourage the Spouse's support of Person X's dieting (S).

## Differences with Traditional Network Analysis

There are several differences between a traditional network approach and a dynamic network theory approach. A first major difference, as mentioned earlier, is that goal nodes are used to show how networks are connected to goal pursuits. This helps us understand how social forces are motivated around goals (or not). A second difference concerns the interpretation of positive and negative linkages. In the above example, consider the link between the Spouse and Relative. For the traditional approach, these two entities are linked positively, because they share a similar motivational orientation. In contrast, the dynamic network chart illustrates that this similarity in motivation is being leveraged against Person X's goals and wishes to lose weight, and therefore represents a negative resistance force in this goal system. A third difference can be seen when looking at overall system dynamics. For example, consider the presumed overall positivity or negativity of network forces in Person X's weight loss network. In the traditional approach, we see that there is high positivity among the interpersonal network connections in Figure 11.1a. That is, the positivity ratio is .90, where four out of the five link-ages are positive in nature. However, the dynamic network chart reveals far less positivity in the system. Here, the *positive focus ratio* from recent work on dynamic network theory (Westaby, Woods, & Pfaff, 2016) is used to generally show the functional forces in a social system involved in a given goal (G and S) where no resistance or conflict is manifest (P, V, N, and R). In this case, five out of the 11 social network role paths demonstrate purely functional orientations. The rest are de-affirming or negative in nature. This results in a positive focus ratio of .45, and suggests that the traditional network analysis of .90 may be over-estimating the positive social forces involved in the goal pursuit. Future research needs to further examine such comparisons (Westaby et al., 2014; Westaby & Redding, 2014).[5]

Although the above concepts and metrics are useful in helping describe and explain complex goal striving systems, such representations are not enough to address dynamical changes over time. In this regard, Snijders and his colleagues have done important work examining how traditional interpersonal linkages in networks may impact behavior, and have used novel methods and program-ming to examine these effects, such as longitudinal analyses, Markov modeling, and SIENA computer modeling (e.g., Snijders, Van de Bunt, & Steglich, 2010). Dynamic network theory adds to this important line of work by directly inserting goal nodes into social network structures along with social network roles to those nodes. A promising line of research would be to use concepts, methods, and pro-gramming developed by Snijders and others interested in explaining behavior in order to examine how including such goal nodes and their linkages may help us better explain emergent goal achievement, behavior, and other system outcomes of interest. Goals play a critical role here by allowing us to see how various enti-ties are emerging in a social network to help, such as providing system support to a goal striver, or hinder, such as enacting goal prevention (e.g., trying to talk a person out of a goal pursuit or behavior). In the next sections, we attempt to further extend our explanation of dynamic network processes through the use of computational modeling in more complex systems over time.

## Simulating the Development of Powerful Networks

Because the framework is grounded in computational metrics, dynamic network theory has the potential to provide new insight into how networks can impact emergent variables and system outcomes over time. Although the theory could be applied in various computational ways, we start with a basic simulation that attempts to examine how individuals derive powerful social networks to help achieve their goals. Computationally, we use a rudimentary agent-based model to simulate how individuals build such networks, given environments with vary-ing degrees of difficulty, for example. This simulation examines how agents, who are the simulated individuals in the computer program, stochastically encounter others in their social networks that may help or hinder them in their pursuits.

These stochastic environments are ones in which various social encounters are randomly and probabilistically determined.

The simulation uses select parameters in dynamic network theory to calculate the emergent power of the networks helping or inhibiting a person's goal pursuit. For example, it is assumed in the computational model that agents who encounter others in a social network that have motivational qualities (i.e., partner goal striving and system supporting roles), strong system competency (another key factor in the theory), and facilitative environments are presumed to be able to build stronger networks to help achieve their goals. In contrast, agents that encounter others that show network resistance (i.e., goal preventing and supportive resistance), negativity (i.e., system negating), and/or difficult environments are computationally assumed to have less potential of achieving goals and performing well overall. When agents probabilistically encounter such situations frequently, they will likely have problems materializing their goals into success. Throughout history, there are countless stories of individuals, groups, and even societies that cannot break such difficult cycles, which can lead to frustration, aggression, and conflict in various cases.

## The Computational Environment

The following illustrates key features of the basic computational model. A stochastic computer environment was first created for the agent in the program. That is, on each round of the computer simulation, the agent was programmed to encounter an entity in the network that had a random configuration of social network role attributes that could impact his or her goal pursuit in conjunction with an environment that ranged from somewhat easy to extremely difficult in achieving the goal. The configuration and impact of the role attributes was based on a theoretical interpretation of effects proposed in dynamic network theory (Westaby, 2012b). Future research could also base computations upon results from empirical studies on real participants, whenever possible (e.g., using results from regression or path coefficients).

Computationally, the more functional behavior the other network entities provide in less harsh environments, the greater emergent network power computationally accrued by the agent in his or her goal pursuit over time. Functional behaviors typically include more goal striving and system supporting and less goal prevention, supportive resistance, and system negation, while harsh environments generally represent those situations where resources are harder to obtain to accomplish the goal.[6] Network power can be generally conceptualized as strong social networks mobilized to assist in goal pursuit. We wanted to simulate how a focal agent builds such power over time. In this study, the rolling total for network power increases on each round when the agent encounters others that provide functional behavior and competence without network de-affirmation, and in the context of facilitative environments. For example, in a positive context where the agent encountered another person in his or her network that showed no network resistance, no dysfunctional negativity, high network motivation (i.e., G and S roles), high system competence, and a facilitative environment, the agent would have the greatest computed increase in emergent network power (e.g., a computation increment of 2). In contrast, if network resistance was encountered without any network motivation, it would stifle an increment in emergent power (e.g., a computation increment of 0). The encounter was not helpful to build the person's network, and would be reflected as such in the computations.[7] Hence, a high score for network power represents an agent's capacity to have a strong network that is willing and able to help the person achieve his or her goal.

Computing and plotting an agent's network power over iterations allows us to see how well agents are able to build network power in their encountered social systems. In Figure 11.2, we plot the network power functions observed across the computer simulations for five different individuals. Each of these plots show the degree to which each specific agent was able to acquire a strong network that has the potential to facilitate his or her goal pursuit. We ran our simulations over 1000 rounds per agent, given that people can encounter a large number of individuals across the span of long-term goals. This fits with other agent-based models that run several hundred iterations to simulate behavior (e.g., 600 for Kaufmann, Stagl, & Franks, 2009).[8]

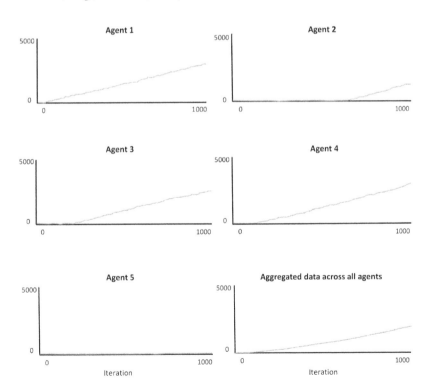

FIGURE 11.2  Emergent network power among five simulated agents. The y-axis reflects cumulative network power.

As one can see, and fitting our expectations, we saw great variation in people's capacities to build powerful networks in their goal pursuits. Some agents started to have success early, and were able to build more powerful networks with much social capital, such as Agent 1. In contrast, Agents 2, 3, and 4 required more time to gain traction, but were then able to start building more powerful networks, although at somewhat different rates and slopes. In contrast, Agent 5 had great difficulty ever gaining traction in building a powerful network, either because the environment was not facilitative, or because when it was facilitative, other people created serious network resistance or there was a lack of goal motivation in the system. In line with nonlinear perspectives (Vallacher, Van Geert, & Nowak, 2015), these results show strong nonlinear effects both within and between individuals, which multilevel statistics or hierarchical linear modeling (HLM) could formally examine for significance (Curran & Bauer, 2011; Hofmann, 1997). In this example, different individuals can end up in very different places, simply as a result of random outcomes and how they may accrue over time. These results do not take into account initial individual differences, which future models should address. In contrast, as seen in the last graph in Figure 11.2, which aggregated the data across all agents, a more linear trend was found when integrating, thereby washing away the various nonlinear complexities that were occurring for different agents in the system. There are several things we learn from these results. First, individuals experienced great variation in their abilities to develop strong networks to help them in their pursuits, which mimics what can be seen in the vast discrepancies of achievement around the world. Second, the results are revealing because they show how nonlinear trends impact the ability to build strong networks. Instead of everyone simply accruing more network power over time in a linear manner, some individuals did not gain traction until after some time passed. Then, they were able to finally start acquiring a helpful network. The implication is that individuals may need to persist through considerable resistance before enjoying some success, akin to the concept of perseverance and Grit (Duckworth et al., 2007). However, there were also some simulated individuals, despite their efforts, who were never able to gain traction. In such contexts, a profound implication is that the individuals may need to consider finding an entirely new social network system that may increase their probability of finding support and minimizing resistance. At a macro level, one can see this when individuals in impoverished countries decide to take huge risks by attempting to migrate to other places that are perceived as more resourceful, social, and less constraining.

## Adding Complexity

Although the above simulation utilized select concepts from dynamic network theory, it did not include other dynamics that could be important during goal pursuit. Hence, in the spirit of a "building block approach" (Harrison et al., 2007) where simple models are expanded, we illustrate several potential extensions. First, various sub-processes in Vancouver and colleagues' multiple-goal pursuit model (Vancouver, Weinhardt, & Schmidt, 2010) could be examined, such as those concerning negative feedback loops in control theory, resource limits (e.g., deadlines), expected performance lags, and learning rules. As of now, some of these sub-processes are more generally accounted for in dynamic network theory's system competency and feedback and change constructs.[9] Joining these theoretical perspectives could provide greater computational specification and precision.

Second, computational work could examine how habit (or past behavior) interacts with "remembering" to impact network roles and behavioral change. Integrating aspects of Tobias' (2009) model of habit, habit decay, and forgetting with constructs from dynamic network theory may be helpful. Third, it would be important for research to model how observers in a network decide whether or not to provide system support (e.g., behavioral, financial, moral, etc.) or partner goal striving—a form of goal contagion. This also has the potential to add breadth to research on bystander interventions, helping, and prosocial behavior (Dovidio, Piliavin, Schroeder, & Penner, 2006).

Another promising area of computational modeling needs to address the network rippling of emotions—a form of emotional contagion. According to dynamic network theory (Westaby et al., 2014), upon goal accomplishment or salient goal progress, goal strivers and system supporters are expected to experience a rippling of positive emotion across the network, while those in resistance roles would feel negative emotion. For example, if Pat achieves a goal, Pat will feel good, as well as Pat's immediate supporters—this positive feeling can then ripple to others in the network as they hear of the success, assuming that they support Pat's goal pursuit. Inverse outcomes are predicted for those in network resistance roles (P and V) in this same system. That is, they are expected to become upset by Pat's success as they learn of it. Those in peripheral roles (I and O) are not expected to experience large changes in emotions, unless they suddenly transform into a supporter or supportive resistor, for example, because of what they have seen in the network.

Future research needs to also examine how the network rippling of emotions, as feedback loops, may further motivate social network role behaviors (or not). To stimulate theorizing, we posit here that the networking rippling of emotions will systematically impact future social network role behaviors. For example, on one hand, we anticipate that the network rippling of positive emotions will act as a form of feedback that elevates or maintains goal striving and system supporting intensity in networks over time. On the other hand, those in network de-affirmation roles are expected to enact more complex dynamics based on the emotional feedback, ranging from complete motivational shutdown to motivational inspiration, if future resistance is deemed to be inefficacious or efficacious, respectively.

## The Network Goal Graphing of Real-World Systems

We believe that one of the most promising and perhaps most ambitious areas for future computational research in the social sciences is to examine how past, present, and future anticipated variables in people's real-world pursuits can predict long-term emergent goal achievement, performance, and other relevant outcomes. Computer simulations are extremely valuable for this level of complexity, because they allow us to integrate numerous social, psychological, organizational, and environmental variables that can help explain the rich context of goal striving over time. Although important efforts have been made to simulate behavioral change and social influence using computational models in specific content domains (Kaufmann, Stagl, & Franks, 2009; Orr & Plaut, 2014; Hu & Puddy, 2011; Schwarz & Ernst, 2009; Wang, Huang, & Sun, 2012; Wang & Hu, 2012), this work has not fully examined how complex motivational structures in networks can impact changes in emergent goal pursuit outcomes over time. Moreover, although work on scenario planning has looked generally at how to make plans for the future, this work has not examined how interpersonal and goal connections relate to past, present, and potential future pursuits. Nor has previous work provided frameworks that can parsimoniously visualize the most relevant complexity, including earlier work on network scripts (Westaby, 2012a).

To stimulate and facilitate modeling in this arena, we introduce a new *network goal graphing* approach to help conceptualize and visualize how complex social networks impact varying levels of emergent outcomes over time in long-term goal pursuits. We hope this framework can provide a foundation from which researchers can then use computational modeling to make projections and forecasts about emergent outcomes into the distal future on real human behavior and system outcomes. The future projections could then be analyzed and compared to empirical results, to further test and rigorously calibrate theoretical advances (Kaufmann et al., 2009; Tobias, 2009). We are very interested in examining how a focal individual (group, organization, or even society) is interacting with other important entities entering or leaving the network or changing their motivation levels over time, while being mindful of past, present, and potential future attractor and stability dynamics that could impact the system (Warren, 2006).

Generally speaking, we theorize that motivational influences from network players can generate profound nonlinear effects on emergent outcomes. Some may be good, such as a new wealthy customer providing major support for a company's goal of selling products (e.g., system support for a company's goal striving), while others can be harmful (e.g., a drug dealer getting an adolescent addicted to hard drugs, where the dealer's goal prevention and supportive resistance is working against the adolescent's normal goal striving for healthy school and family goals). We know of no research to date that has attempted to computationally model or even fully conceptualize the complex influences from such motivated networks on human goal and behavioral striving and resulting outcomes.

Because dynamic network theory proposes that only eight social network roles are needed to explain critical elements of goal pursuit, it is hoped to provide a parsimonious way to explain high levels of complexity in elaborate human systems.

To illustrate, a network goal graph is presented in Figure 11.3, which elaborates on Person X's weight loss goal striving from Figure 11.1. The top portion of the graph shows the *network entities* directly or indirectly involved in the goal pursuit or target behavior, while the bottom portion shows the *emergent levels* of goal achievement, performance, or relevant outcome(s) over time. Going beyond previous dynamic network charts, the goal node is allowed to vary on the y-axis to show these outcomes over time. The *social network roles* are visualized by the paths in the graph (also known as connections, lines, or arcs). These paths show how the network entities on the top portion of the chart are attempting to influence the emergent goal achievement, performance, or system outcome(s) that are varying on the goal node shown in the lower part of the chart. In this way, we can now more easily see how the various network dynamics are differentially impacting emergent criteria over the system's lifespan, as shown by variability in the goal node. Previous charting in dynamic network theory did not provide these dynamic visualizations.

Theoretically, we hypothesize that changes in goal or performance node levels result from the different social network roles being activated. We also assume that the implemented network role behaviors maintain their force on the goal node over time until other events are encountered that trigger new or different social network role behaviors. Thus, one can think of any change to social network

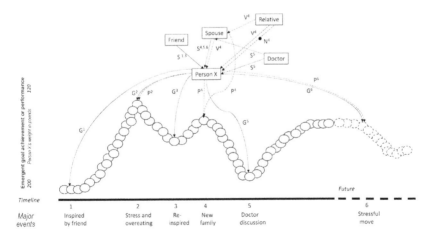

**FIGURE 11.3**   Network goal graph of Person X's weight loss pursuit (G = goal striving; S = system supporting; P = goal preventing; V = supportive resisting; N = system negating). Superscript denotes when interpersonal links are activated on timeline.

role behaviors as also changing the trajectory or direction of the goal node level; this trajectory is then maintained on emergent goal node levels until other events occur that again change network role behaviors.[10] However, as illustrated later, we predict that attractor dynamics can have independent, (re-)stabilizing effects on goal node levels as well.

## Example

The full network goal graph in Figure 11.3 illustrates the network dynamics influencing Person X's weight loss goal, but now over precise points in time. These portrayals provide much more dynamical detail about Person X's struggles and successes with weight loss as compared to either a traditional social network analysis or static dynamic network chart as demonstrated in Figure 11.1. The story is clearer because time and context are taken into account. To illustrate, we can now see that at major event 1, Person X started intense weight loss goal striving after being inspired by the supportive friend (S). Major events from the timeline are connected to the social network roles with superscript indicators (e.g., S[1] to denote system support from this supportive friend at event 1).[11] This behavior (G) contributed to an emergent period of linear weight loss until a stressful event in Person X's life (event 2) presumably led to intentional over-eating (P) and a nonlinear change in weight gain, although Person X did try to maintain some dieting behavior (G) during this time frame. Fortunately, Person X got re-inspired (G) around event 3 by the Friend again (S) and stopped all overeating (no P) and maintained a healthy diet routine (G). This led to nonlin-ear change in weight loss and steady success over time. However, upon getting married, a host of new family dynamics emerged in the network and impacted the system during event 4. For example, Person X's new Spouse provided support for the weight loss goal on one hand (S), but also supported Person X's overeating at other times (V), especially because the Spouse loved to overeat. The Spouse also brought home a lot of fattening food that prevented Person X from serving healthier choices at dinner (Spouse's direct P path to the goal).

To add, Person X's overweight Relative loved family gatherings where every-one ate a lot of questionable food choices, and pressured Person X to join in the festivities at those times (V). Given the new family dynamics, Person X entirely stopped dieting (no G) and started overeating again (P). This led to fast and non-linear weight gain. The pattern finally stopped when Person X developed cardiac problems, which led to serious discussions with a cardiologist during event 5 who said Person X must engage in a healthy lifestyle or it could lead to a catastrophic cardiac event. Such supportive encouragement to Person X for dieting and to the Spouse (S) to help Person X diet was enough to recommit goal striving (G) and stop overeating (no P).

Researchers can also focus their analyses on discrete points in time. This is helpful because the network goal graphs can become visually congested in large systems over time.[12] To illustrate, Figure 11.4 shows the major motivational changes in Person X's network at important times, such as critical turning or tipping points (Gladwell, 2000). Computer technology can allow researchers to easily visualize motivational dynamics at different time periods or view the entire system moving and changing over time. Researchers can also create and use system-level metrics, such as shown on the bottom of Table 11.1, to predict emergent system outcomes, preferably using multilevel statistical methods (Curran & Bauer, 2011; Hofmann, 1997).[13]

In the network goal graph in Figure 11.3, we linked social network role behaviors to a goal achievement/performance node that varies along the y-axis. Alternatively, researchers could use other aggregated summary variables to formalize influence effects over time at the system level. For example, the positive focus ratio could also be plotted over time as a varying node. Furthermore, both the predicted positive focus ratio node and goal performance node could be jointly displayed, ideally in standardized form, to show the relationship between network-level predictions using the positive focus ratio and overall goal performance. Please see the appendix to this chapter for additional details about link strength, metrics, and data aggregation in the ongoing example.

## Attractor Mechanisms

An *attractor* is an important concept from physics that has relevance to human behavior (Warren, 2006). A fixed-point attractor, to illustrate, represents "the state to which a system evolves over time and to which it returns after being

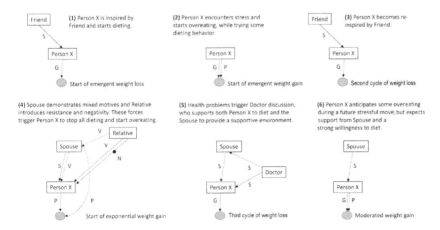

**FIGURE 11.4** Network influence on the goal at major events in time (G = goal striving; S = system supporting; P = goal preventing; V = supportive resisting; N = system negating).

perturbed" (Vallacher et al., 2015, p. 59). Goal achievement/performance node data can provide critical information about attractors, which we theorize can serve as important independent variables to further explain goal pursuit, performance, and relevant outcomes over time. For example, the greater the stability of a goal performance node level over time, the stronger an attractor becomes for that level into the future, thereby serving as a re-stabilizing force when the system is perturbed.[14] Such propositions have particular relevance for simulating how network linkages may interface with previously accrued goal or performance levels over time. To illustrate, if a person's goal achievement has been on a steady decline for an extended period of time, one would predict that this would independently impact future performance (beyond network role activations) and thus need to be accounted for in simulation algorithms. This is akin to how attractors can have strong effects on stabilizing system outcomes, but now contextualized as interfacing with social network role changes over time. Future research will need to examine these joint effects in efforts to better simulate and predict long-term system outcomes.

### Future Forecasting

One of the most ambitious applications of network goal graphing is its use in computational and simulation science to make future forecasts, predictions, and visualizations of system outcomes over time. Such forecasts could be based upon relevant past, present, and future anticipated variables in a system. This is difficult because of the challenges in making long-term projections about outcomes in complex systems (Tetlock & Gardner, 2015; Tetlock & Mellers, 2011), but one in which we think computational and simulation approaches become important because of the host of variables that likely need to be considered. Hence, a critical task in computational work is to accurately select, vet, and weigh valid predictors, such as in the context of data underlying network goal graphs. (See the appendix to this chapter for additional details.)

There are a number of potential variables that researchers could consider from a dynamic network theory perspective. First, researchers could assess the variation, change, intensity, and duration of past, present, and future anticipated network role linkages across the various entities in a network as well as emergent goal achievement, performance, or relevant outcome data. Such data could come from a number of sources with the easiest being self-report. For example, imagine that for the initial data shown in Figure 11.3, Person X reported his or her perceptions of the past and present network roles and monthly weight levels. (We discuss forecast data below.)

Second, given that multiple actors are often involved in our goal pursuits, another powerful source of data could come from these other known individuals in the network (Kilduff, Crossland, Tsai, & Krackhardt, 2008) (e.g., Person X's friend, etc.). Research has also shown that some individuals may have more accuracy when they are more intimately involved (Connelly & Ones, 2010) or when they have characteristics of superforecasters (Tetlock & Gardner, 2015). In our context, participating entities could be asked to judge the degree to which various people are enacting different network role behaviors in a system, including their own role. In such cases, agreement indices could also be created, which provides insights into *dynamic network intelligence* (DNI) (Westaby et al., 2014). For example, if the Friend indicates support for Person X's dieting, which is the same as Person X's perception, Person X would have DNI for that linkage. Researchers could then calculate the degree to which individuals in a network have system-wide DNI, and perhaps then use or weight this information in computational projections.[15]

Third, more objective information could be assessed in other lines of work. For instance, as a critical dependent variable, Person X's weight could be collected weekly by a research team. Researchers could also make assumptions about objective indicators of role behaviors, instead of relying on self-report. To illustrate, Person X's goal striving could be inferred by the number of times Person X went to a gym or spent money on weight loss programs or healthy food choices (where receipts could be objectively examined).[16] This is akin to other researchers making assumptions about how financial spending connects to underlying motives (Aknin et al., 2013).

Fourth, relevant demographic, individual difference, or environmental data can become useful in computational forecasts. For example, one could theorize that target individuals under study will observe the behavior from similar others in the future and adopt similar network roles (i.e., using the observer role under a homophily motive; Kossinets & Watts, 2009; Powell, White, Koput, & Owen-Smith, 2005), when they lack confidence in their anticipated behavior and past behavior is highly variable.[17]

Last, to provide contextual information for the goal or behavioral pursuits, researchers could assess important events or issues occurring during the pursuit as well as future anticipated events and issues. For example, Person X in our ongoing dieting example may be able to better visualize and anticipate that his or her own goal prevention likelihoods will increase somewhat during an anticipated retirement event that Person X anticipates will be stressful. Psychologically, information and experiences from these events would feedback to the judgment and decision-making process that triggers the selection of the eight network roles (and/or their combinations) which are the immediate and direct antecedents of important system outcomes.

## Forecasting Example

To stimulate ways to think about such computational modeling in future research, we hypothetically illustrate what a computational model's forecast could look like in the far right portion of Figure 11.3. In this case, such projections could be based not only on past trajectories and fluctuations of Person X's weight gains and losses (around potential attractor states), but also on anticipated network role behaviors and anticipated weight loss and gain in the future. In our example, given that Person X may anticipate moderately high goal striving and a small amount of goal prevention during an expected stressful move at event 6 in conjunction with somewhat predictable cyclical trends in past weight loss and gain, one simulation model may project that Person X's current weight levels will be maintained until the stressful event happens, at which point greater goal prevention will occur and generate a slight increase in weight gain. However, this would be temporary, since the event may be perceived to be short-term and past tendencies to re-establish relatively stronger goal striving (over goal prevention) would result in a stabilization of moderately successful weight loss.[18]

Akin to how meteorologists make different trajectories of hurricane paths based upon assumptions in competing models (i.e., often referred to as "spaghetti noodles" in the media), computational researchers should estimate in an a priori fashion different trajectories of emergent outcomes based on different theoretical parameter estimates and different stochastic assumptions about future environments. Then they could test and calibrate the different trajectories with observed data over time—a form of "model grounding" (Harrison et al., 2007). In this case, the rival models would be calibrated to the empirical data that become available over time (Kaufmann et al., 2009; Tobias, 2009). In such work, researchers could refine their computational algorithms in ways that best predict future network forces and emergent states, which would then hopefully have applicability across agents and contexts, and therefore generate greater external validity. It also has implications in artificial intelligence applications, providing computers with important parameters to search for in the social network, along with strategies for maximizing functional social network dynamics and minimizing or avoiding dysfunctional ones.

## Summary

This chapter has used dynamic network theory to computationally explore how social networks are involved in human goal striving processes over time and in complex environments. In contrast to traditional network analysis, such network goal analysis inserts goal nodes into network structures. This is a major development because motivational links to those goals can then be directly assessed, such as goal striving and goal preventing, and then their impact on system outcomes examined, such as goal achievement, performance, and the network rippling of emotions. The approach also models interpersonal role linkages that serve goal striving, such as system support, or potentially hinder it, such as system negation. In all, the framework is expected to improve on the prediction of important system outcomes over traditional approaches. We used the theory's proposed set of network role linkages to illustrate how computational models can be derived to simulate emergent network power in a person's goal striving. For more complex modeling, we introduced *network goal graphing* to conceptualize, visualize, and computationally forecast how social networks impact goal pursuit outcomes over longer time spans in upward, downward, or stabilized patterns or trajectories. The importance of attractor sub-mechanisms and dynamic network intelligence were illustrated to further explain important complexities in human pursuits.[19]

## Appendix: Underlying Data and Concepts in Network Goal Graphs

This appendix provides further details about network goal graphs and how they contain information about path strength, aggregation, and corresponding goal performance. We illustrate this in the context of Person X's weight loss goal, where the data in the table below corresponds to the paths shown in Figures 11.3 and 11.4. Column 1 indicates major events occurring over time, such as Person X being inspired by a friend to lose weight at event 1. This event theoretically translates into (or is mediated by) Person X deciding to goal strive (G) with critical support from a friend (S). The strength of these two role paths, each scored 1, can be seen in the next two columns in the table.[20] The other social network role behaviors manifest in the example are shown in subsequent columns (i.e., P, V, and N). As for aggregating to the system-level, the next column illustrates the *positive focus ratio* (Westaby et al., 2016), which generally represents the functional forces in a social system around a given goal. This metric is computed by dividing the strength of G and S goal pursuit paths by all social network role paths in the system (peripheral I and O roles excluded). For example, for event 1, there is one goal striving path (scored 1) and one system supporting path (scored 1), without any other resistance or negativity paths. Thus, the ratio is 1.0 (i.e., 2/2). At event 2, the positive focus ratio decreases to .5, given that Person X shows both goal striving (G) and goal preventing (P)—a common struggle for people trying to lose weight (i.e., 1/2). The last column shows goal performance for Person X in terms of subsequent pounds lost until a new change occurs in the system (e.g., Person X lost 72 pounds after being inspired through G and S mechanisms until a new change occurred during event 2). One would predict that the goal striving and system supporting activated at event 1 at the path level (and/or positive focus ratio at the system level) would impact subsequent performance. Theoretically, the implementation of the social network roles is presumed to result in a stable state of behavior in the system that impacts the trajectory of goal node performance until new changes or events occur in the system, either from the environment or from internal decision-making processes that result in the activation of new social network roles. Statistically, if enough data points are gathered, within-person regressions could be calculated on data in the table to see which roles are having the strongest impact on performance variation (or multilevel modeling could be used, including between-person data). Practically, when longitudinal data are unavailable or untenable, individuals could be surveyed about system paths over different time periods, such as reporting major past, present, and expected future events or changes, along with data on social network role paths and performance. Objective indicators of performance are preferred whenever possible (Westaby, 2012a). Coefficient weighting from the resulting statistical analyses, and/or results from additional policy capturing methods that manipulate future contingencies using survey methods, could be used, in part, in simulating how a person's performance would change over time under different conditions. In addition, the stability of past goal performance could be used when simulating future behavior, which we expect would independently impact system outcomes over time, as discussed in the "Attractor Mechanisms" section of the chapter. Although some exploratory ideas are presented here, more research is needed to examine other possibilities.

| Events over time | Social network roles in Person X's network | | | | | Positive focus ratio[1] | Subsequent performance |
|---|---|---|---|---|---|---|---|
| | Goal striving (G) | System supporting (S) | Goal preventing (P) | Supportive resisting (V) | System negating (N) | | |
| 1. Inspired by friend | 1 | 1 | 0 | 0 | 0 | 2/2 = 1.0 | 72 pounds lost |
| 2. Stress and overeating | 1 | 0 | 1 | 0 | 0 | 1/2 = .5 | 33 pounds gained |
| 3. Re-inspired | 1 | 1 | 0 | 0 | 0 | 2/2 = 1.0 | 17 pounds lost |
| 4. New family | 0 | 1 | 2 | 3 | 1 | 1/7 = .14 | 47 pounds gained |
| 5. Doctor discussion | 1 | 3 | 0 | 0 | 0 | 4/4 = 1.0 | 43 pounds lost (last data point) |
| 6. Potential future stress | 1 | 1 | 1 | 0 | 0 | 2/3 = .67 | 20 pounds gained (expected) |

Note: [1] Other aggregated summary variables could be calculated, plotted, and tested as well, such as the network affirmation ratio.

## Notes

1 There are different types of centrality as well, such as betweenness centrality and degree centrality, representing different ways to analyze the flow of information through a social network.

2 Future research should also examine potential competency levels on various social network role linkages, extending previous theorizing that focused on entity-level system competency alone (Westaby, 2012a).

3 For example, an SIO multiplex role linkage illustrates a person supporting (S) another while also interacting a lot around the person (I) and watching the person's behavior (O). In contrast, a pure S role behavior could represent someone who morally supports someone (S), but does not interact closely in the goal striving (no I), and nor does the person have much time to observe the person's goal striving (no O). Multiplex linkages have been important in network frameworks (Snijders et al., 2010). However, dynamic network theory bounds the number of possible multiplex linkages by the finite set of roles in the theory.

4 Otherwise, a system reactance path (R) would be shown back to the Relative, which can be represented as a solid path with a black dot to symbolize the negative emotion that affirms/protects the goal—otherwise, the path would not be visually distinguished from system support linkages. See Westaby et al. (2014) or Westaby (2012a) for more charting specifics. As a less complicated technique, role symbols can be simply placed on all-black paths.

5 The *network affirmation ratio* (Westaby, 2012a) represents the degree to which network roles are affirming the goal, including motivational properties of defensive system reactance: $(\Sigma G + \Sigma S \, \Sigma R)/(\Sigma G + \Sigma S + \Sigma R + \Sigma P + \Sigma V + \Sigma N)$. Because no R was illustrated in this example, this ratio is the same as the positive focus ratio.

6 *Constructive resistance* can also occur from goal prevention and supportive resistance when goal modifications help goal strivers better achieve their goals (Westaby et al., 2014), although this was not examined in this exploratory simulation.

7 For negative affect and emotions in networks, the effects were presumed to be more complex in this model (Westaby, 2012b). For example, system negation can help people learn and adapt in some cases, especially when others showing the emotion are competent in the goal pursuit and are supportive (i.e., increasing computed network power). In contrast, if a person becomes distracted from system negation or if the other person has little competence in their suggested *changes*, it could reduce goal striving motivation or result in a poor new strategy (i.e., thus not increasing computed network power).

8 Although we only simulated five individuals, researchers could also generate an entire distribution of possible behavioral outcomes for a large set of simulated individuals (Smaldino, Chapter 4 in this volume), given the ease of running simulations. Then, deviations from normal expectations could be generated. We focused on five networks for simplicity and to make the simple point that a wide dispersion of emergent outcomes can occur in small samples.

9 Research should also account for the concept of authorization levels in dynamic network theory, such as computing an additional interaction term for authorized entities who have power to dictate system direction (e.g., a company executive has the power to prevent others from engaging in many behaviors, which would squelch those activities, perhaps wisely or unwisely). Such effects *may* be more relevant in certain environments, such as in organizational, medical, and governmental domains.

10 Otherwise, we would also need to show all network role paths for each emergent data point (e.g., time 1 G, time 2 G, time 3 G), which would add complexity to the charts. Research needs to examine these issues.

11 Superscripts are used because subscripts are already used in original dynamic network charts to indicate intensity levels and performance, such as $S_{2(3)}$, indicating high system support (1 = significant, 2 = intense) with high role performance on the linkage (-3 = very poor performance, 3 = very strong performance) (Westaby, 2012a).

12 Such congestion also happens in traditional network analyses of large systems, although a dynamic network theory approach is fortunately bounded by the given goal, and may be less prone to the "boundary problem" (Westaby, 2012a).

13 Data on the separate social network role behaviors would be available at each snapshot in time within each system as well, and could be used as lower-level predictors in multilevel testing.

14 Researchers should also examine the utility in eliminating previous restrictions in ego-centric dynamic network charts, such as allowing multiple roles (instead of just G and P) to proceed directly to goal nodes.

15 Forecasts from individuals with high DNI could be weighted more strongly in projections than individuals who demonstrate low DNI on past and current roles. If these assumptions result in greater calibration with future outcomes, such insights should be weighted and accounted for in finalized algorithms for future research, which could then be further tested and calibrated. When collecting data, researchers may also want to consider the benefits of placing individuals into even-handed implemental mindsets (Gollwitzer, 2012) when trying to improve long-term predictions.

16 Simulations should also examine group and social interactions in real time based upon Westaby et al.'s (2016) new observational framework, which examines how levels of productive and satisfying interactions may result from various combinations of goal striving behavior during interactions (e.g., pure talking without affect), system supporting (e.g., agreement statements, nodding), goal preventing (e.g., disagreeing without affect), and system negating (e.g., condescending bullying behavior), and their multiplex combinations, such as GS (e.g., talking while warmly smiling toward another).

17 For example, if external research shows that the demographic makeup of Person X in our ongoing example is correlated with weight gain at time Y, this data could be used in the forecasting algorithm, if Person X has low confidence about his or her network role behavior and performance at Time Y and past behavior is too variable to discern stable attractor points or lacks identifiable cycles.

18 Other predictor data could be integrated into computer algorithms as well, including the aggregation of past, present, and/or future anticipated data from other people in the network as well as weighting by dynamic network intelligence. Computer algorithms could also be based upon results from empirical studies of real participants using structural equation models or relevant regressions, which can show the relative weight of the various factors in dynamic network theory, akin to how research has used parameters from SEM and regression to set simulation and change parameters (Schwarz & Ernst, 2009).

19 The authors thank the editors, Yoshi Kashima, and Jennifer Talevich for their helpful comments, and Genie Song for her help programming the agent-based computer model.

20 See Westaby (2012a) for further details about scoring path intensity, such as 1 meaning significant strength of a path and 2 meaning intense strength of a path. In this chapter, all paths are scored 1, for simplicity.

## References

Ajzen, I. (1991). The theory of planned behavior. *Organizational Behavior and Human Decision Processes, 50,* 179–211.

Aknin, L. B., Barrington-Leigh, C. P., Dunn, E. W., Helliwell, J. F., Burns, J., Biswas-Diener, R., Kemeza, I., Nyende, P., Ashton-James, C. E., & Norton, M. I. (2013). Prosocial spending and well-being: Cross-cultural evidence for a psychological universal. *Journal of Personality and Social Psychology, 104,* 653–652.

Austin, J. T., & Vancouver, J. B. (1996). Goal constructs in psychology: Structure, process, and content. *Psychological Bulletin, 120,* 338–375.

Borgatti, S. P., Mehra, A., Brass, D. J., & Labianca, G. (2009). Network analysis in the social sciences. Science, *323,* 892–895.

Burt, R. S., Kilduff, M., & Tasselli, S. (2013). Social network analysis: Foundations and frontiers on advantage. *Annual Review of Psychology, 64,* 527–547.

Castelfranchi, C., Cesta, A., Conte, R., & Miceli, M. (1993). Foundations for interaction: The dependence theory. In P. Torasso (Ed.), *Advances in artificial intelligence* (pp. 59–64). Berlin: Springer-Verlag.

Connelly, B. S., & Ones, D. S. (2010). Another perspective on personality: Meta-analytic integration of observers' accuracy and predictive validity. *Psychological Bulletin, 136,* 1092–1122.

Curran, P. J., & Bauer, D. J. (2011). The disaggregation of within-person and between-person effects in longitudinal models of change. *Annual Review of Psychology, 62,* 583–619.

Dovidio, J. F., Piliavin, J. A., Schroeder, D. A., & Penner, L. (2006). *The social psychology of prosocial behavior.* Mahwah, NJ: Lawrence Erlbaum.

Duckworth, A. L., Peterson, C., Matthews, M. D., & Kelly, D. R. (2007). Grit: Perseverance and passion for long-term goals. *Journal of Personality and Social Psychology, 92,* 1087–1101.

Fishbein, M., & Ajzen, I. (2010). *Predicting and changing behavior: The reasoned action approach.* New York: Psychology Press.

Geen, R. G. (1991). Social motivation. *Annual Review of Psychology, 42,* 377–399.

Gladwell, M. (2000). *The tipping point: How little things can make a big difference.* New York: Back Bay Books/Little, Brown.

Gollwitzer, P. M. (2012). Mindset theory of action phases. In P. Van Lange, A. W. Kruglanski, & E. T. Higgins (Eds.), *Handbook of theories of social psychology* (Vol. 1, pp. 526–545). London: SAGE Publications.

Granovetter, M. S. (1973). The strength of weak ties. *American Journal of Sociology, 78,* 1360–1380.

Harrison, J. R., Lin, Z., Carroll, G. R., & Carley, K. M. (2007). Simulation modeling in organizational and management research. *Academy of Management Review, 32,* 1229–1245.

Hofmann, D. A. (1997). An overview of the logic and rationale of hierarchical linear models. *Journal of Management, 23,* 723–744.

Hu, X. L., & Puddy, R. (2011). Cognitive modeling for agent-based simulation of child maltreatment. In J. Salerno, S. J. Yang, D. Nau, & S. K. Chai (Eds.), *Social computing, behavioral-cultural modeling and prediction* (pp. 138–146). Berlin: Springer-Verlag.

Kaufmann, P., Stagl, S., & Franks, D. W. (2009). Simulating the diffusion of organic farming practices in two new EU member states. *Ecological Economics, 68,* 2580–2593.

Kilduff, M., Crossland, C., Tsai, W., & Krackhardt, D. (2008). Organization network perceptions versus reality: A small world after all? *Organizational Behavior and Human Decision Processes, 107,* 15–28.

Kossinets, G., & Watts, D. J. (2009). Origins of homophily in an evolving social network. *American Journal of Sociology, 115,* 405–450.

Labianca, G., Brass, D. J., & Gray, B. (1998). Social networks and perceptions of intergroup conflict: The role of negative relationships and third parties. *Academy of Management Journal, 41,* 55–67.

Nowak, A., Vallacher, R. R., & Zochowski, M. (2005). The emergence of personality: Dynamic foundations of individual variation. *Developmental Review, 25,* 351–385.

Orr, M. G., & Plaut, D. C. (2014). Complex systems and health behavior change: Insights from cognitive science. *American Journal of Health Behavior, 38,* 404–413.

Powell, W. W., White, D. R., Koput, K. W., & Owen-Smith, J. (2005). Network dynamics and field evolution: The growth of interorganizational collaboration in the life sciences. *American Journal of Sociology, 110*, 1132–1205.

Rhoades, L., & Eisenberger, R. (2002). Perceived organizational support: A review of the literature. *Journal of Applied Psychology, 87*, 698–714.

Richetin, J., Sengupta, A., Perugini, M., Adjali, I., Hurling, R., Greetham, D, & Spence, M. (2010). A micro-level simulation for the prediction of intention and behavior. *Cognitive Systems Research, 11*, 181–193.

Schwarz, N., & Ernst, A. (2009). Agent-based modeling of the diffusion of environmental innovations: An empirical approach. *Technological Forecasting and Social Change, 76*, 497–511.

Smith, E. R., & Conrey, F. R. (2007). Agent-based modeling: A new approach for theory building in social psychology. *Personality and Social Psychology Review, 11*, 87–104.

Snijders, T. A. B., Van de Bunt, G. G., & Steglich, C. E. G. (2010). Introduction to actor-based models for network dynamics. *Social Networks, 32*, 44–60.

Stajkovic, A. D., & Luthans, F. (1998). Self-efficacy and work-related performance: A meta-analysis. *Psychological Bulletin, 124*, 240–261.

Tetlock, P. E., & Gardner, D. (2015). *Superforecasting: The art and science of prediction.* New York: Crown.

Tetlock, P. E., & Mellers, B. A. (2011). Intelligent management of intelligence agencies: Beyond accountability ping-pong. *American Psychologist, 66*, 542–554.

Tobias, R. (2009). Changing behavior by memory aids: A social psychological model of prospective memory and habit development tested with dynamic field data. *Psychological Review, 116*, 408–438.

Vallacher, R. R., & Nowak, A. (1997). The emergence of dynamical social psychology. *Psychological Inquiry, 8*, 73–99.

Vallacher, R. R., Read, S. J., & Nowak, A. (2002). The dynamical perspective in personality and social psychology. *Personality and Social Psychology Review, 6*, 264–273.

Vallacher, R. R., Van Geert, P., & Nowak, A. (2015). The intrinsic dynamics of psychological process. *Current Directions in Psychological Science, 24*, 58–64.

Vancouver, J. B., Weinhardt, J. M., & Schmidt, A. M. (2010). A formal, computational theory of multiple-goal pursuit: Integrating goal-choice and goal-striving processes. *Journal of Applied Psychology, 95*, 985–1008.

Wang, M. H., & Hu, X. L. (2012). Agent-based modeling and simulation of community collective efficacy. *Computational and Mathematical Organization Theory, 18*, 463–487.

Wang, S. W., Huang, C. Y., & Sun, C. T. (2014). Modeling self-perception agents in an opinion dynamics propagation society. *Simulation: Transactions of the Society for Modeling and Simulation International, 90*, 238–248.

Warren, W. H. (2006). The dynamics of perception and action. *Psychological Review, 113*, 358–389.

Wasserman, S., & Faust, K. (1994). *Social network analysis: Methods and applications.* Cambridge: Cambridge University Press.

Weinhardt, J. M., & Vancouver, J. B. (2012). Computational models and organizational psychology: Opportunities abound. *Organizational Psychology Review, 2*, 267–292.

Westaby, J. D. (2005). Behavioral reasoning theory: Identifying new linkages underlying intentions and behavior. *Organizational Behavior and Human Decision Processes, 98*, 97–120.

Westaby, J. D. (2012a). *Dynamic network theory: How social networks influence goal pursuit.* Washington, DC: American Psychological Association.

Westaby, J. D. (2012b). Emergence and contagion in dynamic network systems. Paper presented at *Dynamical Systems and Computational Modeling in Social Psychology Preconference,* San Diego, CA.

Westaby, J. D., Pfaff, D. L., & Redding, N. (2014). Psychology and social networks: A dynamic network theory perspective. *American Psychologist, 69,* 269–284.

Westaby, J. D., Probst, T. M., & Lee, B. C. (2010). Leadership decision-making: A behavioral reasoning theory analysis. *Leadership Quarterly, 21,* 481–495.

Westaby, J. D., & Redding, N. (2014). Social networks, social media, and conflict resolution. In P. T. Coleman, M. Deutsch, & E. C. Marcus (Eds.), *The handbook of conflict resolution: Theory and practice* (3rd ed., pp. 998–1022). San Francisco, CA: Jossey-Bass.

Westaby, J. D., Versenyi, A., & Hausmann, R. C. (2005). Intentions to work during terminal illness: An exploratory study of antecedent conditions. *Journal of Applied Psychology, 90,* 1297–1305.

Westaby, J. D., Woods, N., & Pfaff, D. L. (2016). Extending dynamic network theory to group and social interaction analysis: Uncovering key behavioral elements, cycles, and emergent states. *Organizational Psychology Review, 6,* 34–62.

# 12

# COMPUTATIONAL MODELS OF SOCIAL INFLUENCE AND COLLECTIVE BEHAVIOR

*Robert J. MacCoun*

A photo of the blackboard in Richard Feynman's office features his assertion that "What I cannot create, I do not understand."[1] This chapter is an encouragement to social psychologists to solidify and advance their understanding of social influence and collective behavior by creating and testing computational models—models that can be formally stated with enough specificity to allow them to be run as computer simulations.

Almost a century ago, Floyd Allport (1920) suggested that there are two kinds of data in social psychology:

> (1) the behavior of an individual in direct response to social stimulus, that is in response to some form of behavior in others, and, (2) behavior which is the response to a non-social stimulus, e.g., a column of figures to be added, or a meal to be eaten, when such response is modified by the presence and actions of other persons.

Much of contemporary social psychology involves the second category; direct study of the first category is actually less common than an outsider to the field might suppose. But Allport suggested that it was the first category that posed "the master problem" for social psychology—"the problem of the relation of a single individual's action to the collective result of many individuals acting together" (quoted in Brooks & Johnson, 1978). This chapter takes as its focus efforts to make progress on that problem—specifically, the nature of the relationship between the opinions and behaviors of individuals and those of others around them.

To make this topic manageable, I ignore individual differences in susceptibility and influence, for example those produced by differences in power and status (see Abrams, 1980). Also, some economists and political scientists may be surprised by my treatment of models as mechanisms or algorithms rather than equilibrium solutions deduced from axioms, but that reflects my training— psychologists are wary of both axioms and equilibria, for a variety of reasons appropriate to our discipline. At the same time, I will blur some distinctions that are vitally important for a psychology of social influence, including descriptive versus injunctive norms (Cialdini, Reno, & Kallgren, 1990), French and Raven's (1960) taxonomy of forms of social power (e.g., rewards, legitimacy, expertise), and Kelman's (1958) distinction between compliance, identification, and internalization, all of which I discuss elsewhere (MacCoun, 2012, 2015). Perhaps the most surprising omission from a chapter on social influence is the almost complete lack of attention given to the content of argumentation, but that's because a key goal of the chapter is to show how well social influence can be described by strength in numbers rather than strength in arguments.

Throughout this chapter, I'll attempt to maintain a consistent notation across the different models I discuss, which is not necessarily the notation in which each model is described elsewhere. Following Latané (1981), I'll generally refer to $S$ = *number of Sources* who are advocating one position (opinion, trait, behavior) and $T$ = *number of Targets* who currently favor an alternative, with $s = S/N$ representing the proportion of the local population currently favoring the first option. (This language comes from studies of conformity and persuasive appeals; in studies of mutual deliberation, it is arbitrary which faction is considered the sources and which is considered the targets.) I will use $p$ as a dependent variable for the probability that an individual chooses to convert from Option 2 to Option 1, and $P$ to refer to the probability that the group chooses Option 1.

## Five Key Ideas

Before delving into the details of specific models, it is worth reviewing some verbal propositions about this domain. These are not "laws"—at least not in the deterministic sense; rather, they are empirical regularities.

### People Influence Each Other

A corollary of this first point is that *people monitor each other*; we are exquisitely attuned to those around us, and those of us who aren't have difficulty surviving. (The reader will already be familiar with many classic discussions of this point, but for insightful new perspectives, see Boyer, Firat, & Van Leeuwen, 2015; Leary, 2005.) This is so obvious that it may not seem worth mentioning; it would seem to be the very bedrock of the social sciences. But the reader can verify from any recent journal issue that most social science analyses omit others' responses from the right-hand side of any tested model. In the laboratory, one reason for this omission is that experiments rarely involve interacting individuals or multiple observation periods in which people can respond at time $t + 1$ to behaviors at time $t$. In the field, social influence is often ignored for a different reason; the relationship between the group and individual is usually endogenous, making causal identification very difficult (MacCoun, Cook, Muschkin, & Vigdor, 2008). But the arrival of big data from social media is solving the first problem while it is demanding that we grapple with the second.

## Social Influence Rises with the Number of Sources

As a very rough first approximation, the probability that an actor changes opinions rises with the proportion of others who hold a position the actor doesn't currently hold. Indeed, Mullen (1983) showed that an extremely simple model (the "Other-Total Ratio") can account for a lot of variance in social behavior:

$$p = m\left(\frac{S}{N}\right) \tag{12.1}$$

where $m$ is a scaling constant that serves as a "ceiling" parameter.[2] However, we will see that other models provide a much better approximation. There are even cases where social influence appears to be non-monotonic (MacCoun, 2012): for example, when people don't want to be "on the bandwagon" (Brewer, 1991), or when a lone dissenter seems to have negative social influence (Cialdini et al., 1990).

## Social Influence Is (Often) Marginally Diminishing

A somewhat better approximation comes from positing that influence is marginally decreasing (concave) in influence sources. This is a feature of many models, and it has multiple causes. In social impact theory (Latané, 1981; Nowak, Szamrej, & Latané, 1990), this follows from the interpretation of social impact as a psychophysical phenomenon (Stevens, 1957), with a power function

$$p = m\left(\frac{S}{T}\right)^k \tag{12.2}$$

where $k$ is an exponent that varies from situation to situation. Note that the ceiling parameter ($m$) in each of the above models (and some that follow) provides a second mechanism for producing decreasing marginal influence. A third contributing factor, not explicitly modeled in any of the models presented here, is information-theoretic: Wilder (1977) has demonstrated that marginal influence drops off more rapidly as a function of how similar (and hence partially redundant) sources are to each other. A similar result is implied by a Bayesian analysis of consensus judgments (Dawes, 1989).

## Social Influence Is Disproportionate (Majority Amplification)

In Figure 12.1, the 45-degree diagonal line shows the baseline of strictly proportional influence: that is, if the individual probability of voting for Option 1 is $p = .75$, the group probability of choosing Option 1 is $P = .75$.

The thick grey line in Figure 12.1 shows the predictions of Condorcet's (1785) famous "jury theorem." The sigmoidal shape predicted by Condorcet's model exhibits *disproportionality*—a simple majority of, say, 6/10 actually has a greater than .6 probability of choosing Option 1. Note that the Condorcet model does not predict simple diminishing marginal influence; rather, the Condorcet function is concave for a large number of sources, but it is convex for a smaller number of sources, producing an S-shaped function.

Condorcet's model follows from elementary probability theory, under two assumptions: (1) group decisions can be described by a majority rule, and (2) the probability that the group chooses Option 1 is given by

$$P = \sum_{n_1}^{N} p^{n_1} (1-p)^{N-n_1}, n_1 > .5N \qquad (12.3)$$

where $P$ is the probability of the group choosing Option 1, $p$ is the probability that an individual votes for Option 1, and $n_1$ is the size of a majority voting for *Option 1*. Thus, for a nine-person group, the summation is across the five initial splits that would produce a majority for Option 1: 5:4, 6:3, 7:2, 8:1, and 9:0.

On the basis of a third assumption—that members are more likely to be correct than not (i.e., that $p > .5$)—Condorcet made a strong normative claim that

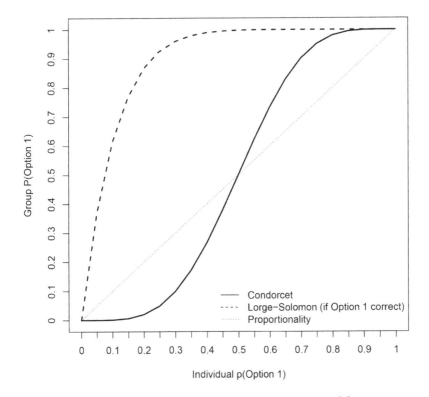

**FIGURE 12.1**  Comparing the Condorcet and Lorge-Solomon models.

the group choice is therefore superior to individual choice. There is ample evidence that this assumption is often wrong. As seen in Figure 12.1, the formal model itself predicts that if $p > .5$, then $P \gg .5$. But it also predicts that if $p < .5$, then $P \ll .5$. Thus, Condorcet's real contribution is not his dubious normative argument, but his insight that group processes can produce what Rosenwein and Campbell (1992) aptly labeled *majority amplification*. Note that the inflection point in Figure 12.1 can be considered an implicit threshold or "tipping point." The most famous conformity experiments—those of Asch (1956)—show this kind of sigmoidal pattern because the second source had more marginal impact than the first. In sigmoidal patterns, marginal influence is increasing (convex) before the inflection point, but decreasing (concave) beyond it.

## Social Influence Is Often Asymmetrical

The models considered thus far are symmetrical in the following sense: The influence of a given faction is a function of its relative size, but not of the position it advocates, and hence a majority's drawing power is the same in a 60:40 split or a 40:60 split. But social influence is often asymmetrical (see MacCoun & Kerr, 1988; Kerr & MacCoun, 2012). One reason is that one side may be arguing the "correct" position, where "correctness" is defined by some shared conceptual system (arithmetic, symbolic logic, a rule book, an encyclopedia) that allows advocates to demonstrate that they are right (see Laughlin, 2011). Lorge and Solomon (1955) offered the following normative model of optimal group performance on such tasks:

$$P = 1 - \left(1 - p\right)^{N} \tag{12.4}$$

As a normative model, this assumes that "truth wins"—that the group will find the correct answer so long as one member finds it. In other words, a faction of a given relative size (say, 25% of the group) will have more drawing power when it is arguing for the position most demonstrably "correct" relative to the shared conceptual scheme. Empirically, even in tasks with a clearly demonstrable correct answer, it often takes more than two initial advocates for the truth to prevail ("truth-supported wins"; see Laughlin, 2011; see also Asch, 1956). Thus, social influence involves both strength in numbers and strength in arguments (Deutsch & Gerard, 1955). But the asymmetry need not be rooted in either factual or logical arguments; it might instead reflect a shared cultural attitude; for example, in criminal juries, advocates of acquittal have greater drawing power than comparably sized factors for conviction, reflecting the asymmetric "reasonable doubt standard" (MacCoun & Kerr, 1988; Kerr & MacCoun, 2012).

## The Social Decision Scheme Framework

Davis (1973) proposed a more general modeling framework for social-psychological research on group decision processes, one that has been quite productive for many decades (Davis & Witte, 1996; Kerr, MacCoun, & Kramer, 1996; Parks & Kerr, 1999; Stasser, Kerr, & Davis, 1989). In the *social decision scheme* (SDS) framework, the group decision process is parsed into two components—the sampling process and the decision process.

The sampling process describes the probability $\pi_i$ that the group will start with a particular initial split—e.g., 10 votes for Guilty versus two votes for Not Guilty. For the sampling function in a dichotomous choice situation, Davis proposed the binomial expansion

$$\pi_i = p^{n_i} (1-p)^{N-n_i}, n_i > .5N \tag{12.5}$$

where $n_i$ is a given number of votes for option 1 in initial split $i$. The major theoretical contribution of this component of the SDS approach is to remind us that how situations evolve is heavily influenced by the processes determining which participants comes to find themselves in the situation. But in reality, most SDS papers ignore this component because in social psychology experiments, the composition of groups is either experimentally controlled (rarely), or else the sampling process is a haphazard matter of convenience. And in any case, the binomial expansion is often dubious because it assumes (a) that the sampling of one participant is independent of the sampling of other participants, and (b) once sampled, groups will actually persist long enough to reach a decision. In reality, neither assumption is tenable in the real world.

The real meat of the SDS approach comes from the notion of a social decision scheme. A particular social decision scheme **D** gives the probability $d_{ij}$ that the group will adopt option $j$ given initial split $i$. (For finer-grained analyses of moment-by-moment individual and group transition probabilities, see Stasser et al., 1989.) The expected outcomes are given by $\pi_i d_{ij}$. The power of the SDS framework is that it encourages researchers to consider a variety of theoretical decision schemes. For example, in the Proportionality scheme—a useful baseline model—$d_i = i/N$. A "Simple Majority" scheme is given by

$$d_i = \begin{cases} 1.0 & if \; \dfrac{i}{N} > .5 \\ 0.5 & if \; \dfrac{i}{N} = .5 \\ 0.0 & if \; \dfrac{i}{N} < .5 \end{cases} \tag{12.6}$$

Note that for this scheme, $\pi$**D** is equivalent to Condorcet's model (Equation 12.3). A "Truth Wins" scheme (assuming the first option is "correct") is given by

$$d_i = \begin{cases} 1 & if \; i \geq 1 \\ 0 & if \; i < 1 \end{cases} \tag{12.7}$$

Since the SDS approach was first articulated, scholars have occasionally confused **D** matrices with formal voting rules. This is not correct; **D** is a summary statement of all the combined individual and group factors that lead the group to behave a particular way. Thus, **D** can readily be estimated or tested in situations where there is no formal voting rule (and indeed, when groups may not even think of themselves as forming a group), and the **D** that best characterizes a group's behavior is often different than the group's formal voting rule—for example, groups operating under a formal unanimity requirement tend to behave as if they were using a Two-Thirds Majority rule.

A large variety of such schemes have been proposed and examined. SDS researchers can either test the goodness of fit between each **D** and some data set, or use the data to describe an empirically derived **D** (Kerr, Stasser, & Davis, 1979). For example, MacCoun and Kerr (1988) meta-analyzed 11 experiments to estimate the typical asymmetric scheme that best characterizes juries operating under a reasonable-doubt standard.

Arguably, an important strength of the SDS approach is that it shifts the focus from a search for "What is the model account of social influence?" to "Which models are best for describing which situations?" Thus, Simple and Two-Thirds Majority schemes fare best in judgmental tasks with no clear criteria for conclusively demonstrating a correct answer; in tasks that do have such criteria, groups are better characterized by a "Truth-Supported Wins" **D** (in which at least two members need to initially endorse the solution) than a Truth-Wins **D**.

## The BOP Framework

MacCoun (2012) demonstrated that, despite their strengths, existing influence models like the Other-Total Ratio and Social Impact Theory have important limitations. In particular, models that fare well in a conformity paradigm (where multiple sources unidirectionally influence a target) perform more poorly in a deliberation paradigm (where factions bidirectionally influence each other), and vice versa. And despite its many strengths, the SDS approach has limitations of its own. It is more suitable for characterizing group decisions than the effects of others on individual decisions, and the machinery of multiple matrices doesn't always facilitate descriptive statements and generalizations. Finally, existing models aren't always well integrated with more general theories of choice and methods of data analysis.

MacCoun (2012, 2015) proposed a family of models for identifying and characterizing the apparent "burden of (social) proof" (BOP) in social influence settings. The BOP framework is an attempt to be integrative in two different senses. First, it attempts to provide a common set for formalisms that are equally applicable across distinct social influence paradigms: the conformity paradigm, the deliberation paradigm, the diffusion-of-innovations paradigm, etc. And second, the BOP models can be directly, explicitly, and formally linked to many other bodies of theory in psychology and the social sciences, including the Luce strict utility model, the McFadden random utility model, item-response theory, and the Schelling tipping point model (see MacCoun, 2012), as well as signal detection theory and prospect theory (see MacCoun, 2015).

The core model in this approach is the bBOP (originally "bidirectional burden of proof") model

$$p = \frac{m}{1 + exp\left[c\left(\frac{S}{N} - b\right)\right]} \tag{12.8}$$

in which $b$ is a threshold parameter denoting the inflection point at which the target is more likely than not to adopt the source's advocated position, and $c$ is a *clarity* parameter which reflects the steepness of the threshold. A low level of $c$ approaches random responding, while a high level of $c$ approaches an abrupt step function. When the parameters are estimated from aggregate data, $c$ is inversely related to the standard deviation of individual thresholds. Thus, $c$ indexes the degree to which there is a socially shared threshold or perceived burden of proof in one direction or the other. When $c$ is very high for a population, behavioral changes are correlated across actors and it is meaningful to talk of tipping points; e.g., Schelling's (1978) demonstration of tipping in housing segregation used a step function. When $c$ is lower, individual changes are only weakly correlated and social change is more gradual (or, at the lower limit, a random walk). In empirical applications so far, I've needed to include the $m$ parameter to fit data in the conformity paradigm, where multiple sources impinge on a single target; in other paradigms, the $c$ and $b$ parameters seem to suffice ($m$ is set to 1) (MacCoun, 2012).

One variant, *uBOP* (unidirectional burden of proof), like social impact theory, uses the $S/T$ ratio (in effect, an odds format) rather than the $S/N$ ratio.

$$p = \frac{m}{1 + exp\left[c\left(\frac{S}{T} - b\right)\right]} \tag{12.8}$$

For complicated reasons that are now moot, MacCoun (2012) conjectured that uBOP would better describe behavior in the conformity paradigm and bBOP would better describe behavior in the deliberation paradigm, but in fact, the models both performed quite well. Figure 12.2 shows two examples. The top row shows that the Other-Total Ratio and Social Impact Theory each predict a pattern of monotonically increasing but diminishing marginal social influence. Thus both do well at fitting Milgram and colleagues' famous study of whether urban passersby would look up in the sky (Milgram, Bickman, & Berkowitz, 1969), as a function of how many sources (Milgram's students) were already gazing up. But neither predicts Asch's 1956 finding that a second apparently wrong source had greater impact than the first one. As seen in the bottom row of Figure 12.2, uBOP fits both patterns quite well.

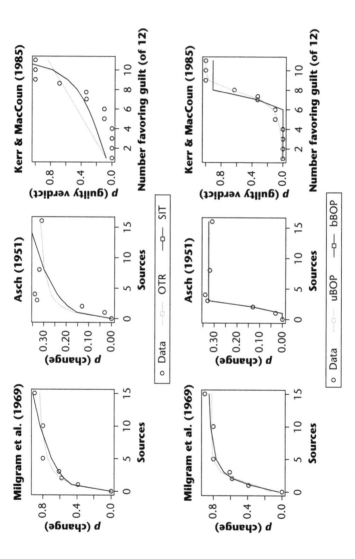

**FIGURE 12.2**  Comparing fit to three data sets. Top row: OTR and SIT. Bottom row: uBOP and bBOP. See MacCoun (2012) for a detailed presentation.

Even though bBOP is more broadly useful, uBOP is helpful for characterizing Asch-type conformity situations involving small numbers of participants and a single target, because it puts the $b$ threshold on an absolute "person" metric rather than a relative "percentage" metric. For example, in the Asch (1956) conformity study, the estimated thresholds were .67 for bBOP and 2.10 for uBOP. The former value is awkward to interpret because both the numerator and the denominator change as more confederates are added to the experiment, but the latter directly tells us that Asch's respondents began to "tip" toward conformity (to a clearly incorrect option) once there were at least two people disagreeing with them. Note that the formulae also predict Asch's finding that adding a second target to the denominator significantly reduced conformity.

The Milgram et al. (1969) and Asch (1956) studies exemplify a conformity paradigm, where multiple sources impinge on a single target. In a deliberation paradigm, there is a fixed group size, so any increase in sources produces a reduction in targets. As seen in the third column of Figure 12.2, OTR and SIT do a poor job of characterizing data from criminal mock juries (Kerr & MacCoun, 1985). The jury data show a sigmoidal pattern, but one that is asymmetric—largely due to the reasonable-doubt standard which gives advocates of acquittal a deliberative advantage (MacCoun & Kerr, 1988; Kerr & MacCoun, 2012).

## Modeling Continuous Judgments

While there are large literatures examining the predictors that influence continuous group judgments (e.g., juries' compensatory damage awards in personal injury trials), there has been relatively little work on modeling the process by which groups combine their opinions into continuous quantitative judgments. One reason is that, to a first approximation, one can often predict these judgments fairly well with the median or mean of the individual member's personal recommendations (see Graesser, 1978). Hinsz (1999) describes a large number of possible models falling into six basic categories: central-tendency, consensus-based, faction-attraction, coalition-based, distance-influence, and dictator schemes. But far too few studies have examined the relative fit of these models across tasks and settings, and it is premature to offer strong views about model validity (Hinsz, 1999; Davis et al., 1997).

Nevertheless, there are some important empirical regularities that any viable model should predict (or more accurately, postdict). The first is the *wisdom of crowds* (WOC) effect (Surowiecki, 2005), first documented by Francis Galton (1907), in which an aggregate (median or mean) of a large number of individual judgments tends to be far more accurate than that of most or even all of the individuals. The WOC effect is really a statistical phenomenon—a demonstration of the cancellation of random errors predicted by the law of large numbers. Indeed, a WOC effect is more likely to be obtained if the individuals in the crowd are completely unaware of each others' judgments (Lorenz, Rahut, Schweiter, & Helbing, 2011).

A second is *group polarization*, the tendency for post-deliberation mean judgments to be more extreme in the direction of the initial mean judgment (for a review, see Isenberg, 1986). Note that group polarization is most commonly documented in cases involving bipolar judgments with a meaningful midpoint—for example, pro-to-anti attitudes, bad-to-good evaluations, etc. Indeed, the phenomenon is partly explainable by the majority amplification effect discussed above—a boost in the relative drawing power of whichever pole has a majority of initial advocates (see Stasser et al., 1989). Group polarization provides an important corrective to the rosy view of groups implied by the WOC effect. While groups (or actually, aggregation) provide an effective way of attenuating *noise* (random error), group deliberation can often amplify *bias* (systematic error; see Kerr et al., 1996).

Something akin to group polarization has been observed for groups making judgments on a monetary scale—for example, juries deciding how much to award in punitive damages. Schkade, Sunstein, and Kahneman (2000) have documented a *severity shift* such that the group's recommended award is often considerably larger than the mean of their initial opinions. Though there may be some element of "emotional contagion" involved, the authors argue that the effect is partly attributable to the difficulty of making judgments on a scale that is bounded at zero on one end but unbounded at the other (see MacCoun, 2005).

## Modeling Growth over Time

It is useful to distinguish two classes of models that are easily confused with each other. The first class, *social influence modeling*, characterizes the probability of change in the prevalence of a trait, behavior, or opinion as a function of the relative popularity of that characteristic. The second class, *social growth modeling*, characterizes the change in prevalence of a trait, behavior, or opinion as a function of time. The approaches are confusable because each produces plots showing monotonic increases in influence—often sigmoidal—but the horizontal axes are different (prevalence of an opinion versus elapsed time). In principle, any social influence model can be recast as a social growth model (e.g., through simple iteration), but the converse is not necessarily true because some models use time as an independent variable (rather than as an index).

If Condorcet (1785) is the grandfather of social influence modeling, Verhulst (1838) is the grandfather of social growth modeling. Verhulst's model begins with the proposal that the rate of growth of a condition (a disease, an opinion, a behavior) in a population is a function of the product of those who already have the condition (in our terms, $S$) and those that do not (in our terms, $T$), weighted by some constant $r$. This basic assumption was so influential in epidemiological modeling that Wilson and Worcester (1944) named it "the law of mass action." As seen on the left side of Figure 12.3, this rate reaches its peak when half the population is already "infected." (Statistically, this is the point of maximum variance for a dichotomous variable.) If we iterate this rate from an initial small $S$, we find something like the

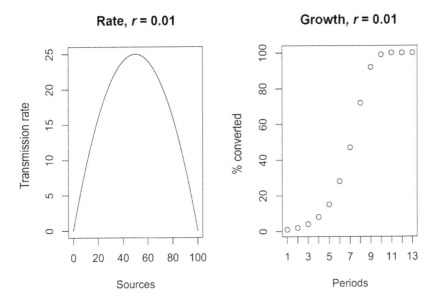

**FIGURE 12.3**  The "law of mass action," with $r = 0.01$ (left) and the pattern of growth over time it produces (right).

sigmoid curve on the right panel of Figure 12.3. Note that, as Verhulst himself recognized, this "law" is based on an assumption of uniform mixing of the two groups of people that is convenient as an approximation but unlikely to be strictly true.

Verhulst's *logistic model* is the integral of this rate; put differently, the "law of mass action" is the derivative of Verhulst's logistic model. Strictly speaking, Verhulst originally modeled the growth of a single population, but his model is readily adapted to persuasion (or infection) processes in which the increase in sources (or infected people) brings about a reduction in targets (or susceptible people). His full model incorporates a ceiling-type parameter, $K$, often called the "carrying capacity" or the "saturation rate." It is the maximum possible number of people (in a population growth analysis), sources (in a social influence analysis), or infected (in an epidemic analysis). Using our notation, it is equivalent to $mN$, where, as above, $m$ is a ceiling parameter between 0 and 1.

$$S_t = \frac{K}{1 + \left(\dfrac{K}{S_0 - 1}\right) e^{-rt}} \tag{12.10}$$

The basic logic of Verhulst's model has been extended in various ways in fields such as epidemiology and sociology (Daley & Gani, 1999; Newman, Barabási, & Watts, 2006; Smaldino, Janssen, Hillis, & Bednar, 2015), where state-of-the-art models are considerably more complex, making far more sophisticated assumptions about contact, susceptibility, network structure, and population heterogeneity. Another large literature in growth modeling examines the diffusion of innovations (see Mahajan, Muller, & Bass, 1995). MacCoun (2012) shows that the following iterative version of bBOP, called iBOP, does a good job of fitting data on technological innovations, political participation, and the spread of drug use among college students:

$$s_t = s_{t-1} + \frac{m - s_{t-1}}{1 + exp\left[-c\left(s - b\right)\right]}$$ (12.11)

This kind of growth modeling is rare in social psychology, partly because longitudinal data are rarely collected in experiments. And there are good reasons to be wary of growth modeling as a tool for social psychology. First, trend data are difficult to interpret causally; for example, what can look like social momentum due to imitation or conformity might actually be a lagged response to common information (for examples, see MacCoun, et al., 2008), or simply autocorrelated error. Second, the Verhulst tradition favors deductive models from calculus that provide closed-form equilibrium solutions. But such solutions come at a price; for the models to be tractable, they have to make many simplifying assumptions about population structure and mixing (see Rahmandad & Sterman, 2008).

## Simulating Communities of Interacting Agents

Simulation modeling provides a more flexible (and arguably more realistic) approach, exploring growth processes numerically (i.e., through iterative computation) rather than analytically (i.e., through closed-form equilibrium solutions). Monte Carlo simulation is one approach; a computer draws simulated samples and/or sampled mixes of parameter settings in order to examine the implications of a model under a variety of plausible settings (for examples, see MacCoun, 2012). Monte Carlo simulation has become incredibly fast and easy; it is a tool every researcher should use regularly, if only as an "intuition pump" when thinking through research problems.

Agent-based modeling (ABM; see Nowak, Szamrej, & Latané, 1990; Railsback, & Grimm, 2011; Smaldino, Calanchini, & Pickett, 2015)[3] is a powerful tool for exploring questions that would be nearly impossible to examine experimentally. ABM has its origins in mathematician John Conway's computer game *Life* (Gardner, 1970) and the simple but highly insightful checkerboard simulations conducted by Thomas Schelling (1978). In the cellular automata approach, a grid of locations (cells) is randomly seeded with "agents," who then interact iteratively with their neighbors and their environment. The agents are simply lines of computer code consisting of rules for exploration, interaction, and locomotion. In the newer network approach (Newman et al., 2006), agent relationships can take on a much broader array of structures.

The left side of Figure 12.4 shows a "Moore neighborhood" in which each agent is exposed to up to eight neighbors (using compass directions: NW, N, NE, E, SE, S, SW, and S). In the example, the 16 cells have been randomly seeded with 10 agents. In a torus formation, the neighboring locations wrap past the borders; thus in a torus, Agent 10's neighbors would include Agents 6 and 9, but also Agents 2 and 4 and 7. In a grid formation, there are border effects, which some modelers prefer to avoid. But of course, the real world has many borders. Allowing empty cells and borders enables the simulation to encompass greater heterogeneity of exposure or connectedness. For example, Agent 1 is far more isolated in the grid formation than the torus. Agents with more neighbors are exposed to more information, and if the simulation allows it, they have more potential exchange partners. Another factor is whether agents are allowed to "see" beyond their immediate Moore neighborhood to some radius greater than one cell; MacCoun (2012) showed that this *vision* parameter had a profound effect on social influence patterns, enabling minority opinions to persist by reducing minority isolation.

The right side of Figure 12.4 shows the same set of relationships as a *network*, with various common indices of network structure. Network models are a more general formalism than two-dimensional cellular automata (which can

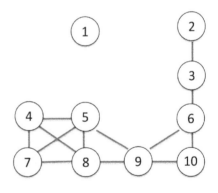

Randomly seeded grid or torus:    Equivalent network:

| | |
|---|---|
| Average number of neighbors: | 2.60 |
| Number of connected components: | 9 |
| Mean distance btwn connected nodes: | 2.53 |
| log(N): | 2.30 |
| log(connected): | 2.20 |
| Clustering coefficient: | 1.40 |

**FIGURE 12.4**  Left: a randomly seeded Moore neighborhood of 10 individuals (in 16 locations). Right: the equivalent social network.

be considered the subclass of "lattice networks"), though an n-dimensional cellular automata model can in principle represent any network (Bonacich, 2001). But real-world social networks have some properties that are better represented by lattice structures than by some of the more esoteric network structures that have received recent attention (e.g., "small-world networks"; Newman et al., 2006).

One such property is *clustering* (see Nowak et al., 1990). Figure 12.5 shows the 50th iteration of each of four different runs of an agent-based simulation using the bBOP model. In each case, there is a 51 × 51 grid initially seeded with 910 red and 910 blue agents; white cells are empty. In all four simulations, agents were assigned a clarity value of $c = 20$ and a threshold value of $b = .5$. In the City 1 simulations (top row), the bBOP model determines the probability that an agent will find its neighbors too dissimilar and move to the nearest randomly chosen open cell. In the City 2 simulations, however, agents cannot move, but they can change colors (opinions, behaviors, political parties), and the same bBOP model gives the probability of change. In all four simulations, 50 iterations was sufficient to produce a considerable amount of clustering—reds with reds and blues with blues. But the simulations suggest that *mobility produces different clustering than mutability*. In the City 1 configuration, the empty cells are redistributed in a manner than provides buffers or "moats" separating the groups. As a result, the City 1 simulations produce greater segregation and less between-group contact and exposure.

## Are Model Results "Results"?

Is this differential pattern of clustering a "finding" in the same sense as, say, Asch's (1956) finding that conformity pressures on a lone target tend to level off after three sources? No, of course not. Simulations are an exercise in theory building, and they enable theories of considerable complexity—too much complexity for us to simulate by intuition—using fairly simple rules. We can use empirical evidence to validate features and predictions of our models, but the models themselves don't produce empirical results. But this is not a profound shortcoming. First, theory is important for science, and social psychological "theories" are often little more than a vague set of verbal propositions that offer simple ordinal or directional predictions and little clear linkage to theories of other phenomena in the field. Second—and here the author can speak from three decades wearing a second hat as a professional public policy analyst—it is wrong to think that we generalize from our data when we offer predictions or suggestions for coping with real-world problems. Rather, we generalize from our theories, as Lewin's dictum "nothing so useful as a good theory" reminds us. Empirical data are essential for theory building and theory testing, but to paraphrase Keynes, those who think they prefer hard facts to academic theories are usually unaware that they are in the thrall of some dead theorist.

(a) **Move t1 d70 p50 v1 c10 b50 5404**
**Period 50**

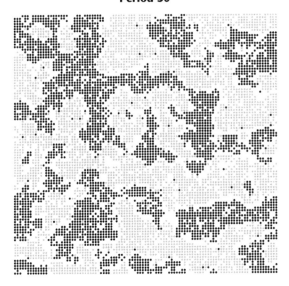

(b) **Move t1 d70 p50 v1 c10 b50 1623**
**Period 50**

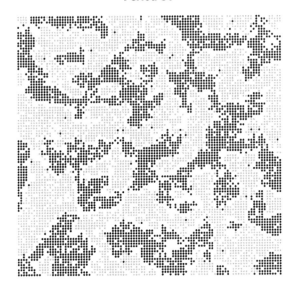

FIGURE 12.5  Similar patterns of emergent clustering from bBOP in models where agents can relocate but not change opinions ("Move", plots a and b) or can change opinions but not relocate ("Change", plots c and d). Note the "buffer zones" that form in the "Move Cities."

(c)    **Change t1 d70 p50 v1 c10 b50 3853**
          **Period 50**

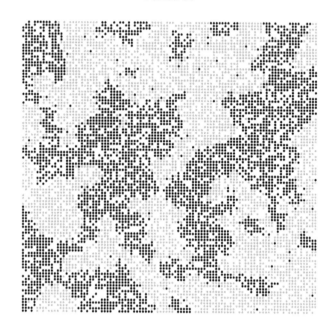

(d)    **Change t1 d70 p50 v1 c10 b50 3852**
          **Period 50**

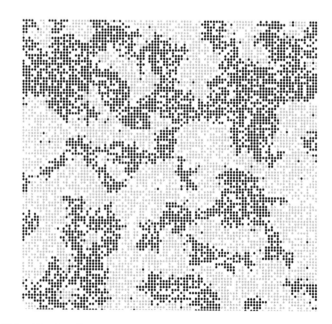

FIGURE 12.5   *(Continued)*

## The Excessive Distrust of Free Parameters

This raises the issue of *free parameters*, with which many psychologists have at least a passing familiarity. For many academic psychologists, a model's free parameters are at best an embarrassment, if not an object of scorn (see Roberts & Pashler, 2000). In brief, free parameters are model components whose values are fitted to a data set by using an iterative algorithm. For example, spreadsheet programs and most statistical packages have algorithms that will seek the values of free parameters that minimize the discrepancy (e.g., mean squared error) between a model's predictions and the observations in the data set. Clearly, some caution is warranted. First, *ceteris paribus*, models with more free parameters will fit data better than models with fewer parameters, and a model that closely fits data with *no* free parameters is impressive indeed. Second, many reasonable models will provide an impressive correlation to data that are monotonically increasing (or decreasing) as a function of an independent variable. According to Occam's razor, we should always prefer the simplest model, and fit indices like the Aikake information criterion steeply penalize free parameters. But according to what's sometimes called "Einstein's razor," we want our models to be as simple as possible, but no simpler.

MacCoun (2012) provides a good illustration of the choice between these criteria. Looking at a dozen data sets, some models (e.g., social impact theory) sometimes outperformed the BOP models with respect to the Aikake criterion. Yet across all 12 data sets (involving multiple research paradigms), the BOP models consistently performed well (and performed best on average), whereas other models were much less consistent, sometimes failing badly. Arguably, the BOP models are superior with respect to what philosophers of science call the "best system" criterion for scientific theories, which balances simplicity (fewer axioms for deduction, or free parameters for induction) with strength (greater informativeness or explanatory power; see Lewis, 1973). And it is not clear why we even need to be parsimonious. Computation is now extremely cheap and relatively easy. Rather than using a handful of empirical tests to "eliminate" models, we can share our modeling code and routinely examine a whole set of plausible models, discovering how they perform in different situations—and in the process, familiarizing our junior collaborators with a range of ways of conceptualizing the domain. Following this approach, models may remain viable contenders for much longer, but when we finally abandon them, we will have a firm sense of why we are doing so and why they were wrong or incomplete.

Psychologists have an unduly narrow view of parameters and the role that they can play in scientific progress. Free parameters needn't be a gimmick to bolster a theory; they can be a source of valuable information leading to better understanding of phenomena. Oddly, psychologists often balk at a "mathematical model" with two to four free parameters, yet few blink when encountering, say, 10 free parameters in a structural equation model (which is, of course, a mathematical model) involving four variables or a logistic regression equation with nine explanatory variables.

Fitting free parameters can and should be seen as a tool for investigation and estimation rather than a definitive test for validation. This requires us to seek parameters that can develop a meaningful psychological interpretation. For example, the best-fitting uBOP model of the Asch (1956) data, with 4 (S/T − 2.1), can be re-parameterized as an ordinary logit model, with -8 + 4S/T. But uBOP interprets Asch's data as a threshold-matching process with the threshold at just over two sources, whereas the logit model has little apparent social-psychological content.

MacCoun (2012, p. 371) demonstrated that, indeed, the BOP models provide a fairly good fit to even randomly generated monotone series. But this would be true for all the influence models; the fit to real data is notably better than to these "decoy" data sets, and most importantly, the estimated BOP coefficients have values that imply we are fitting data generated by a random non-threshold process.

## Parameter Space: Our Next Frontier?

A great strength of parameterization is that it allows us to begin mapping out where different research studies and paradigms fit in "parameter space." For example, in physics, basic mechanical laws tell us how much force is required to move an object in contact with other objects, but only if we know the friction coefficients of each of the objects. Originally, these were free parameters. But with repeated application, these coefficients became known properties of concrete, wood, glass, water, ice, etc. And in time, our developing maps of parameter space can inform us where to collect data and what we should expect to see if our theories are right—as with the Table of Elements in chemistry, or the way cosmologists used a mapping of physical parameters to translate supernova observations into an inference that the universe is expanding at an accelerating rate.

After such lofty examples, Figure 12.6 offers a much humbler example, plotting bBOP coefficients from various data sets involving either criminal jury deliberation or else "brainteaser"-type intellectual problems (MacCoun, 2014). Because the direction of an asymmetric threshold is a matter of convention (a high threshold for guilt is a low threshold for innocence), we can convert the threshold into an absolute index of asymmetry, forming the horizontal axis. Because the clarity parameter is quite variable, we can plot it in base-10 logs, forming a vertical axis.

It turns out (MacCoun, 2012) that many of the most influential Social Decision Scheme **D** matrices are actually points in this parameter space: Proportionality, Simple Majority, Two-Thirds Majority, Truth Wins, and Truth-Supported Wins. Three of these are plotted as "landmarks" on Figure 12.3's map. The map makes readily apparent that the criminal jury studies occur on a different "continent" than the intellective task studies. The intellective tasks produce greater asymmetry, as we would expect when there is a shared conceptual scheme that facilitates the demonstration of a correct solution. But the criminal jury process is

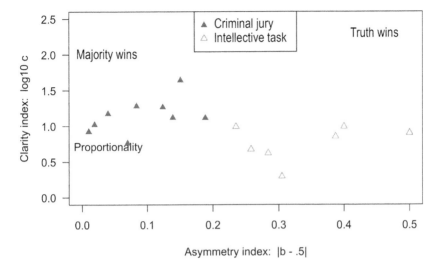

**FIGURE 12.6** "Map" of the bBOP parameter space, showing two types of group decision tasks as distinct "continents" Adapted from MacCoun (2014).

also asymmetric, and it also has greater clarity—the groups all seem to recognize that a sufficiently sizeable amount of disagreement implies that they should acquit the defendant (MacCoun & Kerr, 1988).

Developing maps of parameter space can also aid in the design of new experiments, identifying strong tests, but also helping us distinguish a theory's "terra firma" from regions outside its boundaries of validity or utility. For example: What factors promote threshold clarity? Do homogenous groups show greater clarity than mixed groups? Do socialization and training in a conceptual system promote threshold clarity and correlated behavior, and if so are those effects limited to the shared domain?

## Concluding Thought

Having opened the chapter with Feynman's construction metaphor, I apologize for mixing it with a cartography metaphor. But my fantasy is that the social psychology textbooks a decade or two from now might include both blueprints for constructing models and an atlas of colorful maps of parameter spaces for various phenomena. The blueprints and maps would be so familiar that any two social psychologists would nod in agreement when a third says, "Well, to a first approximation. . . ." In such a discipline, social psychologists would be cautious about offering worldly expert advice for models that haven't been built and areas that are not well mapped out. We would have a clearer sense of the frontier of our knowledge, of uncharted but potentially promising territories, and the kinds of vehicles needed to "get there from here."

## Notes

1 https://en.wikiquote.org/wiki/Talk:Richard_Feynman.
2 Bass (1969, p. 216) made this assumption in formulating his influential model of the diffusion of innovations, stating that the probability of an initial product purchase "is a linear function of the number of previous buyers." But Bass also included an intercept term to allow for the probability that the purchaser is an innovator who makes the purchase independently of the number of other purchasers. On this latter point, see Boyd and Richerson's (1985) model of cultural evolution and discussion in MacCoun (2015).
3 For example, see U. Wilensky's *NetLogo*, available from http://ccl.northwestern.edu/netlogo/.

## References

Abrams, R. (1980). *Foundations of political analysis: An introduction to the theory of collective choice*. New York: Columbia University Press.

Allport, F. H. (1920). The influence of the group upon association and thought. *Journal of Experimental Psychology*, 3, 159–182.

Asch, S. E. (1956). Studies of independence and conformity: A minority of one against a unanimous majority. *Psychological Monographs*, 70(whole no. 416).

Bass, F. (1969). A new product growth model for consumer durables. *Management Science*, 15, 215–227.

Bonacich, P. (2001). The evolution of exchange networks: A simulation study. *Journal of Social Structure*, 2(5). Retrieved from www.cmu.edu/joss/content/articles/volume2/Bonacich.html

Boyd, R., & Richerson, P. J. (1985). *Culture and the evolutionary process*. Chicago, IL: University of Chicago Press.

Boyer, P., Firat, R., & Van Leeuwen, F. (2015). Safety, threat, and stress in intergroup relations: A coalitional index model. *Perspectives on Psychological Science*, 10, 434–450.

Brewer, M. B. (1991). The social self: On being the same and different at the same time. *Personality and Social Psychology Bulletin*, 17, 475–482.

Brooks, G. P., & Johnson, R. W. (1978). Floyd Allport and the master problem in social psychology. *Psychological Reports*, 42, 295–308.

Cialdini, R. B., Reno, R. R., & Kallgren, C. A. (1990). A focus theory of normative conduct: Recycling the concept of norms to reduce littering in public places. *Journal of Personality & Social Psychology*, 58, 1015–1026.

Condorcet, M. (1785). Essay on the application of analysis to the probability of plurality decisions. In K. M. Baker (Ed. and Trans.), (1994). *Condorcet: Selected writings* (pp. 131–138). Brookfield, VT: Edward Elgar.

Daley, D. J., & Gani, J. (1999). *Epidemic modelling: An introduction*. Cambridge: Cambridge University Press.

Davis, J. H. (1973). Group decision and social interaction: A theory of social decision schemes. *Psychological Review*, 80, 97–125.

Davis, J. H., & Witte, E. H. (Eds.) (1996). *Understanding group behavior: Consensual action by small groups* (Vol. 1). Hillsdale, NJ: Lawrence Erlbaum.

Davis, J. H., Zarnoth, P., Hulbert, L., Chen, X. P., Parks, C., & Nam, K. (1997). The committee charge, framing interpersonal agreement, and consensus models of group quantitative judgment. *Organizational Behavior and Human Decision Processes*, 72, 137–157.

Dawes, R. A. (1989). Statistical criteria for establishing a truly false consensus effect. *Journal of Experimental Social Psychology*, 25, 1–17.

Deutsch, M., & Gerard, H. B. (1955). A study of normative and informational social influences upon individual judgment. *Journal of Abnormal and Social Psychology*, *51*, 629–636.

French, J. P. R., Jr., & Raven, B. (1960). The bases of social power. In D. Cartwright & A. Zander (Eds.), *Group dynamics* (pp. 607–623). New York: Harper & Row.

Galton, F. (1907). Vox populi. *Nature*, *75*, 450–451.

Gardner, M. (1970). Mathematical games: The fantastic combinations of John Conway's new solitaire game "Life." *Scientific American*, *223*, 120–123.

Graesser, C. C. (1978). A social averaging theorem for group decision making. *Dissertation Abstracts International*, *38*(11-B), 5647.

Hinsz, V. B. (1999). Group decision making with responses of a quantitative nature: The theory of social decision schemes for quantities. *Organizational Behavior and Human Decision Processes*, *80*, 28–49.

Isenberg, D. J. (1986). Group polarization: A critical review and meta-analysis. *Journal of Personality and Social Psychology*, *50*, 1141–1151.

Kelman, H. C. (1958). Compliance, identification and internalization: Three processes of attitude change. *Journal of Conflict Resolution*, *2*, 51–60.

Kerr, N. L., & MacCoun, R. J. (1985). The effects of jury size and polling method on the process and product of jury deliberation. *Journal of Personality and Social Psychology*, *48*, 349–363.

Kerr, N. L., & MacCoun, R. J. (2012). Is the leniency asymmetry really dead? Misinterpreting asymmetry effects in criminal jury deliberation. *Group Processes and Intergroup Relations*, *15*, 585–602.

Kerr, N. L., MacCoun, R. J., & Kramer, G. (1996). Bias in judgment: Comparing individuals and groups. *Psychological Review*, *103*, 687–719.

Kerr, N. L., Stasser, G., & Davis, J. H. (1979). Model testing, model fitting, and social decision schemes. *Organizational Behavior and Human Decision Processes*, *23*, 399–410.

Latané, B. (1981). The psychology of social impact. *American Psychologist*, *36*, 343–356.

Laughlin, P. R. (2011). *Group problem solving*. Princeton, NJ: Princeton University Press.

Leary, M. R. (2005). Sociometer theory and the pursuit of relational value: Getting to the root of self-esteem. *European Review of Social Psychology*, *16*, 75–111.

Lewis, D. (1973). *Counterfactuals*. Oxford: Blackwell.

Lorenz, J., Rahut, H., Schweitzer, F., & Helbing, D. (2011). How social influence can undermine the wisdom of crowd effect. *Proceedings of the National Academy of Science*, *108*, 9020–9025.

Lorge, I., & Solomon, H. (1955). Two models of group behavior in the solution of Eureka-type problems. *Psychometrika*, *20*, 139–148.

MacCoun, R. J. (2005). Media reporting of jury verdicts: Is the tail (of the distribution) wagging the dog? *DePaul Law Review*, *55*, 539–562.

MacCoun, R. J. (2012). The burden of social proof: Shared thresholds and social influence. *Psychological Review*, *119*, 345–372.

MacCoun, R. J. (2014). Alternative maps for the world of collective behavior. Invited comment. *Behavioral and Brain Sciences*, *37*, 88–90.

MacCoun, R. J. (2015). Balancing evidence and norms in cultural evolution. *Organizational Behavior and Human Decision Processes*, *129*, 93–104.

MacCoun, R. J., Cook, P., Muschkin, C., & Vigdor, J. (2008). Distinguishing spurious and real norm effects: Evidence from artificial societies, small-group experiments, and real schoolyards. *Review of Law & Economics*, *4*(3), 695–714.

MacCoun, R. J., & Kerr, N. L. (1988). Asymmetric influence in mock jury deliberation: Jurors' bias for leniency. *Journal of Personality and Social Psychology*, *54*, 21–33.

Mahajan, V., Muller, E., & Bass, F. (1995). Diffusion of new products: Empirical generalizations and managerial uses. *Management Science, 14,* G79–G88.

Milgram, S., Bickman, L., & Berkowitz, L. (1969). Note on the drawing power of crowds of different size. *Journal of Personality and Social Psychology, 13,* 79–82.

Mullen, B. (1983). Operationalizing the effect of the group on the individual: A self-attention perspective. *Journal of Experimental Social Psychology, 19,* 295–322.

Newman, M., Barabási, A. L., & Watts, D. J. (2006). *The structure and dynamics of networks.* Princeton University Press.

Nowak, A., Szamrej, J., & Latané, B. (1990). From private attitudes to public opinion: A dynamic theory of social opinion. *Psychological Review, 97,* 362–376.

Parks, C. D., & Kerr, N. L. (1999). Twenty-five years of social decision scheme theory. *Organizational Behavior and Human Decision Processes, 80,* 1–2.

Rahmandad, H., & Sterman, J. (2008). Heterogeneity and network structure in the dynamics of diffusion: Comparing agent-based and differential equation models. *Management Science, 54,* 998–1014.

Railsback, S. F., & Grimm, V. (2011). *Agent-based and individual-based modeling: A practical introduction.* Princeton, NJ: Princeton University Press.

Roberts, S., & Pashler, H. (2000). How persuasive is a good fit? A comment on theory testing. *Psychological Review, 107,* 358–367.

Rosenwein, R. E., & Campbell, D. T. (1992). Mobilization to achieve collective action and democratic majority/plurality amplification. *Journal of Social Issues, 48,* 125–138.

Schelling, T. C. (1978). *Micromotives and macrobehavior.* New York: W. W. Norton.

Schkade, D. A., Sunstein, C. R., & Kahneman, D. (2000). Deliberating about dollars: The severity shift. *Columbia Law Review, 100,* 1139–1176.

Smaldino, P. E., Janssen, M. A., Hillis, V., & Bednar, J. (2015). *Adoption as a social marker: The diffusion of products in a multigroup environment.* Retrieved from http://arxiv.org/abs/1507.04775

Smaldino, P. E., Calanchini, J., & Pickett, C. L. (2015). Theory development with agent-based models. *Organizational Psychology Review, 5,* 300–317.

Stasser, G., Kerr, N. L., & Davis, J. H. (1989). Influence processes and consensus models in decision-making groups. In P. Paulus (Ed.), *Psychology of group influence* (2nd ed., pp. 279–326). Hillsdale, NJ: Lawrence Erlbaum.

Stevens, S. S. (1957). On the psychophysical law. *Psychological Review, 64,* 153–181.

Surowiecki, J. (2005). *The wisdom of crowds.* New York: Anchor Books.

Verhulst, P.-F. (1838). Notice sur la loi que la population suit dans son accroissement. *Correspondance Mathématique et Physique, 10,* 113–121.

Wilder, D. A. (1977). Perception of groups, size of opposition, and social influence. *Journal of Experimental Social Psychology, 13,* 253–268.

Wilson, E. B., & Worcester, J. (1944). The law of mass action in epidemiology. *Proceedings of the National Academy of Science, 31,* 24–34.

# 13

# MODELING CULTURAL DYNAMICS

*Yoshihisa Kashima, Michael Kirley,
Alexander Stivala, and Garry Robins*[1]

Culture is an enigma in contemporary social psychology. Despite its brief prominence in the 1960s (e.g., Triandis, 1964), social psychological curiosity about culture waned over the heyday of social cognition in the 1970s and 1980s, only to regain its prominence in the 1990s with the publication of Triandis (1989) and Markus and Kitayama (1991) in *Psychological Review*. Over the last two and a half decades, cultural comparative approaches to culture and psychology have accumulated a large body of literature documenting cultural differences around the globe, though primarily comparing East Asian- and Western European-based cultural groups, and have brought about a number of insights into cultural diversity across humanity. However, this literature has been largely silent on the question of the dynamics of culture—namely, the stability and change of culture, and the mechanisms that drive the trajectories of cultural change over time (see, e.g., Kashima & Gelfand, 2012). *Cultural dynamics* is concerned with these questions—how do individuals' thoughts, feelings, and actions in interaction with others in particular contexts generate the movements of culture—its formation, maintenance, and transformation over time (e.g., Kashima, 2000).

At the heart of this lies the fundamental question for social psychology. How do human individuals interact with the actual and imagined others? In so doing, how do we influence each other? Ever since Sherif and Asch, social influence has been a core concern of social psychology; culture is at one level "what social influence influences" (Axelrod, 1997, p. 207). From the concept of human rights to the landing on the Moon, and from genocides in intractable intergroup conflicts to anthropogenic climate change, culture enables the astonishing human adaptiveness and achievements in society and in nature, while at times exhibiting surprising maladaptiveness with pathological and tragic consequences in both. With all its glories and failings, the dynamic complexity of human sociality is fundamental to human culture. Culture enables human sociality; human sociality constitutes culture. Given their interdependency, culture must be an integral part of human social psychology.

Computational modeling—especially agent-based modeling (e.g., Railsback & Grimm, 2012)—is a useful methodological tool in research on cultural dynamics for the development of a coherent theory, derivation of testable hypotheses, understanding of the past and present, as well as forecasting of future possibilities. Because of the number and heterogeneity of actors, the complexity of social interactions, and different timescales involved (social interaction *in situ* may change in a short timespan, but institutions remain stable over a longer period of time), some formal representations (e.g., difference and differential equations) are often useful in theorizing and describing cultural dynamics. However, these very characteristics often make the type of formal analytical methods necessary for the modeling of cultural dynamics outside the training of social psychologists, and difficult, if not impossible, to use (e.g., A. Nowak & Vallacher, 1998). Agent-based modeling approaches, however, enable social psychologists to explicate their assumptions about culture, construct explicit models of cultural dynamics, and explore their implications in a principled fashion. This chapter is designed to provide a broad and selective introduction to diverse literatures on computational approaches to cultural dynamics.

## Culture and Its Dynamics

Culture is an essentially contested concept—depending on one's theoretical perspective, it can be defined in a multitude of ways. In the current approach, we define culture as *a set of non-genetically transmissible information that is commonly available, accessible, and applicable in a human group*. Cultural information typically takes the form of ideas (e.g., liberty, equality, and fraternity) or practices (e.g., how to deliberate, vote, and determine an outcome). Availability means information is there to be learned if an individual wants to; accessibility implies that information has been learned and can be brought to mind; and applicability suggests that information can inform the individual's action. Several aspects of this definition are worth highlighting:

1.  *Culture is information.* Some theorists (e.g., Herskovits, 1948; Triandis, 1994) have defined culture as the human-made part of the environment. We acknowledge that the human-made part of the environment (largely consisting of artefacts) *carries* or *embodies* cultural information, and cultural information enables humans to construct it; however, we distinguish what represents information from information itself.
2.  *Culture is not a group.* Culture is often equated with a group or a collection of human individuals that continue to exist over a period of time where a group can vary in size from relatively small communities to the whole

of humanity. We acknowledge that a culture is definable when a group is defined; however, we regard culture as information carried by members of a group or embodied in the artefacts constructed by them, and as such, cultural information can continue to exist and inform human action even after the group ceases to exist (e.g., Classic Egyptian, Mesopotamian, Greek, Roman, Indian, Chinese cultures).

3. *Cultural information differs from genetic information in mode of transmission.* Culture consists of information that is socially transmitted, rather than genetically transmitted, from one person to another. Social transmission of cultural information can occur in various forms: formal schooling and explicit instruction, co-participation in joint activities, with or without language or other symbolic means. Although genetic transmission occurs only from a biological parent to a biological child, cultural transmission occurs within and between generations, from older to younger, but also from younger to older, generations.

In this perspective, *cultural dynamics* is concerned with the trajectory of persistence and change of a set of cultural information and associated characteristics (e.g., structure, organization, and frequency and spatial distributions) in a group over time, and the social psychological mechanisms that drive these temporal dynamics.

## Sources of Cultural Dynamics

Critical aspects of cultural dynamics are the *generation* and *retention* of information in the culture of a group. That is, when new cultural information is generated, it is added to the set; when it is retained over time (e.g., across generations), it is kept in the group's culture and potentially used in the future. The mechanism that drives the generation and retention of cultural information is the *social transmission of cultural information* between people (for recent research on this topic, see Kashima, 2016a). This perspective is broadly in line with a host of theories of cultural evolution (e.g., Boyd & Richerson, 1985; Campbell, 1975; Cavalli-Sforza & Feldman, 1981; Dawkins, 1976; Richerson & Boyd, 2005; Sperber, 1996). Kashima, Peters, and Whelan (2008) called this metatheory *neo-diffusionism*.

In this perspective, there are at least four sources of cultural dynamics (Kashima, 2014). New information may be generated by *invention* within the group (e.g., Campbell, 1960; Simonton, 2010) or by *importation* from another group (e.g., Bartlett, 1923, 1932); once cultural information is present, it may be retained by *selection*—selecting it *in* for its benefit, or selecting it *out* for its cost (e.g., Boyd & Richerson, 1985; Cavalli-Sforza & Feldman, 1981)—or by *drift*, non-selective stochastic transmission and retention (e.g., Bentley, Hahn, & Shennan, 2004; Hahn & Bentley, 2003). The four sources of cultural dynamics differ in whether new information is added to a given culture, and whether adaptation is involved (i.e., benefit enhancement or cost reduction; see Table 13.1). Presumably, information is imported or selected during the process of adaptation;

**TABLE 13.1** Sources of cultural dynamics.

|  | *Random* | *Adaptive* |
|---|---|---|
| Addition | Invention | Importation |
| Retention | Drift | Selection |

*Note*: Each source differs in terms of whether it pertains to the addition of new cultural information or the retention (or removal) of cultural information within a population, and whether it occurs randomly or due to adaptive processes. We chose the term "random" here, but it may be better to say it is neutral (i.e., non-adaptive) or blind (i.e., without foresight). The characterization of invention as blind is due to Campbell (1960).

it may be invented or may drift due to stochastic processes that are neutral to adaptation (i.e., do not necessarily result in adaptation or maladaptation).

The sources of cultural dynamics presented here provide a framework for our discussions about diverse computational approaches to cultural dynamics. In this chapter, we begin our coverage with social psychological models of cultural dynamics (Abelson & Bernstein, 1963; A. Nowak, Szamrej, & Latané, 1990), and then move to two prominent approaches to cultural dynamics—Axelrod's (1997) model of cultural dissemination, and evolutionary game theoretic approaches to evolution of cooperation. We show that these approaches focus on complementary aspects of cultural dynamics, and that each has unique strengths in dealing with some aspects, but not others. On one hand, the Axelrod model has been used to explore the dynamics deriving from transmissions of cultural information and the role of drift and to some extent of importation; however, it does not address invention, or most importantly, selection. On the other hand, evolutionary game theoretic approaches have a unique strength in examining the importance of the selection process in cultural (and genetic) evolution. In this chapter, we will thus discuss how the existing approaches complement each other, and also point to the gap in the existing theory—neither has addressed the process of invention (other than as a random process of mutation).

We hasten to add that there are many analytical (for a systematic exposition, see McElreath & Boyd, 2007) and simulation (e.g., Carley, 1991; Hutchins, 1995) models of culture and cultural dynamics; however, they are too extensive and varied to be covered in the present chapter. It suffices to say that these attempts model some of the above processes at the micro-level of cognition and communication, and explore their consequences at macro-levels of organization, society, and culture. Nevertheless, there is a tradition in social psychology to attempt to describe the trajectory of cultural change with computer simulations of individuals' micro-level interactions. We start with this social psychological literature.

## Social Psychology of Cultural Dynamics

The social psychological tradition of cultural dynamics research began with public opinion dynamics. Note that in the current view of culture, a cultural element may be a public opinion. Given a certain proposition (i.e., cultural information) such as "Climate change is occurring, and it is largely human-caused," individuals in a group (e.g., Americans) can have a variety of opinions, and the frequency distribution of opinions on a binary variable such as pro versus con, or a continuous bipolar dimension that indicates a degree of agreement or disagreement with the proposition can be regarded as an aspect of this group's culture. Obviously, the distribution of opinions about public issues such as climate change dynamically changes over time (e.g., Brulle, Carmichael, & Jenkins, 2012). Describing the temporal trajectory of public opinions and examining the social psychological mechanisms underlying such opinion changes are both integral aspects of research on cultural dynamics (e.g., Kashima, 2014).

Abelson and Bernstein (1963) were the first to examine such public opinion dynamics in computer simulations. In their model, agents had opinions about fluoridation of water supplies, interacted with other agents as a function of their relationships with them, conversed with them about fluoridation as a function of their interest in the issue, and updated their opinions and their relationships with their interaction partners; these steps occurred iteratively over time. Although most of the then existing models of attitude formation and change predicted a uniformly pro or con distribution of opinions in the community (Abelson, 1964), Abelson and Bernstein's simulation model showed a polarization of opinions—opinions would become more extreme—so that those agents that held initially pro opinions are likely to hold more pro opinions, and those that held con opinions become more con in opposition as the controversy runs its course. In other words, public opinions could polarize, and the polarization might persist and exacerbate—a finding that accorded much better with the empirical reality of controversies in realpolitik.

Although Abelson and Bernstein (1963) showed that the emergence of consensus is not a universal consequence of simulation models, thus laying a foundation for simulating cultural dynamics, their model did not have an explicit spatial arrangement. It was A. Nowak and colleagues (1990) who explicitly defined a space (depending on its interpretation, it can be construed as a physical or social space). They suggested that agents can be located in a grid-like structure (i.e., lattice), where they would interact with other agents in their spatial neighborhoods and exert social influences on each other as specified by Latané's (1981) social impact theory. More importantly, because their simulation model had an explicit definition of space, they could also model the effect of spatial distance—it is known that opinions of others who are psychologically close (Latané's immediacy; for empirical evidence, see also Latané, Liu, Nowak, Bonevento, & Zheng, 1995) have a greater persuasiveness. Together with the nonlinearity in attitude change processes assumed in the model (see Lewenstein, Nowak, & Latané, 1992), their model produced spatial clustering of public opinions—even if there is a strong majority (i.e., a large proportion of agents have pro or con opinions), an opinion minority could survive if its members are spatially close to each other and cluster together in space (for empirical evidence, see Latané & L'Herrou, 1996).

These developments have enabled modeling of a single cultural element (e.g., opinion), and examination of the consequences of micro-level communication dynamics among agents on the macro-level trajectory of the opinion distribution in the group. This line of investigation can be extended in two different ways: multidimensionality and adaptiveness of culture. We will examine them in turn.

## Multidimensionality of Culture: The Axelrod Model of Cultural Dissemination

One of the characteristics of the foregoing model is that it models only a single cultural element. However, culture is obviously not a single element, but typically consists of multiple elements. Furthermore, cultural elements are not independent of each other, but are considered to be "patterned" (e.g., Kroeber & Kluckhohn, 1952; Triandis, 1996) or to form a configuration. How can a pattern of cultural elements emerge in computer simulations? Latané (1996) suggested one potential mechanism for the emergence of a cultural pattern. That is, when multiple cultural elements exist, but when each cultural element is influenced by the same mechanism of social influence such as dynamic social impact theory, even in the absence of any inherent relations between them, there will be a spatial clustering of each cultural element. However, by virtue of the spatial clustering of these cultural elements, the elements that happen to occur within a given spatial cluster become correlated just by happenstance. A. Nowak, de Raad, and Borkowski (2012) showed this to be the case in their computer simulation (see also DellaPosta, Shi, & Macy, 2015; for a review, see Harton & Bullock, 2007).

This line of investigation was further extended by the Axelrod model of cultural dissemination (Axelrod, 1997). In Axelrod's original model, cultural information is assumed to be represented as a set of multiple attributes (e.g., religion, language, taste) which each agent possesses. It is represented as a *culture vector* of F features, each of which can take q possible values (traits). For instance, one feature can be opinion about climate change, and then each agent can have one of several different types of opinions (e.g., "climate change doesn't exist," "climate change is happening, but not anthropogenic"). Another feature may be opinion about economic development (e.g., "market economy is the best form of resource distribution," "government intervention is sometimes important to regulate the economic process"). This way, there may be a number of cultural elements. When two agents interact, one agent's cultural information is transmitted to the other, and as a result changes the latter's culture vector. This transmission process, however, is constrained, so that the model assumes that cultural transmission occurs only when the agents already share some cultural information. In other words, if two agents have no cultural information in common, they cannot interact or transmit cultural information. This assumption can be interpreted as suggesting that (1) similar people tend to interact with each other (i.e., homophily), (2) people use their shared culture to communicate new cultural information, or both (1) and (2). Note that this process implies that cultural similarity begets cultural similarity—that is, culturally similar agents become more culturally similar to each other. Does this mean that cultural differences eventually disappear? Even with multidimensional cultures, Axelrod (1997) showed that cultural diversity can persist under some circumstances.

## Basic Model

The dynamics of the model are as follows. As in A. Nowak and colleagues (1990), each agent is placed on a lattice site (every site on the lattice is occupied) with four neighbors (i.e., above, below, right, and left; Von Neumann neighborhood), and only neighboring agents can interact. Initially, each agent is assigned a culture vector uniformly at random (that is, each of the $F$ traits is given one of the $q$ possible values at random). Thereafter, at each step, a random agent is chosen as the focal agent, and one of its neighbors is also chosen at random. The probability of the two agents interacting and influencing each other is determined by their cultural similarity, which is defined as the number of matching features between their culture vectors—that is, the number of corresponding features in which the two agents have the same trait value. When they interact, a random feature on which the two agents' values differ (if there is one) on the focal agent is changed to the value of the corresponding feature on the other agent.

This process is repeated until no more changes are possible, because any two neighboring agents either have identical culture vectors, or completely different culture vectors (no features in common, so they cannot interact). At this point, when no more change is possible, which is known as the *absorbing state*, there are two possible results. There is either a monocultural state, in which all agents have the same culture vector, or a multicultural state, in which any two agents in a contiguous region have the same culture, but neighboring agents on the region boundaries have completely different cultures (they can no longer interact as they have no features in common).

Figure 13.1 shows an example run of an Axelrod model using a visualization similar to that originally presented in Axelrod (1997), where the similarity of adjacent sites on the lattice is represented by the darkness of the line between the two sites. In the initial conditions (Figure 13.1a), adjacent sites are mostly completely different, although some have some small degree of similarity. In the intermediate stages (Figures 13.1b and 13.1c), cultural regions have started to form, and the boundaries between some cultural regions are colored light gray, indicating they are quite similar. In the absorbing state (Figure 13.1d), which is a multicultural absorbing state which was reached after approximately 58,000 iterations, there are five cultural regions, the largest of which covers 75% of the lattice. Note that in this implementation of the model (Weaver, 2010), implemented in *NetLogo*,[2] the lattice "wraps around" so that all sites on the lattice have

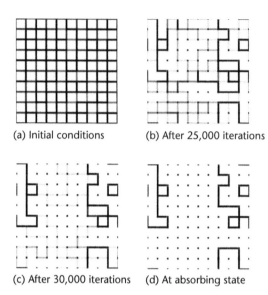

(a) Initial conditions    (b) After 25,000 iterations

(c) After 30,000 iterations    (d) At absorbing state

**FIGURE 13.1**   Example of an Axelrod model run with number of features $F = 5$, number of traits $q = 15$, on a $10 \times 10$ lattice. The darkness of the lines between sites indicates the cultural similarity (white is identical, black is completely different).

exactly four neighbors, with no special cases on the edges of the lattice, unlike the original model specified by Axelrod (1997).

Whether a monocultural or multicultural absorbing state is reached—and if a multicultural absorbing state is reached, how many cultural regions exist—are influenced by a number of factors. Increasing $q$, the number of possible traits of each feature, results in an increased number of cultural regions, but in a nonlinear manner. All else being equal, when $q$ is below a critical value, a monocultural absorbing state is the result. Increasing $q$ above the critical value results in a multicultural absorbing state, with an increasing number of regions as $q$ increases. Increasing the size of the neighborhood of agents with which the focal agent can interact decreases the number of cultural regions. Surprisingly, however, increasing the number of features, $F$, decreases the number of cultural regions, as does increasing the size of the lattice (which in the original Axelrod model also increases the number of agents, each lattice site being occupied) after a certain point.

So even this simple model demonstrates complex behavior, showing how homophily and social influence alone, in which two agents can only ever become more similar, does not necessarily result in a monoculture. In the language of statistical physics, there is a nonequilibrium phase transition at the critical value of $q$, separating the ordered (monocultural) phase from the disordered (multicultural) phase (Castellano, Marsili, & Vespignani, 2000).

## Extensions of the Axelrod Model

The original Axelrod model describes cultural transmission in dyadic social interactions in a grid-like social space with culture vectors taken from a fixed cultural space ($F \times q$ matrix). However, it has been extended to investigate the implications of non-dyadic social interactions in more complex social and cultural structures.

## Non-Dyadic Social Interactions

The effect of *mass media* or other external cultural influences can be modeled as an external field acting on the culture vectors in the Axelrod model, causing a feature to become more similar to the external cultural message vector with a certain probability (Gandica, Charmell, Villegas-Febres, & Bonalde, 2011; González-Avella, Cosenza, Eguíluz, & San Miguel, 2010; González-Avella, Cosenza, & Tucci, 2005; González-Avella et al., 2006). Such an external cultural influence can, counterintuitively, lead to multicultural states when they would otherwise not have existed (González-Avella et al., 2005; González-Avella et al., 2006). A different, earlier, model of the mass media effect was a "generalized other," a hypothetical extra neighbor agent with the most preferred value of each feature (Shibanai, Yasuno, & Ishiguro, 2001). In this model, rather than mass media being an external cultural influence, it is viewed as a social norm constructed from the culture vectors of all agents in the model.

The concept of *multilateral social influence* (i.e., more than two agents interacting) was explicitly introduced by Parisi, Cecconi, and Natale (2003), although it was implicit in the "generalized other" of Shibanai et al. (2001). Parisi et al. (2003) show that, in the absence of homophily, stable multicultural states (neither monocultural nor anomic) can be sustained even in the presence of noise when social influence is multilateral. Kuperman (2006) extends the Axelrod model by having an agent adopt a neighbor's trait only when it will then become similar to more of its neighbors. Extensions of the Axelrod model which incorporate multilateral social influence are thoroughly examined by Flache and Macy (2011), who show that such stable multicultural states can be sustained for wide ranges of noise levels even when homophily is assumed, as long as social influence is multilateral and not just dyadic. Rodríguez and Moreno (2010) incorporate both multilateral social influence and a mass media effect, again finding that multilateral social influence can maintain diversity in the presence of noise.

## Social and Cultural Spaces

Rather than the standard lattice structure, cultural dynamics on more complex *social networks* have been investigated. One of them is a small-world network, which consists of densely connected clusters with sparse links between the clusters. Klemm, Eguíluz, Toral, and San Miguel (2003) find that the critical value of

$q$ increases with increasing density of long-distance connections. Guerra, Poncela, Gómez-Gardeñes, Latora, and Moreno (2010) explore the cultural dynamics on scale-free graphs (i.e., degree distribution follows a power law), which can be constructed by a process of preferential attachment: each new node is added to the graph by choosing an existing node to which to connect it with probability proportional to the existing node's degree (Barabási & Albert, 1999). Although these models have static social networks on which cultural dynamics unfold, more recent models have the social network co-evolve with culture (Centola, González-Avella, Eguíluz, & San Miguel, 2007; Vazquez, González-Avella, Eguíluz, & San Miguel, 2007), or allow for empty sites on the lattice and migration of agents (Gracia-Lázaro, Lafuerza, Floría, & Moreno, 2009), or both (Pfau, Kirley, & Kashima, 2013).

The cultural space in the original Axelrod model is simple and unstructured—a $F \times q$ matrix. Most of the subsequent models used a uniform random distribution of culture vectors as the initial conditions. As noted by Pace and Prado (2014), however, our understanding of the Axelrod model depends on this assumption, and different initial conditions can lead to very different behavior. An important exception to this general assumption is a model in which empirical opinion data is used as the initial culture vectors, which are found to have an approximately ultrametric distribution, leading to increased diversity at the absorbing state compared to random initial conditions (Valori, Picciolo, Allansdottir, & Garlaschelli, 2012). The effects of ultrametricity and other statistical properties of the initial culture vectors were further explored in Stivala, Robins, Kashima, and Kirley (2014). They found that when the agents have culture vectors generated by adding random noises to prototype culture vectors, they showed cultural dynamics similar to those generated by real opinion data, suggesting that the structure of cultural space needs to be further explored.

Nonetheless, these models still assume that different cultural features can change independently from each other. To the best of our knowledge, no research has investigated the cultural dynamics when cultural representations are truly configural, so that a change in one cultural element may precipitate a change in other elements.

## Sources of Cultural Dynamics in the Axelrod Model

Some extensions of the Axelrod model addressed the cultural dynamics stemming from one of the sources of cultural dynamics: *cultural drift* (e.g., De Sanctis & Galla, 2009; Grauwin & Jensen, 2012; Klemm et al., 2003; Klemm, Eguíluz, Toral, & San Miguel, 2005; Parisi et al., 2003). In the Axelrod model, random perturbations can be added in the culture vectors as a form of drift. When a drift rate is small, the monocultural absorbing state becomes more likely; however, for large noise rates, a state of "anomie" is more likely to ensue, in which stable cultural regions fail to form (Centola et al., 2007; Flache & Macy, 2011; Mäs, Flache, & Helbing, 2010).

A high drift rate in this context implies that cultural transmission is noisy or inaccurate, and the findings here imply that inaccurate cultural transmissions are likely to result in a monocultural state. Hence, the model suggests that cultural information needs to be transmitted fairly accurately in order to maintain cultural diversity.

Arguably, the investigation of external cultural influences reviewed above taps a source of cultural dynamics akin to importation, although further extensions including social identity and the like may be possible (e.g., Yamamoto, 2015). However, this research tradition has not investigated other sources of cultural dynamics such as *cultural invention*. That is to say, as noted by Pace and Prado (2014), Axelrod models (without noise) lack a method for the creation of novelty, since traits can only ever become extinct, and cannot be created. A possible major extension of the Axelrod model would be a mechanism to introduce new features or new traits, and compare the behavior of trait change compared to the creation of a whole new trait or feature. Furthermore, an obvious gap in this literature is an investigation of selection processes in which cultural information is selected in or out due to its adaptiveness or a lack thereof. A different tradition of research—evolution of cooperation—has addressed selection as its central focus, to which we now turn.

## Adaptiveness: Evolution of Cooperation

In the models of opinion dynamics and cultural dissemination discussed in the preceding section, agents interact with each other and transmit cultural information as a matter of course regardless of the social and psychological consequences of doing so. Nonetheless, as we noted earlier, one of the sources of cultural dynamics is *selection* (Table 13.1). That is, the more adaptive cultural information is (i.e., its retention, transmission, and use are less costly and bring about more benefits at the psychological, social, and practical levels), the more likely it is to be selected and retained in the group's culture (e.g., Kashima, 2014; Kashima, 2016a, 2016b). However, the models of opinion dynamics and cultural dissemination do not take the consequences of cultural transmission into consideration in describing cultural dynamics.

In contrast, the literature on the evolution of cooperation is the most developed research tradition that addresses *selection* as a source of cultural dynamics. To be sure, there is a long tradition in social psychology which investigates collective action in social dilemmas (e.g., Dawes, 1980; Kollock, 1998; Parks, Joireman, & Van Lange, 2013; Van Lange, Joireman, Parks, & Van Dijk, 2013). A social dilemma is defined as a situation in which individually beneficial actions produce collectively costly consequences. However, research on the evolution of cooperation addresses a question somewhat different from the typical experimental social psychological question, "How do humans behave in social dilemmas?" Rather, it can be construed as asking, "Under what circumstances can cooperation as a cultural practice or a genetic characteristic remain in the population of agents?" In so doing, this research tradition attempts to answer under what circumstances can the cultural practice of cooperation be adaptive, and therefore selected in to remain in human culture.

This section describes some of the key concepts and main findings to provide an introduction to this voluminous literature. In particular, we review the standard game theoretic treatment of the Prisoner's Dilemma (PD) as a prototypical game in evolution of cooperation, introduce an evolutionary game theoretic approach, and describe some of the key findings in this literature.

### Cooperation in Social Dilemma

The standard mathematical approach used to investigate the evolution of cooperation is based on game theory (Von Neumann & Morgenstern, 1953), whose fundamental assumptions are those of rationality and strategic interactions. That is, a rational player takes into account all the available information in the situation (i.e., the game) and tries to maximize the expected payoff by identifying an optimal sequence of choices of strategies (e.g., cooperation or defection). One of the best-known examples of this approach is the classic Prisoner's Dilemma game (Axelrod, 1984; Rapoport & Chammah, 1965), a type of symmetric two-player simultaneous nonzero-sum game. Each of the two agents (typically called *players*), players A and B, makes a choice once from two potential *strategies*: cooperation (C) or defection (D). There are four possible outcomes for the game for each player, depending on the combination of what each player decides to do (Table 13.2).

Typically, the outcomes are displayed in the form of a payoff matrix, as shown in Table 13.3.

**TABLE 13.2** Players A and B's choices and outcomes for A.

| A's choice | B's choice | A's outcome |
|---|---|---|
| C | C | Reward of mutual cooperation (R) |
| C | D | Sucker's payoff (S) |
| D | C | Temptation to defect (T) |
| D | D | Punishment for mutual defection (P) |

*Note:* T > R > P > S.

**TABLE 13.3** Payoff matrix for a two-person game.

|   |   | **B** | |
|---|---|---|---|
|   |   | *C* | *D* |
| **A** | *C* | R | S |
|   | *D* | T | P |

The Prisoner's Dilemma payoff matrix is defined by the constraint T > R > P > S. Looking at this situation from player A's perspective, it is easy to see that D always brings a better outcome than C. If B chooses C, the outcome of A choosing D (T) is better than choosing C (R); if B chooses D, the outcome of A choosing D (P) is better than choosing C (S). In other words, D dominates C. Each player then choosing D is what is known as a *Nash equilibrium*—the state in which unilaterally altering one's behavior does not improve one's payoff (Gintis, 2009; M. A. Nowak, 2006a). Assuming that the players behave so as to increase benefits and reduce costs, this is an equilibrium, in that it is a stable state in which neither player is willing to change his or her behavior unilaterally—the system of interlocking behaviors would remain stable. Nevertheless, given the payoff matrix, both players choosing D (outcome P) brings an outcome worse than their both choosing C (outcome R). Therein lies a dilemma—a strategic choice that brings a better outcome for each individual locks them into a mutually worse outcome.

This situation can be generalized to the case in which a game involves more than two players. One such game is the Public Goods game (e.g., Dawes, 1980; Hardin, 1968; also see Camerer, 2003; Gintis, 2009). Here, each player can either cooperate or defect, but the payoff matrix is generalized to the *n* person situation where the payoffs for cooperators and defectors are a function of the numbers of cooperators and defectors in the group. A player is always better off defecting than cooperating, but payoff is higher if everyone cooperates than if everyone defects. This is the essence of a *social dilemma*—an individually beneficial action resulting in a collectively unpalatable outcome.

## Iterated Games

So far, we have considered the social situation in which agents make a choice only once (*one-shot game*). However, when agents play a game repeatedly (*iterated game*), the strategy to defect does not necessarily generate the highest payoff. For instance, imagine a Prisoner's Dilemma game where players A and B repeatedly play a PD as shown in Table 13.2. If they decide to take turns, so that A cooperates and B defects in the first round, A defects and B cooperates in the second round, A cooperates and B defects in the third round, etc., every two rounds both players cumulate the payoff S+T. If S+T > 2R, then the strategy of taking turns to cooperate and defect can maximize their outcomes (so, for a repeated PD, there is usually another constraint, S+T < 2R). Thus, in an Iterated Prisoner's Dilemma game, the strategy of always defecting is not necessarily the best option.

More generally, if the number of rounds of the game is unknown (or at the very least, the probability of playing additional rounds of the game is high), there are a variety of *conditional cooperation* strategies whose outcomes are better than the always-defect strategy in the long run. As we will see later, Trivers (1971) was perhaps the first to describe these types of strategies as driving the evolution of cooperation within a Prisoner's Dilemma; Axelrod (1984) extended this line of thinking. Put more broadly, the game theoretic formulation enables us to examine the adaptiveness of these game playing strategies, whether the long-term consequences of adopting cooperative strategies are beneficial or costly for the players. The foregoing discussion amounts to saying that a game playing strategy to cooperate is better for both players than a defective one under some circumstances, even if the social situation that dictates the outcome of their enactment constitutes a difficult social dilemma to resolve.

## Evolutionary Game Theory

Evolutionary game theory (e.g., Axelrod, 1984; Axelrod & Hamilton, 1981; Maynard Smith, 1982; M. A. Nowak, 2006a) extends the foregoing idea of iterative game plays by considering a population of players and their selections of strategies. Some terminological clarification is in order here. Although it is the standard practice in evolutionary game theory to call different ways of playing a game "strategies," this seems to us to be a reflection of the conceptual roots of this research tradition, the fact that game theory was developed as a principled consideration of strategic moves when players are trying to outsmart each other. There is an unfortunate connotation that these game playing strategies are deliberate attempts to outperform each other. However, there is no reason why they must involve such deliberative foresights. In order to avoid the deliberative connotation, we will call strategies *genetic traits*, or *genetic tendencies* if they are genetically transmitted, whereas, we will call them *cultural traits*, *cultural practices*, or simply *practices* if such strategies are socially transmitted.

This terminological distinction should clarify what is being modeled. When a strategy like cooperation and defection is construed as a genetically transmitted trait, the resultant dynamics can be thought of as modeling biological evolution. However, when a strategy is interpreted as a cultural practice—a type of cultural information that describes a pattern of behavior—the resultant dynamics can be regarded as modeling cultural evolution. In either case, the payoff an individual receives corresponds to the notion of Darwinian *fitness*—average reproductive success in biological evolution and an average level of rewards in some sense in cultural evolution. The distribution of players' strategies defines a population state, which is formally equivalent to a notion of mixed strategy in game theory. Thus, evolutionary game theory investigates the emergent population dynamics and strategy distribution.

Now imagine that a large group of players play the Iterated Prisoner's Dilemma over multiple rounds of the game.[3] Furthermore, suppose that players can alter their strategy in response to the action played by the other players in previous rounds, such that a strategy that brings a better outcome is more likely retained. In any population of a mixture of players who *always* choose to cooperate or defect (i.e., non-conditional co-operators or defectors), defection produces a higher average payoff than cooperation. Over time, cooperation tends to disappear from the population, and the relative proportion of defection increases as a result of the simulated selection process, with all the group members eventually defecting—this happens even if there is only one defector, and the rest are all cooperators. In this sense, defection is an *evolutionarily stable strategy* (ESS).[4]

Nevertheless, as in the one-shot Prisoner's Dilemma Game, if all players choose to cooperate, everyone will be better off than if all players defect. By everyone cooperating, the entire group reaps benefit; by defecting, everyone will be worse off in the long run. But there is an incentive for each player to defect—the so-called *free rider problem*. If the Darwinian evolutionary process underlies the selection of genetically or socially transmittable behavioral patterns (e.g., cooperation and defection), how can cooperation evolve in a population? Thus, the evolution of cooperation is a theoretical puzzle in the Darwinian theory of biological and cultural evolution. And again, the answer is some form of conditional cooperation—a search for genetic or cultural mechanisms that enable conditional cooperative strategies to produce beneficial outcomes in the long run, even when the social situation that dictates the outcome of combinations of strategy choices involves social dilemmas like the Prisoner's or Public Goods Dilemma.

## Mechanisms Promoting Cooperation

The past theoretical research has identified a number of mechanisms that promote the evolution of cooperation. It is now well established that promotion and maintenance of cooperation within social dilemmas depends on the positive assortment of cooperators (West, Griffin, & Gardner, 2007). That is, there must be mechanisms or interaction structures to ensure that cooperators help other cooperators more than defectors. Below, we provide a brief overview of the five key mechanisms described by Nowak (M. A. Nowak, 2006b; Rand & Nowak, 2013) as well as others, which generally promote positive assortment. M. A. Nowak (2006a) and McElreath and Boyd (2007) provide more formal treatment of the topics.

### Kin Selection

Kin selection (or inclusive fitness) is a mechanism for the evolution of cooperation that arises if agents use conditional strategies based on kin relationship. This mechanism is based on the idea that cooperative behavior can emerge where the donor (the agent that benefits another agent) and the recipient (the agent that receives the benefit) are genetically related in the sense that there is a high probability of sharing a gene. That is, an individual is more likely to cooperate with closer relatives as compared to distant relatives or strangers. This tends to increase the average fitness of those that carry the genetic information that tends to produce cooperation among kinds. Hamilton's rule is typically used as a formalization for this mechanism (Hamilton, 1964a): the coefficient of relatedness, $r$, must exceed the cost–benefit ratio of the act for a cooperative action to be played. Although this may be based on genetic evolution, it can also be a result of cultural evolution.

## Direct Reciprocity

Reciprocity is a mechanism by which agents use information about a history of agents' past behaviors to predict the probability of their cooperation. Direct reciprocity involves iterated encounters where agents play a game repeatedly across a finite number of rounds. Such repeated encounters between the same agents allow for reciprocation of cooperation—that is, when one cooperates, the other can return the favor by cooperating. As we noted earlier, Trivers (1971), Axelrod and Hamilton (1981), and Axelrod (1984) advanced direct reciprocity as a key mechanism for evolution of cooperation.

A well-known example of this type of strategy is "tit-for-tat," developed by Anatol Rapoport, where a player cooperates in the first round and from then on always repeats whatever the other player did in the previous round. When it competed with other strategies in a tournament of strategies, it was the best-performing strategy in that it cumulated the highest payoffs of all strategies (Axelrod, 1984). Nonetheless, this strategy is not very tolerant of a mistake by another player—if players defect by mistake (by rare weakness of will, or a momentary lapse of judgment), strict tit-for-tat strategists descend to all-defection. More flexible and tolerant strategies such as "generous tit-for-tat" (one defection is generously tolerated) and "win–stay, lose–shift" have been shown to be effective once cooperators emerge in the population (M. A. Nowak, 2006a). Arguably, these are all variants of *conditional cooperation*, in which an agent cooperates if other agents cooperate. Indeed, approximately 50% of human players in experimental public goods games appear to be conditional cooperators (e.g., Fischbacher, Gächter, & Fehr, 2001).

## Indirect Reciprocity

Direct reciprocity relies on the firsthand information about the probability of others' cooperation obtained by the direct observation of their past behaviors. In contrast, indirect reciprocity rests on the information about the probability of others' cooperation obtained not from the direct observation of their past behavior, but typically secondhand information based on third parties who directly observed these others' past behaviors (e.g., M. A. Nowak & Sigmund, 1998; Panchanathan & Boyd, 2004). This is basically predicting other agents' behavior based on their *reputation*, which may derive from gossip or other mechanisms of reputation management (e.g., Michelin ratings, university rankings). Agents can adopt conditional strategies and base their decision on reputation profiles of others in the population. For indirect reciprocity to be an effective mechanism in the evolution of cooperation, it requires that reputation information is as accurate as direct information obtaining from personal experience (e.g., M. A. Nowak & Sigmund, 1998; Panchanathan & Boyd, 2004).

It is important to note that, in order for indirect reciprocity to work, agents must have both cognitive and communicative capacities to remember their own interactions and monitor the ever-changing social network within their group, and to use language or other symbolic means to communicate reputational information—that is, to gossip. Some have argued that this was one of the evolutionary bases of human language (Dunbar, 1998). In addition, stereotypes can serve as a basis of reputational information. If a group of agents is seen to be warm, communal, or moral (e.g., Eagly & Kite, 1987; Fiske, Cuddy, Xu, & Glick, 2002; Leach, Ellemers, & Barreto, 2007; Wojciszke, 2005a, 2005b), its members are likely inferred to be at least conditional cooperators. In particular, an agent's ingroup is often stereotyped as trustworthy (e.g., Brewer, 1979), and this autostereotype may be the basis of an ingroup favoritism in cooperation (e.g., Balliet, Wu, & De Dreu, 2014; Yamagishi & Kiyonari, 2000). Of course, this is not to say that stereotypes are accurate; however, it does present a new perspective on the evolution of stereotypes as a reputational mechanism.

## Network Reciprocity

Human interactions are not random, but are typically structured in social networks—some individuals interact with each other more often than others. A social network is represented as a graph structure in which its vertices are occupied by agents, and its edges determine who interacts with whom. A payoff structure can be defined for each interaction, and repeated interactions between agents determine the overall outcome of each agent. Despite the complexity of the dynamics (for an overview, see Perc, Gómez-Gardeñes, Szolnoki, Floría, & Moreno, 2013; Perc & Szolnoki, 2010; Szabó & Fáth, 2007), the underlying principle in network reciprocity is the notion that "neighbors help each other." Here, network reciprocity can promote the evolution of cooperation, because cooperators form clusters within which they cooperate with each other, which can prevail against exploitation by defectors. Recent work combining evolutionary dynamics of group interactions on structured populations provides important insights into our understanding of the evolution of cooperation. A range of extensions can also be considered. For example, the population structure can be dynamic, so that agents can use "active linking," where individuals can choose to break unproductive links and establish new ones (Pacheco, Traulsen, & Nowak, 2006; Rand, Arbesman, & Christakis, 2011), or form social network ties with others based on their reputations (Fu, Hauert, Nowak, & Wang, 2008).

## Group Selection

The idea of group selection (also called multilevel selection) has a controversial background in evolutionary biology and is frequently misunderstood (West, El Mouden, & Gardner, 2011). Wilson and Wilson (2008) describe how natural selection acts not only on individuals, but also on groups. Consider the situation where a population is subdivided into groups. Individuals interact with other members of their ingroup in an evolutionary game that determines their fitness. In a simple scenario, defectors dominate cooperators within groups. However, if groups compete with each other, groups of cooperators out-compete groups of defectors. A little more theoretically, if selection processes operate at the level of groups (i.e., those groups with higher levels of average fitness are more likely to produce offspring than those with lower fitness levels), groups that contain more cooperators are more likely to do better than those with fewer cooperators. Under such conditions, multilevel selection acts as a powerful mechanism for the evolution of cooperation, especially if there are many small groups and if the migration rate between groups is not too large (Traulsen & Nowak, 2006). On the surface, there appear to be many similarities between spatial selection and multilevel selection. However, they are quite distinct mechanisms. In the former case, selection (competition) occurs between individuals. In the second case, there is competition between individuals and competition between groups.

## Signaling

As we noted earlier, the above-mentioned mechanisms typically promote positive assortment—that is, the likelihood that cooperation is met by cooperation, so that cooperative actions co-occur in interacting agents. An additional mechanism for generating the co-occurrence of cooperation is based on signaling (e.g., Gintis, Smith, & Bowles, 2001; Skyrms, 2004). If individuals who are to cooperate in the future can signal their future action to cooperate to each other, they can coordinate their interaction (i.e., choose each other) and avoid the negative consequences of interacting with defectors.

There are a variety of signs that can be used to signal cooperation if agents with a genetic or cultural trait to cooperate have (a) a certain recognizable sign, (b) a capacity to recognize the sign, and (c) the tendency to cooperate when they recognize that sign. One such sign may be physical resemblance in appearance as a sign of kinship (e.g., Hamilton, 1964a, 1964b). Nonetheless, any arbitrary sign—what Dawkins (1976) called a "green beard"—may work as long as it satisfies the above-mentioned three properties (e.g., Riolo, Cohen, & Axelrod, 2001). The displaying of this sign may be costly (Gintis et al., 2001) or cheap (Robson, 1990; Skyrms, 2004); either way, positive assortment can occur under some circumstances. However, if agents develop a capacity to "fake" the sign (i.e., any individual can display the "green beard," but not cooperate with other "green beards"), these agents will have higher fitness than others that cannot, and the sign will eventually be decoupled from the trait for cooperation.

## Additional Mechanisms

In addition to these mechanisms, a number of further mechanisms have also captured the attention of both social and evolutionary biology researchers. One is *voluntary participation*, in which, in addition to the default actions of cooperate or defect, a player is also provided with a third action of not playing at all. In multi-player games such as the Public Goods game, significant levels of cooperation emerge, often in dynamic oscillations (Hauert, De Monte, Hofbauer, & Sigmund, 2002). Under specific circumstance, *punishment* can promote cooperative behavior in social dilemmas (Boyd & Richerson, 1992; Fehr & Gachter, 2002; Sigmund, Hauert, & Nowak, 2001; however, see Ohtsuki, Iwasa, & Nowak, 2009). Typically, punishment is embedded in models based on underlying mechanisms such as indirect reciprocity, spatial selection, and multilevel selection. Punishment may be implemented as a second-stage action with additional costs to an individual, activated when other individuals in the game opt for defection. However, this approach can be undermined by the proliferation of second-order "free riders," who cooperate but do not punish defectors.

## Sources of Cultural Dynamics in Evolution of Cooperation

In this section, we have attempted to describe how evolutionary game theory can be used to understand the evolution of cooperation largely from the perspective of adaptation, more specifically in terms of selection. Assuming that there are some agents who adopt conditional cooperation, when mechanisms are in place to ensure assortment, so that cooperators are more likely to interact with each other than with defectors, the enactment of the cultural practice (or genetic trait) of cooperation is likely to bring about better consequences than the cultural practice of defection on the average in the long run. Those practices that bring about greater benefit with less cost are assumed to be more likely to be transmitted and retained by agents. Therefore, provided that conditional cooperation brings about better outcomes than defection, conditional cooperation becomes more prevalent within the group. A culture of cooperation may thus emerge because, under certain conditions where assortment is possible, cooperation is more adaptive.

Note that the current treatment is rather sketchy, and there is a more nuanced treatment about social transmission of cultural information in this framework. For example, cultural transmission may be biased (e.g., conformity—agents may be more likely to learn a practice that is more prevalent in a group; prestige—agents may be more likely to learn a practice that is used by a more prestigious agent) or unbiased, defective or cooperative tendencies may be both culturally and genetically inherited, etc. (e.g., Boyd & Richerson, 1985; Chudek & Henrich, 2011; Henrich & McElreath, 2003). Nonetheless, it is fair to say that the strength of the evolutionary game theoretic approaches lies in its theoretical treatment of adaptation, especially, the selection process in cultural dynamics.

## Conclusions

Social psychology has a tradition of modeling cultural dynamics. Starting with the public opinion dynamics that involve a binary choice between pro and con in a population of agents without any spatial structure (Abelson & Bernstein, 1963) to dynamic social impact theory within a spatial structure (A. Nowak et al., 1990) and beyond, there has been a steady increase in the complexity with which social psychology has theorized cultural dynamics.

Nevertheless, further advances in modeling cultural dynamics have occurred outside the traditional boundary of social psychology, although there are intriguing developments in social psychology as well (e.g., Denrell & Le Mens, 2007). One of the research traditions extended the univariate representation of culture (i.e., single opinion) to a multivariate representation (Axelrod, 1997), and the other has brought the evolutionary game theoretic framework to incorporate the adaptiveness of culture as a significant driver of cultural dynamics (e.g., McElreath & Boyd, 2007; M. A. Nowak, 2006a). These prominent research traditions have highlighted complementary aspects of cultural dynamics: the process and consequences of cultural dissemination and the process of adaptation by selection. The complementarity of these developments poses an intriguing question for further exploration. How can these two research traditions be integrated so that multidimensional and configural cultural information can be represented and the adaptiveness of the cultural information can be investigated within the same framework?

Theoretical questions aside, there are a number of pressing questions for models of cultural dynamics. First of all, there is an issue of empirical validation of models. Although the early challenges were more about how to model empirically well-established phenomena of opinion polarization (Abelson & Bernstein, 1963) and persistence of diverse opinions (A. Nowak et al., 1990), the more recent models are mathematically sophisticated, but are yet to be tested or validated (however, some empirical tests are underway; for a recent review, see Rand & Nowak, 2013). Second, from apparently intractable intergroup conflicts to climate change, there are a number of challenges to the contemporary world that require a transformation of contemporary cultures (Kashima, 2016b; Wilson, Hayes, Biglan, & Embry, 2014). How can the models of cultural dynamics be used to benefit the public discourse and deliberation on planning and policy development for our common future? These are some of the difficult questions for the modeling of cultural dynamics which future research will need to tackle.

# Notes

1 The preparation of this chapter was facilitated by a grant from the Australian Research Council (DP130100845) to Yoshihisa Kashima, Michael Kirley, and Garry Robins.
2 U.Wilensky, *NetLogo*, available from http://ccl.northwestern.edu/netlogo/.
3 Typically, in the Iterated Prisoner's Dilemma game, an additional constraint on the payoff matrix values is employed, $2R > (T + S)$, so that players are not collectively better off if they simply alternate between playing cooperate and defect actions.
4 Here, the ESS constitutes a Nash equilibrium, but they are not strictly equivalent. For detailed discussions about the relationship between ESS and Nash equilibria, see M. A. Nowak (2006a).

# References

Abelson, R. P. (1964). Mathematical models of the distribution of attitudes under controversy. In N. Frereriksen & H. Gulliksen (Eds.), *Contributions to mathematical psychology* (pp. 142–160). New York: Holt, Rinehart, & Winston.

Abelson, R. P., & Bernstein, A. (1963). A computer simulation model of community referendum controversies. *Public Opinion Quarterly, 27*(1), 93–122. doi:10.1086/267152

Axelrod, R. (1984). *The evolution of cooperation*. New York: Basic Books.

Axelrod, R. (1997). The dissemination of culture: A model with local convergence and global polarization. *Journal of Conflict Resolution, 41*(2), 203–226. doi:10.1177/0022002797041002001

Axelrod, R., & Hamilton, W. D. (1981). The evolution of cooperation. *Science, 211*(4489), 1390–1396. doi:10.1126/science.7466396

Balliet, D., Wu, J., & De Dreu, C. K. W. (2014). Ingroup favoritism in cooperation: A meta-analysis. *Psychological Bulletin, 140*(6), 1556–1581. doi:10.1037/a0037737

Barabási, A.-L., & Albert, R. (1999). Emergence of scaling in random networks. *Science, 286*(5439), 509–512. doi:10.1126/science.286.5439.509

Bartlett, F. C. (1923). *Psychology and primitive culture*. Cambridge: Cambridge University Press.

Bartlett, F. C. (1932). *Remembering: A study in experimental and social psychology*. Cambridge: Cambridge University Press.

Bentley, R. A., Hahn, M. W., & Shennan, S. J. (2004). Random drift and culture change. *Proceedings of the Royal Society of London, Series B, 271*(1547), 1443–1450. doi:10.1098/rspb.2004.2746

Boyd, R., & Richerson, P. J. (1985). *Culture and the evolutionary process*. Chicago, IL: University of Chicago Press.

Boyd, R., & Richerson, P. J. (1992). Punishment allows the evolution of cooperation (or anything else) in sizable groups. *Ethology and Sociobiology, 13*(3), 171–195. doi:10.1016/0162-3095(92)90032-Y

Brewer, M. B. (1979). In-group bias in the minimal intergroup situation: A cognitive-motivational analysis. *Psychological Bulletin, 86*(2), 307–324. doi:10.1037/0033-2909.86.2.307

Brulle, R. J., Carmichael, J., & Jenkins, J. C. (2012). Shifting public opinion on climate change: An empirical assessment of factors influencing concern over climate change in the U.S., 2002–2010. *Climatic Change, 114*(2), 169–188. doi:10.1007/s10584-012-0403-y

Camerer, C. F. (2003). *Behavioral game theory: Experiments on strategic interaction*. Princeton, NJ: Princeton University Press.

Campbell, D. T. (1960). Blind variation and selective retentions in creative thought as in other knowledge processes. *Psychological Review, 67*(6), 380–400. doi:10.1037/h0040373

Campbell, D. T. (1975). On the conflicts between biological and social evolution and between psychology and moral tradition. *American Psychologist, 30*(12), 1103–1126. doi:10.1037/0003-066X.30.12.1103

Carley, K. M. (1991). A theory of group stability. *American Sociological Review, 56*(3), 331–354.

Castellano, C., Marsili, M., & Vespignani, A. (2000). Nonequilibrium phase transition in a model for social influence. *Physical Review Letters, 85*(16), 3536–3539.

Cavalli-Sforza, L. L., & Feldman, M. W. (1981). *Cultural transmission and evolution.* Princeton, NJ: Princeton University Press.

Centola, D., González-Avella, J. C., Eguíluz, V. M., & San Miguel, M. (2007). Homophily, cultural drift, and the co-evolution of cultural groups. *Journal of Conflict Resolution, 51*(6), 905–929.

Chudek, M., & Henrich, J. (2011). Culture-gene coevolution, norm-psychology and the emergence of human prosociality. *Trends in Cognitive Sciences, 15*(5), 218–226. doi:10.1016/j.tics.2011.03.003

Dawes, R. M. (1980). Social dilemmas. *Annual Review of Psychology, 31*(1), 169–193. doi:10.1146/annurev.ps.31.020180.001125

Dawkins, R. (1976). *The selfish gene.* Oxford: Oxford University Press.

De Sanctis, L., & Galla, T. (2009). Effects of noise and confidence thresholds in nominal and metric Axelrod dynamics of social influence. *Physical Review E, 79*, 046108.

DellaPosta, D., Shi, Y., & Macy, M. (2015). Why do liberals drink lattes? *American Journal of Sociology, 120*(5), 1473–1511.

Denrell, J., & Le Mens, G. (2007). Interdependent sampling and social influence. *Psychological Review, 114*(2), 398–422. doi:10.1037/0033-295X.114.2.398

Dunbar, R. I. M. (1998). The social brain hypothesis. *Evolutionary Anthropology: Issues, News, and Reviews, 6*(5), 178–190. doi:10.1002/(SICI)1520-6505(1998)6:5<178::AID-EVAN5>3.0.CO;2-8

Eagly, A. H., & Kite, M. E. (1987). Are stereotypes of nationalities applied to both women and men? *Journal of Personality and Social Psychology, 53*(3), 451–462. doi:10.1037/0022-3514.53.3.451

Fehr, E., & Gachter, S. (2002). Altruistic punishment in humans. *Nature, 415*(6868), 137–140. doi:10.1038/415137a

Fischbacher, U., Gächter, S., & Fehr, E. (2001). Are people conditionally cooperative? Evidence from a public goods experiment. *Economics Letters, 71*(3), 397–404. doi:10.1016/S0165-1765(01)00394-9

Fiske, S. T., Cuddy, A. J. C., Xu, J., & Glick, P. (2002). A model of (often mixed) stereotype content: Competence and warmth respectively follow from perceived status and competition. *Journal of Personality and Social Psychology, 82*(6), 878–902. doi:10.1037//0022-3514.82.6.878

Flache, A., & Macy, M. W. (2011). Local convergence and global diversity: From interpersonal to social influence. *Journal of Conflict Resolution, 55*(6), 970–995. doi:10.1177/0022002711414371

Fu, F., Hauert, C., Nowak, M. A., & Wang, L. (2008). Reputation-based partner choice promotes cooperation in social networks. *Physical Review E, 78*(2), 026117. doi:10.1103/PhysRevE.78.026117

Gandica, Y., Charmell, A., Villegas-Febres, J., & Bonalde, I. (2011). Cluster-size entropy in the Axelrod model of social influence: Small-world networks and mass media. *Physical Review E, 84*(4), 046109. doi:10.1103/PhysRevE.84.046109

Gintis, H. (2009). *The bounds of reason: Game theory and the unification of the behavioral sciences.* Princeton, NJ: Princeton University Press.

Gintis, H., Smith, E. A., & Bowles, S. (2001). Costly signaling and cooperation. *Journal of Theoretical Biology, 213*(1), 103–119. doi:10.1006/jtbi.2001.2406

González-Avella, J. C., Cosenza, M. G., Eguíluz, V. M., & San Miguel, M. (2010). Spontaneous ordering against an external field in non-equilibrium systems. *New Journal of Physics, 12*, 013010. doi:10.1088/1367-2630/12/1/013010

González-Avella, J. C., Cosenza, M. G., & Tucci, K. (2005). Nonequilibrium transition induced by mass media in a model for social influence. *Physical Review E, 72*(6), 065102(R). doi:10.1103/PhysRevE.72.065102

González-Avella, J. C., Eguíluz, V. M., Cosenza, M. G., Klemm, K., Herrera, J. L., & San Miguel, M. (2006). Local versus global interactions in nonequilibrium transitions: A model of social dynamics. *Physical Review E, 73*(4), 046119. doi:10.1103/PhysRevE.73.046119

Gracia-Lázaro, C., Lafuerza, L. F., Floría, L. M., & Moreno, Y. (2009). Residential segregation and cultural dissemination: An Axelrod-Schelling model. *Physical Review E, 80*(4), 046123. doi:10.1103/PhysRevE.80.046123

Grauwin, S., & Jensen, P. (2012). Opinion group formation and dynamics: Structures that last from nonlasting entities. *Physical Review E, 85*(6), 066113.

Guerra, B., Poncela, J., Gómez-Gardeñes, J., Latora, V., & Moreno, Y. (2010). Dynamical organization towards consensus in the Axelrod model on complex networks. *Physical Review E, 81*(5), 056105.

Hahn, M. W., & Bentley, R. A. (2003). Drift as a mechanism for cultural change: An example from baby names. *Proceedings of the Royal Society of London, Series B, 270* (Suppl. 1), S120–S123. doi:10.1098/rsbl.2003.0045

Hamilton, W. D. (1964a). The genetical evolution of social behavior. I. *Journal of Theoretical Biology, 7*(1), 1–16. doi:10.1016/0022-5193(64)90038-4

Hamilton, W. D. (1964b). The genetical evolution of social behavior. II. *Journal of Theoretical Biology, 7*(1), 17–52. doi:10.1016/0022-5193(64)90039-6

Hardin, G. (1968). The tragedy of the commons. *Science, 162*(3859), 1243–1248. doi:10.1126/science.162.3859.1243

Harton, H. C., & Bullock, M. (2007). Dynamic social impact: A theory of the origins and evolution of culture. *Social and Personality Psychology Compass, 1*(1), 521–540. doi:10.1111/j.1751-9004.2007.00022.x

Hauert, C., De Monte, S., Hofbauer, J., & Sigmund, K. (2002). Volunteering as red queen mechanism for cooperation in public goods games. *Science, 296*(5570), 1129–1132.

Henrich, J., & McElreath, R. (2003). The evolution of cultural evolution. *Evolutionary Anthropology: Issues, News, and Reviews, 12*(3), 123–135. doi:10.1002/evan.10110

Herskovits, M. J. (1948). *Man and his works: The science of cultural anthropology.* New York: Knopf Doubleday.

Hutchins, E. (1995). *Cognition in the wild.* Cambridge, MA: MIT Press.

Kashima, Y. (2000). Conceptions of culture and person for psychology. *Journal of Cross-Cultural Psychology, 31*(1), 14–32. doi:10.1177/0022022100031001003

Kashima, Y. (2014). How can you capture cultural dynamics? *Frontiers in Psychology, 5*(995), 1–16. doi:10.3389/fpsyg.2014.00995

Kashima, Y. (2016a). Cultural dynamics. *Current Opinion in Psychology, 8*, 93–97.

Kashima, Y. (2016b). Culture and psychology in the 21st century: Conceptions of culture and person revised. *Journal of Cross-Cultural Psychology, 47*(1), 4–20.

Kashima, Y., & Gelfand, M. J. (2012). History of culture and psychology. In A. Kruglanski & W. Stroebe (Eds.), *Handbook of the history of social psychology* (pp. 499–520). New York: Psychology Press.

Kashima, Y., Peters, K., & Whelan, J. (2008). Culture, narrative, and human agency. In R. M. Sorrentino & S. Yamaguchi (Eds.), *Handbook of motivation and cognition across cultures* (pp. 393–421). San Diego, CA: Academic Press.

Klemm, K., Eguíluz, V. M., Toral, R., & San Miguel, M. (2003). Global culture: A noise-induced transition in finite systems. *Physical Review E, 67*(4), 045101(R).

Klemm, K., Eguíluz, V. M., Toral, R., & San Miguel, M. (2005). Globalization, polarization and cultural drift. *Journal of Economic Dynamics and Control, 29*(1), 321–334. doi:10.1016/j.jedc.2003.08.005

Kollock, P. (1998). Social dilemmas: The anatomy of cooperation. *Annual Review of Sociology, 24*(1), 183–214. doi:10.1146/annurev.soc.24.1.183

Kroeber, A. L., & Kluckhohn, C. (1952). *Culture: A critical review of concepts and definitions.* New York: Vintage Books.

Kuperman, M. N. (2006). Cultural propagation on social networks. *Physical Review E, 73*(4), 046139. doi:10.1103/PhysRevE.73.046139

Latané, B. (1981). The psychology of social impact. *American Psychologist, 36*(4), 343–356.

Latané, B. (1996). Dynamic social impact: The creation of culture by communication. *Journal of Communication, 46*(4), 13–25.

Latané, B., & L'Herrou, T. (1996). Spatial clustering in the conformity game: Dynamic social impact in electronic groups. *Journal of Personality and Social Psychology, 70*(6), 1218–1230.

Latané, B., Liu, J. H., Nowak, A., Bonevento, M., & Zheng, L. (1995). Distance matters: Physical space and social impact. *Personality and Social Psychology Bulletin, 21*(8), 795–805. doi:10.1177/0146167295218002

Leach, C. W., Ellemers, N., & Barreto, M. (2007). Group virtue: The importance of morality (vs. Competence and sociability) in the positive evaluation of in-groups. *Journal of Personality and Social Psychology, 93*(2), 234–249. doi:10.1037/0022-3514.93.2.234

Lewenstein, M., Nowak, A., & Latané, B. (1992). Statistical mechanics of social impact. *Physical Review A, 45*(2), 763–776. doi:10.1103/PhysRevA.45.763

Markus, H. R., & Kitayama, S. (1991). Culture and the self: Implications for cognition, emotion, and motivation. *Psychological Review, 98*(2), 224–253. doi:10.1037/0033-295x.98.2.224

Mäs, M., Flache, A., & Helbing, D. (2010). Individualization as driving force of clustering phenomena in humans. *PLoS Computational Biology, 6*(10), e1000959.

Maynard Smith, J. (1982). *Evolution and the theory of games.* Cambridge: Cambridge University Press.

McElreath, R., & Boyd, R. (2007). *Mathematical models of social evolution: A guide for the perplexed.* Chicago, IL: University of Chicago Press.

Nowak, A., de Raad, W., & Borkowski, W. (2012). Culture change: The perspective of dynamical minimalism. In M. J. Gelfand, C.-Y. Chiu & Y.-Y. Hong (Eds.), *Advances in culture and psychology* (Vol. 2, pp. 249–314). New York: Oxford University Press.

Nowak, A., Szamrej, J., & Latané, B. (1990). From private attitudes to public opinions: A dynamic theory of social impact. *Psychological Review, 97*(3), 362–376.

Nowak, A., & Vallacher, R. R. (1998). *Dynamical social psychology.* New York: Guilford.

Nowak, M. A. (2006a). *Evolutionary dynamics: Exploring the equations of life.* Cambridge, MA: Harvard University Press.

Nowak, M. A. (2006b). Five rules for the evolution of cooperation. *Science, 314*(5805), 1560–1563. doi:10.1126/science.1133755

Nowak, M. A., & Sigmund, K. (1998). Evolution of indirect reciprocity by image scoring. *Nature, 393*(6685), 573–577. doi:10.1038/31225

Ohtsuki, H., Iwasa, Y., & Nowak, M. A. (2009). Indirect reciprocity provides only a narrow margin of efficiency for costly punishment. *Nature, 457*(7225), 79–82. doi:10.1038/nature07601

Pace, B., & Prado, C. P. (2014). Axelrod's model with surface tension. *Physical Review E, 89*(6), 062804. doi:10.1103/PhysRevE.89.062804

Pacheco, J. M., Traulsen, A., & Nowak, M. A. (2006). Active linking in evolutionary games. *Journal of Theoretical Biology, 243*(3), 437–443. doi:10.1016/j.jtbi.2006.06.027

Panchanathan, K., & Boyd, R. (2004). Indirect reciprocity can stabilize cooperation without the second-order free rider problem. *Nature, 432*(7016), 499–502. doi:10.1038/nature02978

Parisi, D., Cecconi, F., & Natale, F. (2003). Cultural change in spatial environments: The role of cultural assimilation and internal changes in cultures. *Journal of Conflict Resolution, 47*(2), 163–179.

Parks, C. D., Joireman, J., & Van Lange, P. A. M. (2013). Cooperation, trust, and antagonism: How public goods are promoted. *Psychological Science in the Public Interest, 14*(3), 119–165. doi:10.1177/1529100612474436

Perc, M., Gómez-Gardeñes, J., Szolnoki, A., Floría, L. M., & Moreno, Y. (2013). Evolutionary dynamics of group interactions on structured populations: A review. *Journal of the Royal Society Interface, 10*(80), 20120997. doi:10.1098/rsif.2012.0997

Perc, M., & Szolnoki, A. (2010). Coevolutionary games: A mini review. *Biosystems, 99*(2), 109–125. doi:10.1016/j.biosystems.2009.10.003

Pfau, J., Kirley, M., & Kashima, Y. (2013). The co-evolution of cultures, social network communities, and agent locations in an extension of Axelrod's model of cultural dissemination. *Physica A, 392*(2), 381–391. doi:10.1016/j.physa.2012.09.004

Railsback, S. F., & Grimm, V. (2012). *Agent-based and individual-based modelling: A practical introduction.* Princeton, NJ: Princeton University Press.

Rand, D. G., Arbesman, S., & Christakis, N. A. (2011). Dynamic social networks promote cooperation in experiments with humans. *Proceedings of the National Academy of Sciences of the United States of America, 108*(48), 19193–19198. doi:10.1073/pnas.1108243108

Rand, D. G., & Nowak, M. A. (2013). Human cooperation. *Trends in Cognitive Sciences, 17*(8), 413–425. doi:10.1016/j.tics.2013.06.003

Rapoport, A., & Chammah, A. M. (1965). *Prisoner's Dilemma: A study in conflict and cooperation.* Ann Arbor, MI: University of Michigan Press.

Richerson, P. J., & Boyd, R. (2005). *Not by genes alone: How culture transformed human evolution.* Chicago, IL: University of Chicago Press.

Riolo, R. L., Cohen, M., & Axelrod, R. (2001). Evolution of cooperation without reciprocity. *Nature, 414*(6862), 441–443.

Robson, A. J. (1990). Efficiency in evolutionary games: Darwin, Nash and the secret handshake. *Journal of Theoretical Biology, 144*(3), 379–396. doi:10.1016/S0022-5193(05)80082-7

Rodríguez, A. H., & Moreno, Y. (2010). Effects of mass media action on the Axelrod model with social influence. *Physical Review E, 82*(1), 016111. doi:10.1103/PhysRevE.82.016111

Shibanai, Y., Yasuno, S., & Ishiguro, I. (2001). Effects of global information feedback on diversity: Extensions to Axelrod's adaptive culture model. *Journal of Conflict Resolution, 45*(1), 80–96.

Sigmund, K., Hauert, C., & Nowak, M. A. (2001). Reward and punishment. *Proceedings of the National Academy of Sciences of the United States of America, 98*(19), 10757–10762. doi:10.1073/pnas.161155698

Simonton, D. K. (2010). Creative thought as blind-variation and selective-retention: Combinatorial models of exceptional creativity. *Physics of Life Reviews, 7*(2), 156–179. doi:10.1016/j.plrev.2010.02.002

Skyrms, B. (2004). *The stag hunt and the evolution of social structure.* Cambridge: Cambridge University Press.

Sperber, D. (1996). *Explaining culture: A naturalistic approach.* Oxford: Blackwell.

Stivala, A., Robins, G., Kashima, Y., & Kirley, M. (2014). Ultrametric distribution of culture vectors in an extended Axelrod model of cultural dissemination. *Scientific Reports, 4*, 4870. doi:10.1038/srep04870

Szabó, G., & Fáth, G. (2007). Evolutionary games on graphs. *Physics Reports, 446*(4–6), 97–216. doi:10.1016/j.physrep.2007.04.004

Traulsen, A., & Nowak, M. A. (2006). Evolution of cooperation by multilevel selection. *Proceedings of the National Academy of Sciences, 103*(29), 10952–10955. doi:10.1073/pnas.0602530103

Triandis, H. C. (1964). Cultural influences upon cognitive processes. In L. Berkowitz (Ed.), *Advances in experimental social psychology* (Vol. 1). New York: Academic Press.

Triandis, H. C. (1989). The self and social behavior in differing cultural contexts. *Psychological Review, 96*(3), 506–520. doi:10.1037/0033-295X.96.3.506

Triandis, H. C. (1994). *Culture and social behavior.* New York: McGraw-Hill.

Triandis, H. C. (1996). The psychological measurement of cultural syndromes. *American Psychologist, 51*(4), 407–415. doi:10.1037/0003-066X.51.4.407

Trivers, R. L. (1971). The evolution of reciprocal altruism. *Quarterly Review of Biology, 46*(1), 35–57. doi:10.1086/406755

Valori, L., Picciolo, F., Allansdottir, A., & Garlaschelli, D. (2012). Reconciling long-term cultural diversity and short-term collective social behavior. *Proceedings of the National Academy of Sciences of the United States of America, 109*(4), 1068–1073. doi:10.1073/pnas.1109514109

Van Lange, P. A. M., Joireman, J., Parks, C. D., & Van Dijk, E. (2013). The psychology of social dilemmas: A review. *Organizational Behavior and Human Decision Processes, 120*(2), 125–141. doi:10.1016/j.obhdp.2012.11.003

Vazquez, F., González-Avella, J. C., Eguíluz, V. M., & San Miguel, M. (2007). Time-scale competition leading to fragmentation and recombination transitions in the coevolution of network and states. *Physical Review E, 76*(4), 046120.

Von Neumann, J., & Morgenstern, O. (1953). *Theory of games and economic behavior* (3rd ed.). Princeton, NJ: Princeton University Press.

Weaver, I. (2010). Dissemination of culture. *NetLogo user community models.* Retrieved from http://ccl.northwestern.edu/netlogo/models/community/Dissemination%20of%20Culture

West, S. A., El Mouden, C., & Gardner, A. (2011). Sixteen common misconceptions about the evolution of cooperation in humans. *Evolution and Human Behavior, 32*(4), 231–262. doi:10.1016/j.evolhumbehav.2010.08.001

West, S. A., Griffin, A. S., & Gardner, A. (2007). Evolutionary explanations for cooperation. *Current Biology, 17*(16), R661–R672. doi:10.1016/j.cub.2007.06.004

Wilson, D. S., Hayes, S. C., Biglan, A., & Embry, D. D. (2014). Evolving the future: Toward a science of intentional change. *Behavioral and Brain Sciences, 37*(4), 395–416. doi:10.1017/S0140525X13001593

Wilson, D. S., & Wilson, E. O. (2008). Evolution "for the good of the group." *American Scientist, 96*(5), 380–389. doi:10.1511/2008.74.1

Wojciszke, B. (2005a). Affective concomitants of information on morality and competence. *European Psychologist, 10*(1), 60–70. doi:10.1027/1016-9040.10.1.60

Wojciszke, B. (2005b). Morality and competence in person- and self-perception. *European Review of Social Psychology, 16*(1), 155–188. doi:10.1080/10463280500229619

Yamagishi, T., & Kiyonari, T. (2000). The group as the container of generalized reciprocity. *Social Psychology Quarterly, 63*(2), 116–132. doi:10.2307/2695887

Yamamoto, K. (2015). Mobilization, flexibility of identity, and ethnic cleavage. *Journal of Artificial Societies and Social Simulation, 18*(2), 8. doi:10.18564/jasss.2669

# PART IV

# Transforming Social Psychology

# 14

## MODELS ARE STUPID, AND WE NEED MORE OF THEM

*Paul E. Smaldino*

> All social science research must do some violence to reality in order to reveal simple truths.
>
> *(Lazer & Friedman, 2007)*

Despite numerous efforts extolling the virtues of formal modeling (Epstein, 2008; Schank, 2001; Smith & Conrey, 2007; Marewski & Olsson, 2009; Farrell & Lewandowsky, 2010; Weinhardt & Vancouver, 2012; Smaldino, Calanchini, & Pickett, 2015), there remains widespread resistance among social and behavioral scientists to adopt formal modeling in their general research approach. In addition to the technical challenge posed by the mathematical and programming skills required to understand and develop models, a common point of resistance appears to stem from the perception of models as crude, overly simplistic, and unrealistic. The conclusion is that models are largely useless as anything but a formal exercise, and unnecessary for most scientists to engage with.

Rather than argue against this perception, I enthusiastically embrace the perspective of the resistance, at least in part. Models are, by and large, stupid. My point of contention is with the conclusion that stupid models are not useful. Quite the contrary. Stupid models are extremely useful. They are useful because humans are boundedly rational and because language is imprecise. It is often only by formalizing a complex system that we can make progress in understanding it. Formal models should be a necessary component of the behavioral scientist's toolkit. Models are stupid, and we need more of them.

### We Are Stupid

Down to the very name of our species, *Homo sapiens*, we humans love to emphasize our intelligence relative to other species. We can certainly solve many complicated problems. And yet we are often very stupid animals who make foolish choices. This isn't a raw failing on our part. We are limited beings, with finite resources with which to compute a coarse model of our world and with which to invent options and evaluate their consequences. Moreover, our world, and the ecological and social environments in which we find ourselves, are changing rapidly, far too rapidly for our brains to possibly adapt via genetic evolution. We do the best we can.

Humans appear to have particular difficulty understanding complex systems. Mitch Resnick, in his book *Turtles, Termites, and Traffic Jams*, details his experiences teaching gifted high school students about the dynamics of complex systems using artificial life models (Resnick, 1994). He showed them how organized behavior could emerge when individuals responded only to local stimuli using simple rules, without the need for a central coordinating authority. Resnick reports that even after weeks spent demonstrating the principles of emergence, using computer simulations that the students programmed themselves, many students still refused to believe that what they were seeing could *really* work without central leadership.

We who study complex systems for a living may feel a certain smugness here. The average person may have difficulty understanding the forces that drive behavior, we think, but through our powerful intellects, our education, and our hefty experience pondering the deep mysteries, *we* can trust our intuition when it comes to understanding the psychological and social forces that make people do what they do. Unfortunately, my own experience working with complex systems and working among complexity scientists suggests that we are hardly immune to such stupidity. Indeed, even seemingly simple puzzles can pose a challenge.

Consider the case of Marilyn Vos Savant and the Monty Hall problem. Vos Savant, famous for her record high score on standard IQ tests, has written a weekly puzzle column in *Parade Magazine* since 1986. In 1990, she wrote about a puzzle commonly known as the Monty Hall problem. The problem goes as follows. You are on a game show and given the choice to open one of three doors. Behind one of the doors is a fabulous cash prize, and behind the others, goats (the assumption is that no one would prefer the goats to the cash). You choose a door, say Door #1. The host, who knows where the cash really is, opens one of the other two doors, say #3, and shows you a goat behind it. The host now offers you the option to switch to Door #2. The question is whether it is to your advantage to do so.

The answer is that, although you are never guaranteed to be correct, you should probably switch. The cash is twice as likely to be behind Door #2 instead of Door #1. This is not an easy result for most people to wrap their heads around, though it follows quite definitively from the assumptions of probability theory (if you are in doubt of the problem's trickiness, I suggest that you pose it the next time you are at a dinner party). Strikingly, Vos Savant's answer was challenged not only by lay readers, but also by many with advanced mathematical training. Indeed, she received many letters from professional mathematicians insisting that she was mistaken, even after she published a follow-up column with a detailed proof. The letters were often written in a smug, knowing tone; Vos Savant details many of these in an article posted to her website (http://marilynvossavant.com/game-show-problem/). One, written after the publication of the follow-up column and signed by a Georgetown University professor, reads:

> You are utterly incorrect about the game show question, and I hope this controversy will call some public attention to the serious national crisis in mathematical education. If you can admit your error, you will have contributed constructively towards the solution of a deplorable situation. How many irate mathematicians are needed to get you to change your mind?

It is my belief that the widespread inability to grasp the solution to the Monty Hall problem stems from a failure to properly model the scenario. You should switch doors because regardless of which door you picked initially, the host can *always* show you one with a goat. Being shown a goat therefore has no bearing on the probability that your initial choice was correct. Since that probability is 1/3, there is a 2/3 chance that you were wrong and the cash is behind the remaining door. Thus, two out of three times, switching is the right move. The common intuition that the choice is instead a 50/50 split between two options is erroneous.

Readers of this chapter are likely to be interested in social behaviors and their underlying psychological mechanisms. These systems tend to be quite a bit more complicated than a simple game show problem. This should concern us. Being an expert does not inoculate us from the failure of our limited imaginations, which evolved to solve problems quite different from those of interest to behavioral scientists. We could use some help.

## Models to the Rescue?

I am, of course, going to argue that we should turn to models, and particularly *formal* models, for help. Specification of a formal model delineates the parts of a system and the relationships between those parts, allows us to examine the logical conclusions of our assumptions, and as a byproduct, examine the appropriateness of those assumptions in the first place. But first, I need to take a brief detour, because when it comes to explaining any behavior, the first question we need to ask is: *What are we talking about?*

### Articulating a System and Its Parts

As behavioral and social scientists, we want to understand some system related to individual or social behavior. Maybe we are interested in how social identity manifests when individuals feel threatened, or how individuals coordinate in joint activities, or how racially charged language is interpreted by individuals of different racial and socioeconomic backgrounds. These examples obviously represent a miniscule selection from among the questions we might ask. The important thing to note is how each question is subject to myriad interpretations. What aspect of the behavior are we interested in, specifically? Are we interested in the neurophysiology of joint attention, down to the way neural spike trains inform action programs? Or are we more interested in a "higher" level of organization, perhaps one in which we can ignore physiology and instead simply consider the temporal relationships between individually designated behavioral units? These are not trivial questions. For any given behavior, there are many questions we can ask related to its development, mechanism, and adaptive function, none of which are obviously favored from a scientific perspective (Tinbergen, 1963).

Once we specify the level of organization and the kind of explanation we are looking for, we still need to do additional work to specify the exact question under investigation. Human beings are complex beings. It's not just that we exist at many levels of organization. Of course, we are made of organs, which are made of tissues, which are made of cells, which communicate using molecules and ions; above the level of the individual, we are enmeshed in local social networks, communities both corporate and categorical, economies, and nations. A further problem arises when we consider that these levels interact—the causal arrows flow both ways (Campbell, 1974; Wimsatt, 1974). The problem is not insurmountable, but needs to be acknowledged. Any explanation of individual and social behavior must necessarily ignore important causal relationships both within and between levels of organization. We must become comfortable with ignoring those relationships, and this comfort is achieved partly through acknowledging their existence.

Part of specifying our research question involves the articulation of the parts of the system of inquiry. Kauffman's 1971 essay still provides the best discussion of this important but overlooked issue. Notice that I do not say that we should specify our question and *then* articulate the parts of the system. The two are parts of a single process. What is our question? To understand joint attention in coordinated behavior, perhaps. But what is our question *right now*? We must decompose the system into explicit parts. We must postulate properties of those parts and the relationships between them. In some sense, this is the essence of all scientific inquiry into behavior. All well-formed scientific research questions concern the properties of parts, the relationships between them, and the consequences of those relationships. The articulation of parts and relationships will necessarily be overly simplified and ignore details of physical reality. But much like a map is only useful because it ignores irrelevant detail, so is a well-formed scientific question useful when it captures only those features of reality most relevant to a useful answer.

To make myself perfectly clear: To ask a scientific question about individual or social behavior, we must specify the parts of a system and the relationships between them. The question at hand may be about the *nature* of these parts or their relationships, and so we may designate a *distribution* of parts or relationships from which to sample, but it amounts to the same thing. The precise specification of parts and relationships is what defines a scientific question and separates it from wishy-washy pseudotheory that is unfalsifiable and distracting (Popper, 1963; Gigerenzer, 1998; Smaldino, 2016).

## Building Models, Formal and Otherwise

Let us assume that we have articulated, in words, the parts of our system and the relationships between them. Perhaps we say, as do the adherents of optimal distinctiveness theory (Brewer, 1991; Leonardelli, Pickett, & Brewer, 2010), that individuals have social identities that correspond to different contexts and different levels of inclusivity, and that they express these identities in order to balance internal drives for assimilation and differentiation. The parts are obviously the individuals, each of whom has the property of possessing an array of identities and the ability to express one of these at any given time. The relationships between the parts manifest as perceptions of others' identities, which dictate how individuals update their own expression. The theory suggests how this updating might occur: individuals should express more exclusive identities when their currently expressed identity is very inclusive, and vice versa.

I have just described what is often called a "verbal model." As Epstein (2008, para. 1.2) phrases it, "Anyone who ventures a projection, or imagines how a social dynamic . . . would unfold is running *some* model." Most behavioral and social scientists are quite comfortable with this sort of model. However, look closer. You'll see that the parts of the system are not particularly well articulated, and neither are their relationships. What does it mean to possess an identity, let alone an array of them? How do individuals choose between their identities when it comes time to express them? Is the expression of a new identity costly, perhaps in terms of time or social capital? How do individuals take stock of the identities of their fellows? Are their perceptions accurate? Are all identities equally easy to perceive? There are additional related questions as well, concerning the nature of system. Where do identities come from, and how might an individual gain a new identity or lose an existing one? What is the adaptive function of expressing an identity in the first place, since, to be preserved, identities must serve some purpose other than internal contentment?

This is not to pick on optimal distinctiveness theorists. Social psychology, and the social and behavioral sciences more generally, are replete with similar cases. This is the limitation of verbal models. They are often a good way to begin an inquiry when the available evidence suggests only some broad type of relationship that might be further refined. The danger with most verbal models is that there are many ways to specify the parts and relationships of a system that are consistent with such a model. Scientific inquiry stalls when data is used to simply support rather than refine a verbal model. Because many different data sets are consistent with a vague verbal model, researchers using such techniques risk lapsing into positing theories that are, by and large, unfalsifiable (Popper, 1963; Gigerenzer, 1998).

The articulation of the parts of a system and the relationships between them always involves incurring some violence upon reality. Science is an iterative process, and pragmatically, we must ignore some details about complexity and organization to make any headway. That said, it's not a terrible goal to try and be a bit more precise. This is where formal modeling comes in. A formal model instantiates the verbal model as a collection of mathematical relationships and/ or algorithmic processes. Rather than saying an individual has something *like* an array of social identities, we can model an individual as a computation object that has *precisely* an array of social identities, which in turn might be modeled as simple numerical values for the sake of comparisons between individuals. My colleagues and I have made models of this type (Smaldino, Pickett, Sherman, & Schank, 2012; Smaldino & Epstein, 2015). More than anything, we have learned that we have a long way to go in understanding the nature and social significance of social identity.

To paraphrase Gunawardena (2014), a model is a logical engine for turning assumptions into conclusions. By making our assumptions explicit, we can clearly assess their implied conclusions. These conclusions will inevitably be flawed, because the assumptions are ultimately incorrect, or at least incomplete. By examining *how* they differ from reality, we can refine our models, and thereby refine our theories, and so gradually we might become *less* wrong (Wimsatt, 1987; Schank, May, & Joshi, 2014; Smaldino et al., 2015). Making formal models of the systems we study is the *only* way to make this possible.

### A Brief Note on Statistical Models

When I talk about formal models, I am primarily talking about models whose purpose is to elucidate the mechanisms underlying psychological and behavioral phenomena. Another category of formal model, more familiar to many readers, I'm sure, is the type of model often used in statistical analysis, such as a path model or a linear model. Statistical models are both important and limited, and therefore worth commenting upon, but as they are not my focus here, I will keep my discussion of them brief.

Statistical analyses are necessary and often well-motivated, but we should never forget that they too have models at their core. The generalized linear model, the work horse of the social sciences, models data as being randomly drawn from a distribution whose mean varies according to some parameter. The linear model is so obviously wrong yet so useful that the mathematical anthropologist Richard McElreath has dubbed it "the geocentric model of applied statistics," in reference to the Ptolemaic model of the solar system that erroneously placed the Earth rather than the Sun at the center, but nevertheless produced accurate predictions of planetary motion as they appeared in the night sky (McElreath, 2015). Such models usually assume that one's data are generated by randomly sampling from some distribution—perhaps a Gaussian distribution whose mean tracks some conditional variable. These models are terrifically important in establishing relationships between variables in empirical data sets, and thus for guiding the development of increasingly strong theories. However, many of these models say little about the processes that *actually* generated the data, or about the *mechanistic* nature of relationships between variables. This is the domain of the kinds of formal models I am principally discussing in this chapter. Such models, if sufficiently precise, may utilize data for validation and calibration (e.g., Schank, 2008; Moussaïd, Helbing, & Theraulaz, 2011; Hills, Jones, & Todd, 2012), but this is not strictly necessary for such models to be useful (Wimsatt, 1987; Bedau, 1999; Epstein, 2008; Gunawardena, 2014).

## Models Are Stupid

A common objection to formal modeling in the behavioral and social sciences is that they are grossly unrealistic. This is, in general, quite correct. Formal models are often fantastically unrealistic. They ignore huge swaths of reality, including details of individual behavior and environmental complexity. However, framing this fact as a downside is a serious error, particularly if the alternative is to rely instead on verbal models. Verbal models can appear superior to formal models only by employing strategic ambiguity (*sensu* Eisenberg, 1984), giving the illusion of understanding at the cost of actual understanding. That is, by being vague, verbal models simultaneously afford many interpretations from among which any reader can implicitly, perhaps even unconsciously, choose his or her favorite. I will illustrate this point with a simple parable.

### The Parable of the Cubist Chicken

One evening long ago, when I was an undergraduate student, a friend and I found ourselves waiting in the basement of a theater for a third friend, an actor about to finish his play rehearsal. There was a large collection of LEGOs in the room, and being of a jaunty disposition and not entirely sober, we amused ourselves by playing with the blocks. One of us—precisely who has been lost to memory—constructed an assembly of red, white, black, and yellow blocks and declared, "Look! It's a Cubist chicken!" The other one of us laughed and heartily agreed that it most definitely looked like a Cubist chicken. We were extremely satisfied with ourselves, not only because it was very silly, but because if in fact we *both* understood the design to be a Cubist chicken, then it surely *was* one. We had identified something *true* about our little masterpiece, and had therefore, inadvertently perhaps, created *art*. This is how liberal arts students amuse themselves.

Our conversation moved on to other topics, but we continued to occasionally comment on the Cubist chicken. After some time had passed, our actor friend entered the room. "Check it out," we said, "a Cubist chicken!" Our friend smiled bemusedly and asked us to explain exactly how the seemingly random constellation of LEGOs represented a chicken. "Well," I said, pointing to various parts of the assemblage, "Here is the head. And here is the body and the legs, and here is the tail." "No!" cried my co-conspirator. "That's all wrong. The whole thing is just the head. Here are the eyes, and the beak, and here is the crest," for my friend had envisioned our chicken as a rooster. And thus the illusion of our shared reality was shattered. We thought we had been talking about the same thing. But when more precision was demanded, we discovered we had not.

### Stupidity Is a Feature, Not a Bug

As many a late-night dorm room conversation can attest, humans are capable of very elaborate theories about the nature of reality. The problem is that, as scientists, we need to clearly communicate those theories so that we can use them to make testable predictions. In the social and behavioral sciences, the search for clarity can present a problem for verbal models, and can lead to a depressing recursive avalanche of definitions. What is a preference? A preference is a tendency for certain behaviors. What are those behaviors? It depends on the context. What is a context? This can go on for a while.

Formal models provide a means of escape from the recursive abyss. By restricting our discussion to the model system, we can clearly articulate all the parts of that system and the relationships between those parts, leaving nothing out. This generally leaves us with something that, on the surface, often appears to be pretty stupid. What I mean is that not only are all models wrong, as George Box famously noted; they are *obviously* wrong. However, the stupidity of a model is often its strength. By focusing on some key aspects of a real-world system (i.e., those aspects instantiated in the model), we can investigate how such a system would work if, in principle, we really *could* ignore everything we are ignoring. This only sounds absurd until one recognizes that, in our theorizing about the nature of reality—both as scientists and as quotidian humans hopelessly entangled in myriad webs of connection and conflict—*we ignore things all the time.* We can't function without ignoring most of the facts of the world. Our selective attention ignores most of the sensory input that nevertheless innervates our neurons (as indicated by the well-known "cocktail party effect"). This ignorance is fundamentally adaptive; the bounds to our rationality are severe, and dedication of cognitive resources entails balancing benefits and costs. Causal explanations work in much the same way. By ignoring all but the most relevant information, we are able to impose some modicum of order upon the world. Problems arise when we try to communicate our systems for ordering the world, as each of us has decomposed the world into a somewhat different set of parts and relationships.

Formal models solve this problem by systematizing our stupidity, and ensuring that we are all talking about the same thing.

In the following section, I will provide several concrete examples of how seemingly stupid models help scientists do their science. Before doing that, however, it is worth taking a moment to discuss some general ways in which models that are obviously wrong can nevertheless inform our thought. For example, studying computational models of complex systems can help us to build mental models of some emergent phenomena whose dynamics are otherwise difficult to visualize (Nowak, Rychwalska, & Borkowski, 2013), and the process of model construction can illuminate core uncertainties in one's knowledge of a system (Epstein, 2008). The clearest delineation I have found is William Wimsatt's (1987) list of 12 "functions served by false models," with the understanding that *all* models are false. I therefore reproduce this list, with only light editing, in Table 14.1.

**TABLE 14.1**  Twelve functions served by false models. Adapted with permission from Wimsatt (1987).

(1)  An oversimplified model may act as a starting point in a series of models of increasing complexity and realism.

(2)  A known incorrect but otherwise suggestive model may undercut the too ready acceptance of a preferred hypothesis by suggesting new alternative lines for the explanation of the phenomena.

(3)  An incorrect model may suggest new predictive tests or new refinements of an established model, or highlight specific features of it as particularly important.

(4)  An incomplete model may be used as a template, which captures larger or otherwise more obvious effects that can then be "factored out" to detect phenomena that would otherwise be masked or be too small to be seen.

(5)  A model that is incomplete may be used as a template for estimating the magnitude of parameters that are not included in the model.

(6)  An oversimplified model may provide a simpler arena for answering questions about properties of more complex models, which also appear in this simpler case, and answers derived here can sometimes be extended to cover the more complex models.

(7)  An incorrect simpler model can be used as a reference standard to evaluate causal claims about the effects of variables left out of it but included in more complete models, or in different competing models to determine how these models fare if these variables are left out.

(8)  Two false models may be used to define the extremes of a continuum of cases in which the real case is presumed to lie, but for which the more realistic intermediate models are too complex to analyze or the information available is too incomplete to guide their construction or to determine a choice between them. In defining these extremes, the "limiting" models specify a property of which the real case is supposed to have an intermediate value.

*(continued)*

**TABLE 14.1** *(continued)*

---

(9) A false model may suggest the form of a phenomenological relationship between the variables (a specific mathematical functional relationship that gives a "best fit" to the data, but is not derived from an underlying mechanical model). This "phenomenological law" gives a way of describing the data, and (through interpolation or extrapolation) making new predictions, but also, because its form is conditioned by an underlying model, may suggest a related mechanical model capable of explaining it.

(10) A family of models of the same phenomenon, each of which makes various false assumptions, has several distinctive uses: (a) One may look for results which are true in all of the models, and therefore presumably independent of different specific assumptions which vary across models. These invariant results are thus more likely trustworthy or "true." (b) One may similarly determine assumptions that are irrelevant to a given conclusion. (c) Where a result is true in some models and false in others, one may determine which assumptions or conditions a given result depends upon.

(11) A model that is incorrect by being incomplete may serve as a limiting case to test the adequacy of new, more complex models.

(12) Where optimization or adaptive design arguments are involved, an evaluation of systems or behaviors which are not found in nature, but which are conceivable alternatives to existing systems, can provide explanations for the features of those systems that are found.

---

## Some (Not So) Stupid Models

Compiling a list of all the interesting and useful models in the sciences is a fool's errand. Let it suffice to say that such a list would be vast. Instead, I want to merely illustrate via a few pointed examples how simple, stupid models can be not only useful, but fundamental to good science. I will start with four well-known examples of models that changed our understanding of basic concepts in the physical, biological, and social sciences. I will then give two examples of how I have used formal models in my own work, focusing on topics that should be of interest to social psychologists: (1) social identity and distinctiveness and (2) hypothesis testing and replication.

### Newton's Model of Universal Gravitation

In 17th-century Europe, the field of astronomy faced a great challenge. Following the pioneering work of Copernicus and building on the meticulously collected data of Tycho Brahe, Johannes Kepler had definitively showed that not only do the Earth and the other planets revolve around the Sun, their orbital paths describe ellipses rather than perfect circles. It was a great mystery why this should be. Enter Isaac Newton. Newton was not the first person to propose that the heavenly bodies might be attracted to one another with a force that varied with the inverse square of the distance between them, but he was the first to build a model based on that proposition (Gleick, 2004). His model was startlingly simple, consisting of only two objects—the Sun and the Earth (Figure 14.1). The model ignored the Moon as well as the five other known solar planets, not to mention all the celestial bodies that were unknown in Newton's time. The size and topology of the Sun and Earth were also ignored; they were modeled as points identified only by their mass, position, and velocity. Nevertheless, the model's strength lies in its simplicity. By restricting the analysis to only two bodies, the resulting planetary orbit was mathematically tractable. Using a simple rule stating that the force of gravitation was proportional to the product of the objects' masses and inversely proportional to the square of the distance between them, Newton was able to show that the resulting orbits would always take the form of conic sections, including the elliptical orbits observed by Kepler. And because he could show that the same law explained the motion of falling objects on Earth, Newton provided the first scientific unification of the Terrestrial with the Celestial. Newton's theory of Universal Gravitation rested on a model that, to naïve eyes, can easily appear quite stupid. Ultimately, the theory has been shown to be incorrect, and has been epistemically replaced by the theory of General Relativity. Nevertheless, the theory is able to make exceptionally good approximations of gravitational forces—so good that NASA's Moon missions have relied upon them.

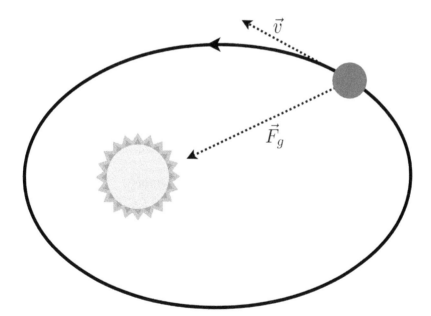

**FIGURE 14.1** A graphical representation of Newton's model of planetary gravitation. The Earth has a forward velocity $v$, which is continuously altered by the gravitational attraction of the Sun, $F_g$, resulting in an elliptical orbit. In reality, the model is even simpler than implied here, because the Sun and Earth were represented as point masses rather than spheres.

## The Lotka-Volterra Model of Predator–Prey Relations

For many years, fur trapping organizations like the Hudson's Bay Company in Canada kept meticulous records on the pelt-producing animals in the regions where they trapped. These records illustrated that linked predator and prey species, like the Canada lynx and the snowshoe hare, tended to have cyclical population levels whose dynamics were tightly correlated. How to explain this? In the early 20th century, Alfred Lotka and Vito Volterra, working independently, applied ideas from the chemistry of autocatalytic reactions to generate a simple model of two interrelated populations, which can be instantiated as a pair of coupled differential equations. This model specifies two animal species: a prey species with a positive rate of growth in the absence of predators, and a predator species with a negative growth rate in the absence of prey. The number of predators negatively influences the number of prey, and the number of prey animals positively influences the number of predators. The model can produce correlated oscillations in the two populations that bear a striking resemblance to data on many predator–prey systems. The model also identifies conditions under which the two growth rates can give rise instead to more stable equilibria as well as yielding complete population collapse—predictions that have since been borne out empirically. However, the model is extremely simplistic. It assumes perfect mixing, so that the probability of a prey animal encountering a predator is simply the relative frequency of predators in the population. It ignores seasonality, circadian cycles, migration, density dependence in the growth rate of the prey species, development, and interactions with other species. Thus, when these features matter, the model may fail to align with empirical fact (Luckinbill, 1973; Berryman, 1992). Nevertheless, the core assumptions of the model often hold. This provides opportunities for extensions and refinements of the model when additional features cannot be ignored. By providing a foundational structure, the Lotka-Volterra model remains one of the core tools for understanding the relationship between predator and prey populations.

## Hopfield's Model of Content-Addressable Memory

Memory—the ability to store information for later recall—is a wondrous property of neural networks that makes possible all but the most rudimentary forms of cognition. By the early 1980s, long-term potentiation—the process by which Donald Hebb's theory that "neurons that fire together wire together" occurs—was relatively well described. It was believed that the formation of such associations was intrinsic to more complex forms of memory, such as that by which a person's face is encoded and then later recognized, but the mechanism was unclear. How could a brain possibly use partial information, like an occluded face, to reconstruct information encoded in memory? To begin to answer this question, the biophysicist John Hopfield (1982) constructed a simple model of two-state neurons in a fully connected network. Edge weights were determined by a process of Hebbian learning assumed to have already occurred, so that a number of configurations (or states) of "on" and "off" neurons were encoded in the network, with edges assumed to be bidirectionally symmetrical (i.e., undirected). Using mathematics derived from statistical physics, Hopfield showed firstly that in such a system, encoded states would be stable, and secondly that if initialized in a non-encoded state, the network would self-organize into the encoded state that most closely matched the initialized state. In other words, he had a model for how memory retrieval could emerge spontaneously in a simple neural network. This model is almost absurdly simplistic, even stupid in its assumptions. Neurons are either on or off, ignoring subtleties of firing rates or even graded activation. Directionality is also ignored; links between neurons are equally strong in each direction. Exactly how the network is presumed to first arrive in its initial state is left a mystery. Yet analysis of the model showed that something *like* biological neural networks could produce content-addressable memory. Hopfield himself later showed that the model's functioning was robust to the relaxation of some of his strict assumptions (Hopfield, 1984), and the work has laid the foundation for much subsequent work in understanding the neurobiology of memory.

### Bass's Model of the Diffusion of Innovations

How do new products diffuse in a population? In the early 1960s, Everett Rogers (1962) provided a near-exhaustive study of this question. He showed that cumulative adoption very often corresponds to an S-shaped curve in which adoption starts slowly, accelerates, and then plateaus. Although Rogers showed that this pattern of product diffusion is common to a startlingly wide variety of domains, he could not explain it. Instead, he merely identified five tautological categories of adopters, defined in terms of their timing of adoption. This explanation is rather unsatisfying and raises many additional questions, including why individuals would fall into a particular category of adopter and how robust the adoption curves are to different proportions of each of those categories. Shortly after Rogers' book was published, Bass (1969) introduced a simple model that provided a strikingly parsimonious explanation of Rogers' data. Suppose, said Bass, that instead of five discrete types, there is only a single type of individual, who with some small probability spontaneously adopts the new innovation (i.e., becomes an innovator) and otherwise adopts with a probability proportional to the number of other adopters he or she encounters. In other words, suppose that innovations spread like diseases. Bass constructed a mathematical model based on these assumptions, and showed not only that they resulted in S-shaped adoption curves, but that by fitting the model to empirical data on the diffusion of different products, characteristics of a given population concerning the rate of observation and the propensity to adopt could be inferred. The Bass model is still the core model for studying the diffusion of products used in communication, technology, and marketing research today (Bass 2004). The Bass model is, of course, extremely simplistic. It ignores real differences between individuals, such as network position (Valente, 1996) or the propensity to adopt based on social group membership (Berger & Heath, 2008), which may influence the dynamics of diffusion. Nevertheless, the Bass model provides critical structure for developing theory and guiding data collection related to the diffusion of innovations.

## The Dynamics of Distinctiveness

Some of my own work has concerned the population dynamics resulting from individual preferences for distinctiveness. Though much of human social behavior stems from conformity—that perfectly reasonable heuristic to copy others "when in Rome"—it is also quite common to actively differentiate ourselves from others (at least in the large, complex societies in which most of us find ourselves; see Smaldino in press). I first became involved in this research in graduate school, when I was approached by two social psychologists working within the domain of optimal distinctiveness theory (ODT; Brewer, 1991; Leonardelli et al., 2010). This theory has long had at its core the sort of vague verbal model I discussed in the subsection "Building Models, Formal and Otherwise." The presumption is that individuals have traits called social identities, and that, all else being equal, they will "identify" with whichever identity optimally balances the opposing needs for assimilation (to be similar to others) and differentiation (to be different from others). It is never stated exactly what does or does not constitute a social identity, what it means to identify as one thing, how the needs for assimilation and differentiation are calibrated, or how one optimizes a balance between them. Empirical tests have shown that US college students do prefer to express, at least on paper, a more exclusive part of their social identity when the initially proposed identity (e.g., being a student of their college) is described as being non-noteworthy (Brewer & Pickett, 2002). However, many questions remain, and the theory remains largely lacking in precision.

One assumption of the ODT is that deviations from optimality will be corrected as individuals change their expressed identities to ones that more optimally balance their opposing needs, and that this will result in a stable equilibrium in which individuals are satisfied in their relative distinctiveness (Leonardelli et al., 2010). To test this, my colleagues and I decided to model a simple scenario based on one possible interpretation of ODT (Smaldino et al., 2012). We assumed a population of individuals who could each express one of some number of discrete identities at any given time. We also assumed that each individual had a preference for some optimal level of distinctiveness, where an individual's distinctiveness was defined as the proportion of neighbors also expressing the same identity. One at a time, agents would consider the distinctiveness of their currently expressed identity, and if a better option was available, switch to that identity (agents were updated one at a time because synchronous updating is unrealistic, eliminates the possibility of behavioral cascades, and can generate peculiar model artifacts; see Huberman & Glance, 1993). The result was that individuals *always* ended up expressing identities that were far too popular to satisfy their preferences for differentiation. I later learned that this result echoed earlier work by ecologists considering animals joining groups of varying size, who had reached similar conclusions (Sibly, 1983).

Our model makes extremely simplistic assumptions about individuals' abilities to observe, express, and change identities. Nevertheless, the model accomplishes something that no previous work on ODT had: it defined all of the parts of the system and their relationships *explicitly*. Based on a set of assumptions that is entirely consistent with the verbal model, we produced a model that provided several initial conclusions and prompted two broad questions. First, is it true that individuals are perpetually more similar to others than they would prefer? This could, in fact, be the case. Several other models have recently shown that even explicit preferences for anti-conformity or distinctiveness can nevertheless result in local conformity (Muldoon, Smith, & Weisberg, 2012; Touboul, 2014; Smaldino & Epstein, 2015). Second, if it is instead the case that individuals *are* generally satisfied with the distinctiveness of their expressed identity, then what key factors related to the dynamics of identity expression were missing from our model? Several possibilities present themselves, including factors such as network structure, interdependence between identities, behavioral inertia, and transaction costs to switching identities. We examined the first of these, network structure, by situating individuals on a square lattice and having them only respond to nearby neighbors. We found that for a wide range of conditions, this kind of network structure solved the problem: individuals could maintain identities that maximized their preferences for distinctiveness. Our implementation of network structure was itself quite unrealistic—real social networks rarely approximate square lattices. Nevertheless, the model represents a step, if only a small one, toward a more precise theory linking individual preferences for distinctiveness with the social organization that results from those preferences.

## Turning the Modeling Lens on the Scientific Process

As a final example, I want to explore how formal models can help us better understand the larger endeavor in which we are engaged: science. Recently, controversy has raged over the roles of replication and publication policy in improving the reliability of research (Open Science Collaboration, 2015). Some propose that all results should be published, to ensure that a "file drawer effect" doesn't lead to over-representation of positive results (Franco, Malhotra, & Simonovits, 2014), while others are skeptical of the value of failed replications because replication studies may have diminished power (Kahneman, 2011; Bissell, 2013; Schnall, 2014). All acknowledge the importance of replication, but opinions vary widely on how much is needed and what its evidential value might be. Until now, each view has been based on intuition and lacked concrete rationale. And empirical analysis is inherently limited, both by the incompleteness of the published record and by the lack of internally consistent models of the scientific process that would allow us to usefully interpret extant data.

To remedy this dearth, Richard McElreath and I developed an analytical model of the population dynamics of science (McElreath & Smaldino, 2015). The model represents a population of scientists who, with regularity, select a hypothesis for investigation, investigate it using the standard methods of their field, and then attempt to communicate their results to the scientific community. We built on previous work by Ioannidis (2005), who introduced a simple model of scientific investigation that highlights the importance of the base rate—that is, the a priori probability that a novel hypothesis is true. When the base rate is low, even the most stringent experimental methods may produce more false positives than true positives. Our model extends this discussion to consider the fact that scientists may replicate their own and each other's work, but also that results must also run the gauntlet of peer review, with negative results being less likely to be published than positive ones. We conclude that regardless of how much replication is done, the biggest impediments to the effectiveness of science are low base rate and high false positive rate. I know of no better way to improve the base rate than to make sure that hypotheses stem from well-validated, precise theories. Such theories, in turn, are often developed at least partly through the extensive use of formal modeling. The model also speaks directly to the debate over the meaning of failed replications. We show that replications are informative even when they have substantially lower power than the initial investigations. Perhaps counterintuitively, we also find that suppression of negative findings may be beneficial, at least when such findings are tests of novel hypotheses and the base rate is low. Under those conditions, most novel results will be correct rejections of incorrect hypotheses. As these will not be surprising, we may want to avoid filling our journals with such results, or at least delegate them to a distinct location.

Our model of science is extremely simple. It frames hypothesis testing in a standard but unsatisfying true/false classification, rather than considering practical significance and effect size estimation. It ignores researcher bias, multiple testing, and data snooping. It ignores the incentives that drive scientists in choosing and publishing results, as well as differences in exclusivity and impact between journals. Nevertheless, our model provides, for the first time, specific quantitative evaluations of many verbal arguments. As I have noted throughout this chapter, all models, whether formal or verbal, ignore some factors. The difference is that, with a formal model, it is precisely clear which factors are being considered and which are being excluded.

## Modelers Are Stupid (Sometimes)

Models can help us to specify theories of how a complex system works, and to assess the conclusions of our assumptions when they are made precisely. However, I want to be careful not to elevate modelers above those scientists who employ other methods. This is important for at least two reasons, the first and foremost of which is that science absolutely requires empirical data. Those data are often painstaking to collect, requiring clever, meticulous, and occasionally tedious labor. There is a certain kind of laziness inherent in the professional modeler, who builds entire worlds from his or her desk using only pen, paper, and computer. Relatedly, many scientists are truly fantastic communicators, and present extremely clear theories that advance scientific understanding without a formal model in sight. Charles Darwin, to give an extreme example, laid almost all the foundations of modern evolutionary biology without writing down a single equation. That said, evolutionary biology would surely have stagnated without the help of formal modeling. Consider that Darwinism was presumed to be in opposition with Mendelian genetics until modelers such as R. A. Fisher and Sewall Wright showed that the two theories were actually compatible.

The second reason is that having a model is not the same thing as having a *good* model, or a model that is well presented, well analyzed, or well situated in its field. I want to focus on presentation and analysis. A model's strength stems from its precision. I have come across too many modeling papers in which the model—that is, the parts, all their components, the relationships between them, and mechanisms for change—is not clearly expressed. This is most common with computational models (such as agent-based models), which can be quite complicated, but also exists in cases of purely mathematical models. I am not a big fan of standardized protocols for model descriptions, as the population of all models is too varied and idiosyncratic to fit into a one-size-fits-all box. I will simply ask modelers to make an effort in their reporting. Make sure your model description is clear. The broad strokes, which may stem from verbal theory, should come first, followed by a filling in of details. When possible, make code available as soon as your paper is published, if not before. Clarity reveals how well the model really represents the system it purports to represent. Obfuscation is the refuge of the poor or insecure modeler.

This is not the place to go into great detail about the best practices for model analysis. I will only say that a major benefit of a model is the ability to ask all manner of "what if" questions. The assumptions of a model, including but not limited to its parameter values, should be explored extensively. After all, obtaining the conclusions that follow from those assumptions is the entire purpose of modeling. If you forgive the indulgence, I'll pick one small nit here concerning methods for analyzing computational models. Where differences between conditions are indicated, avoid the mistake of running statistical analyses as if you were sampling from a larger population. You already have a generating model for your data—it's your model. Statistical analyses on model data often involve modeling your model with a stupider model. Don't do this. Instead, run enough simulations to obtain limiting distributions.

Finally, it is important to always evaluate whether the conclusions of our model rely on reasonable assumptions. For example, it has been claimed that some economists have fallen prey to a sort of theory-induced blindness, giving too much credence to their models—which are generally based on the theory of the rational actor—and ignoring the fact that the core assumptions of the model are based on severe distortions of human psychology (Thaler, 2015). Microeconomic models based on rational choice theory are useful for developing intuition, and may even approximate reality in a few special cases, but the history of behavioral economics shows that standard economic theory has also provided a smorgasbord of null hypotheses to be struck down by empirical observation.

## Conclusion

Humans, scientists included, are limited beings who are bad at forming intuitions about the organization and behavior of complex systems. Verbal models, while critical first steps in scientific reasoning, are necessarily imprecise. Overreliance on verbal models can impede precision and, by extension, impede progress in our understanding of complex systems. Formal models are explicit in the assumptions they make about how the parts of a system work and interact, and moreover are explicit in the aspects of reality they omit. This has the potential disadvantage of making formal models appear stupid. And of course, they *are* stupid, because we are limited beings and stupid models are the best we can do. As Braitenberg writes, fiction will always be part of science "as long as our brains are only miniscule fragments of the universe, much too small to hold all the facts of the world but not too idle to speculate about them" (Braitenberg, 1984, p. 1).

An old adage holds that it is better to stay silent and be thought a fool than to speak and remove all doubt. As scientists, our goal is not to save face, but in fact to remove as much doubt as possible. Formal models make their assumptions explicit, and in doing so, we risk exposing our foolishness to the world. This appears to be the price of seeking knowledge. Models are stupid, but perhaps they can help *us* to become smarter. We need more of them.

## References

Bass, F. M. (1969). A new product growth for model consumer durables. *Management Science, 15*, 215–227.
Bass, F. M. (2004). Comments on "A new product growth for model consumer durables": The Bass model. *Management Science, 50*, 1833–1840.
Bedau, M. A. (1999). Can unrealistic computer models illuminate theoretical biology? In Wu, A. S. (Ed.), *Proceedings of the 1999 Genetic and Evolutionary Computation Conference Workshop* (pp. 20–23). Orlando, FL: GECC.
Berger, J., & Heath, C. (2008). Who drives divergence? Identity signaling, outgroup dissimilarity, and the abandonment of cultural tastes. *Journal of Personality and Social Psychology, 95*, 593–607.
Berryman, A. A. (1992). The origins and evolution of predator–prey theory. *Ecology, 73*, 1530–1535.
Bissell, M. (2013). Reproducibility: The risks of the replication drive. *Nature, 503*, 333–334.

Braitenberg, V. (1984). *Vehicles: Experiments in synthetic psychology.* Cambridge, MA: MIT Press.

Brewer, M. B. (1991). The social self: On being the same and different at the same time. *Personality and Social Psychology Bulletin, 17*(5), 475–482.

Brewer, M. B., & Pickett, C. L. (2002). The social self and group identification: Inclusion and distinctiveness motives in interpersonal and collective identities. In J. Forgas & K. Williams (Eds.), *The social self: Cognitive, interpersonal, and intergroup perspectives.* Philadelphia, PA: Psychology Press.

Campbell, D. T. (1974). "Downward causation" in hierarchically organised biological systems. In F. Ayala & T. Dobzhansky (Eds.), *Studies in the philosophy of biology* (pp. 179–86). Oakland, CA: University of California Press.

Eisenberg, E. M. (1984). Ambiguity as strategy in organizational communication. *Communication Monographs, 51*(3), 227–242.

Epstein, J. M. (2008). Why model? *Journal of Artificial Societies and Social Simulation, 11*(4), 12.

Farrell, S., & Lewandowsky, S. (2010). Computational models as aids to better reasoning in psychology. *Current Directions in Psychological Science, 19*: 329–335.

Franco, A., Malhotra, N., & Simonovits, G. (2014). Publication bias in the social sciences: Unlocking the file drawer. *Science, 345,* 1502–1505.

Gigerenzer, G. (1998). Surrogates for theories. *Theory & Psychology, 8*(2), 195–204.

Gleick, J. (2004). *Isaac Newton.* New York: Vintage Books.

Gunawardena, J. (2014). Models in biology: "Accurate descriptions of our pathetic thinking." *BMC Biology, 12,* 29.

Hills, T. T., Jones, M. N., & Todd, P.M. (2012). Optimal foraging in semantic memory. *Psychological Review, 119,* 431–440.

Huberman, B. A., & Glance, N. S. (1993). Evolutionary games and computer simulations. *Proceedings of the National Academy of Sciences USA, 90,* 7716–7718

Hopfield, J. J. (1982). Neural networks and physical systems with emergent collective computational abilities. *Proceedings of the National Academy of Sciences USA, 79,* 2554–2558.

Hopfield, J. J. (1984). Neurons with graded response have collective computational properties like those of two-state neurons. *Proceedings of the National Academy of Sciences USA, 81,* 3088–3092.

Ioannidis, J. P. A. (2005). Why most published research findings are false. *PLoS Medicine, 2*(8), e124.

Kahneman, D. (2011). A new etiquette for replication. *Social Psychology, 45,* 310–311.

Kauffman, S. A. (1971). Articulation of parts explanation in biology and the rational search for them. In R. C. Buck & R. S. Cohen (Eds.), *PSA 1970* (pp. 257–72). Irvine, CA: Philosophy of Science Association.

Lazer, D., & Friedman, A. (2007). The network structure of exploration and exploitation. *Administrative Science Quarterly, 52,* 667–694.

Leonardelli, G. L., Pickett, C. L., & Brewer, M. B. (2010). Optimal distinctiveness theory: A framework for social identity, social cognition, and intergroup relations. In M. P. Zanna & J. M. Olson (Eds.), *Advances in experimental social psychology* (Vol. 43, pp. 66–115). New York: Academic Press.

Luckinbill, L. S. (1973). Coexistence in laboratory populations of *Paramecium aurelia* and its predator *Didinium nasutum. Ecology, 54,* 1320–1327.

Marewski, J. N., & Olsson, H. (2009). Beyond the null ritual: Formal modeling of psychological processes. *Zeitschrift für Psychologie, 217,* 49–60.

McElreath, R. (2015). *Statistical rethinking: A Bayesian course with R examples.* New York: Chapman & Hall.

McElreath, R., & Smaldino, P.E. (2015). Replication, communication, and the population dynamics of scientific discovery. *PLoS One, 10*(8), e0136088.

Moussaïd, M., Helbing, D., & Theraulaz, G. (2011). How simple rules determine pedestrian behavior and crowd disasters. *Proceedings of the National Academy of Sciences, 108*, 6884–6888.

Muldoon, R., Smith, T., & Weisberg, M. (2012). Segregation that no one seeks. *Philosophy of Science, 79*, 38–62.

Nowak, A., Rychwalska, A., & Borkowski, W. (2013). Why simulate? To develop a mental model. *Journal of Artificial Societies and Social Simulation, 16*(3), 12.

Open Science Collaboration (2015). Estimating the reproducibility of psychological science. *Science, 349*, aac4716.

Popper, K. (1963). *Conjectures and refutations.* New York: Routledge.

Resnick, M. (1994). *Turtles, termites, and traffic jams: Explorations in massively parallel micro-worlds.* Cambridge, MA: MIT Press.

Rogers, E. M. (1962). *Diffusion of innovations.* New York: The Free Press.

Schank, J. C. (2001). Beyond reductionism: Refocusing on the individual with individual-based modeling. *Complexity, 6*(3), 33–40.

Schank, J. C. (2008). The development of locomotor kinematics in neonatal rats: An agent-based modeling analysis in group and individual contexts. *Journal of Theoretical Biology, 254*, 826–842.

Schank, J. C., May, C. J., & Joshi, S. S. (2014). Models as scaffold for understanding. In L. R. Caporael, J. R. Griesemer, & W. C. Wimsatt (Eds.), *Developing scaffolds in evolution, culture, and cognition* (pp. 147–167). Cambridge, MA: MIT Press.

Schnall, S. (2014). Clean data: Statistical artefacts wash out replication efforts. *Social Psychology, 45*(4), 315–320.

Sibly, R. M. (1983). Optimal group size is unstable. *Animal Behaviour, 31*, 947–948.

Smaldino, P. E. (2016). Not even wrong: Imprecision perpetuates the illusion of understanding at the cost of actual understanding. *Behavioral and Brain Sciences, 39*, e163.

Smaldino, P. E. (in press). The evolution of the social self: Multidimensionality of social identity solves the coordination problems of a society. In W. C. Wimsatt & A. C. Love (Eds.), *Beyond the meme: Articulating dynamic structures in cultural evolution.* Minneapolis, MN: University of Minnesota Press.

Smaldino, P. E., Calanchini, J., & Pickett, C. L. (2015). Theory development with agent-based models. *Organizational Psychology Review, 5*(4), 300–317.

Smaldino, P. E., & Epstein, J. M. (2015). Social conformity despite individual preferences for distinctiveness. *Royal Society Open Science, 2*, 140437.

Smaldino, P. E., Pickett, C., Sherman, J., & Schank, J. (2012). An agent-based model of social identity dynamics. *Journal of Artificial Societies and Social Simulation, 15*(4), 7.

Smith, E. R., & Conrey, F. R. (2007). Agent-based modeling: A new approach for theory building in social psychology. *Personality and Social Psychology Review, 11*, 87–104.

Thaler, R. H. (2015). *Misbehaving: The making of behavioral economics.* New York: W. W. Norton.

Tinbergen, N. (1963). On aims and methods of ethology. *Zeitschrift für Tierpsychologie, 20*, 410–433.

Touboul, J. (2014). The hipster effect: When anticonformists all look the same. *arXiv*, 1410.8001.

Valente, T. W. (1996). Social network thresholds in the diffusion of innovations. *Social Networks, 18*, 69–89.

Weinhardt, J. M., & Vancouver, J. B. (2012). Computational models and organizational psychology: Opportunities abound. *Organizational Psychology Review*, 2(4), 267–292.

Wimsatt, W. C. (1974). Complexity and organization. In K. Schaffner & R. S. Cohen (Eds.), *PSA 1972* (pp. 67–86). Irvine, CA: Philosophy of Science Association.

Wimsatt, W. C. (1987). False models as means to truer theories. In M. H. Nitecki & A. Hoffman (Eds.), *Neutral models in biology* (pp. 23–55). New York: Oxford University Press.

# 15

# BIG DATA IN PSYCHOLOGICAL RESEARCH

*David Serfass, Andrzej Nowak,*[1]
*and Ryne Sherman*

> Just as the microscope allowed us to look at smaller and smaller parts of physical objects, big data allows us to zoom in on our minds.
>
> *(Stephens-Davidowitz, 2015)*

We live in the age of information. With the increased use of computers, more data is being recorded than ever. Exabytes of data are created daily (McAfee & Brynjolfsson, 2012). Cell phone providers record call histories, banks record transaction histories, Google records search histories, and Facebook records status updates. In fact, data is the fastest-growing commodity in the modern world, and businesses have been quick to capitalize on these digital records. Netflix provides recommendations for its users based on what they have previously viewed, improving the user experience. Amazon tracks not only what books people buy, but also what they view, allowing it to make better recommendations for customers and sell more products. Retailers (e.g., Target, CVS) track customer purchases through rewards cards to better target their advertising. Google, one of the most valued companies in the world, is on a self-proclaimed mission to gather, organize, and make accessible all of the information (data) in the world.[2]

Beyond the business world, the Big Data revolution is also transforming social science. This chapter has three goals. The first is to describe the ways in which Big Data is transforming the social sciences. As will be seen, Big Data is changing not only the ways social scientists gather and analyze data, but even the way they design their studies. The second goal of this chapter is to discuss some of the opportunities Big Data affords social scientists. We do so by detailing a recent example of Big Data use in the social sciences. Finally, the third goal of this chapter is to describe the new set of challenges that Big Data has created for social scientists and how we may go about overcoming them.

## The New Social Sciences in the Big Data Revolution

The empirical revolution of the early 20th century changed the social sciences by emphasizing quantitative methods, surveys, and statistics, separating the social sciences from the rest of the humanities. Similarly, the modern Big Data revolution is transforming the social sciences. To see how, consider the way in which a social scientist might traditionally answer a research question. First, he or she might begin by evaluating the various theories related to his or her question. Such theories might yield one or more hypotheses. Next, the scientist would design a study to test these hypotheses, including the operationalization, manipulation, and measurement of key variables of interest. An experimental study might contain two to four experimental conditions with around n ≈ 30 in each, while a large survey study might gather reports from several hundred respondents. The researcher would execute the study by gathering data in his or her laboratory and analyze the results using basic inferential tests such as ANOVA, correlation, or regression.

In contrast, Big Data scientists take a different approach to thinking about how research questions can be answered. Rather than considering various ways to gather data to examine the research question, Big Data scientists begin by thinking about the kinds of data that are *already available* and how they could be used to answer the research question. Once a possible data source is located, Big Data scientists consider how they might acquire that data, what analyses they would conduct on the data, and what format the data would need to be in to conduct such an analysis. This different approach to thinking about how to answer research questions is the foundation for at least four fundamental differences between Big Data and traditional approaches to social science.

### Data Sources

The Big Data approach is nothing without data sources. As we noted in the introduction to this chapter, though, data are being produced and stored at greater rates than ever before. As such, the data scientist has many data sources available. Some of the most popular data sources are social media platforms (e.g., Facebook, Twitter), Web search records (e.g., Google Trends), and mobile devices. Because data sources are so essential for the Big Data approach to social science, we will provide some examples of popular data sources and highlight some studies using them.

### Facebook

With over one billion users (Sedgi, 2014), Facebook has been used in several social science studies. One study examined the voting behavior of Facebook users in response to an experimental manipulation. The researchers manipulated whether or not Facebook users saw pictures of their friends who reported voting or a banner that said "Today is Election Day." Users who saw pictures of friends who voted actually voted more than those who only saw the banner (Bond et al., 2010). Another experimental Facebook study manipulated the extent to which users were exposed to positive or negative status updates from their friends. The results indicated that people who were exposed to more negative statuses also posted more negative statuses themselves, thereby demonstrating emotional contagion via large-scale social networks (Kramer, Guillory, & Hancock, 2014). Finally, three observational studies examined the relationship between personality and Facebook usage. Two found that the words that people use in their status updates are related to their personalities (Schwartz et al., 2013; Park et al., 2015), and the third found that the things that people "like" on Facebook are related to their personalities (Youyou, Kosinski, & Stillwell, 2015).

## Twitter

Another social media site that has facilitated a considerable amount of research is Twitter. Twitter's API allows for easy access of publicly streamed Tweets and numerous researchers have used this tool for research purposes. In one study, researchers mapped the patterns of people's affective experiences throughout the course of a day by analyzing millions of individual Tweets and comparing the number of positive and negative words used (Golder & Macy, 2011). They found that positive affect peaks both in the early morning and around 11 p.m., whereas negative affect is highest in the late night hours between midnight and 4 a.m. In another Twitter study, researchers used machine learning to predict psychopathic tendencies based solely on the words that people used in their Tweets (Wald, Khoshgoftaar, Napolitano, & Sumner, 2012).

## Google Trends

Nearly everyone knows that Google is a powerful search engine enabling millions of people to instantly access a huge network of information. However, far fewer people may realize that Google records these searches and that aggregated historical searches can be accessed through the tool Google Trends.[3] The Google Trends repositories have been utilized in several recent studies.

One study used Google Trends to examine Web search frequencies for the words "jobs," "welfare," and "unemployment" to better estimate real-time jobless claims. Traditional economic measures like jobless claims are usually several months delayed due to data collection processes. However, search frequencies from Google Trends improved real-time predictions of joblessness (Choi & Varian, 2012). Another study used Google Trends to explore seasonal differences in sexual behavior by examining search frequencies for mate-seeking terms as well as pornographic material. The results demonstrated a six-month pattern of mate-seeking behavior with peaks in winter and early summer (Markey & Markey, 2013). Another analysis using Google Trends showed that people are more likely to search for terms like "news" and "prayer" in the morning, but words like "suicide" and "symptoms" in the late night hours (Stephens-Davidowitz, 2015).

## Transcripts

Historically, finding past newspaper articles required going to a library and searching through microfilm records. Today, however, many news repositories, and even newscasts, are kept online, making them a particularly juicy data source for Big Data scientists. For instance, different American news sources have reputations for their political leanings. Fox News is considered conservative, MSNBC is considered more liberal, and CNN is considered more moderate. One study used historical news transcripts from a 12-month period to assess the political bias of these different new outlets via semantic preferences. Consistent with expectations, the study found that Fox was the most conservative news source and MSNBC was the most liberal (Holtzman, Schott, Jones, Balota & Yarkoni, 2011).

## Communication Networks

Researchers have also explored the nature of relationships using digital communication records. Utilizing network theory (e.g., Barabási, 2012a, 2012b), researchers have examined underlying organizational structures using corporate e-mail records (Adamic & Adar, 2005). Others have examined communication patterns in response to emergency events using cellular phone records (Candia et al., 2008). Such digital communication records provide a concrete method for understanding how people actually interact with one another in their daily lives.

## Mobile Devices

Cell phones, smart watches, and other mobile devices provide continuous streams of data related to the activity of the user (Miller, 2012). Most mobile devices contain a GPS module that can locate the user and track movements in space, as well as acceleration sensors that can assess the user's movements. Many mobile phones and wearable electronics also monitor physiological parameters such as heart rate. These data are used by companies for various purposes (e.g., to inform coffee drinkers about their proximity to the nearest Starbucks), but social scientists have begun tapping these data sources as well. Lakens (2013) used cellular phones to measure changes in heart rate during relived happiness and anger. Others have used apps controlling the microphones in mobile devices to make audio recordings of participants' daily lives (Mehl & Robbins, 2012).

## Other Data Sources

Of course, this list is not exhaustive, but it serves to illustrate the types of data that are available to researchers. New sources of data are constantly becoming available. Large amounts of data are collected by other techniques such as aerial surveys, cameras, microphones, and sensors. Further, with the new development of the *Internet of Things*, where objects equipped with sensors and microprocessors communicate directly with each other, data concerning objects and their use are becoming available. As we have seen, these new data sources are rapidly advancing research capabilities of psychologists and other social scientists.

### Getting Outside the Lab

While the examples just described showcase various sources available to Big Data social scientists, they also emphasize a second fundamental difference between traditional and Big Data approaches to research. Big Data approaches are much more likely to gather data outside of laboratory settings. While the laboratory experiment will probably always have its uses for social scientists, advancing technology and a desire for increased ecological validity have moved more and more social science research outside the laboratory (Reis, 2012). Indeed, one strength of the Big Data approach to social science is that the data gathered are more likely to reflect actual human behavior (e.g., a Google search, a text message) than self-reports of behavior on a survey or reaction time in a laboratory (Baumeister, Vohs, & Funder, 2007). Moreover, because Big Data often come from real-world data sources (as opposed to artificial sources in the laboratory), we can gain a better understanding of the natural relationships among variables of interest. Laboratory experiments are regularly tightly controlled, often even controlling variables that are naturally correlated with each other. This set of circumstances eliminates the possibility of actually estimating the true (population-level) relationships between parameters (Baumeister, 2016). The Big Data approach embraces natural covariation.

### Description and Measurement Precision

Traditional approaches to social science involve gathering a sample and using statistical induction (i.e., inferential statistics) to generalize to some larger population. Of course, even the logic of these methods is tenuous given that the heavy reliance on convenience samples (e.g., college sophomores) of the WEIRD (Western, educated, and from industrialized, rich, and democratic countries) samples variety severely limits generalizability (Henrich, Heine, & Norezayan, 2010). In contrast, Big Data approaches regularly concern larger, more representative, and more diverse samples, if not entire populations. As a result, Big Data approaches tend to emphasize descriptive rather than inductive approaches. Indeed, if one has the entire population (or close to it), there is nothing left to which one can generalize. Because of their emphasis on effect sizes (Cohen, Cohen, West, & Aiken, 2003), Big Data researchers tend to prefer statistical regression (and related techniques) over traditional techniques such as ANOVA, which emphasize $p$-values and statistical significance. Indeed, the sample sizes used in Big Data research often render all relationships "statistically significant." As a result, Big Data researchers focus more on precision of measurement as embraced by the so-called "New Statistics" (Cumming, 2012).

## Tolerance for Complexity

A fourth fundamental difference between traditional approaches to social science and Big Data approaches concerns complexity. A laboratory experiment or a survey of 100 or so undergraduate students makes the detection of complex relationships (e.g., higher order interactions, non-linear relationships) much more difficult. Indeed, published interaction effects in the social sciences are notoriously difficult to replicate. Because of the sheer amount of the data available, Big Data researchers can readily explore higher-level interactions, the shape of non-linear relationships, and temporal dynamics without fear of making Type-I errors. In practice, Big Data researchers often employ machine learning or deep learning approaches to identify complex relationships and simultaneously employ cross-validation to ensure the robustness of their results. Such tools allow researchers to both explore and confirm relationships between variables that may not have been related to the initial goals or theory behind the study.

## Big Data Opportunities in the Social Sciences

Big Data offers a huge number of possibilities for social science researchers. Ultimately, we believe that the Big Data approach will allow us to understand and predict human behavior better than ever before. In this section, we detail an example of a study we recently conducted using the Big Data approach. Our intent is to use this example to illustrate some of the opportunities Big Data provides for social science researchers and some of the issues involved in using a Big Data approach.

## Measuring Situation Experiences via Twitter

In a recent study, we used Twitter to examine what people all over the United States experience in their everyday lives (Serfass & Sherman, 2015). This study employed machine learning to approximate human ratings of the situational characteristics present in over 20 million Tweets. We began with two research questions: What kinds of situations do people experience in everyday lives, and how do such situation experiences vary across time?

A traditional approach to these questions might involve distributing survey questionnaires to a group of people representative of our population of interest. Such questionnaires could ask people to recall the things they did yesterday, following a technique known as the "day reconstruction method" (Kahneman, Krueger, Schkade, Schwarz, & Stone, 2004). Alternatively, we could have taken advantage of modern advances in mobile technology to conduct an experience sampling study. While either of these approaches may have been useful, they would ultimately be labor-intensive, requiring the recruitment of participants, developing questionnaires, and software for distributing these questionnaires. Further, even with our best efforts, the sample size for such a study may have never really approached Big Data numbers.

Taking a Big Data approach, we wondered what data might already be available that would allow us to rapidly assess daily life situations from millions of people. We ultimately decided to use Twitter, for several reasons. First, Twitter has approximately 271 million users who are responsible for over 500 million Tweets (i.e., social media posts of 140 characters or less) per day (Seward, 2014). Second, the content of such Tweets reflects what people are currently thinking, feeling, and experiencing (i.e., situations). Third, Tweets are often posted in real time, meaning that they tend to reflect experiences that are occurring right now or just occurred recently. Fourth, the Twitter API allows one to rapidly gather millions of Tweets from all across the United States. Thus, Twitter provided an excellent platform for rapidly gathering lots of data aimed at addressing our two research questions.

We used the *streamR* and *twitteR* packages in the statistical computing language *R* to gather over 42 million Tweets posted during a two-week period.[4] Because posts from public social media accounts are often spam or corporate advertisements (see our discussion of data quality below), we limited their impact by removing Tweets from users who (a) posted more than 165 times during the two-week period, (b) had more than 2926 followers, or (c) had more than 40,358 total account statuses (Tweets and Retweets). These figures represented the top 2.5% of each metric. This resulted in a final sample of 20,239,179 Tweets from 1,347,499 users for analysis.

Next, we needed to score each of these 20 million Tweets for their situation characteristics. We used the DIAMONDS model of situation characteristics, which consists of eight core situation dimensions: Duty, Intellect, Adversity, Mating, pOsitivity, Negativity, Deception, and Sociality (for more details, see Rauthmann et al., 2014). Clearly, it would be far too labor-intensive to have research assistants read and rate all 20 million Tweets on the DIAMONDS dimensions. As such, we employed machine learning to build predictive models of the DIAMONDS in each Tweet (based on Tweet content) that approximate human judgments. To do so, we first needed what computer scientists call "ground truth." We had research assistants rate a (different) sample of 5000 Tweets on the Situational Eight DIAMONDS (Rauthmann et al., 2014). Each Tweet was rated by four coders, and composite judgments were used as the criteria for the machine learning models.

After research assistants rated this sample of Tweets, the frequencies with which different words were used in the sample were tallied using the *Linguistic Inquiry Word Count* computerized text analysis program (LIWC).[5] The default LIWC dictionary contains 64 different word categories. These categories include standard linguistic information (e.g., personal pronouns, prepositions), psychological constructs (e.g., anxiety, anger, cognitive mechanism), personal concern categories (e.g., work, leisure), paralinguistic dimensions (e.g., "um"), and general descriptive categories (e.g., word count, six-letter words). The LIWC dictionary provides a validated means for analyzing written and spoken word use, and has been used to analyze textual data in numerous studies (e.g., Chung & Pennebaker, 2008; Yarkoni, 2010).

The word frequencies for each category in the LIWC dictionary were used as the predictors for the machine learning models. We employed various training methods, including linear models, support vector machine, and random forest. Based on both internal and external cross-validation results, we selected models using the random forest method because those models were most accurate at replicating human judgments with Model R values ranging between .26 and .70, depending on the DIAMONDS dimension. We also analyzed the number of coded Tweets necessary to build accurate prediction models. Figure 15.1 shows the cross-validated Model R values for the model predicting Duty based on the number of Tweets that coders rated. As can be seen, Model R values asymptote around 4000 Tweets. This indicates that by having coders rate 5000 Tweets, we captured as much information as possible for our machine learning models.

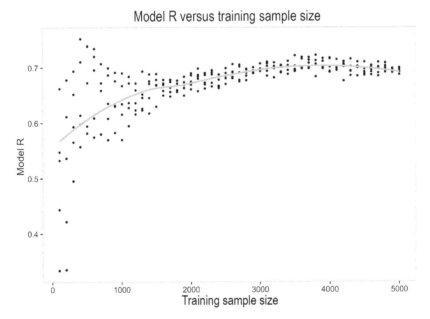

**FIGURE 15.1**    Model R values at different sample sizes. Five models were built at each sample size from 100 to 5000 Tweets. Model Rs for each iteration are shown, along with a locally weighted regression line depicting the predicted Model R at each number of Tweets.

With these models now built, we applied them to our original sample of 20 million Tweets, effectively simulating what we would find if research assistants had read and rated all 20 million Tweets. In other words, we scored millions of Tweets for their psychologically relevant situation characteristics in just a few hours. In contrast, we estimate that attempting to rate all 20 million Tweets by hand would have taken about 400,000 hours at a rate of 50 Tweets per hour.

Using these 20 million Tweets that were scored on the Situational Eight DIAMONDS, we explored the daily patterns of situation experience. We found that people experience more pOsitivity over the weekend and more Negativity during the work week. We also found that people experience, on average, more Duty during the workday and more Sociality in the evenings. Figure 15.2 shows weekly and daily trends in experienced Duty, Sociality, pOsitivity, and Negativity on Twitter.

Further, we also found that women reported more emotional situations, scoring higher on both pOsitivity and Negativity, than men. Women also Tweeted about situation experiences that were, on average, higher on Mating (i.e., romance) than men. Finally, using the geotagged location of the Tweets,

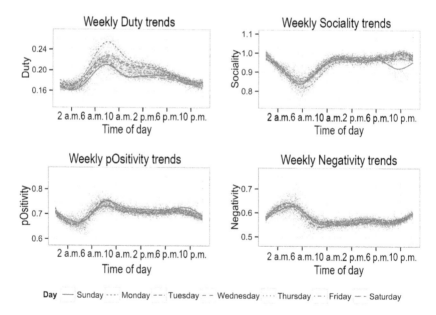

**FIGURE 15.2** Average situation experiences by time and day. The average DIAMONDS dimension score for each minute of each weekday is shown, along with the generalized additive model smoothed lines for each weekday (N = 17,005,376 statuses, 1,347,499 Twitter users, males = 324,244, females = 310,372, unknown = 167,051).

we compared three categories of population density: Urban Areas (population > 50,000), Urban Clusters (population between 2500 and 50,000), and Rural Areas (population < 2500). To our surprise, we found virtually no differences between the situation experiences that people in these areas Tweet about. This suggests that, perhaps, people experience psychologically similar situations regardless of their local population density.

Overall, we hope the discussion of this study serves as an example of the type of research that is enabled by the Big Data approach to social science. Gathering 20 million self-reports of participants' situation experiences, as one might attempt to do employing traditional approaches, would take years, if not decades. Further, as noted above, rating 20 million Tweets manually would be completely unfeasible. However, we want to emphasize that the method outlined here is not limited to situation experiences, or even Twitter. Researchers interested in any psychological construct (e.g., social support, aggression, fear) can follow a similar approach: (1) identify or obtain some sort of 'ground truth' criteria, (2) quantify the stimuli (e.g., word usage, objects in images, etc.), (3) use machine learning techniques to build models to predict the criteria of interest, and (4) apply predictive models to a larger corpus of interest.

## Challenges for Big Data in the Social Sciences

While the Big Data revolution offers many opportunities for social scientists, it is not without its challenges and limitations. This section describes five challenges facing social scientists employing a Big Data approach, and offers potential solutions to these challenges.

### Data Analysis and Storage

First, Big Data challenges prior models of data analysis and storage. In traditional social science research, the researcher collects some data, stores the data in a spreadsheet, and analyzes that data using statistical software on a laptop or personal computer. However, the exponential growth of the amount of data generated and collected every day has rendered these traditional techniques of data gathering, storage, and analysis inadequate, if not completely obsolete. In the aforementioned Twitter study, the raw data file (JSON format) was over 100 GB in size. Files of this size make storage and memory capabilities a necessary consideration. Most laptops and personal computers are not powerful enough to work with files like this. In fact, as the size of the data to be analyzed becomes larger, it may actually be more efficient to move the analysis to the server storing the data, rather than the other way around. This is the idea behind the *Hadoop*-based distributed computing paradigm that many companies use for their data storage and analytics (e.g., Facebook, Google).

## Causal Inferences

A second challenge for social scientists employing a Big Data approach is that experimental methods are often unavailable. The obvious drawback is that making causal claims is more difficult, if not impossible, with Big Data approaches. However, unlike typical survey researchers, social scientists employing Big Data approaches have two advantages. First, it is often the case that the social scientist is not attempting to make causal claims, but rather only interested in building models that best predict an outcome of interest. For instance, in the Twitter example described previously, we were not really interested in understanding the causal processes behind how raters of Tweets made judgments of situational characteristics. Instead, we were only interested in building and applying models that best reflected the ratings, no matter how they were made. Second, Big Data approaches often measure not only a large number of observations, but also a large number of variables. Doing so allows one to rule out many alternative explanations for relationships by including them in the model (Cohen et al., 2003).

## Imperfect Data

A third challenge for social scientists employing Big Data approaches is that the data available to Big Data social scientists are often unintended. In traditional social science research, the scientist carefully determines what to measure and how to measure it. Data that are available to the Big Data social scientist, on the other hand, are often unplanned and consist of things that happen to be measured for no particular (scientific) reason. For example, data from Facebook profiles include the user's relationship status. As a result, researchers with access to Facebook profiles can use this information to study romantic relationships. However, Facebook did not include a question about relationship status to study romantic relationships per se, but rather to enhance user experience. Thus, the data available to the Big Data social scientist are not always exactly the data one might like to have. However, Big Data social scientists are often willing to trade a small amount of perfect data for a vastly larger amount of imperfect data. Big Data social scientists are counting on the fact that larger and more representative samples of data are more likely to replicate and generalize to the population, even if the data are imperfect.

Relatedly, because the data available to the Big Data social scientist are rarely by his or her design, they are often messy, include many outliers, lots of missingness, and/or lack a common format. In response, Big Data social scientists must equip themselves with tools for data wrangling and generally dealing with the problems associated with messy data. It is perhaps no surprise then that many social scientists have begun teaming up with computer scientists, who often have expertise in acquiring and managing Big Data. In the Twitter example we described earlier, we had to eliminate nearly 50% of the Tweets prior to analysis, to reduce the impact of Tweets produced by spammers and corporate accounts. However, even using this conservative data cleaning procedure, we had more than enough Tweets left for analysis. Whereas experimental social scientists use their creative talents to devise sophisticated experiments, Big Data social scientists must use their creativity to identify potentially useful data and methods for extracting and analyzing such data.

## Theoretical Considerations

The fourth challenge for social scientists using Big Data approaches is how to combine Big Data with psychological theory. For the most part, Big Data approaches are purely descriptive. As noted previously, they are usually less interested in *why* and *how* variables are connected to each other than in *which* and *to what degree* variables are connected. Such an emphasis on purely practical matters can be offputting to social scientists who are interested in explanation and building theory. Although the descriptive approach has been proven to be very effective in short-timescale prediction, it cannot replace the theory. The value of the descriptive knowledge holds only as long as the conditions stay the same. Without the theory, one cannot say what will happen in a novel situation. Also, the value of the theory is to compress a large pool of observations to a small set of causal rules. Although the complex relationships discovered by machine learning algorithms may be useful for prediction by computers, their usefulness in allowing humans to better understand the world they live in is limited. Thus, whether the potential of Big Data will be realized by social scientists depends on the ability of social scientists to use Big Data in developing theories and in its ability to show the added value of understanding how human mind works beyond purely descriptive patterns of human behavior.

## Privacy Concerns

The fifth challenge for social scientists using Big Data approaches is privacy risks. From Facebook status updates to credit card transactions to text message records, Big Data is inherently personal. Both corporations and social scientists have already received considerable pushback from perceived Big Data overreach. One Facebook study, already mentioned in the subsection on "Data Sources" earlier in this chapter, manipulated users' news feeds with either more positive or negative news. The researchers found small, but statistically significant, evidence for emotional contagion such that emotions seen on Facebook news feeds seem to impact users' own expressed emotions (Kramer et al., 2014). Another Facebook study, also previously mentioned, manipulated users news feeds about voting, which seemed to have a real impact on voting behavior (Bond et al., 2012). Both studies received considerable public and academic backlash (e.g., Dumas, Serfass, Brown, & Sherman, 2014; Gleibs, 2014), and have largely resulted in

Facebook keeping its research findings internal (i.e., not publishing them). More recently, researchers released a public data set containing user names, age, gender, location, personality traits, and responses to over 2000 data profiling questions compiled by the dating website OkCupid (Kirkegaard & Bjerrekær, 2016; see also Zimmer, 2016). These data were gathered, or scraped, from public profiles on the OkCupid website. This study received tremendous public backlash concerning privacy and ethical issues in Big Data use, and has since been removed by the authors.

Both researchers and the public need to be aware of such privacy and ethical issues in using Big Data. Researchers must take great care to protect the privacy of those who provide them with data, or else they risk losing access to such data (e.g., users leaving websites, having access to data sources revoked). Simultaneously, the public need to be aware of their own privacy rights and how their reactions to Big Data science can alter scientific advancement. While companies, such as Facebook, may have the right to experiment with their news feed algorithm, they will be reluctant to share the results of such experiments with the public if it will only lead to negative publicity. Data scientists should work with the public to help them understand how Big Data can be used to positively affect the lives of the data providers.

## Concluding Thoughts on Big Data

The majority of research presented in this volume utilizes computational modeling to understand social processes. The use of simulations facilitated a new research paradigm for social scientists. The advent of computers capable of processing intensive simulations allowed researchers to simulate societies (Nowak, Szamrej, & Latané, 1990), evolution (Axelrod & Hamilton, 1981), mental processes (Nowak, Vallacher, Tesser, & Borkowski, 2000) and interpersonal processes. Computational modeling led researchers to numerous new insights that were previously unavailable. Big Data research is similarly poised to facilitate a revolution in psychological research.

Big Data has the potential to transform social psychology from a qualitative to quantitative science. By using the data from extremely large samples, or even from the populations, the Big Data approach concentrates on describing the strength of the relationships, rather than their significance. This moves social psychology from qualitative science, concentrating on whether a relationship exists, to a quantitative science, where the goal is the precise description of the relationship. This paves the way to describe theories using formulas, or computational models rather than qualitative verbal descriptions. The mathematical or computational models can be used for practical applications. The qualitative nature of the theories and models makes it possible to precisely predict effects of different types of interventions and to find out the most effective ways to achieve desired changes.

Finding complex, also nonlinear, relationships involving many variables and their interactions is another potential of the Big Data approach. The size of the sample makes it possible to use machine learning algorithms to find very complex relationships in the data and to express the relationships by mathematical formulas. For traditional social psychological research, even if data analysis revealed significant higher than third-order interactions, interpreting them and describing the nature of high-order interactions was a daunting task, because verbal description of the nature of relationship between more than four variables where each variable modifies the effects of the other variables become too complex. Quantitative models based on Big Data analysis have no problem with describing types of relationships that are too complex to be expressed by verbal description, by expressing them in mathematical formulas.

The Big Data approach also naturally leads to more comprehensive models. One of the strongest advantages of the Big Data approach is the potential to merge multiple data sets in a single analysis, with these data sets representing many levels of psychological reality. For example, questionnaire data concerning individuals can be merged with the data describing the organizations where they are employed and the demographic and statistical data concerning the counties where they live (e.g., crime rates, income, etc).

In the traditional experimental approach in social psychology, the number of variables that could be manipulated in a single study is severely limited by the growth of the number of cells with the addition of each new factor. In the correlational approach, the limit on the number of variables was limited by the time the participants could spend answering the questions. In most cases of Big Data studies, the data are collected automatically, without significant effort from the participant, which allows one to collect much more data than in the research requiring subjects to answer questions. Also, it is possible to place psychological data concerning an individual in the context of aggregate multiple-level data (e.g., the organization to which the individual belongs, the county, and the state). Hierarchical multilevel regression models can explore relationships both within and between levels, which allows one to build and test comprehensive, complex, multilevel models, where the psychological processes can be understood in the context of the environmental effects.

Adding dynamics to existing theories in social psychology and developing new theories in the tradition of Dynamical Social Psychology (Nowak & Vallacher, 1998; Vallacher & Nowak, 1997; Vallacher, Read, & Nowak, 2002) represents another potential of Big Data approach. Because most of the data in this approach are gathered continuously and contain time stamps, it allows the researchers, as we have also shown in this chapter, to analyze patterns of change in time. Dynamical theories thus became empirically meaningful and testable. Observing temporal patterns in psychological and social phenomena also inspires new models and theories in social psychology.

In sum, Big Data provides an empirical platform for the development and testing of a new kind of theories in social psychology. Together with computer simulations, the Big Data approach paves the way for the development of theories that are quantitative, complex, comprehensive, multilevel, and dynamic. In doing so, it facilitates integration with computational theories in other social sciences, and also with natural sciences.

## Notes

1 Andrzej Nowak acknowledges the support from the grant of Polish Committee for Scientific Research (DEC-2011/02/A/HS6/00231).
2 More pessimistically, we might say that Google's goal is to "monetize all of the information in the world" (Morozov, 2013).
3 See https://www.google.com/trends/.
4 For *streamR*, see https://cran.r-project.org/web/packages/streamR/; for *twitteR*, see https://cran.r-project.org/package=twitteR; for R, see www.r-project.org/.
5 See http://liwc.wpengine.com/.

## References

Adamic, L., & Adar, E. (2005). How to search a social network. *Social Networks*, *27*(3), 187–203.

Axelrod, R., & Hamilton, W. D. (1981). The evolution of cooperation. *Science*, *211*, 1390–1396

Barabási, L. (2012a). Introduction. In *Network science: Interactive textbook*. Retrieved from: http://barabasilab.neu.edu/networksciencebook/

Barabási, L. (2012b). Graph theory. In *Network science: Interactive textbook*. Retrieved from: http://barabasilab.neu.edu/networksciencebook/

Baumeister, R. F. (2016). Charting the future of social psychology on stormy seas: Winners, losers, and recommendations. *Journal of Experimental Social Psychology*, *66*, 153–158.

Baumeister, R. F., Vohs, K. D., & Funder, D. C. (2007). Psychology as the science of self-reports and finger movements: Whatever happened to actual behavior? *Perspectives on Psychological Science*, *2*(4), 396–403.

Bond, R. M., Fariss, C. J., Jones, J. J., Kramer, A. D., Marlow, C., Settle, J. E., & Fowler, J. H. (2012). A 61-million-person experiment in social influence and political mobilization. *Nature*, *489*(7415), 295–298.

Candia, J., González, M. C., Wang, P., Schoenharl, T., Madey, G., & Barabási, A. L. (2008). Uncovering individual and collective human dynamics from mobile phone records. *Journal of Physics A: Mathematical and Theoretical*, *41*(22), 224015.

Choi, H., & Varian, H. (2012). Predicting the Present with Google Trends. *The Economic Record*, *88*(S1), 2–9. doi:10.1111/j.1475-4932.2012.00809.x

Chung, C. K., & Pennebaker, J. W. (2008). Revealing dimensions of thinking in open-ended self-descriptions: An automated meaning extraction method for natural language. *Journal of Research in Personality*, *42*(1), 96–132.

Cohen, J., Cohen, P., West, S. G., & Aiken, L. S. (2003). *Applied Multiple Regression/ Correlation Analysis for the Behavioral Sciences* (3rd ed.). Mahwah, NJ: Lawrence Erlbaum.

Cumming, G. (2012). *Understanding the new statistics: Effect sizes, confidence intervals, and meta-analysis*. New York: Routledge.

Dumas, G., Serfass, D. G., Brown, N. A., & Sherman, R. A. (2014). The evolving nature of social network research: A commentary to Gleibs (2014). *Analyses of Social Issues and Public Policy, 14*(1), 374–378.

Gleibs, I. (2014). Turning virtual public spaces into laboratories: Thoughts on conducting online field studies using social network sites. *Analyses of Social Issues and Public Policy, 14*(1), 352–370.

Golder, S. A., & Macy, M. W. (2011). Diurnal and seasonal mood vary with work, sleep, and daylength across diverse cultures. *Science, 333*(6051), 1878–1881.

Henrich, J., Heine, S. J., & Norenzayan, A. (2010). The weirdest people in the world? *Behavioral and Brain Sciences, 33*(2–3), 61–83.

Holtzman, N. S., Schott, J. P., Jones, M. N., Balota, D. A., & Yarkoni, T. (2011). Exploring media bias with semantic analysis tools: Validation of the Contrast Analysis of Semantic Similarity (CASS). *Behavior Research Methods, 43*, 193–200.

Kahneman, D., Krueger, A. B., Schkade, D. A., Schwarz, N., & Stone, A. A. (2004). A survey method for characterizing daily life experience: The day reconstruction method. *Science, 306*(5702), 1776–1780.

Kirkegaard, E. O. W., & Bjerrekær, J. D. (2016). The OkCupid dataset: A very large public dataset of dating site users. Unpublished manuscript.

Kramer, A. D., Guillory, J. E., & Hancock, J. T. (2014). Experimental evidence of massive-scale emotional contagion through social networks. *Proceedings of the National Academy of Sciences, 111*(24), 8788–8790.

Lakens, D. (2013). Using a smartphone to measure heart rate changes during relived happiness and anger. *IEEE Transactions on Affective Computing, 4*(2), 238–241.

Markey, P. M., & Markey, C. N. (2013). Seasonal variation in internet keyword searches: A proxy assessment of sex mating behaviors. *Archives of Sexual Behavior, 42*(4), 515–521.

McAfee, A., & Brynjolfsson, E. (2012, October). Big Data: The management revolution. *Harvard Business Review*. Retrieved from https://hbr.org/2012/10/big-data-the-management-revolution/ar

Mehl, M. R., & Robbins, M. L. (2012). Naturalistic observation sampling: The Electronically Activated Recorder (EAR). In M. R. Mehl & T. S. Conner (Eds.), *Handbook of research methods for studying daily life* (pp. 176–192). New York: Guilford Press.

Miller, G. (2012). The Smartphone Psychology Manifesto. *Perspectives on Psychological Science, 7*, 221.

Morozov, E. (2013, November 11). Why we are allowed to hate Silicon Valley. *Frankfurter Allgemeine Feuilleton*. Retrieved from www.faz.net/aktuell/feuilleton/debatten/the-internet-ideology-why-we-are-allowed-to-hate-silicon-valley-12658406.html

Nowak, A., Szamrej, J., & Latané, B. (1990). From private attitude to public opinion: A dynamic theory of social impact. *Psychological Review, 97*(3), 362.

Nowak, A., & Vallacher, R. R. (1998). *Dynamical social psychology*. New York: Guilford Press.

Nowak, A., Vallacher, R. R., Tesser, A., & Borkowski, W. (2000). Society of self: The emergence of collective properties in self-structure. *Psychological Review, 107*, 39–61.

Park, G., Schwartz, H. A., Eichstaedt, J. C., Kern, M. L., Kosinski, M., Stillwell, D. J., Ungar, L. H., & Seligman, M. E. (2015). Automatic personality assessment through social media language. *Journal of Personality and Social Psychology, 108*(6), 934.

Rauthmann, J. F., Gallardo-Pujol, D., Guillaume, E. M., Todd, E., Nave, C. S., Sherman, R. A., Ziegler, M., Jones, A. B., & Funder, D. C. (2014). The Situational Eight DIAMONDS: A taxonomy of major dimensions of situation characteristics. *Journal of Personality and Social Psychology, 107*(4), 677–718.

Reis, H. T. (2012). Why researchers should think "real-world": A conceptual rationale. In M. R. Mehl & T. S. Connor (Eds.), *Handbook of research methods for studying daily life* (pp. 3–21). New York: Guilford.

Schwartz, H. A., Eichstaedt, J. C., Kern, M. L., Dziurzynski, L., Ramones, S. M., Agrawal, M., Shah, A., Kosinski, M., Stilwell, D., Seligman, M. E. P., & Ungar, L. H. (2013). Personality, gender, and age in the language of social media: The open-vocabulary approach. *PLoS One, 8*(9), e73791

Sedgi, Amy (2014, February 4). Facebook: 10 years of social networking, in numbers. *The Guardian*. Retrieved from www.theguardian.com/news/datablog/2014/feb/04/facebook-in-numbers-statistics

Serfass, D. G., & Sherman, R.A. (2015). Situations in 140 characters: Assessing real-world situations on Twitter. *PLoS One, 10(11)*, e0143051. doi:10.1371/journal.pone.0143051

Seward, Z. M. (2014, July 31). How many of Twitter's active users are actually human? *Quartz*. Retrieved from http://qz.com/242483/how-many-of-twitters-active-users-are-actually-human/

Stephens-Davidowitz, S. (2015, July 4). Days of our digital lives. *New York Times*. Retrieved from www.nytimes.com/2015/07/05/opinion/sunday/seth-stephens-davidowitz-days-of-our-digital-lives.html?ref=topics&_r=0

Vallacher, R., & Nowak, A. (1997). The emergence of dynamical social psychology. *Psychological Inquiry, 8*, 73–99.

Vallacher, R. R., Read, S. J., & Nowak, A. (2002). The dynamical perspective in personality and social psychology. *Personality and Social Psychology Review, 6*, 264–273.

Wald, R., Khoshgoftaar, T, M., Napolitano, A., & Sumner, C. (2012). Using Twitter content to predict psychopathy. In *Machine Learning and Applications (ICMLA), 2012: 11th IEEE International Conference on Machine Learning and Applications* (Vol. 2, pp. 394–401). Piscataway, NJ: IEEE. Retrieved from http://ieeexplore.ieee.org/abstract/document/6406768/

Yarkoni, T. (2010). Personality in 100,000 words: A large-scale analysis of personality and word use among bloggers. *Journal of Research in Personality, 44*, 363–373.

Youyou, W., Kosinski, M., & Stillwell, D. (2015). Computer-based personality judgments are more accurate than those made by humans. *Proceedings of the National Academy of Sciences, 112*(4), 1036–1040.

Zimmer, M. (2016, May 14). OkCupid study reveals the perils of Big-Data science. *Wired*. Retrieved from https://www.wired.com/2016/05/okcupid-study-reveals-perils-big-data-science/

# 16

# THE FUTURE OF COMPUTATIONAL SOCIAL PSYCHOLOGY

*Andrzej Nowak[1] and Robin R. Vallacher*

The contributions to this volume have each made a strong case for exploiting the power of modern computer technology and advanced statistical techniques to capture the dynamics and complexity of human experience. Traditional experimental social psychology has created an important foundation for understanding how people think, feel, and interact with one another, of course, but this approach could only take us so far. In recent years, the limitations and problematic features of mainstream social psychological research have begun to receive more attention than have the findings generated by such research—a state of affairs that has generated both concern and defensiveness in the field. Whether by coincidence or in response to this crisis of confidence, the computational approach has emerged as a viable path forward in the quest to create a truly scientific social psychology.

In so doing, we not only get around the limitations of traditional approaches, we also are equipped to address the defining features of mind and action that were of central concern in the field's early decades. Phenomena such as nonlinearity, intrinsic dynamics, self-organization, emergence, and reciprocal causality, which were recognized implicitly, if not explicitly, by early theorists such as Lewin (1936) and James (1890), have resurfaced as crucial considerations in the computational approach. And in focusing on the expression of these phenomena across the topical landscape of social psychology, there is renewed hope that an integrated social psychology is within reach—an integration that is consistent with the principles of dynamics and complexity that have been established in other areas of science.

This rosy future is not a foregone conclusion. New ideas and research strategies have punctuated the history of social psychology, many of them met with enthusiasm as the new way forward, only to falter in their attempt to provide an integrated and nuanced template for the diversity of human experience. Psychodynamics, social learning, general systems theory, and catastrophe theory, for example, all have had their moments in the spotlight, but none has succeeded in providing the unifying set of principles that the field strives to attain. This is not to denigrate the importance of these frameworks—each has generated important insights into the human condition—but rather to remind ourselves that big ideas can fall short of their promise in providing coherence for a fragmented and often contentious field.

Will it be different this time? Can the computational approach live up to its promise as both the solution to the limitations of traditional social psychology and the basis for integrating the diverse surface structure of the field? The contributions highlighted in this book are cause for optimism, but they should be looked upon as initial forays with unclear points of similarity and divergence. This is to be expected in the early stages of a new perspective, of course, but it also serves as a reminder that much remains to be done before computational social psychology can be rightly embraced as the field's source of integration and a viable path forward.

Our aim in this concluding chapter is to speculate on the future of computational social psychology. We begin by noting recent advances in technology that are likely to enhance the salience of computational models and make this approach more accessible to lay people as well as psychologists. We then discuss the advances to be expected in theory construction, especially the potential of computational modeling to provide theoretical integration for the complexity and nuance of human social experience. In a concluding section, we bring traditional social psychology back into the spotlight, noting its added value as the field matures as a truly scientific endeavor.

## Advances in Technology

The pace of innovation in technology has accelerated in recent decades, and this growth shows no signs of diminishing. Several of these advances are poised to refine the computational approach and extend its reach to existing and yet to be defined topics in social psychology. Incorporating and building on these developments is likely to have tremendous payoff for both theory and research.

### Computers and Software

In parallel with the development of computational social science (Conte & Giardini, 2016; Conte et al., 2012), advances in computational social psychology will be based on the increasing capacity of information and communication technologies to acquire and handle large amounts of data. Computers are becoming faster and more powerful, making them better equipped not only to process large data sets, but also to merge such data sets for use in a single analysis. These advances in technology should pave the way for the discovery of complex patterns in diverse sources of data, and the construction of models that replicate these patterns.

For the potential of advances in computing technology to be realized, software must become increasingly powerful and sophisticated. The information generated by text uploaded on the internet, communication over social media (e.g., Twitter, Facebook), and queries on search engines provide rich sources of data to be mined for insights into personal concerns, shared interests, and the spread of social influence. Software designed for this purpose has been developed in recent years—for example, the *Linguistic Inquiry Word Count* algorithms (Chung & Pennebaker, 2008)—and growth in this area is likely to accelerate in the years to come. New computer methods, such as Deep Learning (LeCun, Bengio, & Hinton, 2015), provide a way to find meaningful representations from unstructured Big Data. New analytic algorithms can automatically extract features from signals in different modalities (e.g., text, pictures, and sounds). Speech recognition software can, with high accuracy, convert speech to written text. Software can quite accurately recognize emotions from pictures and movies. All of this makes data acquisition automatic. Meanwhile, the increasing popularity of mobile devices—smart phones and tablets—creates the potential for tracking and identifying patterns of movement. So, rather than being limited to counting the frequency of specific semantic content expressed in electronic media, for example, software on the horizon will be able to identify how communication patterns are related to the extent and rate of people's movement in physical space.

In like manner, programs to simulate social processes will become increasingly sophisticated, to take advantage of the increasing power of computers. Computer modeling packages are being developed for the social sciences that simulate complex phenomena on many timescales, and these can be adapted to topics in social psychology. The standardization and availability of such packages means that implementing increasingly sophistical theoretical models in a computer simulation will ironically require less programming expertise and low-level technical skills, allowing social psychologists without such training to focus on how abstract concepts and principles are expressed.

## Online Information and Communication

Communication and information technology have dramatically expanded the range and availability of data of interest to social psychology. The internet, social networks, and mobile devices are especially likely to play important roles in the development of computational models of social processes.

## The Internet

The internet has become an important environment in which social life takes place. Interaction over social media, in particular, has become increasingly important in recent years, rivaling the importance of face-to-face interactions in the real world. Social media communication clearly provides direct insight into individuals' personal lives. Thus, researchers can mine social media data to investigate people's moods, preferences, and modes of self-presentation (e.g., modesty versus boastfulness). And the recent advent of Big Data (Chapter 15 in this volume) has enabled researchers to emphasize descriptive rather than inductive approaches to identify processes and patterns in human interaction. Whereas laboratory research in social psychology must rely on relatively small convenience samples (most often, college students), the Big Data approach focuses on larger and more representative samples—sometimes approaching entire populations. With such large samples, any observed relationship can essentially be considered "statistically significant," obviating the need to employ inferential statistics.

The internet has also become a popular forum for playing n-person games. The behavior of individuals in such games can provide insight into a variety of social psychological phenomena, including strategic decision-making, collaboration, competition, trust, defection, and aggression. This source of data concerning social processes is destined to increase in the years to come, thus making available the online gaming records of thousands of people from different cultures and with different demographic backgrounds.

It should be noted that the internet can also be employed to conduct traditional social psychological research. Rather than coming to a laboratory, participants can take part in experiments and complete surveys online. *Survey Monkey* and *Qualtrics* for example, are widely utilized platforms for measuring people's attitudes, values, reactions to news events, personal preferences, and personality traits. Several widely used computer-administered assessment devices, such as the Implicit Association Test, have been implemented in online versions. Especially popular among social psychologists is the service of *Mechanical Turk*, where volunteers, for a small compensation, complete questionnaires or participate in online experiments.

## Social Networks

All interactions on social media leave a trace, which greatly expands the capacity to investigate the structure and dynamics of social networks. Instead of being limited to tracing friendships structures in a classroom (e.g., Moreno, 1934), researchers can look for the connections among people in an entire country, based on records of calls and text messages (e.g., Onnela et al., 2007). Analyses exploiting the terabytes—or even petabytes—of such data have already yielded new insights into social networks. It has been shown, for example, that communication patterns are not uniformly distributed in time, but rather occur in bursts, such that different subsets of a network are activated at a given time (Barabási, 2010; Karsai et al., 2011). Large-scale social networks, meanwhile, can be constructed as association networks, where individuals are connected if they belong, or have belonged, to the same entity. Two individuals are connected, for example, if they are both members of the same supervisory board or if they went together on a trip.

Perhaps most noteworthy, analyses of massive data sets have revealed that social networks have several common properties, including *scale-free distribution*, *small-world structure*, *homophile*, and *giant component*. *Scale-free distribution* means that that the distribution of the number of links in a network is highly skewed and follows a Pareto distribution, such that most individuals have a small number of connections and very few individuals have a disproportionally high number of links. In a *small world*, whereas most social links of an individual connect to his or her neighbors, a few links connect the individual to distant others. Because of these distant links, the average distance between any two individuals is short, consisting of very few links (Watts, 1999). *Homophile* refers to the fact that an individual tends to be connected to others who are similar with respect to demographic factors, such as age, education, and income, as well as personality characteristics and values. *Giant component* means that all the individuals in a community are connected to each other, forming one big network, rather than several disconnected networks.

## Mobile Devices

Mobile technology is becoming a dominant means of interaction. This emerging reality is relevant to social psychology because mobile phones are routinely equipped with a variety of sensors, such as a geo-location sensor for GPS, a compass, an acceleration sensor that can precisely detect movement, a light sensor, two cameras allowing one to see and be seen by others, and as many as three microphones that can collectively detect the direction of a sound. These devices can thus collect rich data not only about the communication of the user, but also about many aspects of his or her behavior and the situation in which the behavior occurs. For example, based on the data from a set of microphones and sensors, one can recognize with high accuracy the type of activity a person is engaged in (Ward, Lukowicz, Tröster, & Starner, 2006). As another example, data from mobile phones can be used to detect an individual's chronic or momentary mood, such as depression (Grünerbl et al., 2015).

Because modern mobile phones are essentially small computers, various sensors (e.g., electroencephalogram) can be connected to them. And wearable devices that collect sensory and physiological data, such as Google Glasses or sport bracelets, can transmit such data to mobile phones. This clearly amplifies the ability of mobile technology to collect and integrate rich geo-located personal data concerning the user. Current health applications, for example, not only automatically measure a person's physical activity such as the number of steps he or she has taken, but also ask the user to input data such as his or her current mood. Other applications ask the person to make ratings of objects and events on a number of dimensions and to judge other aspects of his or her experience. User-provided data, combined with automatically collected data, can generate a precise and psychologically meaningful stream of information concerning the user and his or her current environment (e.g., Lukowicz, Kirstein, & Tröster, 2004).

Mobile devices are increasingly employed in psychological research. Because they have the capabilities of computers but can be carried around by people in their daily lives, such devices (e.g., smart phones) can be used to record people's actions and subjective experience in natural settings rather than in artificial laboratory environments. This approach is proving useful, for example, for gaining insight into the perception of situations in daily life and the influence of situational factors in shaping how people think and behave (Sherman, Rauthmann, Brown, Serfass, & Jones, 2015). And because mobile devices enable people to be contacted at different points in time, they are well suited to generate time series data that can be analyzed for dynamic properties in action and subjective experience (e.g., fixed-point attractors, periodic structure, ruptures in routine due to perturbing events). This avenue of research remains unexplored at present, but is likely to become a major focus in light of the emerging interest in the intrinsic dynamics of psychological processes (Vallacher, Van Geert, & Nowak, 2015).

## Cameras and Sensors

Cameras and sensors are becoming ubiquitous in daily life, whether placed strategically at busy intersections in a metropolitan area or worn by individuals as they move about in the course of their everyday activities. They collect a steady stream of images and other types of sensory information (e.g., sound, temperature), providing a continuous record of individual and group experiences. A light sensor, for example, can detect the presence and movement of people, since a passing person casts a shadow that is detected by the device. The utility of cameras and sensors is limited only by our ability to make sense of the voluminous data they generate.

The amount and quality of data will be amplified in the near future with the rapidly developing implementation of the *Internet of Things* (IoT). This refers to the network of physical devices, vehicles, and other items that are embedded with sensors, software, and network connectivity, enabling these objects to collect and exchange data. The IoT can be looked upon as the infrastructure of the information society (Howard, 2015), in that it allows objects to be sensed and remotely controlled across existing networks. Devices in the house or in offices, for example, can sense events in their environment, react to these events, and even communicate with one another. They can also be designed to communicate with users and to detect the intentions of nearby individuals.

It is estimated that the IoT will consist of close to 50 billion objects by 2020 (Evans, 2011), making this a potential gold mine for data collection and interpretation regarding behavior as it is embedded in everyday contexts.

To date, the IoT has been primarily employed to enhance the efficiency of physical systems, as in the creation of smart electrical grids, washers and dryers that use wifi for remote monitoring, and energy management systems. One can envision, however, the exploitation of IoT technology to facilitate human interaction by means of a common link to an IoT device. Whether the nature of human interaction will be qualitatively changed by such developments or simply extended in reach remains to be seen.

## Technological Advances in Perspective

The availability of modern technology clearly has added value for research, but some pause is warranted before embracing it wholeheartedly. The internet, social media, and the use of cameras and sensors all provide an abundance of ecologically valid ("real-world") information about individuals and their social lives, but the collection and use of such information raises two concerns—one practical, the other ethical.

The practical issue stems, ironically, from the rich abundance of information that can be generated with modern technology. For one thing, the exponential growth of the amount of data generated and collected on a daily basis has rendered traditional techniques of data gathering, storage, and analysis inadequate, if not completely obsolete. Beyond the data management problem, the massive amounts of data available for analysis can make it difficult to determine whether observed patterns in the data are meaningful. With enough information at one's disposal, one can always find patterns—the trick is to distinguish the "signal" from the "noise" (Silver, 2012). This problem is analogous to the persistent popularity of conspiracy theories. If one believes the terrorist attacks on September 11, 2001, were really an "inside job" coordinated by the Bush administration, for example, the information relevant to that event is so enormous that one can find a way to "connect the dots" and maintain that belief. The advanced statistical methods employed in Big Data research get around this problem for the most part, but there is always a risk of identifying a pattern that is illusory rather than real. The future is certain to see the development of increasingly sophisticated means of discerning true patterns in large, interconnected data sets.

The ethical issue is not as easy to resolve, as it centers on subjective standards of privacy and personal autonomy. We live in an increasingly transparent world where every personal preference, attitude, and social interaction is open to inspection by those who have not been given explicit permission to collect and collate such information. Mobile phones track our every move and every contact we make. The content on most social networking sites, meanwhile, is penetrated by crawlers or sold by providers. And the true value of most mobile apps in not in the service they provide, but in the data they collect. Often the apps are free and the developers make profits by selling the data. A flashlight app for mobile phones, for example, asks for access to the person's list of contacts, contact dates, stored photos, and texts. None of this information is needed to turn on the light in the phone; the company providing the app for "free" makes money by selling the information to marketing companies.

Privacy concerns are not confined to the collection and use of personal data by hackers and those with profit motives. The myriad sources of information about people's personal and interpersonal lives raise ethical concerns regarding the collection and use of such information in the name of science. Ethical considerations are salient enough in laboratory studies for which participants volunteer; consider the amplification of such considerations in the age of social media, Twitter feeds, and internet searches by people who are unaware that their behavior is likely to be scrutinized by total strangers. Although the mining of Big Data is designed to identify patterns that reflect generic social processes, it can also be used to identify patterns in an individual's behavior, preferences, and attitudes, and do so without the individual's knowledge, let alone his or her consent. Facebook posts, for example, reveal a great deal of information about people's personal lives and their social relationships, and such information can be traced to all the individuals in a person's social network. The use of cameras in public places, meanwhile, can generate important insight into social interaction and the synchronization of movement among large numbers of people, but cameras can also be used to identify individuals—and do so without their permission.

It is important to emphasize that the collection and use of personal data by those with commercial or nefarious interests presents a greater threat to privacy than does the mining of such data by scientists. In order to collect and analyze data obtained from social media, cameras and sensors, and internet searchers, researchers must obtain approval from the Internal Review Boards (IRBs) at their institutions. IRBs are charged with protecting the welfare of the participants in research, and have developed clear standards that must be met to justify the collection of personal data. It is standard practice in science to use anonymized data, for example, so that the identities of "participants" are not known to the researchers. Nonetheless, the trade-off between scientific merit and potential harm can prove tricky to determine, and is often a source of contention. Resolutions to the ethical dilemmas posed by Big Data must continue to evolve as this branch of computational social psychology continues its ascendance as an accepted approach to exploring the social dynamics of everyday life.

## Advances in Theory

The enormous complexity of human thought and behavior presents a daunting challenge to the construction of a parsimonious and generalizable theoretical account of human experience. After all, if complexity is assumed to reflect complex interactions among a large number of variables, with the salience and magnitude of these variables changing on different timescales in the absence of external forces, how can one hope to develop an account that does not incorporate such complexity and associated dynamism into its principles? This is a serious conundrum for traditional social psychology, which of necessity isolates a small number of variables in an artificial setting stripped of the ecological context in which they naturally occur, and measures the effect of these variables on a single variable of interest at one point in time.

As noted in Chapter 1 of this volume, although early theorists were quite sensitive to the complexity, embeddedness, and dynamism of psychological processes, the methods and tools were not available at that time to construct theory and conduct psychological research in these terms. In effect, experimental social psychology had little choice but to focus its efforts on cause–effect relations and one-step processes, and to do so in laboratory settings—in effect, investigating thought and behavior "where the light is better." With the advent of computational approaches, we are in a position to recapture and explore the insights that launched social psychology in the first place. Because computational social psychology is in its nascent stage, however, it is not clear what will eventually emerge as a result of this paradigmatic shift in research—but this does not stop us from speculating.

## Dynamics

Even in the most stable setting, a person's thoughts, feelings, and actions are never static, but undergo constant change on various timescales. This defining feature of human experience was recognized by the founding fathers of social psychology and laid the theoretical foundation for the field. James (1890) coined the term "stream of consciousness" to capture the ever-changing nature of mental process, with thoughts, images, and feelings succeeding each other on a moment-to-moment basis. Cooley (1902) stressed the constant press for action, even in the absence of external forces. Lewin's psychological field theory (1936) emphasized the constant interplay of internal and external forces that gave rise to change and stability at the intrapersonal and interpersonal level. Asch (1946) theorized about the dynamic interplay of thoughts and feelings that give rise to unique Gestalts that cannot be reduced to the component mental elements. Krech and Crutchfield (1948) portrayed social experience as the constant reconfiguration of thought and action in response to a conflicting field of forces in everyday life.

Despite this focus on the dynamic underpinnings of human experience, the lack of adequate theoretical and methodological tools at the time rendered the dynamical approach unproductive. Subsequent theory and research tended instead to concentrate on the static aspects of thought and behavior, with dynamism essentially reduced to a one-step process. In the absence of external forces that presumably "caused" people to change the way they think and act, variability over time in a phenomenon of interest was considered noise, and relegated to error variance in statistical analyses. The "power of the situation" reigned supreme as the guiding assumption in theory and research.

The 1990s saw renewed appreciation of the dynamic nature of human experience, largely due to rapid advances in computational tools appropriate for studying human experience. *Dynamical social psychology* (Nowak & Vallacher, 1998; Vallacher & Nowak, 1994a, 1997; Vallacher, Read, & Nowak, 2002) provided an explicitly dynamical framework for rethinking the topical landscape of the field, and showcased methods for investigating the interaction of external factors and intrinsic dynamics in shaping intrapersonal, interpersonal, and collective processes. Computer simulations (e.g., Nowak, Szamrej, and Latané, 1990; Nowak, Vallacher, Tesser, & Borkowski, 2000) and new empirical tools such as the mouse paradigm (Vallacher, Nowak, & Kaufman, 1994; Vallacher, Nowak, Froehlich, & Rockloff, 2002) made dynamic properties tractable and subject to empirical investigation. During this period, too, connectionist models were developed to investigate the dynamics of social thinking and behavior (Read & Miller, 1998; Smith, 1996).

This redirection of the field—from a focus on external forces and one-step processes to the investigation of the interplay of context and intrinsic dynamics—is likely to become increasingly prominent in the future. As computational tools become a mainstream tool familiar to succeeding generations of social psychologists, existing theories will be reframed to accommodate dynamic properties, and new theories will be developed with such properties at their core—much as the field's early theorists had in mind.

## Differentiation

As evident in the preceding chapters, computational social psychology is not a single approach, but rather represents a broad umbrella for several distinct research strategies, each with its own set of methods and tools. This is appropriate, even necessary, at this point in the development of this perspective. In fact, we can expect the computational paradigm to become more differentiated in the near future, with different strategies being developed to exploit the potential of computer and information technology.

In part, this differentiation in research strategies will mirror the differentiation of the topical landscape of social psychology. Big Data, mobile technology, computer simulations, and time series analyses are each better suited for some concerns than for others. The study of social networks, for example, will advance along with developments in the mining of interactions over social media, while research on societal dynamics and culture will continue to rely on computer simulations of formal models, and research agendas concerning interpersonal coordination and the dynamics of self-evaluation are likely to progress with an emphasis on the dynamic properties inherent in time series data. Within each approach, the methods and tools are likely to become increasingly fine-tuned to the subject matter at hand, enabling enhanced precision in data gathering and greater generalizability of the results obtained.

The differentiation of computational strategies, moreover, is likely to promote collaborations between these strategies and other scientific disciplines. Researchers employing computational approaches to cultural evolution, for example, may forge ties with researchers in evolutionary biology, anthropology, and sociology. Those who develop computational models of interpersonal synchronization, meanwhile, may find increasingly common ground with those who study cognitive neuroscience or collective dynamics in biological and physical systems. Social psychology has been described as a "hub" science (Cacioppo, 2007), with links to other disciplines, providing a foundation for such disparate fields as sociology, education, sports, business, criminal justice, and international relations. The ascendance of the computational approach is likely to amplify the central role of social processes in understanding otherwise disconnected facets of human experience.

## Theoretical Integration

Despite the prospect of increased differentiation of specific research strategies in the future, the computational perspective is likely to bring about increasing theoretical integration to a field sorely in need of such efforts. Traditional social psychology has done much to illuminate the mechanisms associated with a wide array of topics, from self-concept to intergroup relations. In so doing, however, the field has become increasingly fragmented with few unifying principles (Vallacher & Nowak, 1994b). This fragmentation is evident in four forms: the topical landscape of the field, with each topic developing in relative isolation from other topics; the sealing off of different levels of psychological reality, with little or no consideration of how macro-level phenomena are related to micro-level processes; the unclear relation between social psychology and other human sciences; and the independence of social psychology from other fields of science. In each case, there is reason to think that the computational approach can create a foundation that allows for the missing integration.

## Topical Integration

The diverse topical landscape of social psychology is mirrored in the diversity of theoretical concepts that have been generated over the years. Established principles of attitude change, for example, have little intersection with the principles said to underlie self-concept change or the dissolution of close relationships. Because the computational approach emphasizes formal principles that characterize the expression of social phenomena generally, it holds potential for reframing seemingly distinct topics in the same terms. These foundational principles derive in large part from complexity science and dynamical systems theory (e.g., Schuster, 1984; Strogatz, 1994). In recent years, these principles have been adapted to the subject matter of social psychology (Guastello, Koopmans, & Pincus, 2009; Read & Miller, 1998; Vallacher & Nowak, 1997; Vallacher, Read, & Nowak, 2002), creating the potential for framing different topics in the same language. The formation of attitudes, self-concepts, and close relationships, for example, can each be understood in terms of self-organization, the emergence of higher-order structures, and the resistance of higher-order structures to disruption. Change in each case, meanwhile, can be understood as the disassembly of higher-order structures into their respective lower-level elements.

Progress toward topical integration is likely to accelerate with the increasing use of computer simulations to reveal the expression of psychological processes over relevant timescales (e.g., Liebrand, Nowak, & Hegselman, 1998; Read & Miller, 1998). Natural language is useful for expressing the nature of a process, of course, but words and metaphors lack the precision of formal rules that can be investigated for their long-term consequences or for their generality across different domains. The translation of verbal theories into computational algorithms provides a common platform for comparing and hopefully integrating different topics. Two processes may have very different surface features, but the underlying rules leading to the emergence of their properties may be the same. Public opinion—a collective process—and self-concept—a personal process—are clearly different phenomena, for example, but research has established that remarkably similar rules underlie the emergence of both (see Nowak et al., 1990, 2000).

One might think that the enormous complexity associated with each fact of human experience would necessitate an equally complex computer simulation model in order to capture its nuance. Even with the aid of computer technology, then, one must develop a complex theory with many rules, and wind up with an explanation that is as complex and nuanced as the phenomenon one is trying to explain. This is not the case, however. The study of nonlinear dynamical systems has shown, in fact, that extremely complex phenomena can be understood with recourse to very few simple rules. This approach is referred to as *dynamical minimalism* (Nowak, 2004). It is minimalist because it attempts to identify the most basic rules governing a process; it is dynamical because it assumes that the process evolves in time due to the interaction among the basic rules. In effect, dynamical minimalism achieves parsimony in theory construction without stripping the process of its complexity and nuance.

## Developing Links between Micro- and Macro-Level Phenomena

We know intuitively that there are links between different levels of social reality. Group dynamics is clearly different from the thought or behavior of any of the individuals in the group, but the former would not be possible without the latter. Establishing the nature of such linkage, however, has proven to be a challenge for social psychology, so much so that different levels of social reality are usually treated as though they had nothing in common, and thus are discussed in separate journals, in separate sections of a journal, and in separate chapters in a social psychology text. If attempts are made to relate micro and macro phenomena, reductionism is commonly assumed, such that the properties at the macro level reflect analogous properties of the elements comprising the micro level. To explain frustration and anti-social behavior in a group, for example, a theorist might reduce this phenomenon to frustration and readiness for anti-social behavior among the individuals in the group.

The computational perspective is explicitly concerned with the link between micro and macro phenomena, but does so without assuming reductionism. The focus instead is *emergence*, a central concept in the study of dynamical systems (e.g., Holland, 1995; Johnson, 2001; Vallacher & Nowak, 1997). The idea that "the whole is more than the sum of its parts"—that something new somehow emerges at a global level from the basic components of a system—seems mysterious, if not implausible, but it has been repeatedly confirmed in computer simulations based on the dynamical minimalism approach. The researcher specifies the properties of the elements at the micro level, and the rules of interaction among these elements. As the elements interact over time, properties appear at the macro level that were not programmed—or sometimes not even imagined—at the micro level. In effect, a theory constructed at a basic level of psychological reality can be investigated for its consequences at a higher level of psychological reality. Simple rules concerning the interaction of basic and often mutually contradictory thoughts about oneself that arise in the stream of thought give rise to global properties of the self-concept such as self-esteem and self-concept certainty (Nowak et al., 2000), for example, and simple rules of social interaction among individuals promote the emergence of public opinion and customs (Nowak et al., 1990).

Computer simulations within the dynamical minimalism approach are also useful in distinguishing between properties that are critical to the emergence of higher-order processes and those that are trivial and can be ignored in constructing a theory concerning micro–macro linkages. So although psychological processes are complex and involve a wide variety of factors, it is not necessary to incorporate all—or even many—of them in a theory concerning a given process or the emergent consequences of the process. Such distinctions may not be obvious when attempting to explain a phenomenon, so one runs the risk of generating an incomplete account if certain factors are omitted for the sake of designing a manageable study within traditional social psychology.

In the computer simulation approach, however, a researcher can systematically vary the properties of basic factors and their interactions, and then observe which properties and factors generate meaningful changes at the macro level. Those properties that have trivial consequences can then be eliminated from the model.

In this way, computer simulations enable one to distill the minimal set of features—the elements and rules of interaction among them—that are necessary to capture the essence of a process. A simple explanation can therefore be developed and verified without forfeiting a nuanced and comprehensive understanding of the topic under consideration.

## Establishing Connections with Other Human Sciences

As noted earlier, a strong case can be made that social psychology provides a meaningful hub for other human sciences (Cacioppo, 2007). Against this backdrop, it is ironic that many scholars in these disciplines have begun to argue that there is no need for social psychology, and that it has outlived its usefulness and relevance as a distinct discipline. It is noteworthy that this disturbing argument is coming from those in the social sciences who have adopted the computational paradigm (Conte et al., 2012). Their point is that with its emphasis on cause–effect relations investigated in laboratory as opposed to real-world settings and its reliance on statistical inference from small convenience samples as opposed to population description, social psychology is essentially a trivial pursuit that does not contribute meaningful and ecologically valid understanding.

The adoption of the computational perspective blunts this dismissive judgment of what social psychology has to offer. When researchers are no longer bound by the constraints of experimental design, the focus on unidirectional cause–effect relations, and statistical inference from small convenience samples, they can develop and test models that reflect the complexity, nonlinearity, and dynamic patterns of human behavior in ecologically valid contexts. And because social psychology focuses on the individual, computational models can identify the mechanisms of thought and action that mediate or moderate the social processes identified by computational researchers in economics, political science, and other social sciences. The computational approach, then, is not merely an adjunct discipline for computational science, but rather provides unique insight into the mutual feedback between individual and collective processes.

## Integration with Other Areas of Science

Computational social psychology has a set of methods that are unique to human experience, but its conceptual foundation reflects assumptions and principles that are common to other areas of science. Like models of physical phenomena, the various models presented in the preceding chapters emphasize the complexity and dynamism underlying social phenomena of all kind, from those that are intrapersonal in nature to those that are interpersonal and collective. Indeed, the specific features of complexity and dynamism at work in computational models correspond with the features of phenomena in such disparate fields as physics, chemistry, and biology. Thus, human dynamics are increasingly framed in terms of such notions as self-organization, emergence, attractor dynamics, and synchronization—notions that are central to everything in nature from sand piles to galaxy formation.

Of course, the subject matter of social psychology is decidedly different from that of the physical sciences. People are not atoms or gravitons. But the principles by which individuals develop attitudes or form social groups are similar in formal terms to the principles observed throughout the known universe. By viewing the topical landscape of social psychology as complex systems governed by basic processes by which the world operates, the potential for developing an integrative theory of human experience becomes a realistic (though yet unattained) goal. It is ironic that a true appreciation of human uniqueness ultimately derives from what humans have in common with everything else in nature.

## The Future of Social Psychology

We hasten to add that the computational approach does not supplant the traditional experimental approach that has been the mainstay of social psychology throughout the field's history. To the contrary, a comprehensive understanding of human experience will entail a synergistic relationship between computational modeling and experimental methods. Big Data, for example, cannot directly test the causal factors responsible for the patterns that are discovered in large data sets. Knowing that a high volume of Twitter feeds devoted to a topic promotes a change in public opinion concerning the topic does not tell us *why* this change occurs. Perhaps awareness of the high volume creates a bandwagon effect, with everyone wanting to be part of the conversation or to feel solidarity with others, or perhaps the content of the Tweets has information value that clarifies the meaning of the topic for those who previously did not know what to think. Research conducted in social psychology labs can help to decide among these alternative mechanisms.

Beyond that, traditional social psychology has an important role to play in theory construction. This role is especially apparent in the use of computer simulations to model psychological processes. We noted earlier that describing psychological processes in terms of formal rules affords greater precision than does a verbal description that reflects intuition or metaphors. This is true, but it is also true that the rules must come from somewhere. Before a researcher can specify in formal terms the ways in which a process unfolds, he or she must have a guiding vision and set of assumptions about what the process looks like. Social psychologists have generated a rich repertoire of basic visions of what shapes and drives human behavior, and research has functioned to verify a handful of these guiding visions, while eliminating others. The verbal descriptions that have survived this selection process motivate the attempt to identify the rules that enable the process in question to occur.

Consider, for example, one of the most inspiring metaphors of all: James' (1890) stream of consciousness. This enduring image of mental function was not articulated in formal terms by James, but its ring of truth has provided the inspiration for such depictions in recent years (e.g., Nowak et al., 2000). It is one thing to recognize that thoughts tend to unfold over time without the need for external forces or triggers, but how and why does this happen? In Nowak and colleagues' (2000) computational model, mental process is driven in part by a press for integration, so that independent thoughts come to acquire common higher-order meaning (e.g., evaluation) as they co-occur in thinking. Thoughts that differ in initial meaning influence one another to achieve a shared meaning, and thoughts that have similar meaning tend to call each other to mind. The process of developing a common meaning for one's thoughts may involve repeated iterations occurring over long periods of time, with momentary oscillation between conflicting coherent states if the thoughts have contradictory meaning (Vallacher, Nowak et al., 2002). This scenario ensures that mental process is dynamic rather than static.

It is also the case that computer simulations alone may not be sufficient to verify a theoretical model. The use of computer simulations is critical in identifying the properties that are central to the model and investigating the consequences of these properties for the higher-order functioning of the system under investigation. Once these consequences have been identified, they provide the basis for hypotheses that need to be tested in empirical research. The comparison of patterns inherent in experimental data and produced by computer simulation of a model provides a new means of verifying a theory.

Sometimes the relation between computer simulations and empirical verification is reversed. Thus, data collected in laboratory studies can suggest the basic properties and rules of a model, which are then implemented in a computer model to test whether the anticipated emergent properties are observed. The results of such simulations, in turn, can provide the bases for new hypotheses to be tested empirically, and so on, in an iterated approach that holds potential for generating progressive understanding of the phenomenon in question. The reciprocal feedback over time between computer simulations and empirical data is central to theory construction in computational social psychology.

The rapidly growing field of computational social science (Conte et al., 2012; Gilbert, 2007) provides an important context for the development of computational social psychology. This interdisciplinary field, which is populated more by computer scientists and physicists than by social scientists, embraces the subject matter of social psychology, but does so without the benefit of social psychological theory. Indeed, this field is largely atheoretical, focusing more on the description of social processes based on very large data sets and sophisticated agent-based models than on the factors mediating the patterns that are revealed. So, although computational social science is currently more advanced in its methods, it can benefit from the explicit theoretical focus that has defined social psychology throughout its history.

It is noteworthy that computational social science began with a focus on agent-based models (Conte et al., 2012; Epstein, 2006; Gilbert, 2007; Nowak, 2009), concentrating on the emergence of group properties from individual behavior and the self-organization of groups and societies. The focus shifted over time to social networks, however, largely due to the availability of large-scale data on communication on the internet and with mobile phones (Lazer et al., 2009; Wyatt, Choudhury, Bilmes, & Kitts, 2011). The current focus is on data analysis, mostly provided by Big Data (Alvarez, 2016; Wallach, 2016). This progression provides a road map for the likely evolution of computational social psychology. Although agent-based models provide the predominant focus at present—as indicated by the majority of the chapters in this volume—there is increasing attention devoted to social network analyses, communication patterns over the internet and electronic media, and Big Data. The future is likely to see an acceleration in this trajectory, with greater overlap in the respective research methods and concerns of computational social science and computational social psychology. The background in theory provided by social psychology, meanwhile, should facilitate new and deep insight into the nature of human experience as these two approaches utilize common methods to focus on issues of shared interest.

In sum, the computational approach does not replace canonical approaches in social psychology, but rather provides a critical complement to traditional means of generating and testing insight into human experience. Indeed, all the methods available to social psychologists—experiment, field study, computer simulation, Big Data, model fitting to time series data—are optimally viewed as having positive feedback loops, with the results of one approach providing the inspiration and hypotheses for another approach. Because the computational perspective is relatively new, it is competing for attention in the research community. Once it has secured its rightful place in the conduct of social psychological science, its reciprocal connection to traditional approaches will be appreciated and acted upon. Accordingly—and with an optimistic mindset—we can expect to reap the benefits of this budding relationship in the years to come.

## Note

1 Andrzej Nowak acknowledges the support from the grant of Polish Committee for Scientific Research (DEC-2011/02/A/HS6/00231).

## References

Alvarez, R. M. (Ed.) (2016). *Computational social science*. Cambridge: Cambridge University Press.

Asch, S. E. (1946). Forming impressions of personalities. *Journal of Abnormal and Social Psychology, 41*, 258–290.

Barabási, A. L. (2010). *Bursts: The hidden patterns behind everything we do, from your e-mail to bloody crusades*. New York: Penguin.

Cacioppo, J. T. (2007). Psychology is a hub science. *APS Observer, 20*, 1–3.

Chung, C. K., & Pennebaker, J. W. (2008). Revealing dimensions of thinking in open-ended self-descriptions: An automated meaning extraction method for natural language. *Journal of Research in Personality, 42*, 96–132.

Conte, R., & Giardini, F. (2016). Towards computational and behavioral social science. *European Psychologist, 21*(3), 131–140.

Conte, R., Gilbert, N., Bonelli, G., Cioffi-Revilla, C., Deffuant, G., Kertesz, J., Loreto, V., Moat S., Nadal, J. P., Sanchez, A., Nowak, A., Flache, A., San Miguel, M., & Helbing, D. (2012). Manifesto of Computational Social Science. *European Physical Journal Special Topics, 214*(1), 325–346.

Cooley, C. H. (1902). *Human nature and the social order.* New York: Scribner.

Epstein, J. M. (2006). *Generative social science: Studies in agent-based computational modeling.* Princeton, NJ: Princeton University Press.

Evans, D. (2011). *The Internet of Things: How the next evolution of the internet is changing everything.* White paper, Cisco Internet Business Solutions Group.

Gilbert, N. (2007). Computational social science: Agent-based social simulation. In D. Phan & F. Amblard (Eds.), *Agent-based modelling and simulation* (pp. 115–134). Oxford: Bardwell.

Grünerbl, A., Muaremi, A., Osmani, V., Bahle, G., Oehler, S., Tröster, G., Mayora, O., Haring, C., & Lukowicz, P. (2015). Smartphone-based recognition of states and state changes in bipolar disorder patients. *IEEE Journal of Biomedical and Health Informatics, 19*(1), 140–148.

Guastello, S., Koopmans, M., & Pincus, D. (Eds.) (2009). *Chaos and complexity in psychology: The theory of nonlinear dynamical systems.* New York: Cambridge University Press.

Holland, J. H. (1995). *Emergence: From chaos to order.* Reading, MA: Addison-Wesley.

Howard, P. N. (2015). *Pax Technia: How the Internet of Things may set us free, or lock us up.* New Haven, CT: Yale University Press.

James, W. (1890). *Principles of psychology.* New York: Holt.

Johnson, S. (2001). *Emergence: The connected lives of ants, brains, cities, and software.* New York: Scribner.

Karsai, M., Kivelä, M., Pan, R. K., Kaski, K., Kertész, J., Barabási, A. L., & Saramäki, J. (2011). Small but slow world: How network topology and burstiness slow down spreading. *Physical Review E, 83*(2), 25–102.

Krech, D. & Crutchfield, R. S. (1948). *Theory and problems of social psychology.* New York: McGraw-Hill.

Lazer, D., Pentland, A., Adamic, L., Aral, S., Barabási, A. L., Brewer, D., Christakis, N., Contractor, N., Fowler, J., Gutman, M., Jebara, T., King, G., Macy, M., Roy, D., & Van Alstyne, N. (2009). Computational social science. *Science, 323*(5915), 721–723.

LeCun, Y., Bengio, Y., & Hinton, G. (2015). Deep learning. *Nature, 521*(7553), 436–444.

Lewin, K. (1936). *Principles of topological psychology.* New York: McGraw-Hill.

Liebrand, W., Nowak, A., & Hegselman, R. (Eds.) (1998). *Computer modeling of social processes.* New York: SAGE.

Lukowicz, P., Kirstein, T., & Tröster, G. (2004). Wearable systems for health care applications. *Methods of Information in Medicine / Methodik der Information in der Medizin, 43*(3), 232–238.

Moreno, J. L. (1934). *Who shall survive?* Beacon, NY: Beacon House.

Nowak, A. (2004). Dynamical minimalism: Why less is more in psychology. *Personality and Social Psychology Review, 8*, 183–192.

Nowak, A. (Ed.) (2009). *Applications physics and mathematics in social science.* In R A. Meyers (Series Ed.), *Springer encyclopedia of complexity.* Heidelberg: Springer-Verlag.

Nowak, A., Szamrej, J., & Latané, B. (1990). From private attitude to public opinion: A dynamic theory of social impact. *Psychological Review*, *97*, 362–376.

Nowak, A., & Vallacher, R. R. (1998). *Dynamical social psychology*. New York: Guilford Press.

Nowak, A., Vallacher, R. R., Tesser, A., & Borkowski, W. (2000). Society of self: The emergence of collective properties in self-structure. *Psychological Review*, *107*, 39–61.

Onnela, J. P., Saramäki, J., Hyvönen, J., Szabó, G., Lazer, D., Kaski, K., Kertesz, J., & Barabási, A. L. (2007). Structure and tie strengths in mobile communication networks. *Proceedings of the National Academy of Sciences*, *104*(18), 7332–7336.

Read, S. J., & Miller, L. C. (Eds.) (1998). *Connectionist models of social reasoning and social behavior*. Mahwah, NJ: Lawrence Erlbaum.

Schuster, H. G. (1984). *Deterministic chaos*. Vienna: Physik Verlag.

Sherman, R. A., Rauthmann, J. F., Brown, N. A., Serfass, D. G., & Jones, A. B. (2015). The independent effects of personality and situations on real-time expressions of behavior and emotion. *Journal of Personality and Social Psychology*, *109*, 872–888.

Silver, N. (2012). *The signal and the noise: Why so many predictions fail—but some don't*. New York: Penguin.

Smith, E. R. (1996). What do connectionism and social psychology offer each other? *Journal of Personality and Social Psychology*, *70*, 893–912.

Strogatz, S. (1994). *Nonlinear dynamics and chaos*. Cambridge, MA: Perseus Books.

Vallacher, R. R., & Nowak, A. (Eds.) (1994a). *Dynamical systems in social psychology*. San Diego, CA: Academic Press.

Vallacher, R. R., & Nowak, A. (1994b). The chaos in social psychology. In R. R. Vallacher & A. Nowak (Eds.), *Dynamical systems in social psychology* (pp. 1–16). San Diego, CA: Academic Press.

Vallacher, R. R., & Nowak, A. (1997). The emergence of dynamical social psychology. *Psychological Inquiry*, *4*, 73–99.

Vallacher, R. R., Nowak, A., Froehlich, M., & Rockloff, M. (2002). The dynamics of self-evaluation. *Personality and Social Psychology Review*, *6*, 370–379.

Vallacher, R. R., Nowak, A., & Kaufman, J. (1994). Intrinsic dynamics of social judgment. *Journal of Personality and Social Psychology*, *67*, 20–34.

Vallacher, R. R., Read, S. J., & Nowak, A. (Eds.) (2002). The dynamical perspective in social psychology. *Personality and Social Psychology Review*, *6*, 264–273.

Vallacher, R. R., Van Geert, P., & Nowak, A. (2015). The intrinsic dynamics of psychological process. *Current Directions in Psychological Science*, *24*, 58–64.

Wallach, H. (2016). *Computational social science: Discovery and prediction*. Cambridge: Cambridge University Press.

Ward, J. A., Lukowicz, P., Tröster, G., & Starner, T. E. (2006). Activity recognition of assembly tasks using body-worn microphones and accelerometers. *IEEE Transactions on Pattern Analysis and Machine Intelligence*, *28*(10), 1553–1567.

Watts, D. (1999). Networks, dynamics, and the small-world phenomenon. *American Journal of Sociology*, *105*, 493–527.

Wyatt, D., Choudhury, T., Bilmes, J., & Kitts, J. A. (2011). Inferring colocation and conversation networks from privacy-sensitive audio with implications for computational social science. *ACM Transactions on Intelligent Systems and Technology*, *2*(1), 7.

# INDEX